Anticolonial Afterlives in Egypt

This book presents an alternative story of the 2011 Egyptian revolution by revisiting Egypt's moment of decolonization in the mid-twentieth century. *Anticolonial Afterlives in Egypt* explores the country's first postcolonial project, arguing that the enduring afterlives of anticolonial politics, connected to questions of nationalism, military rule, capitalist development, and violence, are central to understanding political events in Egypt today. Through an imagined conversation between Antonio Gramsci and Frantz Fanon – two foundational theorists of anticapitalism and anticolonialism – *Anticolonial Afterlives in Egypt* focuses on issues of resistance, revolution, mastery, and liberation to show how the Nasserist project, created by Gamal Abdel Nasser and the Free Officers in 1952, remains the only instance of hegemony in modern Egyptian history. In suggesting that Nasserism was made possible through local, regional, and global anticolonial politics, even as it reproduced colonial ways of governing that continue to reverberate into Egypt's present, this interdisciplinary study thinks through questions of travelling theory, global politics, and resistance and revolution in the postcolonial world.

Sara Salem is Assistant Professor in the Department of Sociology at the London School of Economics and Political Science.

The Global Middle East

General Editors

Arshin Adib-Moghaddam, *SOAS, University of London*
Ali Mirsepassi, *New York University*

Editorial Advisory Board

Faisal Devji, *University of Oxford*
John Hobson, *University of Sheffield*
Firoozeh Kashani-Sabet, *University of Pennsylvania*
Zachary Lockman, *New York University*
Madawi Al-Rasheed, *London School of Economics and Political Science*
David Ryan, *University College Cork, Ireland*

The Global Middle East series seeks to broaden and deconstruct the geographical boundaries of the "Middle East" as a concept to include North Africa, Central and South Asia, and diaspora communities in Western Europe and North America. The series features fresh scholarship that employs theoretically rigorous and innovative methodological frameworks resonating across relevant disciplines in the humanities and the social sciences. In particular, the general editors welcome approaches that focus on mobility, the erosion of nation-state structures, travelling ideas and theories, transcendental techno-politics, the decentralization of grand narratives, and the dislocation of ideologies inspired by popular movements. The series will also consider translations of works by authors in these regions whose ideas are salient to global scholarly trends but have yet to be introduced to the Anglophone academy.

Other books in the series:

1. *Transnationalism in Iranian Political Thought: The Life and Times of Ahmad Fardid*, Ali Mirsepassi
2. *Psycho-nationalism: Global Thought, Iranian Imaginations*, Arshin Adib-Moghaddam

3. *Iranian Cosmopolitanism: A Cinematic History*, Golbarg Rekabtalaei
4. *Money, Markets and Monarchies: The Gulf Cooperation Council and the Political Economy of the Contemporary Middle East*, Adam Hanieh
5. *Iran's Troubled Modernity: Debating Ahmad Fardid's Legacy*, Ali Mirsepassi
6. *Foreign Policy as Nation Making: Turkey and Egypt in the Cold War*, Reem Abou-El-Fadl
7. *Revolution and its Discontents: Political Thought and Reform in Iran*, Eskandar Sadeghi-Boroujerdi
8. *Creating the Modern Iranian Woman: Popular Culture between Two Revolutions*, Liora Hendelman-Baavur
9. *Iran's Quiet Revolution: The Downfall of the Pahlavi State*, Ali Mirsepassi
10. *Reversing the Colonial Gaze: Persian Travelers Abroad*, Hamid Dabashi
11. *Israel's Jewish Identity Crisis: State and Politics in the Middle East*, Yaacov Yadgar
12. *Temporary Marriage in Iran: Gender and Body Politics in Modern Persian Film and Literature*, Claudia Yaghoobi
13. *Cosmopolitan Radicalism: The Visual Politics of Beirut's Global Sixties*, Zeina Maasri
14. *Anticolonial Afterlives in Egypt: The Politics of Hegemony*, Sara Salem

Anticolonial Afterlives in Egypt

The Politics of Hegemony

SARA SALEM
London School of Economics and Political Science

CAMBRIDGE
UNIVERSITY PRESS

University Printing House, Cambridge CB2 8BS, United Kingdom

One Liberty Plaza, 20th Floor, New York, NY 10006, USA

477 Williamstown Road, Port Melbourne, VIC 3207, Australia

314–321, 3rd Floor, Plot 3, Splendor Forum, Jasola District Centre,
New Delhi – 110025, India

79 Anson Road, #06–04/06, Singapore 079906

Cambridge University Press is part of the University of Cambridge.

It furthers the University's mission by disseminating knowledge in the pursuit of
education, learning, and research at the highest international levels of excellence.

www.cambridge.org
Information on this title: www.cambridge.org/9781108491518
DOI: 10.1017/9781108868969

© Sara Salem 2020

This publication is in copyright. Subject to statutory exception
and to the provisions of relevant collective licensing agreements,
no reproduction of any part may take place without the written
permission of Cambridge University Press.

First published 2020

Printed in the United Kingdom by TJ International Ltd, Padstow Cornwall

A catalogue record for this publication is available from the British Library.

ISBN 978-1-108-49151-8 Hardback

Cambridge University Press has no responsibility for the persistence or accuracy of
URLs for external or third-party internet websites referred to in this publication
and does not guarantee that any content on such websites is, or will remain,
accurate or appropriate.

For my parents, Mamdouh and Marlie, and my sister Nancy

Contents

List of Figures	*page* x
Acknowledgements	xi
Introduction: Trapped in History: Revolution in Egypt	1

Part I   Anticolonialism and Its Discontents

1 Hegemony in the Postcolony? Postcolonial and Marxist Encounters	31
2 Hegemony in Egypt: Revisiting Gamal Abdel Nasser	80

Part II   Hegemony and Its Afterlives

3 Laying Neoliberal Foundations: Infitah and a New Egypt	159
4 Finance Capital and Empty Time	206
Conclusion: Haunted Histories and Decolonial Futures	256
References	280
Index	295

Figures

2.1	Portrait of the second president of Egypt, Gamal Abdel Nasser (1918–70), at the Arab Summit Conference, Cairo, circa 1964	*page* 82
2.2	Leaders of the Non-Aligned Nations	89
2.3	Construction of Aswan High Dam	142
2.4	President Nasser's funeral procession	148
3.1	Egyptian President Anwar Sadat, US President Jimmy Carter, and Israeli Prime Minister Menachem Begin	165
3.2	Anwar Al-Sadat	169
3.3	Meeting of Henry Ford with Mohammed Anwar Sadat	198
4.1	President Mubarak	210
5.1	Egypt goes to the polls for parliamentary elections	258

Acknowledgements

This was a difficult book to finish. It left me feeling as though some moments, some events, simply can't be captured in academic prose. At times, trying to understand, analyse, and make sense of revolutionary shifts felt like an injustice to emotive experiences, to the hopes, dreams, and setbacks millions of people went through and continue to go through. In some ways, the book remains unfinished precisely because of my doubts around making sense of or understanding monumental events. Because this book explores revolutionary loss, juxtaposing it alongside its twin, revolutionary hope, it is one that is always open to interpretation, and I hope that what is written within these pages is not the final story of revolution in Egypt.

In other ways, it was important to me to think through a story of revolution in Egypt that centred afterlives and how they reverberate into the present in the most unexpected ways. This is my humble contribution to the broader project of recovering the centrality and emotive significance of the anticolonial moment, made up of much more than state-led projects that came to dominate the postcolonial world. My sense is that the afterlives of anticolonialism have been powerful enough to seep into and structure the present. The futures that were imagined and the ones that were ultimately created can tell us a lot about where we are today, where we came from, and where we might go.

Despite the focus on Egyptian anticolonial afterlives, this story could not have been told without the events of 2011. Those momentous days illustrate just how entangled revolutionary hope and revolutionary loss always are and how long it can take to think through, feel, and write about what takes place during moments of revolutionary change. It was often eerie writing about anticolonial revolution at a time when Egypt was going through another revolution; I realize now that it was not a coincidence these two moments felt connected.

I owe a great debt to so many people; but before all else, this book is dedicated to the countless Egyptians who lost their lives and gave a part of themselves in the hope and belief that the world could be better. At this particular post-revolutionary moment, there is a lot of pain, anger, and disillusionment. And yet, deep down, there is a quiet voice that tells us where there is revolutionary loss, there was – and will be – revolutionary hope.

*

There are many people to thank, and I apologize in advance if my memory has failed me and I have left anyone out. So many late-night conversations, afternoon walks, day-long workshops, one-hour seminars, and stretched-out online debates have seeped into this book and shaped it. Above all, I want to pay tribute to generations of scholars who have come before and whose work made ours possible today.

I want to thank Noor Amr, Miheret Ayele, Elia el-Khazen, Dina Makram-Ebeid, Karim Malak, Andreas Malm, Nivi Manchanda, Aya Nassar, Nicola Pratt, Nancy Salem, Robbie Shilliam, Brecht De Smet, Vanessa Eileen Thompson, Lisa Tilley, and Rafeef Ziadah for looking at drafts of various chapters as well as successive drafts of the manuscript as a whole.

Brenna Bhandar, John Chalcraft, Sophie Chamas, Hanan Hammad, Adam Hanieh, Paul Higate, Rosalba Icaza, Laleh Khalili, Karim Knio, Kamran Matin, Zeyad El Nabolsy, Roberto Roccu, Alina Sajed, Mai Taha, Cemal Burak Tansel, and Alberto Toscano have given me feedback on my work more generally in ways that have inspired and pushed much of the thinking in this book, and I am grateful for that.

For years of invaluable friendship and for helping me navigate life in all of its beauty and complexity, I thank Omnia Abbas, Reem Abbas, Salma Amer, Noor Amr, Miheret Ayele, Maheen Hyder, Rekia Jibrin, Aya Nassar, Hala Nasr, Nancy Salem, Deana Shaaban, Sya Taha, Vanessa Eileen Thompson, and Lisa Tilley. I am lucky to know you.

I am grateful to Nivi Manchanda for her friendship and that we are traversing this road of having our first books published together.

Dina Makram-Ebeid, Soraya Hosni, Rosalba Icaza, Heba Khalil, Laleh Khalili, Nicola Pratt, Olivia Rutazibwa, Alina Sajed, Tamara Soukotta, Mai Taha, Charoula Tzanakou, Dubravka Zarkov, and Rafeef Ziadah have supported me in too many ways to count, and I am grateful for their friendship.

A special thanks to Maria Marsh, Daniel Brown, and Atifa Jiwa at Cambridge University Press, who have made this such a smooth

Acknowledgements xiii

process. I would also like to thank Hossam Dirar for allowing me to use his beautiful work on the cover of this book.

I finished this book in a new home, the Department of Sociology at the London School of Economics. Conversations with colleagues and students at the LSE during these final months opened up new ways of thinking about questions I have been exploring for a long time, and I am excited to take these further in new projects and pieces of writing, as well as in my teaching. I would especially like to thank Omar Al Ghazzi, Nader Andrawos, Kelly-Jo Bluen, John Chalcraft, Ayça Çubukçu, Suzi Hall, Niamh Hayes, Nabila Munawar and Marral Shamshiri-Fard.

I am especially indebted to the amazing students I have had the honour of teaching in various places, who are endlessly inspiring and energizing, and who make me live Gramsci's 'pessimism of the intellect, optimism of the will' on a daily basis. Teaching makes everything in academia worth it.

Finally, I want to thank my parents and my sister, for everything. Finishing this book has made me realize just how deeply a product of my life journey and family history it has turned out to be.

*

The final chapter is derived in part from an article entitled 'Haunted Histories: Nasserism and the Promises of the Past', published in *Middle East Critique*, 01/07/2019, copyright Taylor and Francis, DOI:10.1080/19436149.2019.1633057; the third chapter is derived in part from an article entitled 'Reading Egypt's Postcolonial State through Frantz Fanon: Hegemony, Dependency and Development', published in *Interventions: International Journal of Postcolonial Studies*, 08/01/2018, copyright Taylor and Francis, DOI:10.1080/1369801X.2017.1421041.

Introduction: Trapped in History
Revolution in Egypt

People are trapped in history, and history is trapped in them.

James Baldwin[1]

As a way of getting seriously past the weightlessness of one theory after another, the remorseless indignations of orthodoxy, and the expressions of tired advocacy to which we are often submitted, the exercise involved in figuring out where the theory went and how in getting there its fiery core was reignited as invigorating – is also another voyage, one that is central to intellectual life.

Edward Said[2]

The crisis consists precisely in the fact that the old is dying and the new cannot be born; in this interregnum a great variety of morbid symptoms appear.

Antonio Gramsci[3]

The basic premise of the theory of hegemony is one with which few would disagree: that man is not ruled by force alone, but also by ideas.

Thomas Bates[4]

The afterlives of an event are often as revealing as the event itself, shedding light on pre-histories and futurities; on the multiple trajectories that could have been, and the one that eventually was. This is a book about the afterlives of Egypt's process of decolonization, and in particular the creation of a hegemonic project that reverberated far into Egypt's future. Antonio Gramsci's concept of hegemony is one that has been written about extensively, but materialized rarely. And yet in the two decades following Egyptian independence from Britain in 1952, we see the rise and fall of a period of hegemony in which anticolonialism, nationalism, and independent development came to define Egypt's

[1] 1984.   [2] 2000, 230.   [3] 1992, 32.   [4] 1975, 351.

future. The fall of this project was just as momentous as its creation; and its afterlives were to travel far into the future, eventually culminating in a second revolution in 2011. This book is a journey between these two revolutions, situating 2011 within the broader trajectory of 1952.

The inspiration for this book started with the 2011 Egyptian revolution, but the book itself has largely turned out to be centred on a different revolution in Egyptian history: the coup d'état and popular revolution of 1952. This project initially began as an attempt to understand the temporality of the 2011 revolution; I was interested in asking why these particular events happened at this particular moment. In attempting to place 2011 within a historical trajectory, I found there was one part of this historical puzzle that struck me as unique, one era in modern Egyptian history that was particularly different from the others. I repeatedly found myself returning to a single question, one that was always at the back of my mind: why was the Nasserist era so singular? This singularity expressed itself in different ways: it is the era that has been most written about in post-independence Egypt; it is an era embroiled in intense controversy; and it is an era that expresses itself in contradictory ways in the Egyptian popular imagination. It is also a project that very much set the limits of the political from 1952 onwards. It seemed to me that there was something different about the Nasser years, an intuition that my focus on 2011 was incomplete unless I connected these two historical moments into one single trajectory.

The contradictions of the Nasser years, as well as the highs and lows, suggested to me that something happened during that historical moment that was powerful enough to leave legacies into the present, legacies that were very much a part of the 2011 revolution. Nasserism as a political project was formed through the radical movements of the 1930s and 1940s, produced in and through the global politics of decolonization, and representative of major shifts in elite nation-building in Egypt and the broader postcolonial world. While the Nasserist moment heralded the creation of a new nation based on industrialization and anti-colonial nationalism, its defeat in 1967 – after the Six-Day War with Israel – brought into being an entirely new historical moment. The rise of neoliberal restructuring in the late 1960s, and the acceleration of this in the mid 1990s, saw the end of Egypt's project of decolonization and the beginning of its integration into a new world order.

Trapped in History: Revolution in Egypt 3

My journey to understand the singularity of the Nasserist project led me to Antonio Gramsci. A Southern Italian Marxist, Gramsci's most well-known work, The Prison Notebooks, is a mine of information spread across hundreds of individual notes that include everything from his major intellectual theorizations to small reminders to himself about future research. Written during his time in prison, the notes and their fragmentary nature reveal the astonishing feat Gramsci accomplished by writing them in those conditions, as well as the limits to trying to extract clearly delineated theories from these notebooks. His concepts of hegemony, passive revolution, and the historical bloc come together into a complex framework analysing society and social change, and his positionality as a Southern Italian led him to focus on inequalities produced within the nation; both of these make him invaluable to theorizing on the uneven nature of global capitalism.[5] His concept of hegemony is a unique articulation of what makes some political projects rule more effectively than others: a balance between consent and coercion, where coercion and consent exist in a dialectical relationship. This book argues that the Nasserist project remains the only - albeit short-lived - instance of a hegemonic project in modern Egyptian history, and that the 2011 revolution signified the end-point of its decline, decades after it was created.

Gramsci did not understand hegemony as something 'positive' or 'negative' but rather a condition of rule that creates powerful effects. As John Chalcraft has written: 'Hegemonic rule is often seen negatively by those who mistakenly identify this strategy of power with the values approved within a given hegemonic system'.[6] Hegemony, as he goes on to note, does not refer to a given set of values, but a particular *structure of power*.[7] It is precisely this structure of power – so present under Nasser – that I am interested in. The polarization that exists between accounts that romanticize Nasserism and those that hold it accountable for Egypt's current predicaments has often meant that the complexity of that particular moment is erased. The book is interested in understanding the power Nasserism exerted, both then and now, and the ways it seeps into the present. Understanding Nasserism as hegemonic, then, is an attempt at unpacking how different threads came together at a particular moment in time to create the possibility of hegemony in Egypt.

[5] Morton 2007.   [6] 2007, 181.
[7] Ibid. Gramsci, for instance, struggled for a socialist hegemony.

Despite beginning with Gramsci and his theory of hegemony, this book owes an equal debt to Frantz Fanon, without whom I would not have understood hegemony and its afterlives in the way that I have. Fanon's work illuminated the centrality of decolonization as a political process on the one hand, and the pitfalls embedded within anticolonial nationalism on the other. Fanon's work has experienced something of a revival over the past several decades. In some ways, making extensive use of Fanon in a book about revolution in Egypt is unsurprising: he was, after all, *the* theorist of decolonization. In other ways, it may seem strange, given that his work is not commonly used in studies of the Middle East.[8] Fanon's call to 'stretch Marxism' and his detailed attention to the specificity of capitalism in the postcolony permeate this book, allowing me to approach hegemony and its afterlives in a way that makes space for colonial histories. Beyond using Fanon's theoretical and empirical work in this book, Fanon has also greatly influenced the ways in which I think of decolonization and its contradictions. His thinking has been invaluable in positing the limitations but also the immense possibilities that coloured that particular moment. Moreover, his work is extraordinary in the agenda it put forth around the coming together of Marxism, postcolonialism, and capitalism.

This book is therefore an attempt at imagining a dialogue between Gramsci and Fanon, and by extension the theoretical canons of Marxism and anti/postcolonialism. I ultimately argue that the synthesis between these two canons is fruitful, suggesting that there is something in Marxism that is important for postcolonial nations, as many Arab and African scholars and activists have said before me. It also suggests that there is – and this is more important – something in postcolonial contexts for Marxism, as witnessed by the long tradition of postcolonial Marxist theorizing. By adopting the lens of travelling theory, I explore both what Gramsci's work can tell us about the 2011 revolution and modern Egyptian history – through the lens of elite configurations and hegemony – as well as what Egypt can tell us about Gramsci, and Marxist theory more broadly. Each chapter engages with some of the problematics around applying Gramsci's thought in contexts such as Egypt, and considers the forms in which they are most useful. This exploration is done vis-à-vis Fanon's work and in particular his concept of stretching Marxism.

---

[8] There are exceptions to this, most notably in work on Palestine and Algeria, as well as recent texts by scholars such as Stefania Pandolfo (2018).

Marxism in the Postcolony; the Postcolony in Marxism

Marxism was part and parcel of the imagined futures that coloured the moment of decolonization, despite clear limitations characterizing its political programme. David Scott captures the complexities of Marxism in the postcolonial world when he writes, 'For those of us born into the uncertain aftermath of sovereignty, Marxism has defined in a very fundamental way the ethical-political horizon of our visions of – and commitments to – the making of just and independent societies. We were still haunted by the spectre of a theory that would enable us to deduce a set of rational political practices and procedures for the radical transformation of our societies. It was, if you like, the remnants of our nostalgia'.[9] Similarly, Alia Mossallam notes that what was hegemonic under Nasser was a *socialist imaginary,* which people related to and willingly sacrificed for.[10] What does it mean to be haunted by a moment during which there were multiple alternatives, if we understand our contemporary moment as a 'world without alternatives'? Scott rightly points to both the limitations of nostalgia and the risks that come from postcolonial scholars disavowing Marxism: 'When Marxism is criticised, what is at stake is the theoretical apparatus for reading history rather than the political question of the criteria by which the shape of an alternative future can be affirmed or refused'.[11]

A central claim of this book is that Marxism – as a 'theoretical apparatus for reading history' – can offer a more telling account of revolution in Egypt. Marxist thought and practice were very much part and parcel of the politics of the Middle East and Africa throughout the twentieth century.[12] Debates within intellectual circles, labour unions, resistance groups, and anti-imperial movements engaged with the core tenets of Marxist theory, and sought to replicate socialist and communist models across the two regions. These stories have been marginal to the way we tell Marxist history, which has tended to focus on the decline that followed the failure of Stalinism in the Soviet Union. These stories have also been marginal to the historiography of the Middle East, where nationalism and anti-colonial resistance have been understood as autonomous, and the Marxist inflections of the region have been ignored or minimized. Yet we only need to turn to the

---

[9] 1996, 1.   [10] 2012, 86.   [11] Ibid., 11.
[12] See Samir Amin, Anouar Abdel-Malek, Mahdi Amel, and Nazih Ayubi, among others.

debates among intellectuals and political leaders to see just how influential the concepts put forward by Karl Marx and numerous subsequent Marxists were to people across Africa and the Middle East who were grappling with the material and ideological effects of European colonial rule. This has already been elucidated by scholars within the Black Radical Tradition such as Cedric Robinson, Claudia Jones, W. E. B. Du Bois, Walter Rodney, and C. L. R. James as well as scholars working on African nationalism vis-à-vis the various African contexts.[13] It is safe to say that Marxism provided an important paradigm for political change across the world throughout the early twentieth century.

Marxism and postcolonial theory have long engaged with one another, and in many ways these discussions form the basis of the arguments made throughout this book. A shift within postcolonial studies away from grand narratives and towards a more postmodernist inflection was neatly encapsulated by Edward Said early on: 'The earliest studies of the postcolonial were by such distinguished thinkers as Anwar Abdel-Malek [sic], Samir Amin, C.L.R. James; almost all were based on studies of domination and control made from the standpoint of either a completed political independence or an incomplete liberationist project. Yet whereas post-modernism, in one of its most famous programmatic statements (by Lyotard), stresses the disappearance of the grand narratives of enlightenment and emancipation, the emphasis behind much of the work done by the first generation of postcolonial artists and scholars is exactly the opposite: the grand narratives remain, even though their implementation and realization are at present in abeyance, deferred, or circumvented'.[14] Edward Said's mention of Anouar Abdel-Malek, Samir Amin, and C. L. R. James as the 'first generation' of postcolonial thinkers is striking given that all three were Marxists. And while Marxist scholars have had a lot to say about postcolonial studies and its postmodern inflection,[15] it is important to also note that the Eurocentrism of much

---

[13] Rodney 1972; Robinson 1983; Du Bois 1933; James 1938/2001. In particular, W. E. B. Du Bois wrote: 'Imported Russian communism ignores the incontrovertible fact of a vertical fissure, a complete separation of classes by race' (cited in Sekyi-Otu 1996, 15).

[14] 1995, 5.

[15] See Vivek Chibber (2014) for the most recent iteration of this. Previous materialist critiques of postcolonial studies include Brennan 2006; Parry 2004; Bartolovich and Lazarus 2002; Sinha and Varma 2017; Dirlik 1994.

Marxist theory is no small challenge to any attempt to analyse the postcolonial world. Nor is the scholarship of Marxists working within postcolonial contexts or racialized contexts in the Global North necessarily as influential within Marxist theory as it should be.[16] This is not meant to underplay the significance of postcolonial Marxist work, but rather to highlight the continuing dominance of perspectives on capitalism that underplay the impact of racism and colonialism.

Perhaps, as Rashmi Varma and Subir Sinha suggest, the fields of Marxism and postcolonial studies are too broad and unstable to be compared in any productive way:

> Does one go with early or late Marx, the mechanistic or the Romantic Marx, or indeed the canonical or the 'Other' Marx? Is one more partial to world systemic derivations from Marx, or to 'political' Marxism? Does one, conversely, follow the postcolonial theory that is inextricable from postmodern and poststructuralist formulations, or one that hitches itself to revolutionary anticolonial thought? Does one concede that modernity arose in 'Europe' or 'the West', thereby underscoring the stability of these terms, or does one see modernity as emerging as a single but uneven system? In the heat of these polemics, these differences *within* Marxism and postcolonial theory, which exist prior to the differences *between* them, are dissolved.[17]

The point about differences *within* rather than between Marxism and postcolonial theory brings us back to the large theoretical canon produced by anticolonial and postcolonial scholars working with the structures of capitalism, imperialism, and racism. What distinguishes them is not whether they are loyal to Marxism or postcolonial theory, but rather that they use particular debates that already exist within both fields to produce unique insights into the workings of global politics today. For it is in the work of postcolonial Marxists that we see a rigorous analysis of capitalism, racism, and colonialism, and where we begin to see the vast potential for an alliance between Marxism and postcolonial theory. This is exemplified through the work of Middle Eastern and African-based Marxists such as Samir Amin, Anouar Abdel-Malek, Frantz Fanon, Mehdi Amel, Mehdi Ben

---

[16] This is in spite of the importance given to imperialism by influential early Marxists such as Rosa Luxemburg and Lenin, not to mention Marx himself in his later writings; see Anderson 2016. Similarly, Giovanni Arrighi, Emmanuel Wallerstein, and Robert Cox, to name a few, have all paid attention to the centrality of imperialism in capitalist expansion.

[17] 2015, 6.

Barka, Amilcar Cabral, and Kwame Nkrumah; whose work analysing capitalism through imperialism sits alongside the work of Claudia Jones, George Padmore, Fidel Castro, and Eduardo Galeano.

Along these lines, Rahul Rao has called for 'recovering reparative readings' of postcolonialism and Marxism.[18] Arguing against a reading of Marx's ambivalence about imperialism as pro-imperialist, and noting how his views on imperialism shifted as European empires spread, Rao shows that the blanket designation of Marxism as Eurocentric fails to attend to the nuances embedded within Marx's position on imperialism. While the debate around Marx's Eurocentrism is an important one, I am equally interested in what gets represented as 'Marxism' in this debate. In other words, what are we assuming to be the Marxist 'canon'? If we take seriously the work of Samir Amin, C. L. R. James, Frantz Fanon, and Claudia Jones, then the Marxist canon itself is not as stable as often imagined. The canon is a global canon, made up of scholars, activists, and political actors. It spans over two centuries, and is made up of people from every part of the world. This is the Marxist canon that inspires so many of us, and that is always already connected to postcolonialism.

This book, then, is an attempt at 'reparative reading' by bringing Gramsci and Fanon into an imagined conversation. Reading Fanon through Edward Said's concept of travelling theory, and focusing particularly on his concept of 'stretching Marxism', I explore how Gramsci's concepts travel to the Middle East, in effect bringing Fanon and Gramsci into a sphere of engagement.[19] The concept of travelling theory was formulated by Edward Said[20] to discuss the ways in which theories travel across space (and time) and what happens to them when they do; the concept of 'stretching', and in particular the stretching of Marxism, as illustrated by Fanon[21] to explore how Marxism changes when it 'meets' postcolonial contexts. These concepts refer to two separate albeit connected movements. The first is the movement of theory from a particular space and time to another – in this case from Southern Italy in the early twentieth century to Egypt in

[18] 2017.
[19] Adam David Morton has previously explored what it would mean to think about Gramsci through Said's notion of travelling theory, in particular in relation to passive revolution (2013). I discuss this piece further in the following chapter.
[20] 1983. [21] 1963.

the twentieth and twenty-first centuries. The second is the movement that happens to the theories themselves, as they stretch and shift form in a new context. These two movements frame the book, and drive the questions asked in each chapter.

Ultimately, although the book aims to contribute to broader debates about Marxist theory in postcolonial contexts, its analysis also makes its contribution through an intervention in ongoing debates about the 2011 Egyptian revolution, and Egyptian political change in general. This is the context that grounds the concepts and theories discussed. This context is neither a prop for a larger theoretical argument nor is it simply background information that lends colour to the text; instead it is a living, breathing subject through which I think with Gramsci and Fanon's concepts. Rather than Egypt being the context to which Gramsci is applied, I am equally interested in what Egypt's political history has to say about Gramsci. This distinction is important, as it foregrounds the postcolonial context and the debates and events that unfold within this context as leading narratives of political change without defaulting to colonial conceptions of linear progress. The 2011 revolution is an important part of this context, but as the following chapters show, it is not the main protagonist; the revolution was monumental but must always be historicized.

Revolutionary Events, New Paradigms

This book aims to make a theoretical intervention in debates on Egyptian political projects modern Egyptian revolutions, and capitalist development in Egypt. The 2011 revolution can be read as an invitation to return back to some of the stories we have told ourselves about Egypt, the Middle East, and the broader postcolonial world. This book draws on many of these stories, and thus its empirical material is wide and varied, from economic reports from the Egyptian Central Bank to ethnographies of class and masculinity. Using Gramsci's concept of hegemony as a guiding light reveals some of these different patterns, allowing us to think of Egyptian elites and Egyptian revolutions in different ways. This book aims to explore the particular characteristics of Egypt's elites by looking at the various projects that they have undertaken, tracing their relationships to other centres of power such as subaltern groups and transnational elites, and mapping the rise and fall of different elite configurations over time. Engaging with Gramscian and Fanonian concepts allows for a more complex, historical and global exploration of changes within Egypt's elite projects and the ways in which these led to the 1952 revolution, the 2011 revolution, and the shifts in between.

Egyptian politics between the 1952 and 2011 revolutions is the context through which I bring together Gramsci and Fanon and where I locate my analysis. The 2010/2011 revolutions in the Middle East have reignited curiosity in a region that has long interested scholars of global politics. This book builds on recent work that has looked at Gramsci's concepts in the context of Egypt, most notably Brecht De Smet's *Gramsci in Tahrir*, Alia Mossallam's *Stories of Peoplehood*, Roberto Roccu's *The Political Economy of the Egyptian Revolution: Mubarak, Economic Reforms and Failed Hegemony*, John Chalcraft's *Popular in the Making of the Modern Middle East*, and Maha Abdelrahman's *A Long Revolution*.[22] Each of these texts approaches the 2011 revolution through Gramsci's concept of hegemony, albeit with different focuses.

While I share the same assumptions and mirror many of the conclusions reached in these works, the overarching aim of this book is to engage in the debates discussed above by exploring how Gramsci's concepts travel to the particular postcolonial context of Egypt. I am thus interested not only in engaging with these concepts, but also in tracing this process of travel, and in bringing in other theorists such as Fanon and various Arab Marxists in conversation with Gramsci. This in turn raises questions such as how postcolonial theory addresses questions of political economy through the 1952 and 2011 revolutions; how postcolonial contexts open up new ways of understanding Gramsci's concepts; and how this process of stretching Gramsci in the context of Egypt opens up new avenues of research on Egypt and the broader Middle East. Above all, this book is greatly indebted to Adam Hanieh's *Lineages of Revolt* and Nazih Ayubi's *Overstating the Arab State*,[23] both of which opened my eyes to the importance of a critical political economy analysis of the Middle East, and the centrality of capitalist expansion to the contemporary political moment in contexts such as Egypt.

The story of 2011 does not have a clear beginning, but there are particular moments during which a number of conditions materialized and came together, producing change. One such moment can be

---

[22] See Pratt (2007) for a Gramscian analysis of Egypt pre-2011. See also Chalcraft 2016; Fahmy 2011 and El Shakry 2007.

[23] As well as many other texts these authors have written.

located in the two decades leading up to the revolution itself; decades during which there was an important shift within Egyptian elites that was to accelerate Egypt's neoliberal restructuring. This in turn resulted in unprecedented numbers of workers' strikes and actions, with a total of more than 2 million Egyptian workers taking part in actions throughout the 2000s. Another moment can be located further back. It would be a mistake to assume that the precedents for 2011 can be located solely in the decades leading up to the revolution; instead, events taking place throughout the last century can help us understand why, in 2011, Egypt saw a revolution demanding bread, freedom, social justice; a revolution that clearly called for a realignment in Egypt's elite formation. It was one century ago that Egypt was drawn into the emerging capitalist world system through imperial expansion, with dramatic effects on the evolution of elite formations. Only a historical perspective unearths these changes and puts forward an analysis that includes patterns and disjunctures and takes time as a central mode of analysis.[24] This is the first major break that this book performs with analyses of the 2011 Egyptian revolution within the fields of international political economy, Middle East politics, and political sociology that locate the causes of the revolution in the decades leading up to 2011, inevitably proposing a linear teleology in Middle Eastern countries that assumes a set of developments that progress towards – or regress away from – liberal democracy.[25]

The story of 2011 is also not simply an Egyptian story. Beyond the fact that the revolution was a global media spectacle, it was also a global event in a more important way: revolutions in postcolonial contexts are always invariably connected to the international sphere, better conceptualised through the term 'colonial international.'[26] At times there is a tendency to analyse the Middle East as isolated from global processes, thus displacing problems internally and removing responsibility from transnational forces. Both postcolonial theory and Marxist theory make the theoretical and conceptual move to transcend methodological nationalism; they are both sets of approaches that think globally and that see global power relations as crucial. Egypt's ties to global capitalism are central throughout this book, in opposition to literature that sees the weakness of capitalism in Egypt as a cause of the revolution.[27] Capitalist

---

[24] Braudel 1982.   [25] Inter alia, Cook 2011; Stacher 2012; Schlumberger 2007.
[26] Jabri 2012.   [27] Cook 2011; Stacher 2012; Schlumberger 2007.

development *is* key to understanding the 2011 revolution; however, as I will demonstrate, it is precisely *because* free market orthodoxy was introduced to Egypt that authoritarianism[28] and economic and political repression intensified.[29]

Although this book tells the story of 2011 through elite formations, Gramsci's concepts of hegemony and the historical bloc problematize notions of who the elite are and how they came to rule. Work that emphasizes neo-patrimonialism in the Arab world – implicitly supporting the 'Arab despot' thesis – tends to individualize rulers and assume that they rule through corruption and/or repression.[30] Alternatively, the excessive focus on institutions, and in particular electoral institutions,[31] simplifies modes of rule in Middle Eastern countries.[32] Conceptualizing elites as a ruling class rather than as individuals or as located within institutions is a holistic approach that looks at how elites rise and fall, as well as which political and economic projects they support or resist. It also contextualizes elites within broader social forces within society, avoiding a top-down analysis. Although there has been incisive work on Egypt's labour movement and the ways in which this led to the revolution, the tendency to separate analyses of labour from analyses of elite configurations misses the important dialectical relationship between them.[33] A historical bloc includes elite groups and subaltern groups; it cannot exist otherwise.[34] Any attempt to create a historical bloc is an attempt to integrate subaltern groups into elite projects – part of what this book does is trace some of these attempts.

Finally, the story of 2011 is also not a story of the resilience or breakdown of authoritarian rule. The paradigm of authoritarianism has become so dominant in the literature on Middle East politics that it

---

[28] As Adam Hanieh (2013, 23) notes: 'An entire academic industry has developed around attempting to explain the apparent persistence and durability of Middle East authoritarianism. Much of this has been heavily Eurocentric, seeking some kind of intrinsic "obedience to authority" inherent to the "Arab mind"'. See also Cavatorta 2010.

[29] See Mitchell 1999.

[30] For an example of analysis based on such assumptions, see Schlumberger 2008.

[31] See Brownlee 2002; Albrecht 2005; Schlumberger 2007; Blaydes 2010.

[32] For an important overview and critique of this, see Pratt 2007.

[33] See Abdelrahman 2014 El Mahdi 2011; Anderson 2011; Bush and Ayeb 2012; Korany and El Mahdi 2012; Joya 2011.

[34] For more on this, see work by scholars who look at hegemony in Egypt through the lens of popular politics, including Chalcraft's (2016) and Mossallam's (2012) work on the everyday politics of hegemony.

Travelling Theories 13

has structured stories about the revolution. The transition paradigm[35] and its emphasis on democratization is part and parcel of this authoritarian lens. The basic question that has guided research questions within this paradigm has been: why are Arab countries especially averse to democratization? As Maha Abdelrahman has noted, 'Arab countries were at the "bottom of the class" after the third wave of democratization had come and gone. The inability of the region to join other countries in ridding themselves of dictatorial regimes gave rise to a robust industry devoted to deciphering the enigma of this anomaly, looking for signs everywhere but mostly in the dark recesses of the regime's cultural and religious systems or, occasionally, in a reductionist version of the "rentier" thesis'.[36] Although the events of 2011 led scholars working within this paradigm such as Eva Bellin to ask whether the paradigm should be questioned,[37] authors continued to list the same problems as preventing democratization: the weakness of civil society, the failure of electoral reforms, cronyism and the failure of economic liberalization, and the continued perseverance of corruption.[38] Tellingly, for this paradigm Egypt represented an example of durable and stable authoritarianism in the decades leading up to 2011. Contrary to this approach, this book argues that the decades leading up to the revolution were marked by weakness rather than 'strength'. This weakness was produced via deeply destabilizing shifts within the elite, which played out in terms of an increased propensity towards coercion.

Travelling Theories

Stuart Hall once wrote that we mustn't use Gramsci like 'an Old Testament prophet who, at the correct moment, will offer us the consoling and appropriate quotation'.[39] Instead, we must 'think' our problems in a Gramscian way.[40] It is this sentiment that guides this book: I am less interested in a wholesale application of Gramsci's concepts and theories to Egypt,[41] and more interested in what it would mean to both 'think' modern Egyptian politics in a Gramscian

---

[35] See Carothers 2002; Anderson 2006. [36] 2014, 1. [37] 2012.
[38] Bellin 2012, 127; Stacher 2012; Osman 2010; Masoud 2015. [39] 2002, 227.
[40] Ibid.
[41] As noted by Morton (2013), this would produce an uncritical form of travelling theory.

way, as well as 'think' about Gramsci from the context of Egypt. Hall goes on to argue that the whole thrust of Gramsci's thinking was to refuse any easy transfer of generalizations from one conjuncture, nation, or epoch to another; this idea, too, is central to this book.

In placing Gramsci in the Middle East, it is useful to recall Omnia El Shakry's reference to the 'lost archive of Arab Marxism', a body of work created by Arab thinkers debating Marxist ideas; although it is an archive that is still being retrieved, it represents a body of work that thought through the connections between postcolonial contexts and Marxist ideas.[42] This is perhaps unsurprising, given the focus on anti-imperialism in nationalist movements across the Arab world, and the strength in Marxist theorizing on the question of capitalist development, dependency, poverty, and the global imbalance of power.[43] In this archive, capitalism was always intertwined with the colonial question. El Shakry cites in particular Ilyas Murqus, who rethought Lenin's formulation of imperialism, and who did not simply adopt European Marxism but rather produced an innovative reading of decolonization in its own right.[44] This is in distinction to Halliday and Molyneux's claim that Marxist theorizing in the third world has shown little innovation.[45] Similar to El Shakry, I argue that engagements with Marxists in general, and Gramsci in particular, should be read less as a wholesale adoption of Marxist tenets to the Middle East and more as a productive engagement, critique, and stretching of these tenets as they travel to postcolonial contexts. What would it mean to work with the spirit of Gramscian analysis, rather than the imposition of an intact Gramscian framework onto a region?

While there has certainly been more engagement with Gramsci's work across the Middle East,[46] there has yet to be a sustained engagement with Gramscian concepts as a means through which to understand Arab politics, as noted by Nazih Ayubi.[47] This does not mean there has not been interest in Gramsci, and in particular his familiarity to Arab scholars:

Gramsci's writings are texts with which you can enter into a dialogue, for they deal with issues that do concern us. Although they were written in Italy over half

---

[42] El Shakry 2015, 930.   [43] Halliday and Molyneux 1984.
[44] El Shakry 2015, 931.   [45] Halliday and Molyneux 1984, 21.
[46] See, inter alia, De Smet 2016; Roccu 2013; El Shakry 2007; Lockman 1994; Chalcraft 2016; Pasha 2005; Zureik 1981.
[47] 1996, 9. This is aside from De Smet's (2016) work.

Travelling Theories   15

a century ago, the worries, aspirations and debates contained in them seem to be parallel to our own, to Arab and to international present-day concerns.[48]

For Ayubi, who makes use of Gramsci extensively in his monumental book *Overstating the Arab State*, it is Gramsci's positionality as an Italian from underdeveloped Sardinia who had lived in Italy at a time of early capitalism combined with fascism that makes him applicable to other peripheral contexts.[49] This is the crux of my own understanding of Gramsci as a travelling theory: it is precisely his own positioning within what he calls an 'internal colony' that allows him to develop concepts that can travel to actual colonial contexts. This is not to flatten the distinction between Southern Italy as an internal colony and Egypt as an external one; rather it is to suggest that Gramsci's attention to multiple levels of inequality – including empire – infuses his work with a particular sensitivity to power operating along lines of empire.

Indeed, in lesser-known writings, Gramsci reflects on Italy's own empire and the ways in which it contributed to rising fascism inside the country:

This capitalist vice gripping the colonies worked wonderfully: millions and millions of Indians, Egyptians, Algerians, Tunisians and Tonkinese [Vietnamese] died from hunger or disease as a result of the devastation wrought on the wretched colonial economies by European capitalist competition. How could an Egyptian or Indian peasant make his prices competitive with the English or French or Italian state? Rice, wheat, cotton, wool – all this was secured for us Europeans, while the colonial peasant had to live on herbs and roots, had to subject himself to the harshest corvée labour in order to scrape a bare subsistence minimum, and had to suffer the raging of impetuous and untameable famines that rage in India like natural storms.

For several years we Europeans have lived at the expense of the death of the coloured peoples: unconscious vampires that we are, we have fed off their innocent blood. But today flames of revolt are being fanned throughout the colonial world. This is the class struggle of the coloured peoples against their white exploiters and murderers. It is the vast irresistible drive towards autonomy and independence of a whole world, with all its spiritual riches. Connective tissues are being recreated to weld together once again peoples whom European domination seemed to have sundered once and for all. (2000, 112–13)[50]

---

[48] Firyal Ghazul, cited in Ayubi 1996, 9.   [49] Ibid., 8.
[50] I would like to thank Alberto Toscano who brought this quote to my attention.

This passage reveals both tensions in how Gramsci understood and wrote about the colonial world, as well as an opening through which questions of colonial violence and the urgency of independence could surface. Before turning to my own dialogue with Gramsci's thought, and the tensions around understanding Gramsci's theories as travelling theories, I touch on the idea of travelling theory itself.

Edward Said wrote that theories sometimes travel to other times and places, and in that process can lose some of their power and rebelliousness:[51]

The first time a human experience is recorded and then given a theoretical formulation, its force comes from being directly connected to and organically provoked by real historical circumstances. Later versions of the theory cannot replicate its original power, because the situation has quieted down and changed, the theory is degraded and subdued, made into a relatively tame academic substitute for the real thing.[52]

However, when he returned to the idea of travelling theories almost two decades later, Said had changed his mind. Travelling theories may sometimes get weaker and less rebellious as they travel; but the opposite can also happen – they can also become more far-reaching.[53] Revisiting the ways in which György Lukács' theories travelled, Said notes that while this sometimes led to depoliticized interpretations of what Lukács actually said, they also had the effect of radicalizing theorists who applied them. Reflecting on this, Said writes:

This movement suggests the possibility of actively different locales, sites, situations for theory, without facile universalism or over-general totalising. To speak here only of borrowing and adaptation is not adequate ... [instead] the exercise involved in figuring out where the theory went and how in getting there its fiery core was reignited as invigorating – and is also another voyage, one that is central to intellectual life.[54]

I expand on Gramsci's understanding of hegemony, as well as its historical legacies, in the following chapter, where I discuss it in relation to the colony. Here I conclude by briefly outlining the ways in which hegemony is used in this book. Hegemony, put simply, is the process whereby a particular social force goes beyond its narrow interests to universalise its project. These social forces are within the ruling class itself, but also within the subaltern classes. Hegemony initially referred to the process by

---

[51] 2000, 416.   [52] Ibid.   [53] Ibid.   [54] Ibid., 230.

Travelling Theories

which the working class could overthrow the ruling class and establish itself as hegemonic. It was Gramsci's adoption of the concept that saw it being applied to the bourgeoisie.[55] His point of departure, in other words, was bourgeois hegemony.[56] This does not mean that he understood bourgeois and proletarian hegemony as identical; as Brecht De Smet notes, for bourgeois hegemony consent is created through paternalism and reformist politics; for proletarian hegemony, consent is formed through a continuous and reciprocal exchange between leaders and led.[57]

Hegemony, then, is the result of the combination of the production of consent and coercion – a 'consensual political practice' that differs from brute coercion.[58] Consent and coercion always exist together in any instance of hegemony. Gramsci noted that a class is dominant in two ways: leading and dominant – it leads the allied classes, and dominates over the adversarial classes.[59] In other words, leadership – through consent – and domination – through coercion – are not two distinct realities that exist independently of one another, but always exist together. 'Hegemony is the form of political power exercised over those classes in close proximity to the leading group, while domination is exerted over those opposing it'.[60] Consent is deployed in relation to the former; and coercion in relation to the latter. The crucial point here is that for hegemony to exist, any deployment of coercion must be grounded in consent; in other words, it must be seen as legitimate. In relation to Egypt, De Smet writes: 'The hegemonic rule of the dominant class can very well rely on a disproportionate use of force (war, occupation, state violence), as long as this is accepted as necessary and in the interest of the common good by its allies'.[61] It is not that under hegemony there is less coercion than times of non-hegemony; rather it is that under hegemony this coercion is seen as necessary, justifiable, etc.[62] As Gramsci wrote:

The 'normal' exercise of hegemony on the now classical terrain of the parliamentary regime is characterised by a combination of force and consent, which counterbalance each other, without force predominating excessively

---

[55] As Peter Thomas (2009, 60) notes, hegemony was initially a theory to theorize and guide the proletariat in allying itself with other subaltern groups; it was Gramsci's usage of the concept to analyse bourgeois power that was his most unique contribution to the concept.

[56] Ibid., 223.   [57] 2016, 88–9.   [58] Ibid., 144.   [59] Ibid., 163.   [60] Ibid.

[61] Ibid., 25.

[62] A special thanks to Brecht De Smet, who encouraged me to think of coercion-consent in this sense.

over consent; rather, it appears to be based on the consent of the majority, expressed by the so-called organs of public opinion.[63]

This book argues that the Nasserist project is the only instance of hegemony in modern Egyptian history. This was partly because of the specific historical conjuncture during which it emerged, and partly because of how the project mobilized ideologies and implemented material changes that spoke to the overarching anti-colonial nationalist consciousness of the time. Hegemony, then, does not imply the absence of coercion, or even lower levels of coercion; indeed in many ways the Nasserist ruling class was as dependent on coercion as the ones that emerged under Anwar el Sadat and Hosni Mubarak, as well as the one we see in Egypt today. Hegemony, rather, signals the presence of notable levels of consent that can legitimize and justify the coercion that co-exists alongside it. As we will see in the case of Egypt, although high levels of coercion existed throughout modern Egyptian history, it was only when consent was produced as a counterbalance, folded into a powerful political project, that we see the presence of hegemony.

Gramsci Meets Fanon

An imagined conversation between Gramsci and Fanon might take many different forms; here I read it through the particular context of modern Egypt. Inspired by Rahul Rao's writing around Fanon's ambivalence towards both Marxism and postcolonialism, I imagine a conversation with Gramsci that would think through the tensions and possibilities inherent in Gramsci's concepts. Rao writes: 'I find Fanon useful as a reminder of the existence of a form of political thought that is situated in a position of productive ambivalence with respect to both postcolonialism and Marxism on account of its refusal to accord any one axis of subordination analytical or normative priority. Fanon and other black Marxists inaugurated a technique of political analysis, a way of thinking about race and class (and other forms of inequality) that is all but obscured in contemporary polemics that insist on viewing postcolonialism and Marxism as unremittingly opposed to one

---

[63] Quoted in Thomas 2009, 164.

another'.[64] Fanon's ideas, then, are a way of stretching hegemony and the historical bloc in the colony/postcolony, and thinking through the tensions embedded within this process, both productive and unproductive. What would this imagined conversation look like, if it were to take place in Egypt?

Fanon's point of departure is that capitalism in the colonial – and therefore postcolonial – world took a distinct form. He analyses this specifically through distinguishing between ruling classes in the West and those in the colonized world, arguing that the latter were structurally and fundamentally created *to be dependent*. Even in cases where this ruling class may want to become hegemonic, it will always fail precisely for the structural reasons emended within colonial capitalism, most notably a failure to accumulate capital on the scale necessary to create an authentic bourgeois project. For Fanon, then, decolonization did not always succeed in its *stated* goal of interrupting colonial structures and forms of dependency, and often merely transferred those same structures and forms to a native class.

In some ways, this is an accurate reading of the Nasserist project in Egypt, the point from which this book begins. After some ambiguity, Nasserism adopted a state-led capitalist programme that ensured the reproduction of capitalism in the postcolonial context; Nasserism also embodied ideas of modernity, development, and industrialization that relied on a modernist teleology of civilization.[65] Finally, ideas around mastery (mastering nature, workers, and subjectivity) were central to various anticolonial projects, even as they were encoded within the language of anticolonialism.[66]

In other ways, Nasserism seems to interrupt Fanon's prediction of a dependent class that is unable to become hegemonic. Teasing out this contradiction, I argue that Nasserism, formed in the early 1950s, was an instance of hegemony rather than domination. This, however, can still only be explained with reference to both colonialism and anti-colonialism. Rather than Egypt's colonial position – and the nationalist sentiment imbricated in this – acting as a backdrop in the formation of this project, it was precisely its condition of emergence. Nasser and the Free Officers created a project that both drew on and implemented anticolonial goals which had already been crafted and popularized by various social movements that came before them, and which were often

[64] 2017, 10.   [65] El Shakry 2007.   [66] Singh 2017.

expressed in varying forms of nationalist consciousness. From an active worker's movement to the Wafd; from students to feminists; Egypt pre-1952 was bursting with anti-colonial activity. The failure of the Wafd – Egypt's first nationalist and primarily liberal party – to secure meaningful independence further set the stage for Nasser and the Free Officers, who fashioned themselves as a more radical alternative that spoke to the everyday Egyptian. Indeed the class composition of the Free Officers is key to understanding their widespread popularity, as they were the first, and possibly last, ruling class composed of individuals from non-elite classes. Nasserism, then, owed its hegemony to the anticolonial moment.

The Free Officers were initially a nationalist movement, made up of different trends including the Muslim Brotherhood, the Wafdists, and the Communists.[67] Their shared class background explains not only the antipathy many felt towards the monarchy and political parties such as the Wafd that had a clear class bias, but also contributed to their particular understanding of anticolonial nationalism as a material form of decolonization. This class background was a result of the opening up of Egypt's Military Academy to men from the middle classes in 1936, transforming what had always been an elitist institution. It was in 1949 that Nasser established the 'founding committee' of the Free Officers' movement, initially composed of eight men who met to discuss what kind of political action was needed in Egypt: Nasser, Abdel Mon'im Abdel Ra'uf Kemal al-Din Hussein, Khalid Mohieddin Abdel Hakim Amer, Salah Salem, Hassan Ibrahim, and Abdel Latif al-Boghdadi. In the early 1950s, the first Free Officer pamphlets were printed, stating that the goals of the movement were to bring an end to British imperialism, palace and government corruption, feudalism, and to tackle the Palestine question.

On 23 July 1952, a mere three years after the Free Officers were formed, Anwar el Sadat announced to the nation that a coup had taken place, and an outpouring of national support followed. Military bases and instalments, the national broadcasting station, and the Suez Canal were seized. In his book outlining the goals of the revolution, Nasser emphasized the destructive British presence in the Suez Canal, the destruction of imperialism and feudalism, the establishment of social justice, and the establishing of a democratic system.[58] The road

---

[67] Botman 1986, 350.   [68] 1959, 6–7.

to an actual hegemonic project being created, however, was rocky. In the early days of their time in power, there were major disagreements among the officers as to how they should build a 'new Egypt'. While there may have been broad consensus around the creation of a new social base and anti-colonialism, there was equally broad disagreement over how these should be achieved. Some of the groups that had supported the Free Officers were sidelined and dealt with through coercion, such as the Muslim Brotherhood,[69] while others were approached through a mixture of consent and coercion, such as the Egyptian communist movement.

One of the main ways in which hegemony is created is through balancing coercion within consent. The Nasserist project achieved high levels of consent, I argue, in several ways. Some of these are not the result of any political work they did themselves; they were able to mobilize certain ideologies and energies that pre-dated them, and also emerged during a historical moment in which the question of anti-colonialism was dominant. In other ways, the ruling class did contribute to these levels of consent; they did, for example, expend energy into spreading their project through Egyptian civil society, be it through popular media such as *Voice of the Arabs*, or through their transformation of Egypt's educational system. Indeed it is difficult to think of a sphere within civil society[70] (defined in a broad Gramscian sense) that the Free Officers did not intervene in. Because of the complexity behind the creation of consent under Nasserism, we are precluded from any simple dismissal of Egyptians as either having been brainwashed by Nasser or as having been repressed into acquiescing to Nasser's schemes. As Alia Mossallam has argued, Egyptians rearticulated the ideological and material tenets of the Nasserist project in complex ways, making them their own.[71] This everyday politics of hegemony cannot be easily sidestepped, and should be central to how we understand the Nasserist project and its afterlives, which were to last for decades to come

[69] See Kandil 2014.
[70] Civil society, for Gramsci, constitutes schools, religious institutions, journals, clubs, political parties, and other such social institutions, whereas political society refers to formal public institutions such as the government, police, military, and courtrooms.
[71] 2012.

Alongside powerful ideologies, the materiality of the Nasserist project equally explains its hegemony. The dismantling of the landed elite, the limited land reform programme, the introduction of free education and health care, and the guarantee of employment after graduation, were some of the material changes put in place by the Nasserist project. These material changes were contradictory; not only were they limited in practice, they also still relied on the reproduction of capitalist development. At the same time, they radically affected the chances of many Egyptians in terms of accessing both social mobility and social services. Equally pertinent are the infrastructural projects of this era, including the nationalization of the Suez Canal and the building of the High Dam; these projects spoke directly to questions of *national* development.

Here Fanon intervenes again, turning our attention to the *international* context within which Nasserism was produced and reproduced. My analysis suggests that the creation hegemony is always international, but that the international at that moment was structured to reproduce dependency. Nasserism's interventions into international politics raises questions about the simple narrative that Nasserism was purely dependent or reactionary. From the infrastructural projects of modernization to the Suez crisis, Nasserism challenged the colonial international, even while simultaneously upholding some of its key tenets. It is this complexity, in all of its contradictions, that interests me and that I explore in this book. While I challenge the idea that Nasserism represented Fanon's dependent bourgeoisie – instead positing that this bourgeoisie came much later, in the late 1960s – I simultaneously unpack the ways in which Nasserism reproduced colonial lifeworlds and ways of being.

In 1967 – following Egypt's defeat to Israel – the emergence of a new ruling class and a new national project were met with increasing social, political, and economic crisis. These crises increasingly betrayed the lack of hegemony, as did the turn to coercion that was not hidden under a layer of consent, as it had been throughout the 1950s and 1960s. While we may ask why so many within radical movements had an ambivalent relationship to Nasser, by the 1980s and 1990s this question haunts us less; the clear resistance to the Sadat and Mubarak ruling classes by many parts of Egyptian society suggests an absence of hegemony. There was no project to defend;

instead, what we see is the slow engulfing of society by violence, coercion, and domination.

What emerges in the late 1960s is a ruling class, led by Anwar el Sadat, that was incapable of creating a historical bloc or hegemony. Here I bring together Fanon's understanding of what a 'real' bourgeoisie ought to do, and the parallels this has with Gramsci's understanding of hegemony. For Gramsci, a class that successfully creates hegemony must be able to maintain a balance between consent and coercion, but also between narrow interests and universalizing reforms. Fanon wrote of this very same balance in relation to the difference between European and (post)colonial ruling classes. The moment of defeat in 1967 is interesting because we see the slow erosion of the Nasserist ruling class and the emergence of the ruling class Fanon predicted. This moment is significant because although the infitah ruling class was unable to create hegemony internally, it drew on transnational forces and a growing consensus around neoliberalism to rule, assuming that this could compensate for the lack of consent. As Fanon wrote in *The Wretched of the Earth*: 'The national bourgeoisie turns its back more and more on the interior and on the real facts of its undeveloped country, and tends to look towards the former mother country and the foreign capitalists who count on its obliging compliance'.[72] This was possible only because of Egypt's position as a postcolonial nation; recalling Fanon, this allowed Egypt's ruling class to access material and ideological power from the colonial international, reducing its need to produce consent within the nation.

By the time we get to the 1990s things begin to shift once again. What we see here is not a shift in the political project itself, as we did during the transition from Nasserism to infitah. Rather what we see is a change in the tempo of the project. This shift in tempo – marked by acceleration – ultimately was what destroyed the balance both Gramsci and Fanon spoke of as being integral to hegemony. The acceleration of neoliberal restructuring throughout the 1990s and 2000s swung the pendulum towards coercion and let go of any attempts to represent the new ruling class as anything but a class for itself. The balance between consent and coercion disintegrated, revealing the increasing violence for what it was. Because of the new

[72] 1963, 165.

financial ruling class's acceleration of neoliberal restructuring, there was growing discontent from different parts of society. To deal with this, the ruling class increasingly made use of coercion, and in particular began to target larger numbers of Egyptians through everyday police brutality. Alongside decreasing levels of consent, this coercion was seen as brutal violence protecting the enrichment of a small circle, symbolized by the 'cabinet of businessmen'.

The social force that emerged in the mid 1960s, then, did not produce something *new* from the perspective of a hegemonic project. Instead, the years following Nasser's death can be read as an interregnum – a moment during which the 'old is dying but the new cannot be born' – when uncertainty prevailed and attempts to create hegemony failed. Similarly, the rise of a social force under Hosni Mubarak, which did not correlate with his coming to power but instead happened midway through his reign, suggests that this moment was also not productive of a new political project. Other than a shift in tempo, during which neoliberalism was accelerated, we do not see a historical bloc or hegemony emerge; this is why I join these two moments together into one period: the afterlife of hegemony, marked by *empty time*. Although there has been a strong tendency to read Egyptian history chronologically, through the rise and fall of individual leaders, I suggest – particularly in the last three chapters – that an analysis focused on hegemony challenges us to think of alternate chronologies. Bringing together the idea of *empty time* – a time of crisis during which politics pauses – and Gramsci's concept of *transformismo* – 'damage control' – I read the years between 1967 and 2011 as time that was both empty in the sense that we see an absence, rather than presence, of hegemony.[73]

It is precisely these shifts in how various national projects have been understood and resisted over time that interests me. Was the Nasserist project singular, and if so, why? Bringing Gramsci and Fanon into conversation allows for a more complex appraisal of the Nasserist project and its afterlives. This conversation pushes us to think of who the ruling class is and how it is formed; how hegemonic projects are created and what kinds of energies they depend on; how

---

[73] To clarify, I do not use 'empty' here to denote the absence of politics more broadly but rather the absence of a hegemonic project or historical bloc.

subaltern classes relate to hegemony in the postcolony; how postcolonial ruling classes relate to transnational capitalist classes; and finally how the material and ideological substance of anticolonialism, nationalism, and decolonization created the particularities of hegemony in contexts such as Egypt.

By using hegemony as a searchlight, I demonstrate that what characterizes successive elite formations in Egypt is a decreasing ability to create hegemony, and a correlated increase in the use of coercion over consent; it is this that ultimately led to the 2011 revolution. By tracing the presence or absence of hegemony, the pending collapse in the formation of the 1990s and 2000s becomes clear. The historical bloc – formed when one social force[74] transcends its narrow interests and succeeds in universalizing them in support of a hegemonic project – that was created by Gamal Abdel Nasser and the Free Officers in 1952 represents an instance of hegemony and strength; the absence of a hegemonic project under Anwar el Sadat, whose ruling class was significantly weaker resulting in him having to rely on transnational forces to maintain hegemony, as well as under Hosni Mubarak suggest that the singularity of Nasserism can be located precisely in the presence of both a historical bloc and hegemony. This also suggests alternative ways of understanding the 2011 revolution, that locate it within the absence of both a historical bloc and hegemony on the one hand, and rising subaltern resistance on the other. A searchlight for hegemony brings to the surface the increasing turn to coercion and the overall weakness of Egypt's ruling class in the lead-up to the revolution. Rather than see this as a contemporary phenomenon, I instead locate it within the longer trajectory of decolonization.

Outline of the Book

The introductory chapter traces the various theoretical and empirical questions the book explores. Connecting the two revolutions of 1952

---

[74] I use the term *social force* throughout to refer to a faction that gathers around a particular material and ideological form of capitalist accumulation. Each force is discernible not simply through the interests of its individual members but through the dialectical process that creates each force and in turn Egypt's production and accumulation strategies.

and 2011, I suggest that they should be understood as part of one historical trajectory. I sketch out the broader debates that have taken place between Marxism and postcolonialism, before delving into the particular conversation Gramsci and Fanon have throughout the book. I argue that while there are important tensions in how Gramsci and Fanon conceptualize political and social change, there is something productive in bringing them together through Fanon's call to 'stretch Marxism'. The chapter further explores travelling theory more broadly, as well as the specifics of hegemony as a travelling theory, before presenting an outline of the book.

The first chapter returns to travelling theory on the one hand and stretching Marxism on the other, unpacking them and connecting them to threads and concepts in Gramsci and Fanon's work. The main focus of the chapter is to focus on debates around hegemony by producing a genealogy of the concept both in Marxism and as in debates on its application to the postcolonial world. Following the Subaltern School and Fanon, I show why hegemony in postcolonial contexts, in contrast to Western contexts, is dependent on the transnational and why an international lens is thus central to understanding political change in countries such as Egypt. It is for this reason that a change in Egypt's – and other postcolonial nation's – positions vis-à-vis the international and capitalist development is necessary for meaningful independence. To contextualize this debate, I look specifically at the founding of Bank Misr in the 1920s, revisiting a debate about foreign capital and national capitalists in Egypt.

The second chapter revisits Gamal Abdel Nasser and the 1952 revolution. Focusing on the emergence of Nasserism, I argue that it represents the first and last hegemonic project in modern Egypt. Nasserism can be understood as a collective will that was produced in a particular historical moment; one that was formed against the dangers of imperialism and the hopes of a postcolonial project. Nasserism was also, however, an articulation of an elitist state-led project of decolonization that centred the military, the state, and capitalism, leaving powerful legacies that would haunt Egypt's future. Exploring these contradictions, the chapter charts a history of Nasserism through Fanon and Gramsci, thinking through anticolonial nationalism, state-led capitalism, third worldism, the colonial international, and hegemony. I argue that the creation and then decline of Nasserism as a hegemonic project is central to understanding contemporary Egyptian politics. The chapter looks specifically

Outline of the Book

at the anticolonial movements predating 1952; the creation of the Free Officers and new historical bloc; the creation of consent in civil society; and some of the paradigmatic events of anticolonialism in Egypt such as the nationalization of the Suez Canal.

The third chapter traces the decline of Nasserist hegemony and the rise of a new ruling class and its project of *infitah* (literally translated to 'opening'). Marking Egypt's opening to global capital and the failure of state-led capitalist development, these years see the dominance of neoliberal restructuring and Westernization. I argue that while this ruling class did attempt to create hegemony, its project was weaker than the Nasserist project. Engaging in debates on the effects of neoliberalism in the Middle East, the chapter argues that it was this bloc that laid the foundations for Egypt's neoliberal trajectory, but failed to create a hegemonic project strong enough to maintain the same level of hegemony as the Nasser-led bloc and thus had to rely on transnational social and ideological forces in order to rule. The question of transnational capitalist development and its effects across postcolonial contexts frames this chapter, as I argue that there is a correlation between weakening hegemony and neoliberal restructuring. This era is thus understood through Fanon's notion of a dependent bourgeoisie, as well as Gramsci's notion of an *interregnum*, a period of transition.

The fourth chapter shifts to the early 1990s. The 1990s and 2000s are crucial decades that saw the emergence of a new dominant social force, led by Gamal Mubarak and other businessmen associated with him, signalling the finale in the neoliberal project put in place under the previous ruling class. The financialization of Egypt's economy began in earnest, a process that not only created severe social tension but also marginalized other actors within the ruling class such as the military. By engaging in the debates surrounding this new social force, I argue that their decision to accelerate Egypt's neoliberal restructuring contributed to the ultimate collapse of the ruling class and the continuing failure to create hegemony. Tracing the rise in violence and repression, I show how the pendulum swung further towards coercion under this ruling class. I pay particular attention to increasing police brutality in the everyday; electoral politics; increasing workers' strikes; and the shift from productive to unproductive capital to highlight these changes. I argue that it is the ultimate failure of this ruling class to create a political project that could have become hegemonic that culminated in the 2011 revolution.

The final chapter brings the various threads of the book together, and revisits hegemony and its afterlives in Egypt through the concepts of haunting and mastery. I trace some of the ways in which hegemony and its afterlives fed into the 2011 revolution, and ask why it was so important for each ruling class to portray itself as either a rupture or a continuity. Haunting allows me to lay out both how these different projects were formed, and how they seeped into one another; in other words, how some projects haunted others. I posit that Nasserism set the terms of the political and economic debate in contemporary Egypt; the projects that came after consistently found that they had to work within these terms – or face serious crises. After discussing the concept of haunting, the chapter explores Nasserism and its promises as well as the afterlives of Nasserism that haunt contemporary Egypt, particularly in relation to economic liberalism. I then turn to the question of mastery and the ways in which Nasserism's attempt to master the future also haunts us in important ways, and why to become truly free we must think about the future in ways that do not centre mastery or mastering. The book ends with Fanon, and his call to create a new world, one in which all of us are free, and in which decolonization becomes a reality rather than a dream.

PART I

Anticolonialism and Its Discontents

1 | *Hegemony in the Postcolony?*
Postcolonial and Marxist Encounters

Why should Russians wait for the history of England to be repeated in Russia?

Antonio Gramsci[1]

Gramsci saw the political as a live, decentred, disorderly domain, composed of myths and passions as much as of rational doctrines.

Stuart Hall[2]

For those of us invested in the analysis of, and struggle against, multiple and intersecting forms of oppression on the basis of class, race, nation gender, sexuality, disability and other axes of subordination, the continued mutual repudiation of postcolonialism and Marxism is disconcerting.

Rahul Rao[3]

Social freedom, namely socialism, does not mean observing rigid theories which have not arisen out of the nature of national experience.

Gamal Abdel Nasser[4]

The national bourgeoisie turns its back more and more on the interior and on the real facts of its undeveloped country, and tends to look towards the former mother country and the foreign capitalists who count on its obliging compliance.

Frantz Fanon[5]

Antonio Gramsci's theory of hegemony is arguably one of the most influential accounts of the twentieth and twenty-first centuries that

---

[1] Cited in Brennan 2001, 170. [2] 2016, 3. [3] 2017, 2.

[4] Ibid., 38. Alongside Nasser, Kwame Nkrumah, Kenneth Kaunda, Julius Nyerere, and Patrice Lumumba represent other African postcolonial leaders who engaged with Marxist and socialist ideas to elaborate new programs for their countries' development.

[5] 1963, 165.

attempts to explain how ruling classes rule. Although Gramsci was unique among Marxists of his time for the emphasis, he put on the dialectic between the material and the ideational, leading to insights into the role of culture, norms, and values in political rule, his work was still very much a product of a particular historical moment in a particular geographical space.[6] Gramsci's position as a Southern Italian intellectual – occupying the position of periphery within the centre – opens up interesting possibilities for work looking at other global peripheries.[7] This positionality is what allows Gramsci's concepts to travel, and the changes that take place during these travels are what interest me. This does not mean that travelling theories travel seamlessly; rather, as Edward Said notes, they are always mutating and changing.[8] I am interested in this process of travel, on the one hand, and the process of adaptation, on the other. What happens when the 'elsewhere' that we think Gramsci's concepts through is a postcolonial context?

This chapter is divided into two parts. The first part sketches out the theoretical stakes of the book through exploring Gramsci's concepts of hegemony, the historical bloc, and passive revolution, as well as Fanon's concept of 'stretching Marxism', predominantly in relation to Ranajit Guha's work on hegemony/domination within the Subaltern Studies Collective. In particular, I am interested in both the intervention Guha made in debates around hegemony and what this means for the (im)possibility of hegemony in the colony, and Fanon's notion of a 'dependent bourgeoisie' that emerges after independence and what this means for the postcolony. The second half of the chapter applies these particular interventions to the context of Egypt pre-1952, in other words, the prehistory of independence. What sets the scene for Nasserism, and how did the absence of hegemony during British colonial rule transform into the presence of hegemony during independence? Bringing together the concepts discussed in the first half of the chapter,

[6] For comprehensive takes on the uses of Gramsci today, see Buttigieg 2009; Fontana 2009; Hall 1986.

[7] As I show further on, Gramsci wrote extensively on Southernism and the particular problems Southern Italy faced that were similar to the problems faced by formal colonies in other places. 'Italy presents itself as a case study for understanding the colonial relationship, both in international terms – as having been both subject to external powers and a colonising power itself – and in domestic terms – as the dominance of the North over the South' (Srivastava and Bhattacharya 2012, 4–5).

[8] 1983.

Gramsci as Travelling Theory

the case of Egypt pre-1952 contextualizes and historicizes the material that makes up the following chapters. It also allows me to trace the two movements that this book is interested in: travel, on the one hand, and stretching, on the other.

Gramsci as Travelling Theory

From Southern Italy to Egypt

Adam David Morton describes Gramsci's work as a form of travelling theory that is positive and powerful.[9] Thinking through passive revolution, space, and history, Morton proposes that Gramsci's attention to space and time renders passive revolution a useful form of travelling theory and thus that it does not apply only to Italy but to multiple contexts and time periods. Echoing Said's warning that theories can lose their criticality when they travel, Morton suggests that as long as a theory retains a form of critical consciousness – in his eyes, through a focus on spatiality – it can continue to hold radical potential.[10] Instead of using theories and applying them wholesale, the point is to pay attention to the particularities of any given context. While I agree with Morton's argument, my point here is to argue that Gramsci's concepts – in this case, hegemony – retain a critical consciousness especially when they travel to the postcolony. It is the confluence of capitalism and colonialism that creates this critical consciousness, allowing Gramsci's radical potential to hold as he travels. I also depart from this in that I am equally interested in what travelling theory tells us about the reverse process; in other words, travelling theories do not just tell us new things about a particular context but also tell us new things about Marxist concepts more broadly.

Gramsci is perhaps the most popular Marxist theorist within the field of postcolonial studies, aside from Marx himself.[11] For postcolonial scholars who have turned to Gramsci, ranging from Edward Said[12]

---

[9] 2013, 50.   [10] Ibid., 60.

[11] Given the tense relationship between postcolonial theory and Marxism at certain junctures, the popularity of Gramsci is even more indicative of his potential in analysing postcolonial contexts. For more on this relationship, see Lazarus 2011; Rao 2017.

[12] Said in particular has been clear about his debt to Gramsci at the intellectual level. Specifically, the theory of hegemony allowed Said to discuss the stability and power of Orientalism as a structure. For a take on Said's use of Gramsci, see Bhattacharya in Srivastava and Bhattacharya 2012, 80–97.

and Stuart Hall to the members of the Subaltern Studies Collective, he represents a departure from a more orthodox form of Marxism that is economically deterministic. Gramsci, to them, provided concepts that were applicable to the postcolonial world.[13] This can be seen in the elasticity of his concepts and their applicability to the non-West, as well as in the fact that some of his early writings focused on race, imperialism, and the 'Southern' question in Italy, and in particular Southern Italy's position as an internal colony.[14] Gramsci did not simply use the term *subaltern* as a synonym for *proletarian* but also paid attention to the intersections of difference, particularly through nation and class in constructing the subaltern – a move that is clearly of value to scholars working in and on the postcolony. Despite this, only a handful of articles and one book have been written on the subject of Gramsci and postcolonialism.[15]

What is perhaps most impressive about Gramsci is his critical approach to politics, an approach that is based not only on his own theoretical leanings but also on his personal involvement in Italy's workers' movement. His most famous contribution is his concept of hegemony – a system of rule that combines a balance between consent and coercion and that functions through the internalization of specific norms and ideals directly tied to a specific mode of production. This focus on norms and ideals as part and parcel of the material made Gramsci one of the first Marxists to emphasize the role of the ideational. He was attuned to the questions of consciousness, culture, and ideology and – by extension – the role of intellectuals; this attention to the ideational constitutes one of his most unique interventions. Gramsci's concepts provide a framework through which to analyse political change by tracing the relations between the base and superstructure – the material and the ideational – by using various concepts such as hegemony, passive revolution, and the historical bloc.

Although Gramsci should very much be placed within a Marxist terrain, he saw Marxism as a body of work that was fluid, porous,

---

[13] For a well-known critique of the ways in which postcolonial scholars use Gramsci, see Brennan 2001.

[14] In particular, Gramsci's writings on India and British colonialism, on Southernism and on Italian imperialism demonstrate the importance he gives to colonialism and global politics. See Srivastava and Bhattacharya 2012, 3; Brennan 2001, 159.

[15] See Chatterjee 2008b; Brennan 2001; Srivastava and Bhattacharya 2012.

Gramsci as Travelling Theory

and malleable. As Stuart Hall put it, 'Gramsci was never a "Marxist" in either a doctrinal, orthodox or "religious" sense. He understood that the general framework of Marx's theory had to be constantly developed theoretically; applied to new historical conditions; related to developments in society which Marx and Engels could not possibly have foreseen; expanded and refined by the addition of new concepts'.[16] The Marxist tradition as a whole emphasizes the centrality of class, production, and the ways in which human beings reproduce themselves in order to survive, and thus the material always takes ontological priority. Gramsci's work, however, emphasizes the importance of the material structure of ideology, building on Marx's proposition that a popular conviction 'has the same energy as a material force'.[17] In the words of Nazih Ayubi, 'Gramsci filled in the gaps in Marx's theory of politics. His formulations part company with the "scientific" Marxist premise that the "base determines the form of consciousness", and establish instead the premise that the "base determines what forms of consciousness are possible"'.[18]

Hegemony

The word *hegemony* – of Greek origin (*egemonia*) – also exists in Arabic as *haymana* and has an interesting historical lineage in Arabic scholarly writing. As Ayubi notes, we can even see traces of the concept in Ibn Khaldun's work, in particular, in his concept of *iltiham* (coalescence), which adds social integration and ideological cohesion to the overpowering physical capacity of the state.[19] The concept of hegemony dates back to the nineteenth-century Russian labour movement, although Gramsci's usage of the term in the *Prison Notebooks* he credits to Marx's 1859 text *A Contribution to a Critique of Political Economy*.[20] The concept was also in use among Italian socialists in the decade that Gramsci spent in

---

[16] 1986, 6.   [17] 1971, 377.   [18] 1994, 5.

[19] In his published work the *Muqaddimah*, Ibn Khaldun writes, 'Natural authority is derived from group feeling (*'asabiyya*), through the constant overwhelming of competing parties. However, the condition for the continuation of this authority is for the subservient parties to coalesce with the group that controls leadership' (Ayubi 1994, 6). These discussions of authority as natural, and it being derived from 'group feeling', very much tie into a Gramscian understanding of rule through consent rather than coercion.

[20] Boothman 2008, 201.

Turin, and we know that Lenin's understanding of hegemony also greatly influenced Gramsci's understanding of the term, although Gramsci was to question its universalism.[21]

In an influential account, Perry Anderson argued that there are 'three moments' in the *Prison Notebooks* that show a teleological move to understanding hegemony as something both the proletarian and bourgeois classes experience and create.[22] Anderson argues that the concept of hegemony did not originate with Gramsci and that he inherited it from the debates at the Fourth Congress of the Third International, a moment that marked the first time hegemony was used to denote the domination of the bourgeoisie over the proletariat.[23] Prior to this, Russian workers were using the term *hegemony* to mean the process whereby the proletariat extended their hegemonic project to other elements of the subaltern classes. Other Gramsci scholars have pointed to different historical legacies, most prominently Machiavelli.[24] The definition I work with stems from Gramsci's extension of hegemony to understanding how the bourgeoisie rules over the proletariat, as well as how the proletariat (could) exert hegemony over other subaltern classes.

Hegemony, put simply, is the process whereby one class exerts influence over society so that other classes follow its political and economic project. This is accomplished when a social force is able to transcend its narrow interests and universalize them through moral and intellectual reforms; tracing this process produces a hegemony-driven analysis. Culture, civil society, and organic intellectuals are all means through which hegemony is produced and resisted. It is precisely this fact that allows hegemony to exist through a mix of consent and coercion rather than purely through coercion. Gramsci's work emphasizes the importance of the material structure of ideology, with Gramsci building on Marx's argument that a popular conviction has the 'same energy as a material force'.[25] My aim here is to produce such an analysis in order to trace the major political changes that have taken place between the two revolutions in Egypt.

The methodological criterion on which our own study must be based is the following: that the supremacy of a social group manifests itself in two ways: as 'domination' (*dominio*) and as 'intellectual and moral leadership'

---

[21] For an extensive overview, see Bates 1975; Boothman 2008.
[22] Anderson 1977. For a discussion on this argument, see Thomas 2009, 56–71.
[23] Thomas 2009, 58.   [24] Fontana 1993; Femia 2005.   [25] 1971, 377.

Gramsci as Travelling Theory

(*direzione*). A social group dominates antagonistic groups, which it tends to 'liquidate', or to subjugate perhaps even by armed force; it leads kindred and allied groups. A social group can, and indeed must, already exercise 'leadership' before winning governmental power (this indeed is one of the principal conditions for the winning of such power); it subsequently becomes dominant when it exercises power, but even if it holds it firmly in its grasp, must continue to 'lead' as well.[26]

In unpacking Gramsci's description of hegemony I want to draw attention to both the notion of domination and that of intellectual and moral leadership. Domination can be read analogously to 'authoritarianism', a paradigm that has come to dominate understandings of states in the Middle East. However a lens that looks at domination alone does not tell us much about the contestation, negotiation, and leadership that make up the political scene. Reading Middle Eastern politics through domination – particularly by focusing on military and police violence – erases the presence of other forms of what Gramsci calls 'leadership', as minute as they might be. Gramsci also points to the necessity of leadership to the project of hegemony; coercion/domination alone is an unstable and short-term form of rule: only leadership can ensure that a ruling class that has become dominant can continue to exercise power.

I focus on two particular aspects of it that I return to throughout this book: the two 'levels' at which hegemony is formed – civil and political – and the balance between consent and coercion. In writing that hegemony is constructed through political society and civil society, Gramsci points to the need for the ruling class to universalize its narrow class interests to other classes through moral reforms. The power of the ruling class is therefore not just concentrated in the state, but throughout society, for as Gramsci noted, 'In reality civil society and the State are one'.[27] Gramsci also developed the concept of the hegemonic apparatus, which referred to the institutions and practices that allowed a class to gain political power, from newspapers and schools to political parties and religious institutions. It is this apparatus that bridges civil and political society, turning civil power into political power.

Because of his idea that political society and civil society form the basis on which hegemony is built, he suggests that the power of the ruling class is not concentrated simply in the state but rather throughout society. He writes:

[26] 1971, 207. [27] Quoted in Thomas 2009, 68.

What we can do, for the moment, is to fix two major super-structural 'levels': the one that can be called 'civil society', that is the ensemble of organisms commonly called 'private', and that of 'political society' or 'the state'. These two levels correspond on the one hand to the function of 'hegemony' which the dominant group exercises throughout society and on the other hand to that of 'direct domination' or command exercised through the State and 'juridical' government.[28]

Put simply, civil society refers to schools, religious institutions, journals, clubs, political parties, and other such social institutions, whereas political society refers to formal public institutions such as the government, police, military, and courtrooms. Intellectuals – particularly organic intellectuals – become important in attempting to spread a hegemonic project through civil society. The distinction between civil and political society reproduces the coercion versus consent relationship in spatial terms,[29] with consent lying in the realm of civil society and coercion in the state.[30] Some scholars disagree on whether Gramsci actually divided political and civil society into two clearly distinct levels.[31] Suffice it to say here that while the extent of the division is subject to debate, Gramsci did distinguish between political and civil society as two separate realms within which hegemony had to be constructed and exercised.

As for the state, Gramsci defines it as 'the entire complex of practical and theoretical activities with which the ruling class not only justifies and maintains its dominance, but manages to win the active consent of those over whom it rules'.[32] He expands the concept beyond the Marxist-Leninist notion of the state as a coercive instrument of the bourgeoisie. What is perhaps more important is Gramsci's assertion that political and civil society come together to form the 'integral state'. Civil society and the state are not separate but rather civil society is an 'ensemble of practices and relations dialectically interpellated by and integrated within the state'.[33] This means that any hegemonic movement must exercise power in the realm of ideas and society; capturing the state alone is never enough to create hegemony. In other words,

---

[28] 1971, 12.
[29] Here *spatial* does not mean geographical but is rather a metaphorical reference to the realm of the state and state politics on the one hand and the realm of non-state politics on the other.
[30] Thomas 2009, 167.   [31] See Thomas 2009, 167–95.   [32] 1971, 244.
[33] Ibid., 180.

Gramsci as Travelling Theory

both civil and political society must be targeted in any attempt to form hegemony. This is precisely why, as I show further on, postcolonial scholars have questioned the possibility of hegemony in the colony – while political society may be successfully pierced by colonial powers, it is questionable whether this is the case with civil society.[34]

Central to establishing hegemony within these two spheres is the creation of a historical bloc. A historical bloc is a state of being that every ruling class aims to achieve, one that allows it to organize society in its own image. This understanding of the historical bloc as a condition to be achieved rather than simply as a social alliance provides a more abstract and theoretical understanding of the concept. This new configuration of social forces, coming together in a particular way at a particular moment in time, produces a new form of politics. Different norms, different values, and different ideologies emerge, as well as different material conditions of production. In short, society changes. However, this change is neither abrupt nor does it represent a clear break with the previous configuration; thus we see that new forms of politics or new norms and dispositions may only become dominant halfway into a new historic bloc. Moreover, these new changes within society usually do not displace old ones completely, but rather combine with them. It is because the historic bloc is so crucial and expansive that only an organic crisis can dislodge it.

The balance between consent and coercion is the second aspect of hegemony I engage with throughout the book:

> The 'normal' exercise of hegemony in what became the classic terrain of the parliamentary regime is *characterized by the combination of force and consent variously balancing one another, without force exceeding consent too much*. Indeed one tries to make it appear that *force is supported by the consent of the majority*, expressed by the so-called organs of public opinion – newspapers and associations – which are therefore, in certain situations, artificially increased in number.[35]

Here Gramsci highlights two features of consent/coercion: that they are balanced, with coercion not exceeding consent too much; and that coercion should appear to be supported by the consent of the majority. The relationship between consent and coercion, then, is a dynamic one in which the two are dialectically related. Consent works to legitimize or

---

[34] See in particular Chatterjee 2011.   [35] Gramsci 2000, 261.

erase coercion, and coercion needs consent in order to appear necessary. It is only when this dynamic is in place that hegemony can exist.

This is where Gramsci's focus on culture, norms, and ideas becomes integral: it is precisely through ideology that consent is created, which ultimately negates the need to use vast amounts of coercion.[36] When the balance of consent and coercion is disturbed and a ruling class becomes dependent on coercion in order to maintain stability, we see the beginnings of an organic crisis and the decline of hegemony and the historical bloc that created it. As I demonstrate in the penultimate chapter, 2011 was the material consequence of an organic crisis that developed due to the failure of a new ruling class to establish hegemony or a historical bloc. One of the biggest indicators of this failure was precisely the reliance of this specific ruling class on coercion which greatly exceeded consent. Its inability to create consent through transcending its narrow interests and universalizing them is precisely what ultimately led to the increasing levels of coercion. In other words, as consent decreases, coercion must increase.

A hegemonic project expresses the spirit of its time. Because it is created and spread through both political and civil society, and because it is both material and ideological, hegemonic projects can serve to highlight the dominant forces and ideas of any given moment. Here Gramsci's uniqueness comes in; understanding norms, values, and ideas is as important as tracing the mode of production, the state, and the political economy of any given society. Civil and political society come together to form the integral state, and it is this coming together that represents the complexities of creating hegemony. Although this may appear to hold universal relevance, it is important here to take a step back and ask how, in postcolonial contexts, the integral state and hegemony play out, something I turn to further in the chapter.

---

[36] There have been debates about whether hegemony is really the antithesis of domination; Peter Thomas for example argues against Anderson's reading of hegemony as the opposite of domination and suggests instead that Gramsci sees political leadership as constituting both domination and hegemony: 'A class is dominant in two ways, that is, "leading" and "dominant". It leads the allied classes and dominates over the adversarial classes' (Gramsci, in Thomas 2009, 163). In other words, a social force, or class, must lead other forces within the ruling and subaltern classes that support their project but dominate those who do not. Consent is needed for those within the ruling and subaltern classes who are allies; coercion is needed for everyone else.

Gramsci as Travelling Theory 41

Perhaps the most interesting element of hegemony is that it broadens out what 'politics' means and is. In the words of Stuart Hall, 'One of the most important things that Gramsci has done for us is to give us a *profoundly expanded conception* of what politics itself is like, and thus also of power and authority. We cannot, after Gramsci, go back to the notion of mistaking electoral politics, or party politics in a narrow sense, or even the occupancy of state power, as constituting the ground of modern politics itself'.[37] As I noted in the previous chapter, it is precisely the frame of electoral politics and the occupying of state power that have dominated analysis of Egyptian politics. In this process, politics has come to represent something much smaller than it actually is. Hegemony, instead, is expansive, complex, and fluid; it is about tracing change, movement, alliances, violence, and everything in between. As Hall says, hegemony allows us to profoundly expand what we think politics is.

Historical Bloc

Historical blocs are formed when a particular social force goes beyond its narrow interests to 'sell' its project to other groups, thereby universalizing it. These social forces are within the ruling class itself, but also within the subaltern classes. The historical bloc is therefore not simply a synonym for 'ruling class', but a configuration that includes both the ruling class and the subaltern classes, held together by a hegemonic project. As Stuart Hall notes, a historical bloc is 'precisely different from that of a pacified, homogenous, ruling class':

It entails a quite different conception of how social forces and movements, in their diversity, can be articulated into a set of strategic alliances. To construct a new cultural order, you need not to reflect an already-formed cultural will, but to fashion a new one, to inaugurate a new historical project.[38]

An analysis of a historical bloc would look at how a particular group articulated specific things at specific times – in other words, the ideology they used – and how they packaged their own narrow interests within a wider project that was made appealing to other segments of the ruling class as well as segments of the subaltern classes. At some point in time, historical blocs break down, and at this point a political

[37] 2002, 272.   [38] Ibid., 273.

crisis may occur. 2011 is an example of such a crisis, although it was not until mid 2013 that an attempt at forming a new historical bloc was made.

Gramsci understands historical blocs as constituted through a particular coming together of the material and the ideological:

A[nother] proposition of Marx is that a popular conviction often has the same energy as a material force or something of the kind, which is extremely significant. The analysis of these propositions tends, I think, to reinforce the conception of *historical bloc* in which precisely material forces are the content and ideologies are the form, though this distinction between form and content has purely didactic value, since the material forces would be inconceivable historically without form and the ideologies would be individual fancies without material forces.[39]

Structures and superstructures form a 'historical bloc'. That is to say the complex, contradictory and discordant ensemble of the superstructures is the reflection of the ensemble of the social relations of production. From this, one can conclude: that only a totalitarian system of ideologies gives a rational reflection of the contradiction of the structure and represents the existence of the objective conditions for the revolutionizing of praxis.[40]

The material forces as content and the ideologies as form – despite his insistence that this separation is purely conceptual rather than practical – suggest that a historical bloc is built around the coming together of these 'levels'. Putting it in a more Marxian framing in the second excerpt – 'structures' and 'superstructures' – Gramsci reiterates the complex and contradictory nature of such a coming together. To achieve this, a social force must therefore position itself as the carrier of certain values, which then become detached as projections of its political outlook. The attractiveness of these projections is what draws other social forces into the project, and thus determines whether a historical bloc can be formed.[41] Ideology and ideas are thus central to the formation of blocs:

A[n] historical bloc refers to an historical congruence between material forces, institutions and ideologies, or broadly, an alliance of different class forces politically organized around a set of hegemonic ideas that gave strategic direction and coherence to its constituent elements. Moreover, for a new historical bloc to emerge, its leaders must engage in conscious planned struggle. Any new historical bloc must have not only power within the civil society and economy, it also needs persuasive ideas, arguments and initiatives

---

[39] 1971, 377.   [40] Ibid., 366.   [41] Adamson 1983, 178.

Gramsci as Travelling Theory

that build on, catalyze and develop its political networks and organization – not political parties such.[42]

Here Gramsci elaborates on this coming together of the material and ideological by framing it through an alliance of class forces that coalesce around a set of hegemonic ideas. For this to happen, there must be active and conscious political activity on the part of the social force attempting to create a historical bloc; only this allows it to expand power within both political and civil society.

Identifying the rise of historical blocs means looking for new (or old) social forces in society that are attempting to displace one configuration of hegemony with another. In turn, identifying the breakdown of historical blocs is an important method of tracing shifts within society and understanding the causes of crisis and revolution. In the case of Egypt, the major revolutions and political crises have always been connected to either the rise or fall of a given historical bloc, including the 2011 revolution. I argue in the book that the revolution can be understood as a response to the absence of hegemony and a historical bloc: a new ruling class emerged in the mid 1990s, coalescing around Hosni Mubarak's son Gamal and as I show, this class failed at creating both a hegemonic project and a historical bloc that could propel it forward. It is the absence of both that can explain why the 2011 revolution happened when it did and why the ruling class in place at that moment was unable to prevent it.

Passive Revolution

This brings us to the final concept – that of passive revolution. Gramsci took this term from Vincenzo Cuoco, who used it to analyse the Neapolitan evolution of 1799, and instead used it to look at the Italian *Risorgimento*.[43] In the *Prison Notebooks* Gramsci refers to a 'revolution' without a revolution – which he later begins to describe as a 'passive revolution'.[44]

The concept of 'passive revolution' must be rigorously derived from the two fundamental principles of political science; 1. that no social formation disappears as long as the productive forces which have developed within it still find room for further forward movement; 2. that a society does not set itself

---

[42] Gill 2002, 58.   [43] Thomas 2009, 146.   [44] 1971, 59.

tasks for whose solution the necessary conditions have not already been incubated, etc.[45]

The category of passive revolution refers to the ability of the bourgeoisie to produce socio-political change that conserves power in its own hands and that leaves subaltern groups in a state of subalternity.[46] In this way the bourgeoisie preserved its power not by extending or strengthening its own hegemonic project but by preventing the emergence of competing projects.[47] Peter Thomas writes:

In its over-arching logic of disintegration, molecular transformation, absorption and incorporation, the passive revolution in both of its phases was single-mindedly dedicated to this one goal: prevention of the cathartic moment in which the subaltern classes cross the Rubicon separating a merely 'economic-corporative' phase from a truly 'hegemonic' phase, or, in other words, the phase in which a subaltern social layer becomes a genuine class and architect of an historical epoch.[48]

Passive revolution is not as central to this book as hegemony and the historical bloc. Rather, following De Smet, it is used as a 'methodological searchlight' that highlights the agency of dominant groups in class struggle, which consistently attempt to reproduce their power.[49] It is thus more prominent during some periods than others, most notably during the shift from Nasserism to *infitah* in the 1970s. Although some have argued that Nasserism represents an example of passive revolution, I would add that in this instance, passive revolution should be understood as hegemonic. What interests me more with Nasserism is less the question of whether it was a passive revolution or not, and more the question of whether it achieved hegemony.

These three concepts together provide a holistic approach to understanding political change in Egypt between revolutions. The rest of the book is dedicated to exploring what happens when these concepts travel to Egypt and how they can be stretched when we think through and with them in a postcolonial context. This adds to a growing body of work that explores connections and tensions between postcolonial and Marxist theory. By bringing Egypt's political context into conversation with both Gramsci

---

[45] 1971, 106.   [46] Quoted in Thomas 2009, 147.   [47] Ibid., 151.
[48] Ibid., 151–2.   [49] 2016, 70.

and Fanon, this book shows us why a synthesis of Marxism and postcolonialism is useful in understanding political change in contemporary Egypt.

Gramsci's East versus West Duality

As Stuart Hall notes, Gramsci was born in a place, Sardinia, that stood in a colonial relationship to the rest of Italy. His exposure to radical movements came through Sardinian nationalism, and how it was understood in relation to class politics. 'Gramsci was acutely aware of the great line of division which separated the industrializing and modernizing "North" of Italy from the peasant, underdeveloped and dependent "South"', writes Hall, and this articulated itself through a lifelong concern with dependency and unevenness.[50] This comes out in both his work on the *Southern Question,* as well as his understanding of categories such as North/South, and East/West.

As noted in the previous chapter, Gramsci reflected more directly on Italy's own empire in writings that are less well known than the *Prison Notebooks*:

Rice, wheat, cotton, wool – all this was secured for us Europeans, while the colonial peasant had to live on herbs and roots, had to subject himself to the harshest corvee labour in order to scrape a bare subsistence minimum, and had to suffer the raging of impetuous and untameable famines that rage in India like natural storms.

For several years we Europeans have lived at the expense of the death of the coloured peoples: unconscious vampires that we are, we have fed off their innocent blood. But today flames of revolt are being fanned throughout the colonial world. This is the class struggle of the coloured peoples against their white exploiters and murderers. It is the vast irresistible drive towards autonomy and independence of a whole world, with all its spiritual riches. Connective tissues are being recreated to weld together once again peoples whom European domination seemed to have sundered once and for all.[51]

What we see more often in his writings, however, is an analysis of underdevelopment within Italy itself. Gramsci's ideas of the differences

---

[50] 1986, 9.
[51] 2000, 112–13. I would like to thank Alberto Toscano for bringing this quote to my attention.

between underdeveloped and developed geographies emerge most clearly in *Some Aspects of the Southern Question*, where he articulates forms of uneven development that result from colonial and/or racial inequalities. He writes:

> It is well known what kind of ideology has been disseminated in myriad ways among the masses in the North, by the propagandists of the bourgeoisie: the South is the ball and chain which prevents the social development of Italy from progressing more rapidly; the Southerners are biologically inferior beings, semi-barbarians or total barbarians, by natural destiny; if the South is backward, the fault does not lie with the capitalist system or with any other historical cause, but with Nature, which has made the Southerners lazy, incapable, criminal and barbaric- only tempering this harsh fate with the purely individual explosion. of a few great geniuses, like isolated palm-trees in an arid and barren desert.[52]

In *Some Aspects of the Southern Question,* Gramsci explores two blocs: the Northern (industrial) bloc and the Southern (agrarian) bloc. The question he is interested in is how a revolutionary working class in coalition with the peasantry can rise up and displace these two blocs. In this piece of writing, we see Gramsci make use of both meanings of hegemony: from below and from above. Importantly, this analysis is about more than class; it is here that he focuses specifically on the question of colonialism.

Following Stuart Hall, it is clear that Gramsci did not write extensively about racism, or even colonialism, per se:

> Gramsci did not write about race, ethnicity or racism in their contemporary meanings or manifestations. Nor did he analyse in depth the colonial experience or imperialism, out of which so many of the characteristics 'racist' experiences and relationships in the modern world have developed. Superficially, all of this might suggest that Gramsci belongs to that distinguished company of so-called 'Western Marxists' whom Perry Anderson identified, who, because of their preoccupation with more advanced Western societies, have little of relevance to say to the problems which have arisen largely in the non-European world, or in the relations of 'uneven development' between the imperial nations of the capitalist 'centre' and the englobalised, colonised societies of the periphery.[53]

---

[52] 1971, 71.   [53] 1986, 8.

Gramsci's East versus West Duality

Yet even though Gramsci was more concerned with his native Italy than with questions of imperialism, it was his positionality within Italy itself that allows for his ideas to travel beyond and to shed light on colonialism and other forms of uneven development. It is only a superficial reading, as Hall notes, that would render Gramsci irrelevant to global questions of power and inequality. In this section, I want to draw out my understanding of Gramsci and his relevance for postcolonial contexts by juxtaposing it to two other approaches that look at the international: the neo-Gramscians on the one hand, and Peter Thomas' interpretation of Gramsci's East/West duality on the other.

The Neo-Gramscians

Arguably Gramsci's understanding of hegemony was one that took the international seriously, although this has not necessarily been the way in which extensions of Gramsci's work have been read. For Gramsci, the national can only be considered in the 'international perspective' – which cannot be simply added or skimmed over.[54] Gramsci's perspective was always internationalist; national exceptionalisms existed, but the unity of capitalism in the era of imperialism was of primary importance.[55] While the nation may have been the point of departure, for any analysis to be successful it must be completed from an internationalist perspective, most importantly in order to understand the truly global nature of revolution.

Neo-Gramscian work emerged within a wave of critical theories in the 1970s, including historical sociology and post-structuralism, which rejected positivism.[56] As noted by Robbie Shilliam, it represents perhaps the most influential leftist tradition of thought in the field of international relations.[57] Robert Cox's work[58] can be said to be the umbrella underneath which most of the neo-Gramscian approaches sit, and these approaches can be broadly grouped into two schools. The Amsterdam School focuses on what Henk Overbeek calls 'transnational historical

---

[54] Ibid., 216.   [55] Ibid., 217.
[56] See Cox 1981, 1983, 1987; Gill and Law 1989; Gill 1993; Van der Pijl 1998; Rupert 1995; Bieler and Morton 2003; Bieler and Morton 2003, 2004.
[57] Shilliam 2004, 60.
[58] In particular, his two articles 'Social Forces, States and World Orders: Beyond International Relations Theory' (1981) and 'Gramsci, Hegemony and International Relations: An Essay in Method' (1983).

materialism' by looking at fractions of capital and concepts of control; while the Nottingham School focuses on fractions of capital and fractions of labour with a strong emphasis on ideology. Neo-Gramscians have focused extensively on the international division of labour and transnational capital, attempting to internationalize Gramsci's concepts. The Amsterdam School, for example, argues that neo-Gramscian analysis should be understood as transnational historical materialism, which 'brings back to life themes that were central to the debates on imperialism in the early years of the twentieth century. The global dimensions of the processes of capital accumulation and of class formation, and the changing roles that national states play in these processes, were central in Marx's own understanding of capitalism'.[59] Similarly, scholars such as Bieler and Morton have looked at the ways in which fractions of capital and labour evolve internationally.[60] Using Gramsci as a basis, the aim of such work is to bring questions of imperialism to the centre by analysing global processes of capitalist accumulation. Through focusing on world hegemony and how it is created, neo-Gramscians explore questions of how states and societies act at the international level, as well as the reproduction of imperialism.[61]

The responses to the emergence of neo-Gramscian work have varied. Some have argued that it is not as rigorous in its treatment of orthodox Marxist presumptions as it should be[62] while others argue it is too economistic in its treatment of hegemony.[63] Additionally, Drainville[64] and Panitch[65] critique the neo-Gramscians for giving too much agency to elites and not allowing for the possibility of change among and from subaltern groups; and Germain and Kenny have argued that the form Gramsci's ideas have come to us makes it difficult to speak of a Gramscian 'approach' per se.[66] I want to focus on a second criticism made by Germain and Kenny, namely that Gramsci should be returned to his historical context, and whether Gramsci is useful in analysing the world order. On the one hand, I posit throughout this book that Gramsci's positionality as a Southern Italian Marxist made him especially attentive to questions of power within global capitalism and the uneven manifestations of these.

---

[59] Overbeek 2013, 162.   [60] 2004, 2003.   [61] Cox 1981.
[62] Burnham 1991.   [63] Mouffe and Laclau 2014.   [64] 1995.   [65] 1994.
[66] 1998.

On the other hand, neo-Gramscian work is an example of Gramscian analysis that has not interrogated the imperial in their move to theorize the international, as suggested by Robbie Shilliam and Mustapha Kamal Pasha's critiques of neo-Gramscian work. Shilliam posits that neo-Gramscians use the concept of hegemony at the level of the global by universalizing specific qualities of capitalist social relations without properly interrogating this implicit universalizing tendency.[67] This ignores the history of primitive accumulation and its international dimension, and also fails to understand the significance of the 1917 Russian revolution which posed a major challenge to a 'stageist' understanding of capitalist development: 'The Russian Marxists recognised in this deviance from the heartland norm evidence of a constitutive international dimension of social transformation: in its translation across differentially developed socio-political orders, the process of primitive accumulation "mutated"'.[68] While Gramsci and the neo-Gramscians saw differences between 'East' and 'West', what remained under-theorized, especially by the latter, was what had *caused* these differences, and what this meant for international Marxist praxis. Shilliam instead turns to Trotsky's combined and uneven development as one possible way out of this problem. For him, Trotsky took seriously the different stages of development at the global level, and applied this theoretically and analytically. While neo-Gramscians claimed to do the same, their understanding of the international order remains somewhat lacking.

Kamal Pasha's critique similarly questions the ways in which neo-Gramscians approach imperialism and the world order it has created. Arguing that neo-Gramscians have been unsuccessful at avoiding the biases implicit within Western IR, he posits that by assuming that cultural difference is not an impediment to establishing Western-centred global hegemony on the one hand, and by seeing otherness as a principle source of counter-hegemonic resistance on the other, neo-Gramscians produce a variation of 'soft Orientalism'.[69] This ignores how central the difference of the periphery (especially cultural difference) has been for consolidating an international hegemony that is Western-centred. In other words, producing consent in the West relies on using coercion in the periphery; this is how international hegemony is formed. The periphery, however, is ignored by neo-Gramscians

[67] 2004, 62.   [68] Ibid., 68.   [69] 2005, 544.

except when they turn to discussing resistance: 'These regions are smuggled back into analysis as the principal site of counter-hegemonic struggles in the era of globalization. Their challenge, though, is to an order *already constituted*'.[70]

These critiques are central to the problems with much theorizing of the world order and international hegemony. Because they do not see the mutual constitution of core and periphery, imperialism remains under-theorized. Neo-Gramscians thus claim that they are internationalizing Gramsci's theories, without engaging in a discussion about whether Gramsci's theories *can* travel internationally; instead they have simply been appropriated based on the assumption that they can. The work of asking the question of whether Gramsci's theories can travel has instead been done by Shilliam and Kamal Pasha, who show that imperialism must be foundational to any attempt to analyse hegemony. Moreover, there has been little engagement on the part of neo-Gramscians with the Subaltern Studies School, who arguably made this move to internationalize Gramsci much earlier. It is within this latter attempt to position Gramsci's concepts internationally – and specifically in postcolonial contexts – where I locate my own intervention.

'In the East'

Gramsci's famous declaration – 'In the East, the State was everything' – has come to represent his supposed idea that in the East civil society was weak and the state was strong; in the West civil society was strong and thus able to create the hegemony needed for the ruling class to rule through consent. Recall the supposed distinction between consent and coercion on the one hand, and civil and political society on the other. The assumption is that civil society – being the place where consent is manufactured – is strong where hegemony exists, i.e. the West. This is in contradistinction to the East, where coercion is high and hegemony weak, thus indicating the weakness of civil society and the strength of the state, which, after all, is the arm of repression. I first discuss Peter Thomas' correction of these two assumptions, and then extend this by showing that the weakness of civil society in the East is a direct result of

[70] Ibid., 547.

Gramsci's East versus West Duality 51

colonial rule, and that this is ultimately what presents ruling classes with the impossibility of creating consent and thereafter hegemony.

I have already shown why a neat separation between civil and political society is intransigent, and why it is more useful to see them as porous spaces that together form the more important structure of the integral state. However, the importance of civil society in constructing hegemony cannot be underestimated; it is here that the ideological work is done. While consent and coercion may not be as neatly mapped onto civil and political society as some have made it seem, there does appear to be a correlation between consent and civil society.

Gramsci's declaration that 'in the East, the State was everything' has often been taken to imply the strength of the state in the East and, consequently, a comparative weakness of the state in the West. Yet, on closer inspection of Gramsci's formulation, it is precisely the state's overwhelming 'pyrrhic predominance' in the East that turns out, to have been a weakness, when compared to the 'proper relationship between the state and civil society' that obtained in the West.[71]

Thomas suggests that the strength of the state in the East is in fact a sign of weakness; without the consent from civil society, the ruling class is unable to rule through hegemony. This duality does not map neatly onto the developing/developed world, but instead refers to a particular stage of hegemony.

Regarding the duality of East versus West in Gramsci's work, I want to quote Thomas' intriguing argument concerning the possible Orientalist assumptions underlying this duality:

The question here is not posed in terms of East versus West, but rather as one of differential times, cultural and political traditions and political forms within the West itself.[72]

Thomas argues that Gramsci made a similar argument in the context of the US, claiming that the reliance on Fordism effectively meant that consent could not be produced in the US. In other words, it is only in Western Europe where Gramsci saw civil society as being strong enough to produce consent. Similarly, Stuart Hall has noted that Gramsci's East/West distinction should not be taken literally:

[71] Thomas 2009, 200.   [72] Ibid., 201.

Many so-called 'developing' societies already have complex democratic political regimes (in Gramsci's terms, they belong to the West). The point is therefore not to apply Gramsci's distinction literally or mechanically but to use his insights to unravel the changing complexities in state/civil society relationships in the modern world.[73]

Thomas moreover posits that Gramsci's statement should not be seen as a case of East versus West, but rather as a call to see the entire globe as being in the *same temporal cycle* but with different political forms:

Rather than a simple juxtaposition between East and West, Gramsci acknowledges a deeper unity-in-difference regarding the revolutionary strategies appropriate to each of them, founded upon the fundamental unity of the capitalist state-form and the necessity for a proletarian united front to oppose it. Against the popular image, it is necessary to stress this consciously international scope of Gramsci's theory, which comprehended the difference between these social formations and their state-forms as one of degree, not of type ... Against all stageism, Gramsci proposes that it is the historically more 'advanced' centres that allow us to understand the 'delayed' developments in their peripheries.[74]

While this is an important argument, I want to push it further by showing that this is precisely where a postcolonial intervention becomes necessary; or, where we can stretch Marxism. Although Thomas alludes to the distinction between different social and political formations, I instead, taking my cue from the intervention by scholars such as Ranajit Guha and Partha Chatterjee, argue that it is colonialism that is responsible for the inability for civil society to create hegemony in the 'East'. This not only means that colonial rule itself was never – and could never have been – hegemonic; it also means that any ruling class that came after independence and that based its project on colonial norms of modernization and development would have faced serious challenges in constructing hegemony because of the inability to gain consent for what were essentially colonial projects. It is here that the Subaltern Studies debate acts as an important corrective to Marxist accounts, for we can see now that even critical accounts do not take the crucial step of naming colonialism as the reason for the absence of hegemony in the East.

I want to bring in Partha Chatterjee's discussion of political and civil society in here. While he accepts the Hegelian understanding of civil

[73] 1986, 19.   [74] Ibid., 212, 203.

society as institutions of modern life – originating in the West – that are based on equality, freedom, and recognized rights and duties, he argues that in postcolonial countries civil society institutions were set up by nationalist elites in the era of colonial modernity and embodied a desire on the part of these elites to replicate Western modernity.[75] At the same time, something else was happening:

> Even as the associational principles of secular bourgeois civil institutions were adopted in the new civil society of the nationalist elite, the possibility of a different mediation between the population and the state was already being imagined, *one that would not ground itself on a modernised civil society.*[76]

This was because elites realized the limits of civil society institutions in reaching large sections of the population, and turned to politics as a means of mediating between the population and the state. In other words, because civil society could not mediate between the population and the state, political society was to do so instead. This new political society was also built on the framework of modern political associations, such as political parties, but became open to a host of claims and appropriations from different social forces.[77]

Chatterjee's intervention is key because he shows that while civil society may have been the most important site of transformation during the colonial period, it was political society that became the most important site during the postcolonial period.[78] This is precisely why colonialism – as monumental as it was – played a role in affecting the ability of civil society to create hegemony in the postcolony. It was the shift from civil to political society – defined by the institutions of the developmentalist state and the ideologies of modernity and progress – that signalled the inability of nationalist elites to construct hegemony following independence. My own intervention, outlined in this chapter and the next, builds on this one by arguing that, as in India, Nasser *did* build hegemony through civil society in Egypt; but that, as opposed to India, the ruling class that came afterwards were unable to build hegemony. Nasser's hegemony can be seen through his success in drawing subaltern groups into his project, thereby creating a historical bloc, and his success in embedding the large amount of coercion during his reign within consent, thereby largely legitimizing it in ways future ruling classes were unable to do. This underscores why

---

[75] 1998, 62. [76] Ibid., 63 (italics my own). [77] Ibid., 64. [78] Ibid., 65.

hegemony remains a useful concept in analysing postcolonial contexts, as it distinguishes the Nasserist ruling class as the only instance of hegemony in Egypt; in other words, the only time in modern Egyptian history where consent dominated.

Stretching Gramsci: Fanon, Subaltern Studies, and the Colonial Context

The discussion of colonialism and Gramsci's East/West duality leads us to the broader approach framing this project, namely that of 'stretching Marxism'. Here I turn to Fanon specifically, before discussing Ranajit Guha's intervention in understanding hegemony in the colony. What interests me about both of these thinkers is their careful attention to the particularity of the colonial context and what this means for the creation of a ruling class that can (or cannot) establish a historical bloc and hegemony. In particular, Guha's assertion that there cannot be hegemony in the colony and Fanon's notion of a dependent bourgeoisie that prevents hegemony in the postcolony both complicate the idea of a neat transposing of the concept from Southern Italy to Egypt. But where does that leave us with regard to Nasserism? My intervention is precisely to loosen any conviction that sees the postcolony as a space in which hegemony could not be created; Nasserism not only raises questions about Fanon's dependent bourgeoisie, but also suggests that hegemony – and not just passive revolution – is what characterized the postcolonial project in countries like Egypt.

Fanon in the Middle East

Before delving into the specificities of Fanon's call to 'stretch Marxism', I want to attempt to position Fanon within the Middle East. Fanon has been translated widely into Arabic, Farsi, and Turkish, although his influence varies across the region. In this section I focus on some of the details of how this translation took place and how it was received, specifically with regard to Arabic and Farsi. The translation of Fanon's work into Arabic is of particular interest given his close connection to Algeria and the Algerian war of liberation. Fanon paid close attention to Algerian language and culture in his attempt to both theorize and participate in the war of liberation as well as to create psychiatric practices that spoke to the local context. Fanon travelled widely, and

Stretching Gramsci

no doubt met many of those involved in liberation struggles across the Middle East. Notably, Mahdi Amel – one of the most popular Arab Marxists – taught classes on Fanon when he moved to Algeria in 1963 and wrote an article on him for the publication *Revolution Africaine*.[79]

Six editions of *The Wretched of the Earth* have appeared in Arabic translation, with the first being published in Beirut in 1963, two years after the original was published in French.[80] Dar al-Ṭalīʿah (Vanguard Press) had already published translations of Freud, Trotsky, Gramsci and Marx, and was seen as a sanctuary for leftist thinking. Sami al-Durabi and Jamal al-Atassi, the translators, were politically active Syrian leftists, very much involved in anti-imperialist and nationalist politics.[81] Both were strong supporters of Nasser in Egypt, and advocated Arab unity and Arab nationalism. The introduction they wrote for the translation of *The Wretched of the Earth* expanded on the themes of anti-imperialism and independence, and levelled an attack against the national bourgeoisie for making Arab unity impossible.[82] While it is unlikely that they ever met Fanon, the parallels between their political ideas and his is undeniable. It is said that following this edition, the Syrian Ministry of Education published versions of *The Wretched of the Earth* for Syrian secondary school students – a fascinating claim that has been difficult to verify as these copies have not been located.[83]

The latest edition of *The Wretched of the Earth* to be translated into Arabic was published in 2015 in Cairo, by Madarat. This version aims to speak to contemporary events in the Arab world, with the introduction stating: 'We see that after more than half a century, little has changed: military colonisation has been replaced by a "local" or "domestic" colonisation, which is cheaper, and whose cultural, political and economic interests are still controlled by the former colonial powers'.[84] The locating of Egyptian political turbulence vis-à-vis colonialism rather than the Arab national bourgeoisie – as in the first edition published in Beirut – is noteworthy. Given the publishing house's focus on Islam and Islamism, sections are added that focus on Fanon's understanding of Islam.

---

[79] *Jadaliyya* 2012.   [80] Harding 2017, 99.
[81] Both were involved in the Syrian Baʿth party, at the time focused on questions of socialism, liberation from colonial rule, and social justice; ibid., 105.
[82] Ibid., 104.   [83] Ibid., 110.   [84] Ibid., 117.

Despite Fanon's connection to Algeria, it has been argued that his influence on Algerians and the broader Arab world has been minimal.[85] The exception to this muted reception is Palestine, where Fanon's work has directly influenced various groups. Although Fanon did not write extensively on the formation of the state of Israel and the expulsion of nearly half a million Palestinians, his politics around Palestine can be inferred based on Josie Fanon's criticism of Jean-Paul Sartre's support of the Zionist project. In an article in the Algerian publication *El Moudjahid,* Josie Fanon asks for Sartre's preface to be removed from all editions of *The Wretched of the Earth*, noting that Fanon would not have supported the Zionist project and its crimes in Palestine, as Sartre clearly did.[86] Fanon was a clear influence on Fateh, who quoted his work as well as modelled their resistance movement on the Algerian war of liberation.[87] For example, analysis of Fateh pamphlets shows that excerpts from *The Wretched of the Earth* are used liberally.[88] More recently, scholars have continued to use Fanon to analyse Palestinian politics.[89]

Discussing the muted reception of Fanon across the rest of the Arab world, Yasser Munif writes:

Fanon is almost absent in public discourses in the Middle East and is still marginal in the Maghreb. The uprisings should have been an excellent opportunity for Arab intellectuals and activists to engage with Fanon's work on the revolution and the subaltern in the new conjuncture. However, despite the significance of his political philosophy for the current revolts, his books are either out of print or conspicuously absent from many bookstores in the Arab world.[90]

Munif has suggested that this absence has historically been due to Fanon's critique of the national bourgeoisie, an argument I find unconvincing given his influence across Africa and Latin America.[91] I posit in the second chapter of this book that Fanon's depiction of the national bourgeoisie did not accurately describe the ruling class that emerged in countries such as Egypt following independence, as these ruling classes were not dependent but rather anti-imperialist and in favour of

---

[85] Macey 2000, 7; Cherki 2006. [86] Macey 2002, 463.
[87] Harding 2017, 119.
[88] Ibid., 121. For an example, see the pamphlet *al-Thawra wa al-'Unf Tariq al-Tahrir* (The revolution and violence are the way to liberation).
[89] Rodrigo 2015. [90] 2012. [91] Ibid.

Stretching Gramsci 57

independent nationalist development. I argue instead that Fanon's famous national bourgeoisie emerged *later* in Egypt, and that the ruling classes of independence in fact delayed the emergence of the dependent national bourgeoisie. In other words, while Anwar el Sadat in Egypt can be considered the epitome of Fanon's national bourgeoisie, Nasser in many ways was not.

A second reason has to do with the ways in which Fanon's work was translated. Here I turn to the question of why Fanon was enthusiastically engaged with in Iran, a country that had not been colonized in the way Arab countries had been colonized. In an article on Fanon in Iran, Farahzad notes that it is because of the way in which Fanon was translated – by Ali Shariati – that partly explains his reception in Iran. Although Fanon's work was translated several years later in Iran than in Beirut, not only was it engaged with more widely, but several other texts aside from *The Wretched of the Earth* were translated – indeed all of Fanon's work was eventually translated into Farsi. Although Iran had not experienced colonization, Farahzad writes that it did identify with the colonial experiences of oppression and thus did organize around anti-imperialism and resistance.[92] While I focus solely on Shariati's translations here, I want to note that other translations also enjoyed wide popularity, notably Mohammad Amin Kardan's translation of *Towards an African Revolution* (*Enghelab-e Afriqa*), which went through seven reprints, and *Black Skin, White Masks* (*Poost-e Siah, Sooratak haye Sefid*) which went through five reprints.[93] What Kardan did, as did Shariati, was provide extensive contextual information in order to explain unfamiliar concepts, thereby making the unfamiliar familiar to Iranian readers.[94]

Ali Shariati remains one of the most influential Iranian political thinkers of the revolutionary period. He is responsible for two translations of Fanon's work: *Fanon's Will* (*Vasiat Nameye Fanon*) and *The Wretched of the Earth* (*Doozakhian-e-Rooy-e-Zamin*).[95] Shariati was very much involved in the Algerian struggle for independence, joining the National Liberation Front (FLN),[96] writing articles for *El*

---

[92] 2017, 130. [93] Meisami, cited ibid., 130. [94] Farahzad 2017, 131.
[95] Interestingly, SAVAK – the Iranian Security Organisation – issued a letter in 1970 with a warning that Shariati was translating *The Wretched of the Earth*; ibid., 134.
[96] The FLM was a nationalist political party founded in 1954 to fight against French colonization in Algeria.

Moudjahid while he was a student in Paris and establishing links between Algerian and Iranian resistance groups.[97] Both Shariati's daughter Sara Shariati and his biographer Ali Rahnema have said that Fanon and Shariati corresponded often and had extensive discussions.[98] Despite these connections, Farahzad argues that it was far from obvious that Shariati would be interested in translating Fanon: 'There was no clear overlap between Fanon's work and Shariati's religious project of Islamic revivalism; Iran had never been colonised and in that sense Fanon's theorising of decolonisation could only be of indirect relevance'.[99] However, it was the broader global moment of decolonization, with its anticolonial nationalist politics, that drew them together: 'Both Fanon and Shariati seemed to have shared the same grand narrative of their time, namely that of war and liberation, wars of independence against Western domination, imperialism, and the bourgeoisie, a narrative that could encompass both religious and anti-colonial contexts'.[100]

Shariati's project was very much a religious one, focused on Islamic revival. He made use of Fanonian concepts, such as Fanon's understanding of alienation, which he used to analyse how in third world countries identity is replaced by a 'false awareness as a result of tyranny' and that Islamic revival was one way of 'returning to the self'.[101] Shariati's foreword to *The Wretched of the Earth* was extremely intense and impassioned, and he immediately draws the connection to Iran by including Iran within a list of nations that were involved in wars of independence.[102] What is striking throughout is that Shariati does not assume that Fanon's text is applicable to Iran in a straightforward manner, and instead consistently illuminates *why* and how this text is important to the Iranian situation: 'Shariati highlights a number of themes in Fanon's work which might serve as 'lamps' for his own country'.[103] It is through the discussion of these themes that the religious intonation is made explicit, and it is precisely here that we see the very active role Shariati played as translator. It is arguably this that partly explains why Fanon has been more popular in Iran, given the immense amount of work Shariati put into translating his concepts for the political project he was involved with in Iran. Although some Arabic translations attempted to do the same, there remains a marked

---

[97] Ibid., 135.   [98] Ibid., 136.   [99] Ibid., 137.   [100] Ibid.   [101] Ibid., 138.
[102] Ibid., 143.   [103] Ibid., 144.

Stretching Gramsci

difference in how contextualized Fanon's concepts were in Arabic and Farsi translations.

Ranajit Guha, Subaltern Studies and 'Stretching Marxism'

Subaltern Studies emerged in the 1980s as an intervention in the historiography of South Asia.[104] The collective aimed to bring the subaltern back into history in order to rectify the elitist bias of much work on South Asia. By critiquing both Marxism and post-structuralism, Subaltern Studies raised important questions about who the subaltern is, what agency they have, and how history as a discipline conditions the types of historical research that is done on South Asia. While they saw E. P. Thompson's work as extremely important to their project, Gramsci's attempt to take seriously the culture, norms and values of everyday peasants was also seen as a much-needed departure from what they called European Marxism.[105] While the connection to Gramsci seems apparent, given their focus on the subaltern,[106] scholars in the collective nevertheless criticized Marxism's Eurocentric humanist subject.[107] What is important for now is the collective's focus on nationalism and the subaltern in India and the ways in which this relationship was seen as precluding the possibility of hegemony.

Ranajit Guha has perhaps made the most important intervention in the debate around hegemony and the postcolony. In his book *Dominance without Hegemony,* he argues that postcolonial societies differ from nations that were former colonial powers because of their position in the global system.[108] Understanding the limitations faced by local bourgeois elites during colonial and postcolonial times allows us to acknowledge that hegemony was always based more on dominance and coercion rather than persuasion and consent. While nations of the metropole – the centres of empire – may have constructed hegemony in their own nations through persuasion and consent,[109] in the colony

---

[104] For an extensive analysis of subaltern studies, see Prakash 1994; Chakrabarty 2000b.

[105] Chatterjee 2008b, 220.

[106] Partha Chatterjee (2008b, 119) was later to write that subaltern studies was inspired by Gramsci's prison writings.

[107] Chakrabarty 2000.   [108] 1997.

[109] I would posit, however, that coercion was also central in establishing hegemony in the metropole, through the violent disciplining of the working class within

60   *Hegemony in the Postcolony?*

hegemony did not exist because consent was outweighed by coercion.[110] This matters because Gramsci's core assumption is that hegemony exists only if both civil and political society are fused into a hegemonic project. This means that because India was non-hegemonic, the state – by extension – could not carry this out. Crucially, the Indian bourgeoisie was unable to represent the Indian nation, meaning that they could create hegemony. Guha agrees that there is domination and subordination, but argues that the 'organic composition of power is dependent on a host of factors and their combinations, circumstantial as well as structural',[111] and that in the postcolonial context, coercion is key:

> It is clear that coercion comes before persuasion and all other elements. This precedence accrues to it by the logic of colonial state formation. For there can be no colonialism without coercion, no subjugation of an entire people in its own homeland by foreigners without the explicit use of force. Coercion prevails in domination as its crucial defining element. For that power had established itself initially by an act of conquest.[112]

Siba Grovogui similarly makes this point, stating that the context for consent in the postcolony was an 'unparalleled machinery of coercion'.[113] The colonial state could never be hegemonic in the sense of persuasion dominating coercion. Colonial states by definition are first established through coercion and violence, even if institutions are later constructed to create consent among specific segments of the population. Indigenous leaders through which colonial rule is constructed are always in a complicit relationship with imperialism and thus – through a series of processes – become isolated from vast segments of society. This is precisely why, Guha argues, they are unable to create a fully hegemonic system.

A clear argument is being made here: hegemony could not exist in the colony because colonization in and of itself is a violent process that – in most cases – requires domination rather than consent; in other words, it was not possible to embed colonial violence within consent or render it legitimate. While some segments of society may consent through

---

the metropole as well as the incredible violence exerted through colonisation, slavery and indigenous genocide. However the transition towards consent, which began in the early eighteenth century, has meant that many modern European societies are characterized by hegemony today.

[110] Ibid., xii.   [111] Ibid., 22.   [112] Ibid., 24.   [113] 2011, 180.

Stretching Gramsci 61

internalizing the ideals, norms, and values of empire – for instance intellectuals such as the modernist reformers of Egypt in the early twentieth century – this does not successfully pierce the whole of civil society to an extent that would allow for the creation of hegemony. On the other hand, the question naturally arises: what happens when these nations become independent? Can internal hegemony be created, now governed by indigenous ruling classes?

Here we start to see parallels with Fanon. Fanon argued that the local bourgeoisie as a class can never attain full, meaningful independence following the end of colonial rule: 'This bourgeoisie will manage to put away enough money to stiffen its domination. But it will always reveal itself as incapable of giving birth to an authentic bourgeois society with all the economic and industrial consequences which this entails'.[114] Fanon's work traces the emergence of a dependent bourgeoisie in newly independent nations as a sign of continuing subservience to imperial rule. Because this bourgeoisie must answer to global capital rather than to social forces within its own society, labour within these societies are constrained in their ability to bargain with capital. This class is characterized by its tendency to rely on foreign rents rather than investing in productive activities.

The national bourgeoisie, which takes over power at the end of the colonial regime, is an underdeveloped bourgeoisie. The national bourgeoisie is not geared to production, invention, creation, or work. All its energy is channelled into intermediary activities. The national bourgeoisie has the psychology of a businessman, not that of a captain of industry.[115]

This psychology, as Fanon calls it, dramatically affects the extent to which newly independent nations can change patterns of investment. He goes on to write:

The national economy of the period of independence is not set on a new footing. It is still concerned with the ground-nut harvest, with the cocoa crop and the olive yield. In the same way there is no change in the marketing of basic products, and not a single industry is set up in the country. We go on sending out raw materials; we go on being Europe's small farmers who specialize in unfinished products.[116]

This is 'stretching Marxism' in action, which can be seen as an ambiguous response to that question, as Fanon both accepts and rejects the

[114] 1963, 17. [115] Ibid., 98. [116] Ibid., 151

assumptions of Marxism at the same time. For Fanon stretching Marxism was an attempt to contextualize the specificity of capitalism in the colony without completely disregarding the assumptions underpinning Marxism. While it may be tempting to posit that Fanon extended the Marxist project, this somewhat ignores the fact that implicit in his call to stretch Marxism was a critique of the way Marx envisioned capitalism vis-à-vis the colonies. Where Marx located revolutionary potential within the capitalist core, Fanon instead located it within the colonies themselves – in a sense, he turned Marx's position on its head.[117]

Fanon's call to stretch Marxism can be understood as a methodology that allowed for a deeper exploration of colonial capitalism:

> Marxist analysis should always be slightly stretched every time we have to do with the colonial problem. Everything up to and including the very nature of pre-capitalist society, so well explained by Marx, must here be thought out again.[118]

Fanon was thus very much focused on a material analysis of neocolonialism (as well as a psychic analysis), despite the fact that he has often been read in ways that dilute this. His work can thus be read alongside Kwame Nkrumah, among others, who clearly pointed to neocolonialism as a material consequence of colonial rule.[119] Fanon's methodological proposition, however, suggests more than merely an expansion. Instead, as suggested earlier, it turns Marx on his head when it comes to the colonies, and brings up a whole new set of questions.

Following the assumption that capitalism cannot be understood without looking at how it is racialized, I argue that Fanon's conception of a dependent bourgeoisie allows for an analysis of capitalist expansion that connects it to the neocolonial policies that continue to condition countries like Egypt today. For Fanon, these attempts to criticize and deepen Marxist analysis result from his understanding of the different relationship between base and superstructure in the colonial context. He states that race supersedes the economic question in the colony, writing:

---

[117] A special thanks to Vanessa Eileen Thompson, who put it in precisely these terms.
[118] 1963, 40. [119] 1965.

Stretching Gramsci

In the colonies the economic substructure is also a superstructure. The cause is the consequence; you are rich because you are white, you are white because you are rich. This is why Marxist analysis should always be slightly stretched every time we have to do with the colonial problem.[120]

It is precisely the confluence of the superstructure (race) and the base (economic power) that articulates itself differently in the colonial context.

The next chapter shows the ways in which Nasser and the Free Officers understood this difference, as well as how they attempted to break out of it through industrialization. As early as the 1920s there were attempts by Egyptian capitalists to break away from a dependency on foreign capital, which was seen as a barrier to full independence. While the attempt by Bank Misr, which I detail in this chapter, failed, arguably Nasser's attempt was more successful. While Nasserism was a passive revolution, similar to the one Guha and Chatterjee describe in India, it was equally a hegemonic passive revolution; the first and (to date) last instance of hegemony Egypt would experience.[121] It was not, however, the last instance of a passive revolution Egypt would experience. Both Egypt and India experienced a second passive revolution during the shift to neoliberalism, although where India's second passive revolution was hegemonic, to some extent, Egypt's was not. Where in India the ascendancy of a corporate class, which dismantled the licence regime, allowed in foreign capital and foreign consumer goods, and which opened up transport, banking, and infrastructure to private capital, also led to the hegemony of this class, in Egypt these changes – which took place in an eerily similar manner, by an eerily similar corporate class – did not establish hegemony. Instead, this corporate class that emerged in Egypt in the 1970s is

---

[120] 1963, 30.

[121] Passive revolution is used in the context of 1947 in India to name the process whereby Indian elites appropriated the agency of the Indian masses for their own ends. This allowed, ultimately, for domination but not for hegemony. Brecht De Smet (2016) has made a similar argument in his book *Gramsci on Tahrir*, arguing that Nasser represents a moment of passive revolution in the Egyptian context, where the agency of Egyptians was co-opted into an authoritarian project that was not – indeed could not be – hegemonic. Departing from this view, I show that Nasser's passive revolution was in actual fact hegemonic.

64   *Hegemony in the Postcolony?*

more akin to Fanon's dependent bourgeoisie, unable to lead or rule, simply a caricature of its European counterpart.

A Pre-History of 1952: Foreign Capital and Local Capitalists

The rest of this chapter takes the form of a pre-history of Egyptian independence and the Nasserist project, which is the point from which the next chapter begins. Sketching out the specificities of the Mehmed Ali project and its aftermath through the lens of Fanon's call to stretch Marxism, I show the particular ways in which colonial rule set the borders within which Egypt had to act. On the one hand, this is central to explaining why hegemony was absent in Egypt during its time as a colony; on the other hand, it is equally central to explaining why hegemony became possible during and after independence. In particular, I focus on the case of Bank Misr, a bank founded in 1920 with the explicit aim of independent industrialization. Through tracing the way the Bank's founder, Tal'at Harb understood this project as well as the barriers he faced, I show the postcolonial predicament facing countries such as Egypt, and why the colonial context produced restrictions that disenabled independent forms of development.

Mehmed Ali and Egyptian Cotton

The story of Bank Misr begins much earlier than its founding, in the reform programme of Mehmed Ali and in particular his attempt to strengthen and develop Egypt's cotton industries. Starting in the mid 1800s, the introduction of private landownership,[122] the regulation of peasants in order to coerce them into producing cotton for foreign markets, the introduction of banks and debt, and the shift to wage labour all had dramatic effects on the Egyptian economy and on Egyptian workers. By the 1820s, between 10 and 25 per cent of the revenues of the Egyptian state came from the sale of cotton, and Ali placed an embargo on British goods, encouraging Syrian merchants – who dominated Egypt's textile

---

[122] The first land register was created and the law of 16 September 1798 inaugurated land prices, recognizing the right of peasants to inherit, and introduced a framework to regulate the recording of landownership (Abdel-Malek 1968, 6).

A Pre-History of 1952

industries – to set up factories.[123] By 1835, 15 000–20 000 workers in 30 cotton factories operated 400 000 spindles. Most of this cotton was for the domestic market, and some was exported to Sudan, Syria, Anatolia, and India. Sven Beckert quotes the German newspaper *Ausland*, which wrote the following in 1831: 'It is interesting that a barbarian has achieved within a few years what Napoleon and the entire continent were unable to accomplish since the beginning of the century, despite all possible efforts'.[124]

This success worried the British, particularly as Egyptian imports into India – where the British dominated – were of superior quality.[125] Britain used protective tariffs to protect its own industries, but when Ali copied this in Egypt, there was outrage.[126] Egypt grew its own cotton and labour was cheaper, and thus the British swiftly swung into action. Pressure from British merchants and industrialists eventually opened Egypt's markets and in 1838 the Anglo-Ottoman Tariff Treaty went into effect, forcing free trade on Egypt.[127] This ultimately destroyed Egypt's first mechanized textile industry and more broadly Ali's plans for independent industrialization. Ali's reliance on coercion, as opposed to wage labour, also brought about the end of the cotton boom in Egypt. These two factors came together to ensure that by the end of the 1830s, Egypt went from being the world's fifth largest cotton producer to having barely any cotton industry at all. 'The Egyptian state was powerful domestically, but weak when it came to defining Egypt's position within the global economy, no match for British interests and designs'.[128] Sayyid-Marsot comes to the same conclusion: 'Britain did not want a new independent state in the Mediterranean, one that was militarily and economically powerful'.[129] Although Ali had recognized the need for profit through industrialization, the expansion of European imperialism made it increasingly impossible for countries such as Egypt to develop independently, particularly if this posed a threat to imperial interests. We thus see a shift from a strong state before and during Ali, to the state subjugated to British imperialism and 'free trade' by the late 1800s. Ali knew free trade was not in Egypt's interest, seeing it as the free exploitation of the country's resources by foreign agents.[130]

---

[123] Ibid.   [124] Ibid.
[125] This superior quality was also due to the decision of Ali to plant a certain type of plant that produced tougher cotton.
[126] Beckert 2014, 169.   [127] Ibid.   [128] Ibid.   [129] Sayyid Marsot 1984, 177.
[130] Ibid., 185.

Khaled Fahmy has argued against this view in his influential *All the Pasha's Men*.[131] Skilfully showing how modern institutions such as the army, schools, hospitals and so on were created under Ali, Fahmy argues that Ali should be understood as the founder of modern Egypt. Arguing against Egyptian nationalist historians who saw Ali's reign as a positive force for Egyptian national development, Fahmy instead shows how the army subjugated and disciplined Egyptian workers for Ali's own objectives. Moreover, Fahmy downplays the impact of British imperialism on Egypt's failure to 'take-off'; he instead locates this failure in the threat Ali posed to British colonies rather than Britain's fear of Egyptian independent industrial development.[132] As Beckert shows, these two were connected: Ali's search for Egyptian colonies was part and parcel of his industrialization project; he assumed that independent development *needed* this territorial expansion – after all, this is precisely how Europe had industrialized. Nevertheless, Fahmy and Beckert's points about the subjugation of labour under Ali are crucial to understanding the failure of this project; his reliance on forced labour ultimately made his project untenable in the long term. These events were central to Bank Misr, the focus of the next section.

Following Ali's death, a class of landowning elites emerged and consolidated the capitalist mode of production. The unequal trade of raw materials and the introduction of a vast system of credit were the hallmarks of this period, which lasted until 1952. Agricultural production was now based on capitalist relations because of the structural changes that had happened vis-à-vis land ownership during the past few decades. Primitive accumulation can be seen here in 'the state's role in depriving the peasantry of their land, paving the way for the formation of an "agrarian bourgeoisie"'.[133] This landowning class had close ties to the British, particularly the cotton markets. The emergence of this class that made profit off of agricultural production, and the increasing number of Egyptians involved in wage labour, demonstrate the presence of primitive accumulation. From 1919 onwards, Egypt was ruled by the agrarian fraction of capital within the ruling class, which pushed for the centrality of foreign capital. Capitalism now became the dominant mode of production, but this happened on an uneven scale both nationally and globally.

[131] 1997.   [132] Ibid., 297.   [133] Chaichian 1988, 29.

Ali's attempt to pose a limited challenge to British imperial interests is noteworthy because it pre-empted a similar attempt by Bank Misr in the 1920s, which I turn to next. I am more interested in what he saw as the problems associated with dependent capitalist development and the ways in which he challenged them, only to find that there was little power Egypt could wield against the British Empire in terms of capitalist development. This was a lesson Egyptian nationalists were to learn again in the 1920s, and yet again in the 1950s. However, Ali's attempt is also interesting for another reason, for it shows that tracing hegemony without contextualizing political change within capitalist development is futile. One could ask to what extent there was the space to create hegemony while Egypt was under both Ottoman and British rule. Where industrialization in the metropole had occurred under very different circumstances and was largely dependent on the genocide, expropriation and exploitation of the colonies, industrialization in contexts such as Egypt instead relied on massive amounts of internal coercion that could not easily be justified through consent. It is these differences that raise important questions about hegemony in the postcolony.

The Emergence of Bank Misr

Mehmed Ali faced the predicament of dependent development and the limits of challenging it; here I discuss a second instance of attempted independent capitalist development, as embodied by Bank Misr, before turning to Nasser in the following chapter, who along with the Free Officers was to confront the very same predicament once again in 1952. The predicament facing postcolonial nations references moments of resistance to dependent capitalist development on the part of social forces within colonized nations, and the barriers they faced that ultimately led to the failure of such attempts. In order to trace one such predicament in the Egyptian context – the failure of Bank Misr to industrialize through Egyptian capital investment – I first outline the particular evolution of British imperial rule in Egypt and the specific infrastructure it set in place – the very infrastructure that would later ensure that Egypt's attempts at autonomous economic development were bound to fail. I then present the case of Bank Misr and its attempt at autonomous industrial development, arguing that it represents a key instance of the postcolonial predicament in the Egyptian context.

68   *Hegemony in the Postcolony?*

Even before formal occupation, the infiltration of British capital had already created an infrastructure in Egypt that allowed for the expansion of foreign capital through its institutions such as banks, debt, and credit. Because its primary export was cotton, the export of cotton became the basis for Egyptian capitalist development as it was the major source of value exchangeable with foreign creditors. This meant that Egypt's integration into the capitalist world market was reinforced rather than broken.[134]

British merchants worked hard to open Egyptian markets for their goods, as Egypt weakened vis-à-vis European powers. A system of 'free trade' dominated by Britain made it practically impossible for Egypt to industrialize. Egypt's cotton industry was devastated from two sides: its domestic embrace of war capitalism and its ultimate subjugation to British imperialism. The Egyptian state was powerful domestically, but weak when it came to defining Egypt's position within the global economy, no match for British interests and designs.[135]

The failure of industrialization, the creation of specific labour relations, and the control over Egypt's main commodity by the British all served to weaken Egypt's ability to develop autonomously. This did not begin with Ismail Pasha; as noted, Ali is often cited as having created the infrastructure that created modern Egypt. The *tanzimat* – reforms that introduced bureaucratic centralization, registration of land ownership, building of new armies and modern educational systems, and the attempt to reassert the control of government over the economy and to maximize tax revenues, can also be read as *defensive* modernization. As Ayubi argues, these reforms were meant to keep Europe at bay; but instead, they ended up making Egypt more dependent by allowing European capital to infiltrate quicker and more thoroughly.[136] The decline of Mehmed Ali and the rise of Ismail Pasha has been characterized as heralding the de-industrialization of the Egyptian economy.[137] In particular the connections between Ismail Pasha and the British are key, for, as Samir Amin has noted, the attempt for Egypt to emerge under Ali was ultimately violently put down by the British.[138]

The Egyptian state emerged as part and parcel of these processes of imperialism. Increasing imperial expansion into the region required a means of organizing labour and production, as outlined in the

---

[134] Hussein and Chirman 1973, 206.   [135] Ibid., 149.   [136] 1996, 87.
[137] Ibid.   [138] 2012, 17.

A Pre-History of 1952

introduction. Raw materials and cotton in particular played a role in this process, as Sven Beckert notes:

Territorial control in Egypt went hand in hand with the expansion of cotton agriculture. The construction of markets, including global markets, was thus a political process. As more and more states competed for access to raw materials, labour, and markets, this political process was ever more framed by nation-states. National economies, empires, and national capitalists became increasingly the basic building blocks of the new global political economy.[139]

Key to the consolidation of British power in Egypt was precisely its ability to impose certain conditions on Egyptian development, including the emergence of a particular form of state, and the development of a particular infrastructure. As early as 1838 there was an agreement between the British and the Ottoman Empire which aimed to 'abolish the monopoly system imposed by Mehmed Ali and put in place a system of free trade. This removed any protections Egyptian industries had, and within a few years Egypt became a European colony without a shot being fired'.[140]

Bank Misr and Independent Industrialization

A group of capitalist nationalists emerged at a time when Egypt's economy was very much integrated into the global capitalist economy, with foreign capital dominating major investments. Eric Davis, historicizing their emergence, argues that the founding of Bank Misr was the result of the crystallization of the social and political forces of the nineteenth century, most notably the imperial condition, the dominance of foreign capital, and the concurrent rise of nationalism.[141] The structural constraints facing Egypt were multiple, including the fact that all exports, most internal commerce, mortgages of its most valuable asset – land – and its currency were all in the hands of foreigners.[142] Above all, it was Egypt's dependency on a single export that consistently worried nationalists and capitalists alike. This raised the question of diversification and self-sufficiency; indeed the report of the commission that led to the founding of Bank Misr stated that this reliance on a single export was

---

[139] 2014, 290. [140] Ibid. [141] 1983, 4. [142] Tignor 1980, 103.

70   *Hegemony in the Postcolony?*

dangerous and that Egypt needed to gain greater control over the purchase and sale of cotton.[143]

While processes of Egyptianization[144] were under way in some companies, having more Egyptian employees or even board members did not necessarily mean that Egyptians had more control.[145] It was clear that the British had neocolonial aims in Egypt: even as political control was loosening, they hoped to expand the already-powerful financial and commercial British community in Egypt.[146] The hope for a peaceful transition to a neocolonial regime headed by King Farouk was quickly dispelled by events throughout the 1940s, including assassinations as well as anti-British and anti-capitalist attacks.[147] The infamous demonstrations of 26 January 1952 were very much directed not only against the British presence but against the influence of British *capital* in Egypt.[148] It is this connection that interests me, as it demonstrates the complexities of nationalism during this moment and the awareness of the connections between British colonialism and British capitalism.

Tal'at Harb, the founder of Bank Misr, was a nationalist and a critic of European exploitation in Egypt: 'Bank Misr was founded as a supremely Egyptian institution and an expression of nationalist aspirations. Its founders hoped that the Bank might facilitate the emergence of an independent Egyptian bourgeoisie. They also wanted to use its resources to establish new commercial, industrial, and financial companies separate from European capital and working exclusively for the economic well-being of Egypt'.[149] Industrialization was very much central to the founding of Bank Misr, as it was seen as Egypt's way out of its dependency on a single export crop: cotton. In the report that led to the founding of the Bank, it was stated that while foreign capital could be part of this industrialization drive, it needed to be overseen by a protectionist state and had to be combined with Egyptian capital. This protectionist state materialized soon after: the state used its own purchasing power to favour local products over imported ones; it granted concessions to Egyptian firms; and it introduced tariff reforms in 1930 meant to protect these new Egyptian industries.

---

[143] Tignor 1977, 162.
[144] The process of increasing the number of Egyptian employees and board members in companies.
[145] Tignor 1980, 109.   [146] Tignor 1987, 486.   [147] Ibid., 489.
[148] Ibid., 493.   [149] Tignor 1977, 161.

A Pre-History of 1952 71

Industrialization was seen, on the one hand, as an economic solution to Egypt's dependency within the global capitalist system; and, on the other hand, as a solution to a *social* problem: that of poverty. We see here the ways in which industrialization and the nation come together; it is not posed simply as a means by which Egyptian capitalists can accumulate capital more effectively, but as a means of improving the Egyptian nation as a whole.[150] This was a prelude to how the Nasserist project would understand industrial development.

Tal'at Harb did not come from the class of wealthy landed elites, and was the son of a government employee. Rising through the ranks of Egypt's commercial world, he eventually ended up managing the estates of numerous wealthy landowners.[151] His writings show the intricate ways in which nationalism and anti-capitalism were seen as part and parcel of the same problem. In a text on the Suez Canal Company, for example, he discussed European financial imperialism and the domination of foreign capital over Egypt's economy, calling on the state to insist on Egyptian membership on the board of directors, a percentage of the Canal's profits, and that the company would revert to Egyptian ownership once the concession expired. 'Tal'at Harb portrayed the Suez Canal Company as an egregious example of rapacious and exploitative European capitalism and called upon the state to place limits on its freedom of operations'.[152] Other writings focused on foreign banks and their ultimate loyalty to their foreign shareholders, as well as why it was important for Egypt's peasantry that Egypt controlled its own resources.[153]

These nationalist ideas permeated the Bank itself, and gave it a solid nationalist orientation and suspicion of foreign capital. The Bank's Charter specified that only Egyptians could be shareholders – a massive departure from other companies of the time – that the board of directors must be Egyptian, and that the Bank must operate in Arabic – also a massive departure, given the dominance of French in Egyptian banking.[154] The Bank's reports often reiterated its suspicion of foreign capital and its allegiance to nationalism. Soon after its founding in 1927, four new companies were launched: the Misr Spinning and Weaving Company, the Misr Silk Weaving Company, the Misr Linen Company, and the Misr Fisheries Company. The capital for these firms

[150] See Shakry 2007 for an extended study on social modernization, nationalism and welfare in interwar Egypt.
[151] Ibid., 163. [152] Ibid., 164. [153] Ibid., 165. [154] Ibid., 166.

was supplied entirely by Egyptian capitalists, but this was possible largely because aside from the Spinning and Weaving Company, none of them were heavily capitalized.[155]

This dilemma eventually led to the downfall of the Bank, and that constitutes the postcolonial predicament I mentioned earlier. On the one hand, the Bank had been created to further Egyptian industrialization through creating domestic industries.[156] On the other hand, the Bank soon came to the realization that without foreign capital, and to some extent foreign expertise, it would be unable to embark on major industrial projects. At first the Bank entered into agreements with foreign companies on strict terms. For example, it formed the Misr Cotton Export Company with the German cotton exporter Hugo Lindemann. The profits were split equally, the president was Egyptian, and it was stressed that Lindemann had lived in Egypt his whole life, was fluent in Arabic, and was not representative of foreign capital.[157] Similarly, when Tal'at Harb decided he wanted to found a national airline, he was very selective with who his British partner would be, rejecting one that he saw as a threat to the Bank's autonomy.[158] In these instances we see a slow turning towards foreign capital after years of fiercely resisting it.

These examples also illustrate the aggressive ways in which Britain – working through British capital – tried to maintain its grip over Egypt, showing not only the close connections between Britain and British capital, coming together as part and parcel of British imperialism, but also disproving suggestions that Britain was slowly pulling out of Egypt and had no neocolonial fancies. As the Bank faced increasing difficulties in realizing its project of Egyptian industrialization, British capital was mounting increasing attacks against the Bank's investments, most notably the Misr Spinning and Weaving Company.[159] This attack was picked up by the press, and Tal'at Harb was vindicated: his fears about foreign capital were very much proven true, albeit in a tragic manner. Tal'at Harb was able to negotiate with the firm launching this attack, eventually signing a joint venture arrangement, demonstrating agency on his part that is important to note. However this also signified once and for all the Bank's turn towards foreign capital.

---

[155] Ibid., 170.
[156] See e.g. its 1929 report *The Creation of Domestic Industries* (ibid.).
[157] Ibid., 171.   [158] Ibid., 172. The airline in question was Imperial Airways.
[159] Ibid., 175.

A Pre-History of 1952

After several crises, Tal'at Harb's career came to an end in 1939. He was forced to resign from the Bank, which had to be saved from insolvency by the government. Tignor argues that there is truth to the Egyptian press's allegations that Harb was pushed out because of his nationalist ambitions, stating: 'British capital and British officials would have been much calmer had a more pro-British board of directors been at the helm of the Bank. The successors to Tal'at Harb – Hafiz Afifi and Abd al-Maqsud Ahmad – were acceptable to the British'.[160] By the early 1940s the Bank was no longer its old nationalist self.

Of all the Egyptian economic institutions created in this era the Bank and its affiliates were the most avowedly nationalistic. Tal'at Harb envisioned an autonomous Egyptian capitalism able to stand aloof from European capital. He was not able to realise this goal, however, partly because he needed European technical expertise, but mainly because European capitalism was so solidly entrenched in Egypt that the Misr companies had to make an accommodation with it or see their plans for industrial expansion thwarted.[161]

It is clear that addressing the question of the Bank's failure means positioning the Bank within broader international structures and asking to what extent industrial development can take place in post/colonial contexts. This does not mean we should not address the question of agency, and particularly the role of Egyptian capitalists in expanding Egypt's economy during the interwar period. Tignor in particular has tried to show the complex ways in which Egyptian capitalists navigated these structural constraints.[162] Notably, he points out that the expansion of capitalism in Egypt did not 'wipe out' everything before it; indeed here Ayubi's concept of articulation is helpful. It is rare that one mode of production ever destroys another mode completely; what usually happens is that one mode mixes with another. Tignor rightly notes that Egyptian industries were able to compete with foreign ones for a period of time,[163] although this was only after they modernized. Here one could ask what modernization entailed and whether one could see it as a power relation embedded within capitalism that was not necessarily beneficial to Egyptian industry in the long run.

The fact remains that Egyptian capitalists were able to carve out space and make industrial advances, even when these were against the interests of British and European capital. Nevertheless, this agency came up against

---

[160] Ibid., 179. [161] Ibid., 181. [162] 1977, 1980. [163] Tignor 1977, 105.

74   Hegemony in the Postcolony?

structures of global capitalism and imperialism which in turn raises a question at the heart of an analysis of the dependent bourgeoisie in any postcolonial context. It replicates the classic tension between structure and agency: the structures of imperial capital versus the agency of local capitalists. Davis argues that the origins of Egyptian industrialization were to be found in the contradictions that arose from the activities of foreign capital in Egypt. On the one hand, it can be argued that the industrial fraction that emerged could not play a progressive role because it was not independent of foreign capital: 'Those members of the Egyptian bourgeoisie who collaborated with foreign capital during the 1930s should be seen in neocolonialist terms as they provided a front which obscured the real control of the enterprises in question. On the surface, it appeared as if Egyptians had gained a greater measure of control over the economy than in reality they had'.[164] On the other hand, Robert Vitalis has argued that focusing too much on foreign capital and imperialism means losing sight of the power held by local capital.[165] Vitalis uses the example of Ahmad Abboud, who combined foreign-funded projects with local accumulation. He expands this by pointing out that in the early twentieth century it was local capitalists that began to make use of Egyptian state resources – tax exemptions, coercive force, and subsidies for example.[166]

Debates in the literature about Bank Misr reify these competing views and focus specifically on whether the Bank represented nationalistic development or was tied to British interests. Some, such as Anouar Abdel-Malek, have argued that the local bourgeoisie and foreign interests belonged in one group,[167] while others point to the fact that Bank Misr was against the British Chamber of Commerce.[168] Malak Zaalouk has written that the reason for founding the Bank was the Egyptianization of the economy: 'The bank, with its policies designed to create a national bourgeoisie, was frowned upon by the British authorities as well as other foreign elements and their local allies who had a vested interest in obstructing such a development'.[169] Capital was needed for this, however, and ultimately, the Bank had to turn towards foreign sources of capital, signalling its failure to achieve national economic independence. This need for private foreign capital

[164] 1983, 72.   [165] 1995, 11.   [166] Ibid.   [167] 1968, 69.   [168] Deeb 1979.
[169] 1989, 18.

A Pre-History of 1952

was very much a mechanism set within the structure of colonial capitalism, as Fanon wrote:

> It is a fact that young nations do not attract much private capital. Private companies, when asked to invest in independent countries, lay down conditions which are shown in practice to be unacceptable or unrealisable. At a pinch they willingly agree to lend money to the young states, but only on condition that this money is used to buy manufactured products and machines: in other words, that it serves to keep the factories in the mother country going.[170]

In an iconic work on British colonial rule in Egypt, Timothy Mitchell approaches the question at a deeper level, showing the effects of new economic processes on the subjectivities of different parts of society.[171] Highlighting the layered machinations of colonial rule, the book unpacks the complex ways in which economic subjectivities were formed and contested, all within the space of colonial power. Bank Misr was made up of Egyptian capitalists who had the intention of industrializing Egypt with Egyptian capital; nevertheless the reality they were confronted with was that under British colonial occupation the biggest source of capital remained foreign capital. Following Fanon, the bourgeoisie in colonial and postcolonial contexts must be theorized as dependent precisely because of these structural constraints. This does not discount moments of agency, as demonstrated through the founding of Bank Misr; but it does denote a contradiction in calls for national development within the confines of the colonial international.

In his writing, Tignor often mentions the optimism and hope that characterized the founding of the Bank and the economic programme it represented.[172] Seeing it as a 'child of the revolution of 1919' and as representing a 'naïve sentimentality' and 'boundless optimism for Egypt's prospects for development',[173] the Bank in many ways appears to parallel the similar sentimentality around 1952. This notion of sentimentality is intriguing. The predicament of anticolonial nationalism is not that these hopes were unrealistic or naïve; it is that a belief in independence meant that one *had to have these hopes*, while knowing how unlikely it was that they would ever materialize. The story of Bank Misr is the story of a postcolonial predicament: capitalist development seems intrinsically tied to imperialism, and

---

[170] 1963, 103. [171] 1991a. [172] 1977, 166. [173] Ibid.

attempts to develop 'local' forms of capitalism do not escape the imperial trap. As Fanon writes:

The young independent nation sees itself obliged to use the economic channels created by the colonial regime. It can, obviously, export to other countries and other currency areas, but the basis of its exports is not fundamentally modified. The colonial regime has carved out certain channel and they must be maintained or catastrophe will threaten.[174]

This points to the problems of capitalist expansion in the peripheries: despite it being led by local elites, it was still by and for a small class of capitalists and thus of negligible benefit to the majority of Egyptians.

While there is little doubt that Tal'at Harb and Bank Misr laid the foundations for Nasser's industrialization project, they also represented a warning to this very same project. Like Nasser and the Officers, Tal'at Harb did not come from the class of wealthy landed elites, separating him somewhat from other Egyptian capitalists. And like Nasser and the Officers, he saw industrialization as central to Egypt's future economic and political independence. The failure of Harb's project revealed the nature of the colonial international, and the limits of capitalist development within such an order. It suggested that working from within capitalist development did not necessarily pose the solution to Egypt's dependency. Unfortunately, as we see in the following chapter, the Nasserist project did not heed this warning and instead reproduced a similar attempt to liberate Egypt through state-led capitalist development. Yet these attempts should be read within the historical conditions they were produced in and that they fought against. While it is easy to both hold local capitalists accountable for the failure of independent economic development, and to point to the pitfalls of capitalist development, the fact remains that European colonialism created a world in which countries such as Egypt had few options available to them that would allow a break from its subservient role in global capital.

A Postcolonial International Order

Returning to Guha's argument that the fundamental difference between the metropole and the colony/postcolony is their different positions within the global system, I bring together the various

[174] 1963, 103.

threads in this chapter by focusing on the new international order postcolonial nations attempted – and ultimately failed – to create. Tying together Gramsci, Fanon, Guha, and Chatterjee what becomes clear is that the constitution and characteristics of the capitalist class post-independence are highly dependent on the international capitalist system. While this is arguably true of any capitalist class, including those in the metropole, the degree to which postcolonial nations are tied to the international division of labour as well as the dependency and subservience that characterizes this relationship makes it qualitatively different. The postcolonial capitalist class comes into existence through colonial rule; it is thus able to sustain itself and reproduce itself through these ties to the colonial metropole; it does not need hegemony – indeed one could argue that they were never given the option to begin with.

In his book *Philosophy of the Revolution*, Nasser wrote: 'Socialist action is no longer compelled to observe literally laws formulated in the nineteenth century. The progress in means of production, the development of nationalist and labour movements in the face of domination of imperialism and monopolies, the increasing chances of world peace, as a result of the influence of moral forces and, at the same time of the effect of the balance of atomic terror – all these factors combined of necessity created, and should create, a new situation for socialist experiments, entirely different from what existed in the past'.[175] Signalling to the global context, Nasser suggests that both national and international forces affect the ways in which socialist experiments play out in various contexts. This quote highlights an understanding of decolonization as not merely a national phenomenon, but rather both national and international, an argument Adom Getachew makes in her book *Worldmaking after Empire*. She notes that 'decolonization was a project of reordering the world that sought to create a domination-free and egalitarian international order', arguing against the standard view of 'decolonization as a moment of nation-building in which the anticolonial demand for self-determination culminated in the rejection of alien rule and the formation of nation-states, I recast anticolonial nationalism as worldmaking'.[176]

The postcolonial predicament, as I have shown, was intimately connected to the colonial international; the very same reality Fanon points

---

[175] Nasser 1959, 15.   [176] 2019, 2.

to when he calls for Marxism to be stretched. The international has been central to political changes inside postcolonial nations; through both its articulation of imperialism as well as the brief moment after decolonization during which newly independent nations attempted to re-articulate their position to this international. Throughout the early twentieth century, we can already see attempts by Egyptian capitalists to grapple with the international sphere and its reproduction of imperialism. Here I expand on the notion of a colonial international, which I use to frame political changes in Egypt in the following chapters. Connecting this colonial international to hegemony, I show that Gramsci's theory of hegemony must be read through the Subaltern Studies debate and Fanon's work for it to apply to contexts such as Egypt. It is their relationship to capitalist development and the colonial international that ultimately determines their ability, or inability, to create hegemony.

In *The Wretched of the Earth*, Fanon writes: 'The national bourgeoisie turns its back more and more on the interior and on the real facts of its undeveloped country, and tends to look towards the former mother country and the foreign capitalists who count on its obliging compliance'.[177] Fanon seems to be suggesting that whereas what occurred in European countries was that the bourgeoisie succeeded in establishing hegemony and masking the capitalist accumulation that was only benefitting a small strata, in postcolonial contexts, on the other hand, the failure to mask this meant a lack of hegemony: the middle class wanted to get rich quickly without inventiveness or leadership, and thus paid little attention to maintaining stability. This was later argued by Guha, who noted that hegemony cannot exist in colonial conditions. Fanon, however, adds another layer: because of the middle class's ties to the former colonial power, it ends up trying to become a replica of Europe, though in the end only managing to become its caricature.

Vivienne Jabri has argued that we must contextualize the politics of newly independent nations as attempts to access the international.[178] To regain control over the institutions of international political economy – the same institutions that reproduced global inequality – was seen as the path to independence. 'In its role in both accumulation and the establishment of legitimacy, the postcolonial state is an interventionist state: it

---

[177] 1963, 165. [178] 2012, 100.

seeks to construct a hegemonic structure that functions to legitimize a political economy of development; it builds a state apparatus geared for planning as well as the mobilization and management of national resources; it negotiates its role as allocator with the demands of a modern sector that seeks its own stakes in the developmental economy'.[179] However, this is always done vis-à-vis the international; it is this tension that mediates anything and everything the postcolonial state does. 'This is where the postcolonial state comes face to face with the colonial structure of the international. The resistance of the postcolonial state as such must hence be measured in terms of how it fulfils its role in relation to the constraints of the international'.[180] It is these historical conditions that Getachew similarly draws our attention to if we are to understand anticolonial nationalism; avoiding the tendency to see anticolonial nationalism as intrinsically regressive, we should instead place it within its historical and geographical context, and understand what it was up against and what it was trying to achieve.[181]

Tying this to the question of hegemony, I posit that hegemony and its establishment are always already international. The international, however, has been constituted in and through empire; therefore hegemony is always already tied to histories of colonial rule. Following the Subaltern Studies view that hegemony could not exist under colonialism, and where Fanon argues that the first ruling class to emerge after independence could not be hegemonic, I instead posit that Gamal Abdel Nasser's ruling class was hegemonic, and that he constructed the first and last instance of hegemony in modern Egypt. This success in establishing hegemony not only demonstrates the connections between hegemony, colonialism, and the international, but also shows why hegemony remains a useful concept in analysing postcolonial contexts. I turn to Nasser and his hegemonic project now.

[179] Ibid., 102.   [180] Ibid.   [181] 2019, 2.

2 | *Hegemony in Egypt*
Revisiting Gamal Abdel Nasser

Gramsci came face to face with the revolutionary character of history itself. When a conjuncture unrolls, there is no 'going back'. History shifts gears. The terrain changes. You are in a new moment. You have to attend, 'violently', with all the 'pessimism of the intellect' at your command', to the 'discipline of the conjuncture'.

Stuart Hall[1]

The Revolution was framed as a living, growing experiment that everyone had a role in constructing. It was usually depicted as something in the process of formulation, which in many ways it was.

Alia Mossallam[2]

The fundamental duel which seemed to be that between colonialism and anti-colonialism, and indeed between capitalism and socialism, is already losing some of its importance. What counts today, the question which is looming on the horizon, is the need for a redistribution of wealth. Humanity must reply to this question, or be shaken to pieces by it.

Frantz Fanon[3]

The imperial privilege still exists in a world without colonies.

Partha Chatterjee[4]

The Nasserist vision got all tangled up with Marxism, and it became increasingly difficult to distinguish between the two until well after the flood waters had receded.

Arwa Salih[5]

---

[1] Hall 2002, 228. [2] 2012, 52. [3] 1963, 78.
[4] Chatterjee in Eslava et al. 2017, 674. [5] 2018, 28.

The Modern Prince

Writing on the 'modern prince', Gramsci says: 'The modern prince, the myth-prince, cannot be a real person, a concrete individual. It can only be an organism, a complex element of society *in which a collective will, which has already been recognised and has to some extent asserted itself in action, begins to take concrete form*'.[6] This chapter looks at Nasser and Nasserism more broadly, a project that can be seen as an incarnation of Gramsci's modern prince. A collective will – built on the radical movements pre-dating 1952 on the one hand, and growing anticolonial nationalism on the other – takes concrete form, incarnated 'mythically' in the project of Nasserism. The 'great and imminent danger' that pushes this collective will to passion, fanaticism, and white heat is the problem of imperialism or, more precisely, Egypt's colonial situation. Nasserism can be understood as a collective will that was produced in a particular historical moment; one that was formed against the dangers of imperialism, the hopes of a postcolonial project, and the 'white heat' of decolonization. Nasserism was also, however, an articulation of an elitist state-led project of decolonization that centred the military, the state, and capitalism, leaving powerful legacies that would haunt Egypt's future. The Nasserist era thus raises crucial questions around what the nation is, the undesirability and impossibility of a 'national interest', and the afterlives of attempts to resolve these questions.

The period that produced Nasserism – that of decolonization – remains one of the most pivotal moments in modern history. As Sven Beckert notes, 'Without its Eurocentric distortions, decolonization would be at the very centre of the narrative we tell about the twentieth century – and this retelling would allow us to see that global capitalism today is most fundamentally shaped by the struggles for independence'.[7] Gamal Abdel Nasser (Figure 2.1) ruled Egypt for fourteen years, from 1956 until his death in 1970, and is undoubtedly a complex and contradictory political figure in Egyptian public memory. Representing Egypt's formal break with colonial rule as well as an attempted transition towards an industry-driven economy, the Nasser years were a momentous time. The

---

[6] 1971, 121.   [7] 2014, 359.

Figure 2.1 Portrait of the second president of Egypt, Gamal Abdel Nasser (1918–70), at the Arab Summit Conference, Cairo, circa 1964. Credit: David Lees / Hulton Archive / Getty Images.

excitement surrounding this period has inevitably led to major debates surrounding Nasser, his political and economic project, and the effects this era was to have on successive ruling formations.[8] The stakes were high; it was the moment of formal independence and Egypt's future hung in the balance. Nasser was a leader who enjoyed the support of not only many Egyptians, but of many Arabs, Africans, and other people across the newly decolonized world. His role in the 1967 defeat to Israel was a tremendous blow to the entire region and to the course decolonization was to take.

My argument in this chapter is that the project established by Nasser and the Free Officers – which I refer to as the Nasserist project – is the first and last time (to date) in modern Egyptian history that we see the

---

[8] This period is arguably the most thoroughly researched period of post-1952 Egyptian history. For interesting perspectives on the archives of Nasser's Egypt, see El Shakry 2015; Nkrumah 2007, 2002.

creation and consolidation of hegemony albeit for a limited amount of time. Numerous scholars have argued that Nasserism was a hegemonic project;[9] here I unpack this by exploring how this hegemonic project was built, the factors that led to its downfall, and the afterlives of the project that reverberate into the present. I show that the Nasserist era was very much characterized by a balance between consent and coercion, as tenuous as it was, and that the projects that came after were marked by a rise in coercion and decline in consent. From 1967 onwards, what we see is the slow and steady coming apart of this hegemony.

The Nasserist project, however, was built on internal contradictions, among them the continuation of capitalist development, the absorption and weakening of radical movements such as labour, and the reproduction of colonial institutions such as the nation and nationalism. Bringing the idea of hegemony in conversation with Fanon's writing on anticolonial nationalism, I revisit the idea that anticolonial nationalism can be thought of as both a force for liberation and reactionary in shaping the trajectories of countries after independence. While Fanon predicted that the national middle class that took power in most African countries after independence would fail in its task of rejecting neocolonialism, I argue that the Nasserist project complicates this prediction somewhat. While it did ultimately fail in its task of independent economic development, it cannot be neatly characterized as Fanon's dependent bourgeoisie either, a bourgeoisie that was to fully emerge after the downfall of the Nasserist project.

Nasser, Third Worldism, and the Colonial International

The moment of decolonization in the mid twentieth century took the world by storm. Although rarely seen as one of the most pivotal moments of the twentieth century, the world as we know it today would not exist without the anticolonial struggles of the 1950s and 1960s. This section takes Sven Beckert's call to centre decolonization as the most significant event of the long twentieth century, fleshing out the historical and global context within which postcolonial projects such

---

[9] Chalcraft 2011; Mossallam 2012.

as Nasserism navigated and established themselves. In particular, the colonial nature of the international meant that postcolonial projects were never purely nationalist in their orientation, making third world-ism always already international.[10]

Focusing on Egypt, Vivienne Jabri has argued that the changes put forward by Nasser should be understood as attempts to access the international, in which access means exerting control over how global international relations affects the nation.[11] For postcolonial nations, regaining control over the institutions of international political economy – the same institutions that reproduced global inequality – was seen as the path to independence:

> In its role in both accumulation and the establishment of legitimacy, the postcolonial state is an interventionist state: it seeks to construct a hegemonic structure that functions to legitimize a political economy of development; it builds a state apparatus geared for planning as well as the mobilization and management of national resources.[12]

However, this is always done vis-à-vis the colonial international; it is this tension that mediates anything and everything the postcolonial state does. 'This is where the postcolonial state comes face to face with the colonial structure of the international. The resistance of the postcolonial state as such must hence be measured in terms of how it fulfils its role in relation to the constraints of the international'.[13] This suggests that when we evaluate post-independence leaders and their political projects we must always consider their relationship(s) towards the international.

The attempted dismantling of the international, which was seen as part and parcel of decolonization, can be read through seminal events such as the Afro-Asian conference at Bandung in 1955. Bandung brought together representatives of over two-thirds of the world's population, and the emotional and symbolic nature of this moment cannot be overstated. Bandung, the Non-Aligned Movement, and other such movements and conferences were part of a set of ideas that characterized decolonization, ideas that located justice both nationally and internationally. As Adom Getachew argues, these attempts should be read as attempts at *worldmaking* that go beyond the nation.

National sovereignty was what was at stake in debates around the colonial international, an international system of global politics that

---

[10] See Getachew 2019.   [11] Jabri 2012, 100.   [12] Ibid., 102.   [13] Ibid.

was colonial precisely because the majority of nations within it were not considered to be sovereign. From mandates and protectorates to full on colonized nations, the logic of colonialism was a linear logic where many nation-states were stuck in a position of potential sovereignty. As Antony Anghie notes, 'Sovereignty existed in something like a linear continuum, based on its approximation to the ideal of the European nation-state'.[14] Yet while postcolonial nations put forward a critique of the uneven distribution of sovereignty, the move to accept the nation as the main vessel of sovereignty – as well as to accept sovereignty in itself – betrays a concession to colonial understandings of the world. Not only did it often include the oppression of racial, ethnic and religious minorities not seen as part of the nation, it also displaced alternative understandings of sovereignty.

Sovereignty was understood specifically through material changes such as industrialization and nationalism. The Communiqué issued after the conference begins by listing principles of economic cooperation,[15] suggesting the importance of the economic in the creation of a new international.[16] Some of the themes that emerge from these principles include the need for cooperation within the Global South; the creation and sharing of technical expertise, research, and development; the establishment of international bodies to coordinate economic development; and self-determination in terms of economic policy. Most importantly, the principles clearly delineate a programme for national development based on industrialization. The fourth principle calls for the stabilizing of commodity trade in the region, and the fifth principle acknowledges the importance of primary commodities and the position of the postcolonial world in supplying them. The sixth principle states: 'Asian-African countries should diversify their export trade by processing their raw material, wherever economically feasible, before export'. Furthermore, the nationalization of banking was strongly proposed, as was the development of infrastructure to engage in trade. As Chatterjee notes, the Communiqué suggests that most countries at the conference saw themselves as 'exporters of raw

---

[14] Anghie 2007, 148.
[15] The Communiqué can be accessed at http://franke.uchicago.edu/Final_Comm unique_Bandung_1955.pdf
[16] In some ways, this pre-empted approaches such as dependency and world systems theory, which centred the global capitalist system as a site of colonial inequality.

commodities and importers of industrial products'.[17] State-led economic development through industrialization was envisioned as a means of interrupting the dependency they faced on global capital.

Spaces and moments such as Bandung recall Fanon's hopes for a postcolonial renaissance, and for the creation of a new international beyond European imperialism:

> The Third World today faces Europe like a colossal mass whose aim should be to try and resolve the problems to which Europe has not been able to find answers. If we want to turn Africa into a new Europe, then let us leave the destiny of our countries to Europeans. They will know how to do it better than the most gifted among us. But if we want humanity to advance a step further, if we want to bring it up to a different level than that which Europe has shown it, then we must invent and we must make discoveries . . . No, we do not want to catch up with anyone. What we want to do is go forward.[18]

For Fanon, the creation of a new social and political project was very much tied to anti-imperialism and anti-racism. These were the very themes that animated this conference and others like it. These conferences created a new space of internationalism[19] that, for a brief moment, challenged the colonial international. 'The demands made at Bandung still remain the unfulfilled promises of a global order founded on the freedom and equality of nations and peoples. That is why the memory of 1955 still refuses to go away, even though the world has changed so much over the past sixty years'.[20] It is difficult not to see this as a lost or missed opportunity,[21] even when we understand the severe limits these nations faced; such a moment has not come about since then, and in many ways, we saw the deepening of the colonial international with the Washington Consensus in the 1970s.

Nasser's stated commitment to various internationalist movements are part of the story of the hegemonic project that was built. Reem Abou El Fadl has traced the ways in which Cairo became a hub for African, Asian and Afro-Asian connections in the 1950s, building an infrastructure of solidarity and engaging in regional identity-making; this was both enabled and limited by Nasser (2019). Pan-Arabism, pan-Africanism and Arab socialism were used to position Egypt as a strategically important country within the new configuration of post-independence nation-states. Although debates around whether Nasserism can be understood as

---

[17] Chatterjee, in Eslava et al. 2017, 673. [18] Fanon 1963, 254.
[19] Ibid., 671, [20] Ibid., 674. [21] Taha 2017.

a socialist project are extensive, what I am more interested in here is how Arab socialism as well as pan-Arabism and pan-Africanism carried out the political work of creating solidarity within Egypt's new ruling class; within Egyptian society; and both regionally and internationally. These ideologies of postcolonial solidarity were central to the hegemony created under Nasser. Alluding to geographical forms of connectivity, these ideologies were much more about a shared goal of anticolonialism and the desire for a new global order. Arab socialism in particular allowed Nasser to create a common ideological basis within the Free Officers who made up the ruling class. Although some officers disagreed with how far socialist policies should go (including Nasser), the ideological components of Arab socialism formed a common language that connected them and worked as consent.

Nasser's regionalism and internationalism were not as romantic as sometimes portrayed, however. The war in Yemen is an exemplar of Nasser's geopolitics and the ways in which it could destroy radical forces in other Arab nations. Egypt's war in Yemen has been called 'Nasser's Vietnam' not only because of the centrality it played in weakening Nasserism's hegemony but because of the devastation it caused. The war complicates a simple understanding of Nasser's Pan-Arabism as a progressive form of internationalism and instead positions Nasserism's geopolitical ambitions within his attempt at *regional hegemony*. As Isa Blumi notes, the war also brought to the fore the contradictions between Nasserist ideology and practice, and led Yemeni revolutionaries to characterize Nasserist-led nationalizations as 'stealing from the poor'.[22] Following a coup in September 1962 and an occupation that followed, rather than viewing Egypt's intervention in Yemen as part of a broader Arab socialist project, it in fact replicated the same problems Nasserism created inside Egypt, namely a state-led form of capitalist development that relied on modernization and a linear teleology.[23]

Beyond the ruling class, Arab socialism was able to unite large swathes of the Egyptian public, again by functioning as an ideological vessel in which anticolonialism, nationalism, and independent development came together. It matters less that it didn't live up to its theoretical potential, or that it contained contradictory elements; what matters is that it was able to act as a unifying ideology across vastly different populations. Similarly, pan-Arabism and pan-Africanism created a certain form of ideological

---

[22] 2018, 104.   [23] Ibid., 114.

unity at the international level. While disagreements existed over what these projects actually entailed as well as over what solidarity should look like, they still captured a particular approach to decolonization that saw the international as a space in need of decolonizing, and that brought together people across most of the globe under the banner of anticolonialism. Political ideologies developed duirng this era, then, should be understood through an anticolonial lens. As Reem Abou El Fadl argues, 'positive neutralism developed out of the pursuit of a particular combination of foreign policy and nation building, both of which were dominated by an anticolonial rather than Cold War consciousness.'[24]

As David Scott writes, 'Socialism was the name of a variously configured oppositional idea of political community defined largely in terms of anti-imperialism, national self-determination, and anti-capitalism'.[25] These ideologies and movements were a product of a very particular historical moment – referred to as the Bandung Era by Samir Amin[26] – and this goes some way in explaining the weakness of the ideologies produced by ruling classes that came after Nasser. At the same time, the Nasserist ruling class clearly understood the importance of (seemingly) clear ideologies that could capture widespread sentiments, ideals and values, and that could be used to push forward a new hegemonic project at the national level. Here Sherif Younes' attempt to trace how Nasserism's ideological power was exercised by reference to 'the people' is key.[27]

Nasserism both produced and was produced by this historical moment, and should be centred within it. Many of the changes put in place under Nasserism have distinct parallels with what was happening around the postcolonial world, raising interesting questions about South-South solidarity. Similarly, much of what Nasserism achieved was made possible by these new forms of solidarity and connectivity that allowed parts of the postcolonial world to act as a power bloc in opposition to neocolonial interests.[28] While Nasser was undoubtedly one of the major figures involved in this moment at the global level (see Figure 2.2), from Bandung to the founding of the Non-Aligned Movement, Egypt's involvement in anticolonial mobilization dates back much earlier. I turn now to the nationalists that came before Nasser, to highlight both the continuities and discontinuities between the radical anticolonial projects of the early twentieth century and the postcolonial state that emerged in 1952.

[24] 2015, 3.   [25] 1996, 11.   [26] Ibid.   [27] 2012.   [28] Abou El Fadl 2019.

Figure 2.2 Leaders of the Non-Aligned Nations. Credit: Bettmann / Getty Images.

The Nationalists Who Came before Nasser

It was Nasser's twin project of national and international transformation – based on his belief in both a social and political revolution – that Egypt's first historical bloc set out to achieve. This bloc was formed in the 1950s, against a backdrop of the intense nationalist fervour that had engulfed the country for decades. Rather than nationalist sentiment acting as merely a backdrop in the formation of this bloc, it was very much its raison d'être. It was Nasser and the Free Officers' ability to create a hegemonic project that both drew on and implemented nationalist goals that explains not only their popularity but the ownership many Egyptians felt over the new project.[29] From the military coup on 2 July 1952 until the downfall of the project in 1967, the Nasserist project created what can be described as hegemony, where high levels of coercion were embedded within high levels of consent; where many Egyptians identified with the ideological pronouncements being made; and where material changes were brought about that affected millions of ordinary Egyptians. In this section, I trace

---

[29] See Mossallam 2012.

90   *Hegemony in Egypt*

the positioning of the officers within the pre-revolutionary landscape, before looking at two movements involved in broader nationalist debates – feminists and labour – to sketch out how it was these movements that laid the groundwork of the new project, despite their eventual side-lining by the Nasserist bloc.

The Pre-Revolutionary Political Context

A key element in creating a historical bloc is a definitive ruling class tied to a clearly defined project. Sherif Younes has noted that the Free Officers cannot straightforwardly be understood as representing the military of the time; first, a process of politicizing officers had to take place.[30] This meant that a rupture had to be performed between the military under British colonial rule and the military post-1952.[31] Throughout the 1930s and 1940s, King Farouk had been amassing additional powers that increasingly brought the military under his control. He led the army to defeat in the 1948 Palestine War, during which Egypt suffered heavy losses and which was one of the major causes of discontent within the military, and also began to rely on the army to crush rising internal dissent. The right to control the army began to be one of the main nationalist demands.

The 1930s and 1940s saw a continued British presence in Egypt, albeit with nominal independence and the Wafd in control of Egypt's government. The Wafd were a political party dominated largely by wealthy Egyptian capitalists pushing for nationalism and independence. It was headed by Sa'ad Zaghloul, who had participated in the Urabi revolt of the 1880s, also a nationalist affair.[32] The Wafd had introduced Egypt's first constitution and government, and were involved in events that led to the 1919 nationalist revolution.[33] The 1919 revolution is crucial to

[30] 2012.
[31] Although beyond the scope of this chapter, the transformation of the military from protectors of both Ottoman and British colonial rule to the protectors of nationalist Egyptian rule is an important one to chart.
[32] The word *wafd* means 'delegation', and this had been Zaghloul's intention: to gather a delegation that would present the British with a request for Egyptian independence. The delegation was denied the right to travel to London, and Zaghloul and other members were exiled to Malta.
[33] Although the British had somewhat reduced their presence by 1919, they were still able to intervene in four key areas that in effect maintained the occupation: foreign interests, the defence of Egypt against foreign aggression, the Suez Canal and Sudan.

The Nationalists Who Came before Nasser

understanding the growth of anticolonial sentiment and mobilization leading up to 1952, and is key to the pre-history of Nasserist hegemony.

The 1919 revolution was very much a nationalist affair, centred around questions of wealth extraction and self-governance and exacerbated by the toll World War I took on Egyptians and Egypt. When Saʿad Zaghloul and other leaders of the growing independence movement were exiled to Malta, demonstrations and strikes broke out. The British response was heavy-handed, and included killing protesters and bombing villages.[34] Less than one month later, Zaghloul and the other leaders were released and allowed to attend the Paris peace conference, and a commission was set up to explore Egyptian self-rule on the condition that the strikes and demonstrates ended. In February 1922, Egypt was declared independent. The Wafd drafted a new constitution based on a parliamentary system, and Zaghloul became the first elected prime minister of Egypt in 1924.

The Wafd did not, however, straightforwardly replace the monarchy or British interests, and functioned more as part of a formal governing coalition in an Egypt that was still under occupation. By 1936, following King Farouk's signing of the Anglo-Egyptian Treaty – seen as highly damaging to hopes of full Egyptian independence – popular disillusionment with the Wafd grew as they had failed to boycott the King for his signing of the treaty. Given that the Wafd had risen to power based on their nationalist credentials and support for independence, it was especially notable when they were seen as betraying these in favour of the monarchy and British interests. The Abdeen Palace incident of 1942 highlights this shift: Miles Lampson, Britain's ambassador to Egypt, presented King Farouk with a decree demanding the abdication of Hussein Sirri's government and its replacement by a Wafd government headed by Mustafa el Nahhas. Finding his palace surrounded by military forces, Farouk had little choice but to assent. The Wafd therefore came back to power in 1942 at the hands of the British, an event crucial to the revolution that was to come just ten years later.[35]

The Free Officers were able to portray themselves as a more legitimate nationalist force precisely because of rising questions around the Wafd's nationalist credentials during such key moments.[36] As Nazih Ayubi notes, 'the Wafd increasingly became attuned to the interests of

---

[34] www.lrb.co.uk/blog/2019/april/the-arab-spring-of-1919
[35] Additionally, internal rivalries within the Wafd contributed to their decline, as well as the party's structure which left little space for contrasting views (ibid., 23).
[36] Chalcraft 2016, 279.

a landowning class that was continuing to extend its activities into commerce and ally itself with new industrialists who had close links with international capital. The Wafd represented a kind of "unfulfilled promise".[37] In understanding them as a political party that favoured procedural democracy, it is useful to recall Fanon: 'The entire action of these nationalist political parties during the colonial period is action of the electoral type: a string of philosophico-political dissertations on the themes of the rights of peoples to self-determination, the rights of man to freedom from hunger and human dignity, and the unceasing affirmation of the principle: "One man, one vote".[38] It is here that we see an interesting description of the Wafd: a nationalist political party calling for self-determination on the one hand, but also a party through which colonial rule continues to function on the other. 'Pacifists and legalists, they are in fact partisans of order, the new order – but to the colonialist bourgeoisie they put bluntly enough the demand which to them is the main one: 'Give us more power'. It is on these terms that we should understand both the limitations of the Wafd and the space this created for a force such as the Free Officers.

The rupture between the military under British colonial rule and after 1952 was also very much an ideological one: their emphasis on nationalism, development, Arab socialism, and anti-colonialism clearly associated them with other radical trends active at the time, who saw independence as the most pressing dilemma facing Egypt. It is precisely the centring of the nationalist question that allowed the Nasserist bloc to so effectively make use of nationalism in its hegemonic project, particularly in the face of the Wafd's failure to embody a nationalism that was 'anticolonial enough'. The key to forming a historical bloc is for a social force within the ruling class to transcend its own narrow interests and universalize them. This movement outwards has to incorporate both social forces within the ruling class itself as well as subaltern social forces in order to bring a significant number of them into the new bloc, tied together by a cohesive ideological project.

In the rest of the section, I look at two of these radical trends in order to tease out the ways in which nationalism was imagined and contested, and how this ultimately fed into the Nasserist hegemonic project. Both the women's movement and the worker's movement developed complex projects that called for a liberated Egypt. They were not alone; students,

[37] 1996, 107.   [38] 1963, 59.

The Nationalists Who Came before Nasser

Islamists, nationalists, and others similarly articulated independence along lines that spoke to multiple forms of inequality. What I show is that for all of these movements, nationalism became the most important path to liberation, for better or for worse. The forms of nationalism performed by these groups, however, should be distinguished from the form adopted by the state; this is by no means an attempt to collapse these into one broad category of nationalism. Nevertheless, nationalism was central to many social movements in the decades leading up to 1952; because of this, the groundwork for the Nasserist project was already in place. In other words, a large part of the battle to produce consent had already been won, before the Free Officers even came to power.

Feminists or Nationalists?

The dilemma facing feminists across the postcolonial world has often been presented as a difficult choice between nationalism and gender equality.[39] This narrative suggests that by deciding to prioritize nationalism in the fight for independence, feminists were essentially used by nationalist male leaders and promptly set aside once independence had been won. This narrative has appeared in Egyptian feminist historiography in relation to the side-lining of women's demands during the 1919 revolution by Egyptian male modernists.[40] While this narrative touches on important historical realities – such as the way in which women were excluded after independence across many postcolonial countries – it is simplistic in how it puts forward a seemingly neat choice between nationalism and feminism. Instead, feminists in places like Egypt did not always see the two as separable, and often articulated feminism through the lens of national liberation. As Margot Badran notes, the term *nationalist* was used by feminists who generated a feminist concept of nationalism.[41]

---

[39] For work on the Egyptian feminist movement and its history, see Ahmed 1992; Ali 2000; Hatem 1992; Bier 2011; Badran 1988; Baron 2005; Khater and Nelson 1988.

[40] Badran 1988; Baron 2005. In 1923, the Egyptian Feminist Union was formed, with Huda Sha'arawi as its head. In the same year, voting rights for women were withdrawn after they had been granted earlier, and this marked an important turning point for feminists who, as Badran notes, felt betrayed after their participation in the nationalist struggle.

[41] 1988, 16.

In her work, Badran has shown how before 1919, there was an evolving nationalist consciousness and social nationalism among women, as can be seen from the growing women's press.[42] From 1919 onwards, women became increasingly visible in public life: they founded journals, charity associations, and political organizations (among them the Society for the Advancement of Woman in 1908 and the Intellectual Association of Egyptian Women in 1914 – with Sha'arawi and Mai Ziyada as founding members – and the Society of the New Woman in 1919). Women also increasingly took part in anti-British activities: 'During workers' strikes women stationed themselves at entries to government offices, bidding men not to return to work. After Sa'ad Zaghloul was exiled, schoolgirls and women took part in massive popular demonstrations.[43] In addition, women organized anti-British economic boycotts: in 1922 they master-minded their first massive boycott of British goods and services, calling for broad support from women as buyers and household managers. Nationalist women urged Egyptians to withdraw their money from British banks and formed committees to sell shares in the new national bank'.[44]

The first three decades of the twentieth century, then, saw feminism become visible intellectually, then organizationally and politically.[45] Huda Sha'rawi, Nabawiya Moussa, Malak Hifni Nassef, and Saiza Nabarawi are some of the well-known Egyptian feminists who made up this earlier movement, which focused on women gaining the right to work, the right to education, and on the issues of seclusion, veiling, marriage, and divorce; it was these questions that became known as the 'woman question'.[46] There were important differences that existed between these feminists, however, despite their similarities which coalesced around a specific modernist form of nationalism and their shared class background.[47] Ahmed argues that a feminism that favoured Westernization and secularization, with a heavy upper-middle-class emphasis, became dominant. This produced a nationalism that was tied to Egyptian modernization, or the need for modernization to be more accurate, and thus a feminism very much tied into particular audiences. For instance, the Egyptian Feminist Union's periodical – L'Egyptienne – was published in French and thus inaccessible to most Egyptian women.

[42] Ibid., 24. [43] 1992, 174. [44] Ibid., 26. [45] Ahmed 1992, 175.
[46] Baron 2005, 31.
[47] Most of the pioneering feminists came from the upper or upper middle classes, spoke foreign languages and travelled widely.

The Nationalists Who Came before Nasser

One alternative to this were feminists who articulated female subjectivity within a discourse that was more 'Egyptian'.[48] Hifni Nassef represents this latter trend, while Sha'arawi (and the Egyptian Feminist Union) represents the former: 'Sha'arawi's feminism was politically nationalistic; it opposed British domination in the sense that the liberal intellectuals of her class and the upper-middle classes opposed it, rather than opposing the British and everything Western with the extremity expressed by other groups and parties that had a base among the popular classes'.[49] This is in distinction to Hifni Nassef, who formulated her ideas about feminism in and through the lens of Egyptian culture. For both strands of feminism, however, women's rights were part of a broader debate around nationalism; what was different was how they envisioned the future.

It is these energies that fed into a new phase of the feminist movement that emerged in the 1950s, where we begin to see an important alignment between the goals of feminists and the goals of the new ruling class that makes it difficult to separate feminism from nationalism. What is distinctive about this new wave, however, is that feminists began to put forward a different articulation of nationalism which was influenced by a more egalitarian form of class politics. Anti-colonialism was still central, as it had been before, but anti-capitalism became increasingly prominent alongside a growing interest in Marxism and socialism. For more, see Hammad 2011. In terms of gender, this lent itself to more structural understandings of inequality that called for more deep-seated transformations.

This was undoubtedly connected to the increased prominence of socialist and Marxist theorizing globally, including the proliferation of organizations and conferences that connected feminists across the postcolonial world, conferences at which global inequality was a central theme. This gave feminists the analytical tools, including a means of analysing class conflict, to analyse Egypt's position vis-à-vis a rapidly changing world, and also provided a way of analysing what many of them saw as the main problem facing Egypt: social inequality. Some examples include Inji Efflatoun, who, as a delegate of the League of Women Students and Graduates of Egypt, the communist women's organization, to the World Congress of Women held in Paris in 1945, gave the following speech: 'I made a very powerful speech in which I linked the oppression of women in Egypt to the British occupation and imperialism. I not only denounced the

---

[48] 1992, 175. [49] Ibid., 178.

British, but the King and the politicians as well. It was a very political speech in which I called for national liberation and the liberation of women'.[50] Other feminists active as communists included Latifa al-Zayyat and Soraya Adham.

While there has been much focus on what has been called 'state feminism' during the Nasser era and the ways the state attempted to reduce gender inequality by reforming the public sector, this relationship was not one of pure control. As Laura Bier and others have noted, the Nasserist project was a highly gendered one. In particular, the role of the 'working woman' was central to the socialist and postcolonial project, in that it represented the Nasserist project as modern, secular, and socialist.[51] Egyptian women were affected in various ways by changes made by the Nasserist project, particularly their access to higher education and to professional fields such as business, engineering, and politics. Where in 1962 women had formed 4 per cent of the waged labour force, by 1982 it was 15 per cent (1 million women). These women were primarily educated women entering professional, technical, and scientific fields, with women holding 26 per cent of such employment in Egypt.[52]

Symbolically, women were also key:

Female workers, especially those working in new sites carved out by socialist development, were represented in state feminist discourse not only as necessary to the economic success of state socialist policies but also as a critical symbol of the regime's success in transforming Egypt into a modern socialist nation.[53]

Surveys studying women's productivity – thereby objectifying it – proposed that the state needed to modernize social reproduction in order to allow women to be more productive in building the new nation. Day care and domestic technologies were introduced, thereby freeing (some) women from social reproductive labour so that they could be more involved in other forms of labour. Egypt's family planning programme similarly targeted the family as an object to be modernized as part of its broader project of scientific modernization and economic development.[54] As Omnia El Shakry has written, from the interwar period until the Nasserist one, 'population questions merged with the nationalist preoccupation with the women's question, which was closely entangled with the improvement of the quality of the population.'[55]

---

[50] 1992, 196. [51] Bier 2011, 62. El Shakry 2007. [52] Ibid., 212.
[53] Ibid., 69. [54] Ibid., 122. [55] 2007, 174.

The Nationalists Who Came before Nasser

It is in changes like these that we can see the contradictory effects of Nasserism as a project, for it is these very changes that gave women – at least legally – full equality in the public sphere as well as took seriously the question of social reproduction. Nevertheless, the management of social reproduction was now handed over to male policy makers rather than women or female social networks, and the management of the population meant that the family was transformed 'from a metaphor to an instrument of governance'.[56] More broadly, the use of women within the nationalist project echoed a larger trend whereby postcolonial states used women's bodies and statuses to construct themselves as modern. It is precisely this messiness that makes the Nasserist project difficult to understand coherently: the very era during which women made many material gains, they also became objectified within a nationalist project whose goals of modernism did not always adopt a critical feminist perspective.

Indeed, a paradox of feminism during this era was that it both gave women access to spaces in society they fought for, such as employment and education, while simultaneously shutting down political space and exerting control over independent organizing; Nasser shut down the Egyptian Feminist Union and jailed notable feminists such as Doriya Shafik[57] and Inji Aflaton for criticizing the new ruling class. When, in March 1954, the Free Officers proposed a new constitution and an assembly that included no women, Shafik went on a hunger strike in protest, stating: 'I protest against the formation of a Constitutional Assembly without women's representation. I will never agree to be ruled by a constitution in the preparation of which I had no say'.[58] Her hunger strike ended when the governor of Cairo met with her to inform he that the new constitution would guarantee full political rights for women. However, when the new constitution granted women the right to vote only if they asked for it, Shafik announced a second hunger strike to protest 'against the infringement of my human freedom on two fronts – the external and the internal: the Israeli occupation of Egyptian land (Israel took its time about withdrawing from the Sinai after the Tripartite Aggression) and the onset of dictatorship that is leading Egypt into bankruptcy and chaos'.[59] Other members of Bint al-Nil pressured her to resign,

---

[56] El Shakry 2007, 166.

[57] Shafik, unlike Aflatoun, put forward a more 'secular' form of feminism. She founded Bint al-Nil, an organization that aimed to achieve full political rights for women.

[58] 1992, 205.   [59] Ibid.

before Nasser placed her under house arrest and closed down both the organization and its journal.[60]

Despite this, Nasser was present in many feminist discussions during this period.[61] Nasser's anti-imperialism and the discourse of Arab socialism proved relatable to the majority of Egyptians for whom social justice and economic independence were central concerns. This is not to say that they saw him as solely responsible for all the gains that were made during this period, most notably in areas of education and employment; as Egyptian feminist Wedad Mitri argued, the women's movement in Egypt had long demanded the right of women to vote and be elected to office as part of any real grassroots democracy. 'In 1956, Gamal Abdel Nasser extended this right to us. But of course, it didn't just happen. It resulted from the struggle of generations and generations of women'.[62] Here we see a nuanced view that does not match either the discourse of state feminism or part of the historiography of the Egyptian women's movement – both of which ascribed to the state the power to give women rights. Feminists during this era refer to Nasser in a multiplicity of ways, all of which are connected to his economic and political successes and failures and not to his project vis-à-vis the 'woman question' or state feminism; this is because they saw gender as interlinked with the broader changes happening under Nasser and not as separate from them.

Class and Nation

Within Egypt's workers' movement, similar intersections of radicalism and nationalism emerge.[63] Workers from various sectors were an influential force before 1952, with a strong workers' movement made up of an industrial proletariat that was a major part of the nationalist movement.[64] The emergence of this movement should be set within the context of Egyptian integration into global capitalism, particularly through cotton production and the emergence of private property. As in many parts of the world, this process of integration was one based on coercion and expropriation.[65] Mehmed Ali forced peasants to cultivate cotton on state-

---

[60] Ibid. [61] See Salem 2017. [62] Ibid.

[63] For extended studies on Egyptian labour activism, see Chalcraft 2011; Posusney 1997; Beinin and Lockman 1998; Alexander and Bassiouny 2014.

[64] For more on Egypt's labour movement in the twentieth century, see Chalcraft 2016, 269–73.

[65] Beckert 2014, 117.

The Nationalists Who Came before Nasser　　　　　　　99

owned lands for their yearly corvée duty, a forced-labour tax. Peasants also had to plant cotton in specific ways on their own land in order to sell the final product to the state.

The shift to full-scale British occupation in 1882 came with new forms of domination. Timothy Mitchell has traced the initial moment in 1830 during which Egyptians were confined to their villages in order to produce for the expanding market.[66] Egyptians now had to seek permission and official documents in order to leave their home villages, which were from then on to be guarded and organized in a way conducive to the production of commodities for European consumption. Central Bureaux of Inspection were established, with local inspectors in each village. A sixty-page booklet issued in 1829 detailed how peasants were to work, the crops they should cultivate, the confinement to their villages, and how they were to be guarded and supervised.[67] This booklet was produced following an emergency meeting called to address increasing peasant desertion and decreasing revenues.[68] The primary motivating factor behind these technologies of discipline was to increase revenue, justified according to new theories on how to productively use land. Connected to this was the emergence of private property[69] and the institution of debt. Peasants who disobeyed were whipped, and this new organization introduced a novel system of surveillance. There was major resistance to the imposition of such an organization, with countless villagers leaving their villages, despite heavy penalties, and numerous uprisings followed. Alongside these changes, there was a shift in the mode of production itself, with peasants having to accept wage labour in order to survive under the expansion of capitalist production.

---

[66] 1991a, 34.　　[67] Ibid., 40.　　[68] Ibid., 41.

[69] The process of establishing private property was a similarly violent one. Mitchell (1991a, 56) notes the contradiction between establishing private property as a right and then using it to take over land in far-away colonies such as Egypt, writing: 'The land could be taken because those who farmed it had not heard of this universal right'. In violently seizing this land, the British had to construct the previous arrangement as the opposite of modern; the Egyptian state was portrayed as despotic and its right to the land as void. This is despite the fact that under the Ottoman Empire the state did not 'own all the land' – land was not seen as an object that could be owned. As Mitchell notes, 'the doctrine of state ownership of land did not correspond to the modern notion of property but registered the ruler's political claim to a share of the revenue, while also acknowledging both the revenue claims of local political forces and the subsistence claims of the cultivator and other members of the village' (ibid., 57).

These changes were to lay the foundations of an active worker's movement that was strongly nationalist and anti-colonial. As is clear, the changes peasants faced were very much connected to both the consolidation of capitalism and the expansion of imperialism. These two processes were not separate: each relied on the other. Many workers thus saw a connection between anti-imperialism and struggles around work, despite intermittent resistance to such views from political actors such as the Wafd.[70] Major incidents such as the Cairo tramway workers' strike in 1908 defined the contours of British policy towards Egyptian labour activism. During the strike, the police intervened and broke it up, and 'militant' workers were fired.[71] This heavy-handed approach came to define the British response to labour activism and was justified on the grounds that the British were concerned about the political ramifications of successful strikes. This replaced the attempt by the British to mould Egyptian labour activism along the lines of reformist trade unionism, based on the model of the British Trade Union Congress.[72] In other words, it might further encourage nationalist sentiments, and this connection between labour activism and the nationalist movement was at the heart of what worried the British. By the 1930s the Egyptian working class, loosely organized around numerous unions, had become a social force the British had no choice but to confront.[73]

This brief history suggests that for the Egyptian workers' movement, there was – as for the feminists – no easy split between nationalism and other causes such as anti-capitalism or feminism. The nationalist cause was one that seeped into everything and gave it its full character; because for the majority of Egyptians, independence was seen as the most important political, economic, and social goal. This does not discount the reality that independence was imagined in different ways, or that internationalism was an intrinsic feature of anticolonialism. Rather, I highlight these movements and the role nationalism played in them in order to show why the Nasserist project was able to extend its hegemony through similar ideological and material promises. The Nasserist project was not created out of thin air; it was very much a continuation of the goals and aims many radical movements

---

[70] Alexander and Bassiouny 2014, 39–40.   [71] Ibid., 226.

[72] Ibid., 2014, 41. Indeed this attempt at co-optation predated Nasser's attempt, which is often presented as the first attempt at labour co-optation.

[73] Ibid.

had been making for decades. It is here that the uniqueness of the Nasserist project surfaces: it promised something new, by building on energies that had been building for a long time. To do this, it used the same language, discourses, and ideas that many Egyptians had already become familiar with; it also put in place material projects that Egyptians had been calling for, such as nationalization and industrialization. The Nasserist project was old and new; it was made up of the past, but promised a different future. In absorbing these energies, however, Nasserism also depleted many of these movements. Indeed one significant afterlife of the Nasserist project is the weakening of a left that could have resisted the neoliberalization to come in the 1970s. The ghosts of Nasserism are many, but surely his exclusion and disappearing of those who supposedly shared his vision for what Egypt could be has produced an especially intense form of haunting stretching into the present.

'Workers, Peasants, Soldiers, and Nationalist Capitalists': Creating a Historical Bloc

Nasserism as a project was heavily dependent on his mobilization of 'the people', as noted by Sherif Younes.[74] This was Nasser's basis of legitimacy which extended over transitional (organizing people into societal groups), achievable (improving their living conditions), and populist (mobilizing them) forms of legitimacy.[75] In many of his speeches, Nasser referred to what he called an 'alliance of popular forces', made up of workers, peasants, soldiers, and nationalist capitalists. This is where we can pinpoint the contours of the historical bloc, which was very much premised on these four different groups being mobilized in support of one hegemonic project. Moreover, as Younes notes, Nasser could 'read people's dreams' and turn them into a political project; he was able to 'represent the invisible people who were an abstraction', and speak for them.[76] Ultimately, Nasserism shifted people's loyalties to other forms of social solidarity into loyalty to the regime and its new political project.[77] Here I look at the emergence of the Free Officers who were at the centre of the new historical bloc and who made up its core ruling class, before tracing the consolidation of the bloc through the exclusion and inclusion of different

[74] 2012. [75] Ibid. [76] Ibid. [77] Ibid.

102   *Hegemony in Egypt*

groups, before concluding by focusing on how the new historical bloc created consent.

The Emergence of the Free Officers

A historical bloc is formed when a social force is able to universalize their own narrow interests outwards and create hegemony. This social force was Nasser and the Free Officers, held together by their positions within the military and the military coup they executed, by their common class interests, and by a unified belief in anticolonial nationalism and independence in all forms, even as they differed on what this meant and how to achieve it. Indeed much of the literature emphasizes these differences, suggesting that there was no uniform project in the early 1950s and that most of what we retrospectively understand as the Nasserist project was made up as the Free Officers went along. While there is certainly some truth to this, I also think there is something to be said for the shared stated goals the Free Officers announced, and how this reflected an awareness of the need to create a project that could universalize their interests. It seems to me that while the 1950s can be understood as lacking a coherent project, by the 1960s this is no longer the case.

The Free Officers were initially a nationalist movement, made up of different political trends including the Muslim Brotherhood, the Wafdists, and the Communists.[78] They did not come from the agrarian class of wealthy landowners, a social force that was extremely powerful pre-1952 but rather hailed from predominantly middle-class families, with the exception of Nasser and Anwar el Sadat, who were from lower-middle-class families. This shared class background not only explains the antipathy many Free Officers felt towards the monarchy and the nationalist political parties that catered to the upper classes, it is also significant in that this was the first – and last – historical bloc in Egypt to be made up of men who did not come from classes with a history of capital accumulation. Their path to power, however, was not smooth. In many ways, they were able to form a historical bloc because of their successful co-optation of many active political trends, from workers to nationalists, as well as their ability to coerce social forces seen as antithetical to their own project, such as the Muslim

[78] Botman 1986, 350.

'Workers, Peasants, Soldiers, and Nationalist Capitalists'   103

Brotherhood. It is this two-pronged approach – consent and coercion – that I am interested in.

In 1936, Egypt's Military Academy was opened up to men from the middle classes. Nationalists had long criticized the Academy as an elitist institution, and believed that opening it up was the only way to bring it in line with nationalist goals. Property qualifications were lifted, dramatically changing the structure of the institution. Six of the fourteen members of the Revolutionary Command Council (RCC) that headed the coup had joined the Academy after 1936 following this restructuring, including Nasser himself. It was in 1949 that Nasser established the 'founding committee' of the Free Officers' movement, initially made up of eight men who met to discuss what kind of political action was needed in Egypt: Nasser, Abdel Mon'im Abdel Ra'uf Kemal al-Din Hussein, Khalid Mohieddin Abdel Hakim Amer, Salah Salem, Hassan Ibrahim, and Abdel Latif al-Boghdadi. They soon began to meet every fortnight. Gamal Salem and Anwar el Sadat were added to the group later, and Abdel Ra'uf left soon after. Members of the founding committee represented different sections of the military, ensuring the movement had widespread support from all branches.[79]

This class of officers were very much a product of Egypt's colonial situation. Growing up during a period of growing nationalist sentiment and agitation, they were part and parcel of the particular historical moment leading up to decolonization. Their ability to access the Military Academy was also a product of these new forms of contestation that rallied against the elitism of public institutions. In a sense, this explains the ability of Nasser to create consent within this class; shared values of forming a new power base on the basis of anticolonial nationalism and independent development through national autonomy served to create a basis of agreement. Equally importantly, these men shared a class basis that was a radical departure from previous ruling elites. They did not come from the landed elite or the royal family, and while some members came from wealthy families, this was by no means the norm. The Free Officers, instead, represented an Egyptian ruling class that was formed of men who did not have long family histories of capital accumulation.

In the 1950s, the first Free Officer pamphlets were printed, stating that the goals of the movement were to bring an end to British

[79] Ibid., 51.

imperialism, palace and government corruption, end feudalism and to tackle the 'Palestine question'. From the start, nationalism was very much part and parcel of the ways in which the Free Officers articulated their project, from monopoly capitalism and foreign interests to the defeat in the Palestine War.[80] While King Farouk knew that elements within the military opposed him, he was unaware of how deeply the Free Officers had infiltrated the institution. Aside from growing discontent around the military being used to crush dissent internally, its position as an institution so straightforwardly tied to nationalism represented fertile ground on which to unite individuals against what they saw as the declining state of the nation.

On 23 July 1952, a mere three years after the Free Officers were formed, Anwar el Sadat announced to the nation that a coup had taken place, and an outpouring of national support followed. Military bases and instalments, the national broadcasting station, and the Suez Canal were seized. Muhammad Naguib, more experienced than most of the other Officers, was chosen to lead both the armed forces and the nation. Ali Maher was chosen as prime minister, enjoying the support of many groups, including the Muslim Brotherhood. King Farouk was sent into exile, leaving to Italy on his yacht, and the RCC was formed with Nasser as its leader. In his book, Nasser outlined the goals of the revolution, framed through the threats the new nation faced:

1 The lurking British occupation troops in the Suez Canal zone, the first principle was: Destruction of imperialism and its stooges among Egyptian traitors.
2 The despotism of feudalism which dominated the land and those on it, the second principle was: Ending of feudalism.
3 The exploitation of wealth resources to serve the interests of a group of capitalists, the third principle was: Ending monopoly and the domination of capital over the Government.
4 The exploitation and despotism which were an inevitable consequence to all that, the fourth principle was: Establishment of social justice.
5 Conspiracies to weaken the army and use the remaining part of its strength to threaten the internal front eager for revolution, the fifth aim was: Building of a powerful national army.

[80] Ibid., 59.

'Workers, Peasants, Soldiers, and Nationalist Capitalists' 105

6 Political forgery which tried to veil the landmarks of true nationalism, the sixth aim was: Establishment of a sound democratic
system.[81]

A new Egyptian era had begun.

The Contours of a New Ruling Class

Despite a common broad-based agenda, the Free Officers did not
seamlessly form a new ruling class, nor did they necessarily agree on
central issues. Before a historical bloc could be formed, the contours of
the new ruling class had to be set. While there were many issues on
which these men agreed, the methods of achieving a 'new Egypt'
differed dramatically from one Free Officer to the next. Because historiography has often looked at the 1952 revolution by focusing on social
forces that countered the Free Officers, there has been less of a focus on
the divisions within the Officers themselves. The power politics that
followed the coup were in effect central to establishing Nasser's authority as well as forming hegemony. Here, I look at how Nasser established
consent within the ruling class by both spreading the influence of the
military as an institution and by negotiating tensions within the military itself, or what Younes calls politicizing the military.[82]

Soon after coming to power, individuals within the Free Officers
began to position themselves in key political posts. Central to a new
ruling class was establishing a source of social power that was separate
from the traditional landed elite, in which Egypt's new elites could be
cultivated. This ended up being technocrats or bureaucrats, cultivated
through the newly expanded public sector; these men and women
would go on to occupy key governmental posts.[83] This social force is
unique in that it did not come from a class with a history of accumulating capital; rather, it became a social force through its connections to
national development, the newly expanded public sector, and the new
military-led government. We can also read shifts in the role of the state
through the emergence of this social force; while the state in Egypt has
always played a key role vis-à-vis production, this was enhanced even
more under the new ruling class. The state was at the centre of the Free
Officers' attempt to re-articulate Egypt's position within global

---

[81] 1959, 6–7.   [82] 2012.   [83] Faksh 1976b, 143–4.

capitalism, at the heart of which lay independent economic development through policies such as nationalization and industrialization.

It was precisely these types of changes that led to structural divisions within the Free Officers themselves. An important conflict marking the ruling class during this period and that is relevant to the discussions this book tackles was over the decision by the new regime to limit political space. Soon after coming to power, the Free Officers' RCC first decided that parties needed to be reformed since they seemed unable to do so themselves,[84] then ordered the arrest of sixty-four politicians, including Fu'ad Serag al-Din, Ibrahim Abdel-Hadi, and Naguib al-Hilali, all previous Prime Ministers, and finally banned all political parties. This was largely a result of the sentiment among RCC members that civilians were incapable of ruling the country at that point in time.[85] The repercussions of these moves by the RCC were so great that Ali Maher – then prime minister – resigned. This ignited another struggle within the Free Officers, as it was revealed that Maher was not in favour of drastic changes to Egypt's economic structure such as land reform. Maher himself was a big landowner and argued that land reform would reduce productivity and discourage foreign investment.

While there was greater consensus on the centrality of some degree of land reform – thus rendering Maher unpopular – there was no consensus within the Free Officers on the issue of controlling political parties. Muhammad Naguib in particular, officially president of Egypt, favoured a liberal democratic approach that did not include banning parties or removing people from office. What was controversial about this, according Nasser, was that it allowed too much political space through which colonial powers could infiltrate and influence Egyptian politics. A clear power struggle emerged between Naguib and Nasser, who came to represent these opposite poles. Naguib began to be excluded from RCC decisions as tensions mounted between him and Nasser. This is part and parcel of how Nasser created consent within the ruling class, by turning to both ideological justifications for Arab socialism and coercive moves such as side-lining Naguib. The split between these two figures represents two possible historical trajectories: on the one hand, the trajectory that materialized: a form of non-democratic state-controlled capitalism; and on the other hand, a trajectory that may have yielded a more liberal imperialist form of

[84] Ibid.   [85] Ibid.

'*Workers, Peasants, Soldiers, and Nationalist Capitalists*' 107

politics, as supported by Naguib, which would have meant continuity with Egypt's pre-independence economic structure. The question is therefore not simply about democracy versus authoritarianism, but also about questions of production, accumulation, and economic independence, albeit with continuing capitalist development in both instances.

The fact that the closing down of political space was seen as necessary by some social forces in order to achieve certain short-term structural changes raises interesting questions about decolonization, independence, and democracy. The argument that newly independent nations could not afford to allow democratic space because it would allow imperial forces to exercise neocolonial influence is one way of explaining the path taken by the new ruling class. There is little doubt of the need by imperial powers to consolidate new forms of control over Africa and the Middle East following independence, and their response to nations that defied this should be noted, with the assassination of Patrice Lumumba in Congo by the CIA and Belgium as the most daunting example.[86] The tripartite attack on Egypt offers another example, showing the extent to which former colonial powers were willing to go to maintain control over their lost territories. Furthermore, social forces such as the aristocracy and the agrarian fraction of capital were closely tied to imperial global forces and transnational capital, and undercutting their power was seen as central to achieving economic autonomy.

On the other hand, the new ruling class went much further than this. By undercutting the power of social forces – especially subaltern groups – who strongly supported the nationalist project – the new ruling class rendered unlikely the achievement of social justice through dismantling capitalism in Egypt. This is revisited at the end of the chapter, where I argue that had the Nasserist project centred workers and anti-capitalism, an alternative trajectory might have materialized. Capitalism – the ultimate colonial institution – was simply not a means to independence. Ultimately, relying on subaltern forces may have been the key to ensuring the longevity of the new historical bloc as well as the possibility of social justice – and, arguably, real democracy; instead, it was only to last fifteen years before crashing to the ground.

[86] Recall here the discussion of Bank Misr in the previous chapter and the consistent and aggressive attacks by British imperialism to establish neocolonial forms of dominance.

108   *Hegemony in Egypt*

Another central struggle within the ruling class was around the question of the military. Although all of the members of the Free Officers came from the military, and although Nasser was undoubtedly the central figure in this new ruling class, it was not straightforwardly the case that the military came under his complete control. This is clear from looking at the battle between Nasser and General Abdel Hakim Amer in the mid 1960s, a battle Nasser was not guaranteed to win even when his popularity was at its peak. Although it had been relatively easy to isolate Naguib within the Free Officers' group itself, as most of this support came from segments of the public and other political groups, this was not the case with Amer, who headed the armed forces. This conflict between Nasser and Amer represents a clear intra-ruling class conflict, as both had immense power – concentrated in different fractions – to draw on.

At the beginning of 1952, Amer represented a notable figure due to his close relationship with Nasser; their families had even intermarried. Most importantly, Nasser saw it as extremely important to keep the military on his side. The military qua institution was becoming increasingly powerful as military men began to occupy posts in companies as well as government positions across the country. This in turn led to upward social mobility for many officers who were now able to intermarry with the old aristocratic elite. From the start the Free Officers had realized the threat of the military and attempted to curb it, initially by forcing 450 officers to retire.[87] Amer's close relationship with Nasser allowed him to ensure that the military was beyond reproach, and gave him a measure of independence over the military's affairs. As tensions between the two mounted, however, Nasser found himself restricted by Amer's popularity within the military. Nasser even received threats from within the military warning him not to remove Amer.

By 1961, the two men effectively controlled different aspects of the country. The ultimate outcome of the confrontation was Amer's fall from power, but only after the defeat in 1967. Along with fifty military officers, Amer was arrested for plotting a coup against Nasser. After being kept under house arrest for several weeks, he was eventually taken to the hospital after swallowing pills in what appeared to be a suicide attempt, although it has been suggested that he was killed.

---

[87] Gordon 1992, 110.

'*Workers, Peasants, Soldiers, and Nationalist Capitalists*' 109

This, as well as the conflict between Nasser and Naguib, is an important part of the consolidation of the Nasserist bloc. It also shows us that while the Nasserist ruling class depended on and strengthened the military, it was by no means synonymous with it. Not only did Nasser not always directly control the military while he was in power, but the Nasserist ruling class was made up of individuals who had different ideas of the role the military should play in Egypt's future. It was in spite of these differences that Nasser was able to create consent within the ruling class.

This is not to minimize the role of the military in supporting this new ruling class and its project; as Anouar Abdel-Malek's pivotal work on the Egyptian military shows, the military was central to the new state that emerged.[88] The military increasingly controlled specific areas of Egyptian life, and were 'the main modernising force that carried out the new ruling class's project'.[89] Because of the centrality of the state to the new project, the military-state-economy nexus become increasingly enmeshed. Changes in class composition added to this: the power of the agrarian fraction was severely curtailed, and in their place a new technocratic and military elite took their place.

In light of events post-2011, and the immense support the military has enjoyed since (though declining at the time of writing), it is crucial to underline the trinity of military-nation-state capitalism that crystallized during this moment. This remains one of the major legacies of Nasserism, even as the content of these categories and the ways in which they are connected has shifted over time. What I want to emphasize, however, is that the prism of a 'military state' or 'military society' alone does not account for the new emerging project or historical bloc. It is only a careful analysis of Nasserism as a project – which was supported by the military and which benefitted the military – that can shed light on the particular power configurations we see materializing during this period. Hegemony is always in need of reproducing; it is not a static reality that – once established – remains firmly in place. As Stuart Hall notes, 'Hegemony is a very particular, historically specific, and temporary "moment" in the life of a society. It is rare for this degree of unity to be achieved, enabling a society to set itself a quite new

---

[88] Abdel-Malek was one of Egypt's most influential Marxist thinkers, producing complex analyses of Egyptian politics that was always sensitive to questions of capital and class.

[89] Faksh 1976b, 143–4.

110   *Hegemony in Egypt*

historical agenda, under the leadership of a specific formation or constellation of social forces. There is nothing automatic about such periods of "settlement". They have to be actively constructed and positively maintained'.[90] Hegemony is a living, breathing reality that must constantly be reproduced to remain in place. This is why understanding the Nasser era purely through the lens of a static state of authoritarianism is fraught, and removes all agency from anyone within or outside of the ruling class. The fact that the ruling class under Nasserism was made up of divergent points of view makes it difficult to equate it directly with the military, and also implies a strong level of consent tying together contradictory positions.

Friends and Enemies

The process of establishing a historical bloc involves both exclusions and inclusions. While the Nasserist historical bloc was notable for the broad range of social forces included within it – ranging from subaltern forces such as labour, the women's movement, nationalists – to elements of the industrial elite and the new public sector elite – there were also major exclusions that shed light on the hegemonic project proposed by this new bloc. Perhaps two of the most notable are the landowning elite and the Muslim Brotherhood; here I focus on the latter because they highlight my argument that if consent exists, coercion can quite easily be embedded within it and thus legitimized. The Muslim Brotherhood, although initially allied with the officers, eventually tried to assassinate Nasser, resulting in a massive crackdown of Brotherhood members across the country. The assassination attempt on Nasser's life suggests that the Nasserist project may not have been as hegemonic as I suggest throughout this book. To engage with this, I argue two things: first, that this attempt, which took place in 1954, was during the early days of Nasser's rule, and the project that was developing had not yet become hegemonic; and two, that historical blocs are always predicated on both inclusions and exclusions. In other words, a historical bloc does not imply the incorporation of all major social forces. What is notable about the Nasserist bloc is that it was able to consolidate itself without the Brotherhood, who were in reality a major social force in Egyptian society, and that they went even further than this by using extensive coercion against them. How did this happen?

[90] 1986, 15.

The Muslim Brotherhood have enthralled scholars of Egypt and the broader Middle East for well over half a century. A tendency to focus on Islamism and to assume that Islam must always be the major driving force of politics in the Arab world has meant that groups such as the Muslim Brotherhood are sometimes given more attention than their actual influence deserves. Nevertheless, there is little doubt that throughout the twentieth and twenty-first centuries, they were one of the more active opposition groups to various ruling classes, even as their opposition sometimes lapsed into subservience. This interesting paradox characterizes the politics of the Muslim Brotherhood since their inception: they both oppose and reinforce dominant political, economic, and social configurations, which ultimately makes it difficult to understand them solely as an oppositional, emancipatory, or radical social force. In the following chapter, I discuss the transformation of the Brotherhood during the 1970s and 1980s, and their eventual inability to successfully design a historical bloc or hegemonic project. Here I go over some details about the organization and the clash they experienced with Nasser, before returning to the question I posed earlier: how was the Nasserist bloc able to consolidate itself despite the absence of the Brotherhood and despite the high levels of coercion used against them?

The 'Marx and Engels of Islamism',[91] Hassan al-Banna and Sayyid Qutb – were born in the same year, 1906, and both began their careers as primary school teachers. It was al-Banna that went on to found the Muslim Brotherhood in 1928, and as the organization expanded rapidly, its headquarters moved to Cairo. Building neighbourhood mosques, creating small educational centres, building small hospitals for the public, and creating social clubs were some of the ways in which al-Banna expanded the Brotherhood even further, and by the 1940s it is no exaggeration to say that they were one of the most well-known social movements in Egypt. Partly, this is because of their popularity among large segments of Egyptian society such as the university-educated middle class[92] (although this was to come later), as well as rural parts of Egypt.

What is notable about the organization is how it has shifted over time, particularly in terms of its social base: while it initially attracted Egyptians from rural and urban areas, this was later to be focused much

[91] Kandil 2014, 126.   [92] Ayubi 1980, 495.

112   *Hegemony in Egypt*

more on the urban middle class. Moreover, with the mass migration of Egyptians to the Gulf countries from the 1970s onwards, the Brotherhood leadership increasingly became dominated by businessmen. This connection to business was not new, however. As early as 1938, Brotherhood treasurer Abd al-Hakim Abdin required each member to invest between a tenth and a fifth of his income in Brotherhood-run companies.[93] In the 1950s and 1960s, individual members made vast fortunes in the Gulf, and from the 1970s onwards, through *infitah*.[94] By 1980, eight of the eighteen families who dominated Egypt's private sector were affiliated with the Brotherhood, and enterprises linked to the organization – many concentrated in real estate and currency speculation – may have constituted as much as 40 per cent of the private sector, as I show in the following chapter.[95]

The Brotherhood, like many movements during the early twentieth century, was heavily involved in anti-British mobilization. In 1948, after the Brotherhood-formed militia participated in the Palestine War, it was dissolved by authorities after a Special Order found in a jeep exposed their military wing. In response, the militia turned its attention to urban violence: assassinations of politicians and judges as well as destroying public buildings. Egypt's prime minister, who had issued the order dissolving the organization, was assassinated (Mahmoud al-Nuqrashi), as was the judge who presided over the case (Ahmed al-Khazindar). These actions were always denied by the Brotherhood, who claimed they were carried out by over-zealous young Egyptians. Even the assassination attempt on Nasser was met with denial, despite evidence against Muslim Brotherhood member Mahmoud Abd al-Latif.[96] The response to this wave of violence in 1948 was for the secret police to assassinate Hassan al-Banna; it was this that ultimately led the Brotherhood to give support to the Free Officers during the 1952 coup.

There are, unsurprisingly, differing version as to the relationship between Nasser and the Brotherhood on the eve of 1952, with the Brotherhood claiming that Nasser was following their orders and that large numbers of the Free Officers were Brotherhood members, and Nasser claiming that while some officers were part of the Brotherhood, it was still an autonomous committee. Following Nasser's refusal to comply with their demands in forming his cabinet,

---

[93] Ibid.   [94] Ibid., 78.   [95] Beinin 2004, 12.   [96] Kandil 2015, 91.

'Workers, Peasants, Soldiers, and Nationalist Capitalists' 113

he swiftly dissolved the organization and detained most of the leadership. They were released soon after, following a promise to support Nasser over Naguib. But just two years later, on 26 October 1954, Mahmoud Abd al-Latif, a member of the Brotherhood's Special Order, fired nine shots at Nasser during a speech in Alexandria. The Brotherhood denied that they were responsible, but Nasser swiftly detained more than 20 000 members and executed two senior leaders.[97] Nasser's decision to imprison large numbers of Muslim Brotherhood members, as well as inflict severe torture on many of them,[98] meant the decimation of the Brotherhood for most of the 1950s and 1960s. Nasser also brought all major religious institutions under control of the state. The *awqaf* (religious endowments) were abolished or brought under the Ministry of Awqaf; the shari'a courts' jurisdiction was brought under that of the national courts; al-Azhar was reformed and attached to the state through the appointment of a Minster of al-Azhar, and its curriculum was changed, which included the introduction of four 'secular' faculties (medicine, engineering, agriculture, and commerce).[99]

I explore in more depth the limitations of the Brotherhood from the perspective of hegemony and consent in the next two chapters; here I want to end by highlight both the ability of Nasser and the Free Officers to form a historical bloc without one of the most popular social movements and organizations in Egypt, as well as to form a bloc through the infliction of social and political violence. Indeed the violence brought upon members of the Brotherhood and, eventually, many of those in opposition to Nasser, remains a central feature of the Nasserist project. Yet it is precisely this that raises the spectre of the power of Nasserism and the Nasserist ruling class. The assassination attempt on Nasser by the Brotherhood suggests that they were not part of the historical bloc, but this does not mean that there was no historical bloc in place. Furthermore, the fact that they went on to imprison a massive number of Brotherhood members in camps on the outskirts of Cairo, as well as to inflict torture on many of them, brings us back to the ability of consent to legitimize coercion. What happened to the Brotherhood is evidence that coercion is rarely absent during hegemony-making; rather, it is embedded within consent and thus

---

[97] Ibid., 128. [98] See Kandil 2014, 62–6.
[99] Said Aly and Wenner 1982, 343.

114   *Hegemony in Egypt*

rendered invisible, illegible, repressed, or justifiable. Different parts of Egyptian society reacted differently, and there was certainly criticism of the high levels of repression taking place; but this was not enough to weaken the Nasserist project and its attempt at creating hegemony. This coercion was seen as necessary, as deserved, or as unfortunate but inevitable. With the Brotherhood, this was to be repeated again, in eerily similar ways, in 2013.

I turn now to the other side of the equation: consent. Exploring the ways in which social forces were brought into the historical bloc is more complex, because of the multiple layers involved in creating consent. Consent is not equivalent to successfully brainwashing 'the people'; nor is it created in a purely top-down manner. Consent is complex precisely because it implies a societal process where narratives around the past, present, and future come together around a particular project. This project was Nasserism, and that consent was created because the project built on, spoke to, and coalesced with many of the hopes and aspirations of most Egyptians. In the rest of this section, I look at the evolving relationship between the ruling class and workers to trace how consent was created and negotiated. In particular, it was the project's basis in nationalism and social welfare, as well as its promise of tangible changes to the material lives of most Egyptians, which made it attractive to workers.

This did not mean that coercion was not used; Nasser's approach to trade unions and the communist movement, for example, regularly made use of intimidation, imprisonment, torture, or forced closure. One need only recall the brutal crackdown on workers at Kafr al-Dawwar in 1952 that resulted in the public hanging of the two alleged ringleaders.[100] Overall, however, the story is more complicated than a simple case of an elite co-opting and controlling workers. Chalcraft has written about hegemonic contestation as a lens through which to understand worker movements in Egypt

---

[100] The workers at the Misr Fine Spinning and Weaving Company (founded by Tal'at Harb and Bank Misr) began a strike on 12 August 1952, calling for higher wages, better working conditions, union recognition and the dismissal of two managers. The workers, numbering over 10 000, had nursed these grievances prior to the revolution, and believed that the new ruling class would look on their cause favourably. The government responded by surrounding workers, blockading some inside the factory while attacking others, and killing one; 545 workers were arrested, and 29 were charged with offenses ranging from premeditated murder to arson and destruction of property (Beinin and Lockman 1998, 423).

'*Workers, Peasants, Soldiers, and Nationalist Capitalists*'

from Nasser onwards.[101] He argues that Egypt's working class was integrated into state-dominated unions not because they were duped into it and did not know better; rather workers were nationalist and developmentalist themselves, and had similar desires for national self-determination and modernization.[102] 'The formula that diminished labour protest in Egypt after independence was not simply repressive, nor simply moral, but hegemonic'.[103]

Right from the start there were debates within the Free Officers about whether to support or repress trade unions, with some arguing that providing workers with concessions would ensure their political support and others arguing that this would negatively impact investment. Laws were passed that raised the minimum wage, strengthened labour regulations, and gave workers representation on management boards of state firms.[104] Ultimately, it was the creation of two organizations that signalled the ruling class's attempt at channelling the energy of workers into the Nasserist project: the Arab Socialist Union and the Egyptian Trade Union Confederation. Alongside this, a host of changes were introduced to address inequality at the structural level, including: land reforms, free education, free health care, and guaranteed employment. The Agrarian Reform Law in particular was represented as revolutionary: it lowered the ceiling on land ownership, expropriated land and redistributing it to peasants within five years, created agricultural cooperatives, and allowed farm workers to join unions. These changes did not always materialize, and they certainly did not lead to a dramatic shift in the institution of private property, but the work this law did was to dismantle the power of the landowning elite – precisely what Nasser needed to do in order to build a new historical bloc.

Worker's collective action was discouraged, and it became clear that workers were central to the new bloc and project – but only if they stayed within the parameters set by the ruling class. Some have argued that Nasser's overall policy towards workers was corporatist,[105] just as the pre-1952 approach had been. There is little doubt that in both cases there were attempts to industrialize workers and harness the power of their resistance in order to push forward specific goals that did not necessarily

---

[101] 2011. [102] Ibid., 43. [103] Ibid., 44. [104] Paczyńska 2013, 86–7.
[105] Organizing workers into industrial and professional corporations, which then serve as organs of political representation that can be controlled.

benefit the majority of workers. The major difference is that under Nasser this was part of an attempt to create a bloc and hegemony, whereas under colonial rule it functioned as a means to crush anti-colonial resistance. Under the Nasserist bloc, workers were able to both experience the triumph of independence, and achieve tangible benefits through the welfare system. The access to free education, free health care, and guaranteed employment should not be underestimated given Egypt's trajectory since then. These changes elevated a large part of a generation of Egyptians who were now able to attend university and work in the public sector, even as it excluded others such as peasants or workers in the industrial sector who may not have had the social mobility to migrate and take advantage of emerging opportunities.

An even more important reason as to why the Nasserist era requires a different lens towards workers is the question of agency: it is important here to emphasize that workers were not brainwashed nor were they fully coerced; as I have shown, because some of their goals correlated with those of the new ruling class, it is understandable that they saw in Nasser a chance at realizing some form of independence. Alia Mossallam's work on the workers who built the Aswan Dam alludes to the problems with seeing workers as having been brainwashed by Nasser, erasing a set of relationships that were far more complex. I focus on her work further on, but want to note here how she mobilizes T. J. Jackson Lears' writing on cultural hegemony.[106] Lears notes that hegemony is never complete; the outlook of subaltern groups will always be divided, and that subaltern groups may at times maintain a symbolic universe that legitimizes their domination.[107] This does not imply a form of false consciousness but rather that subaltern groups can *both* identify with and challenge a hegemonic project: 'As Gramsci understood, the hegemonic culture depends not on the brainwashing of "the masses" but on the tendency of public discourse to make some forms of experience readily available to consciousness while ignoring or suppressing others'.[108]

This complexity played out with the communist movement as well, whose position towards Nasser was always shifting and elusively complicated. As with the workers, it was because of their prioritizing of anti-colonialism and independent economic development that communists saw Nasserism as an important project: 'The experience of the

---

[106] 1985.   [107] Ibid., 573.   [108] Ibid., 577.

Egyptian communist intelligentsia confirms Abdallah Laroui's thesis that the attraction of Marxism for Third World intellectuals is principally as a guide to the conduct of the national liberation struggle'.[109] While the majority of Egyptian communist trends initially resisted the Free Officers, the coup, and Nasser's reforms, by 1954 most of them had declared allegiance to the new bloc and project largely because of Nasser's anti-imperialism and in particular the nationalization of the Canal:

> The rapprochement between the communists and the regime was based primarily on support for Nasser's anti-imperialist foreign policy, which was, in Nasserist political discourse, nearly synonymous with pan-Arab nationalism. Understanding the popularity and power of this idiom, the communists embraced it with only faintly articulated reservations about the continuing undemocratic character of the Nasser regime, its prohibition of strikes, its efforts to control the leadership of the trade union movement, and its refusal to allow overt communist political activity.[110]

In 1958 all communist currents merged to form the Communist Party of Egypt. In September of the same year, following failed attempts by the government to reach a political agreement, a full-scale attack was launched against the movement.[111] In December, influential communists were arrested, and within the next five months an additional 700 were jailed. Many suffered physical and psychological torture in prison.[112] Following negotiations with the government, all communist prisoners were released in 1964, after an agreement stating that all communist parties be dissolved. As Joel Beinin succinctly notes: 'The Egyptian communists were caught up by their embrace of the national movement and ultimately destroyed by it. The communist intelligentsia made the nationalist and anti-imperialist struggles its priorities and therefore conceded that political discourse should be conducted in these terms. But the communists could not outbid Nasser for nationalist legitimacy'.[113]

Perhaps the best way to understand the complexities of Nasserism and the left is to borrow Arwa Salih's notion of haunting.[114] Salih, a prominent Egyptian communist, evocatively named her memoir *The Stillborn*, referencing a project that was unfinished, that had failed, and yet that haunts us all, a project that was through and through a nationalist one:

---

[109] Ibid., 572. [110] Ibid. [111] Ibid., 581. [112] Ibid., 582. [113] 1987, 584.
[114] See Hammad 2016.

I felt profoundly disconnected from the 'national struggle' that haunts every sentence of this book. This national struggle was a historical necessity for liberation-era communists. Both second and third wave communists were hopelessly trapped in the logic of anti-imperial nationalist populism, isolated from 'the only game in town' and forced to lead a 'double life' that destroyed both their integrity and 'their ability to believe'.[115]

Nationalism – and its connection to anti-colonialism – was the defining struggle of that era. For many, Nasserism seemed at last a real chance at achieving goals that had for so long eluded Egypt. These goals were not created by Nasser and then spread throughout society; these goals were already part and parcel of Egyptian society, for whom, if anything, Nasser and his project appeared to be a means to an end that many Egyptians had long dreamed of. And yet it was precisely the eventual realization that the Nasserist project would not be what it promised to be that created many of the complexities this section has touched on. Communists 'sang his songs' from prison, while workers died to build a dam that they truly believed in. This is not a simple case of coercion, nor brainwashing; this complexity – full of contradictions, emotions, and hope – can perhaps more usefully be captured and understood through the lens of political project-making.

Creating Consent

Consent is complex, multi-layered, and full of contradictions. Although the production of consent is never a mechanical top-down process, there were clear attempts by the new ruling class to cultivate consent in various parts of civil society, and it is some of these attempts I look at here. Civil society has been described as 'the sphere of potent historical action, where ideology and cultural organization take place',[116] and if civil society, à la Gramsci, is made up of all non-state organs, then its expanse ranges from schools and religious institutions to mass media and the family. Each of these spaces represents an opportunity for mobilizing the public and spreading hegemonic ideas, not through censorship or control – although this can be part of the process – but through creating these ideas as necessary. In other words, it largely means fighting a battle of ideas.

---

[115] Salih 2018, 1.   [116] Bates 1975, 353.

'Workers, Peasants, Soldiers, and Nationalist Capitalists'

Waging a battle of ideas is not a reference to the liberal 'marketplace of ideas' thesis, whereby all ideas should be heard and the best one will win; from a Gramscian perspective, power is often what determines which ideas are heard, and which ideas 'win'. Recall that hegemony is essentially political leadership based on the consent of the led, and that this consent is created by the diffusion and popularization of the world view of the ruling class.[117] Hegemony is 'an order in which a certain way of life and thought is dominant, in which one concept of reality is diffused throughout society, in all its institutional and private manifestations, informing with its spirit all tastes, morality, customs, religions and political principles, and all social relations'.[118] The failure to establish hegemony leads ruling classes to fall back onto coercion, which is always the least preferred means of ruling society. The failure of hegemony often happens when there is an organic crisis in which people stop believing in the ideologies put forward by a specific ruling class. Gramsci suggested that organic crises are often brought about when a ruling class fails in a larger undertaking, such as war.[119] As we will see, this is precisely what ended the hegemony of the Nasserist historical bloc.

In his Philosophy of the Revolution, Nasser clearly articulated the simultaneous quest for a political and social revolution. Echoing Kwame Nkrumah, who famously stated 'seek ye first the political kingdom' – Nasser underlined the centrality of the social to the political. The social revolution, in effect, was the real aim of the political revolution. Here I look at how this social revolution was connected to the political one, through how different spaces were mobilized in spreading, normalizing, and legitimizing the ideas of the Nasserist bloc. In particular, I look at the mass media, specifically Nasser's radio station *Voice of the Arabs*; the education system and the construction of nationalist subjects; and the Arab Socialist Union, which became a vessel through which revolutionary goals were to be achieved and debated. This is by no means an extensive list of spaces and institutions within which hegemony was constructed; it does, however, provide insight into some of the battles the historical bloc waged in order to ensure that their project was seen as the only viable project for advancing Egypt's future.[120] What is pertinent is the way in

---

[117] Bates 1975, 352. [118] Williams 1960. [119] Ibid., 365.

[120] Although intellectuals – both traditional and organic – were central to the Nasserist project, I have not included them here because there are numerous and extensive studies that look at intellectuals and writers during the Nasserist

120   *Hegemony in Egypt*

which Nasser both 'banned' civil society (through coercion) and also
centralized it (through consent). This double movement is precisely what
produced the legacies of Nasserism into the present.

Voice of the Arabs

Popular culture has long been central to hegemonic projects.[121] In his
book *Ordinary Egyptians*, Ziad Fahmy chronicles the role of popular
culture in anti-colonial sentiment in the first half of the twentieth
century, and traces some of the ways in which popular culture created
a unitary sense of 'Egyptian-ness'.[122] Fahmy shows the ways in which
mass culture laid the ground for events such as the Urabi revolt,
particularly periodicals such as Abu Naddara Zarqa' which he writes
'provided sustained counter-hegemonic attacks on the British and the
Egyptian regime'.[123] For instance, his attacks on Tawfiq – who had
sided with the British against those involved in the Urabi revolt –
successfully cemented Tawfiq's reputation as *al-wad al-ahbal* (the dim-
witted kid) in the public imaginary.[124] Britain grew concerned, and the
following was published in the *Times*:

> The fact that the rabid utterances of the native press continue unchecked is
> causing anxiety, and surprise is felt that England, who is responsible for the
> maintenance of order in the country has not authoritatively interfered to stop
> this source of danger.[125]

People like Abdallah al-Nadim, whose journal al-Tankit wa al-Tabkit
became very popular, used mass culture to spread nationalist aspirations

> era. The idea of *iltizam*, or committed literature, came to dominate the Arab
> world in the 1950s, reflecting a shift in how intellectuals and writers
> understood themselves. Writers such as Naguib Mahfouz, Taha Hussein and
> later Sonallah Ibrahim, among many others, offered works of fiction that can
> be read as fascinating journeys into the politics of Nasserism. Mahfouz in
> particular expressed his disappointment with the revolution with 'seven years
> of silence': disappointed with the revolution, Mahfouz entered a seven-year-
> long period of silence during which he wrote no new novels (DiMeo 2016, 80).
> Sonallah Ibrahim is another interesting example; born just before the
> revolution, he is infamous for having gone to jail under Nasser – for his
> involvement in the Communist Party – and yet continuing to praise the
> Nasserist project as a whole. Even in prison – from age twenty-one for a total of
> five years – he reportedly wrote letters of support to Nasser and decades later
> fondly displayed a picture of him in his apartment (ibid., 162).

[121] For more, see Pratt 2007.   [122] 2011.   [123] Ibid., 63   [124] Ibid.
[125] Ibid.

'Workers, Peasants, Soldiers, and Nationalist Capitalists'

for independence and even influenced Mustafa Kamil, who was to become one of the major nationalist figures in Egypt.[126] Interestingly, much nationalist sentiment was expressed through a growing concern with the increasingly undiversified Egyptian economy and the lack of 'traditional' Egyptian jobs. Moreover, a decline in Egyptian manufacturing and increase in the importing of foreign goods, as well as the increased exploitation of peasants, all served to intensify nationalist criticism of colonial government.[127] In one issue, Nadim asks his readers: 'What can the people do, now that all the goods are imported? Cooked canned meat, dried milk, tailored garments, even cotton and woollen textiles used to make turbans and caftans are manufactured and imported from Europe. What are we supposed to do about this calamity?'[128] The blame for all of this was laid at the feet of the British and their Egyptian collaborators.

Events such as Dinshaway[129] were immediately transformed into national myths because of the power of this burgeoning popular culture[130] and, as Fahmy argues, it is here that we see the strength of nationalism: 'Perhaps the best measure of successful discourse is its potential to motivate public action'.[131] Nevertheless, much of this was urban-based, particularly the newspaper and magazine production that made up the 'national press' as well as music and theatre productions.[132] Music, to some extent, reached more Egyptians than the press – especially thinking of extremely influential singers such as Sayyid Darwish, Abdel-Halim Hafiz, and Umm Kulthum, who have been central to the Egyptian public imaginary. However, it was to be radio that was to have the most extensive reach into Egyptian society, as became clear in the early 1950s when Nasser established Voice of the Arabs.

Voice of the Arabs should be placed within the broader context of media nationalization under Nasser. By 1960, all major publishing houses had been nationalized, and all journalists had to join the Arab

---

[126] Ibid., 67.   [127] Ibid., 78.   [128] Ibid.

[129] This was a confrontation in 1906 between residents of the Egyptian village of Dinshaway and British officers during the occupation, in response to the officers hunting pigeons-an important source of livelihood-for sport. In the resulting fighting, an Egyptian villager was falsely accused of murdering a British officer, and a special tribunal was set up. Extremely harsh punishments – including death by public hanging – were handed out to villagers, prompting national outcry. This became a central moment around which anti-colonial nationalist resistance coalesced.

[130] Ibid., 92.   [131] Ibid., 98.   [132] Ibid., 31.

Socialist Union (ASU), a Nasserist political party. Control over national television was complete, through both coercive means and through numerous benefits that were given to media employees who supported the revolution. The rationale given for this was to prevent the domination of capital within media broadcasting, but in effect it served to ensure limited criticism of the new ruling class.[133] Nasser was quoted as saying: 'I can't control the economy and leave a small group of individuals controlling information'.[134] Voice of the Arabs was thus very much the product of this changing media scene.

It is not an exaggeration to say that Voice of the Arabs was one of the most influential instruments of mass media in the Middle East during the period of decolonization. Started after Nasser enthusiastically supported the idea, the radio's aim was to 'end imperialism and colonialism; to declare our principles, with liberation and self-determination'.[135] Although initially placed under the Minister of National Guidance, the radio station eventually came under direct control of the President's Office, and scholars have generally assumed that the station was largely influenced by Nasser himself. Voice of the Arabs began service on 4 July 1953 and it quickly went from broadcasting for a few hours a day to twenty-four-hour radio service. Although difficult to confirm, it was estimated that most Egyptians listened to the station at one point or another, and that its reach in other Arab countries was equally impressive. In its heyday, it received over 3000 letters a day from listeners.[136]

The station included a wide variety of programming, from entertainment and religious shows to political commentary. Its director, Ahmed Said, hosted two especially popular shows: *Truth and Lies* and *Do Not Forget*, both focused explicitly on articulating the Nasserist project and defending it against 'lies' that came up in other media sources. What is notable about Voice of the Arabs was the particular reach radio had that other mediums such as television and print simply did not. Importantly, radio was much more accessible to Egyptians who were not formally literate and who did not own televisions. Voice of the Arabs allowed the new ruling class to reach not only large numbers of Egyptians, but also millions of Arabs, Africans, and other colonial and postcolonial subjects. Scholars have argued that it was through the radio that a new national identity was cultivated, and this hints at the immense importance of Voice of the Arabs to spreading Nasser's hegemonic project.

[133] Beattie 1994, 184.   [134] Ibid.   [135] Nasser, in Alahmed 2011.   [136] Ibid.

'Workers, Peasants, Soldiers, and Nationalist Capitalists'   123

Nasser's speeches, which were broadcast, were one part of this strategy. These speeches – a total of 1359 and coming to 10 000 pages – were, as Sherif Younes suggests, not mere words but a political act and central to the ideology being formulated.[137] Moreover, these were interesting in terms of the effect they had. This was done in various ways, from Nasser's tendency to identify himself as one with the audience to his move to retell history and politics through the lens of the revolution. As Mossallam notes, he often referenced how Western historians related specific incidents and juxtaposition these to his own 'true' or nationalist version.[138] Indeed Mossallam goes on to note that the people she interviewed often felt that they were being directly addressed by Nasser when they listened to his speeches.[139]

The radio station's focus on political programming that extolled nationalism, socialism, and pan-Arabism and pan-Africanism was another key feature of its broadcasting. Through this, the radio station was able to influence events in other African and Arab countries, most notably Algeria, Jordan, Iraq, and Yemen.[140] For example, Nasser appealed to Jordanians to speak out against Jordan becoming part of the Baghdad Pact, and almost instantly demonstrations across Jordan broke out.[141] And in 1958, when a military coup overthrew the government in Iraq that had been led by Nuri el-Said, the director of Voice of the Arabs received a letter in which was enclosed a piece of Said's finger – presumably to thank the station for its help in making the coup happen.[142] The station soon became one of Egypt's most important foreign policy tools through which it was able to exert geopolitical influence, particularly through Arab socialism, pan-Africanism, and pan-Arabism. Representatives of liberation movements in Africa and the Middle East were encouraged to use the radio to broadcast anti-imperialist programmes.[143] Britain, concerned, launched a counter-station in Cyprus, called The Voice of Britain, which encouraged Egyptians to support those who had come to 'free them from their mad leader' (the British, presumably).[144] However, once the Arab staff discovered the aims of the station, they resigned en masse, rendering it an embarrassing failure.[145] The downfall of the station eventually took place in 1967. Voice of the Arabs had been central to propaganda efforts convincing Egyptians that they were winning the war. When the truth

[137] 2012. [138] 2012, 69. [139] Ibid. [140] Ibid.
[141] Boyd and Kushner 1979, 649. [142] Ibid. [143] Abou El Fadl 2019.
[144] Ibid. [145] Ibid., 650.

124   *Hegemony in Egypt*

eventually emerged, the station, its director – and Nasser – were beyond saving.

After the UN requested that Nasser shut down the station, his response was emblematic of just how important it was to his project: 'How can I reach my power base? My power lies with the Arab masses. The only way I can reach my people is by radio. If you asked me about the radio disarmament, it means you are asking me for complete disarmament'.[146] Such mediums were what allowed the new bloc to clearly articulate their new projects ideologically, as well as to connect the ideological to material changes that were taking place. While the radio can certainly be seen as a propaganda tool, it was the tangible material changes affecting the lives of many Egyptians that gave a veneer of legitimacy to Nasser's ideological pronouncements. It is precisely this coming together of the ideological and the material that creates hegemony. While the land reforms, social welfare, and industrial advancements were central to the bloc, equally important were stations like Voice of the Arabs that narrated the Nasserist project and embedded political, economic, and social events into a coherent narrative.

Education and the Construction of Nationalist Subjects

The Nasserist project's focus on national development entailed changes to the education system that allowed many Egyptians to access primary, secondary, and university education at a very low cost. This opening up was part and parcel of the new hegemonic project in several ways. First, education was seen as central to the construction of modern subjects that would in turn modernize the Egyptian nation.[147] Second, education was rightly viewed as a key locus through which to form cultural and political consensus. Third, education was part of a broader effort of Egypt's industrialization project, which required manpower and expertise that was not foreign. As noted by Donal Reid, this was part of a 'third worldist moment' during which 'world prospects seemed bright'.[148] Finally, universities in particular became spaces in which political debate needed to be controlled and channelled into support for Nasserism. Education was thus no simple matter for the new ruling class; it was very much central to the achievement of their political, economic, and

---

[146] Ibid.   [147] See: El Shakry 2007.   [148] Reid 2002, 184.

'*Workers, Peasants, Soldiers, and Nationalist Capitalists*' 125

social goals. Take the 1962 National Charter, which mobilized education in a very particular way: 'The object of education is no longer to turn out employees who work at government offices. The educational curricula in all subjects must be reconsidered according to the principles of the revolution'.[149] This focus on cultivating a particular understanding of Egypt by developing a revolutionary retelling of history was central to the new educational system. Nationalism in particular became central, and was implicitly and explicitly connected to the new ruling class.

Mehmed Ali first established Egypt's educational system – with the Ministry of Education and primary and secondary state schools – and although many of these were rolled back by his successors, they did produce Egypt's afandiyya class, a class of literate urban Egyptians. This class was central to the making of modern Egypt, and was very much a product of Egypt's Westernization drive.[150] What changed dramatically post-1952 was the opening up of education to vast segments of the Egyptian population that had previously been unable to access it. Between 1952 and 1967, the percentage of children enrolled in primary school went from 45 per cent to 80 per cent.[151] Not only did primary and secondary school enrolment expand dramatically, as did literacy rates, but the higher education sector in particular saw rapid growth. This was a result both of Egyptians seeing university degrees as perhaps the most important route to social mobility, as well as the ruling class's drive to produce specialists in science, engineering, agriculture, and medicine in order to bolster its industrialization project. Most importantly, financial barriers to education were removed under Nasser, which led to the democratization of university education. This was made official in 1962 with a presidential decree that made a l higher education free.[152] While it is clear that education expanded, this expansion was not necessarily as wide as the state represented it to be, as Louis Awad noted.[153] Nevertheless, the ruling class gained much in terms of ideological currency from the belief that education had been democratized.

In 1958, university chairs in the History of the Arab Nation were established.[154] In 1959 a new committee was established in order to establish a 'national doctrine' and a programme for youth leadership. In 1961 a Ministry of Higher Education was established, and one of

---

[149] Abdallah, cited in Mossallam 2012, 55.   [150] Fahmy 2011, 24.
[151] Faksh 2006, 45.   [152] Ibid., 47.   [153] Reid 2002, 178.   [154] Ibid., 20.

their first moves was to establish a social curriculum made up of three subjects: revolution, socialism, and Arab society.[155] In 1962, military training for men and women during the first three years of their undergraduate education was introduced. Topics such as 'the 23 July Revolution' and 'Arab socialism' were compulsory. In terms of teaching materials for both university and primary and secondary schools, Reid notes: 'An overly Egypto-centric approach and glorification of the Mehmed Ali dynasty certainly marred old regime textbooks. The post-1952 textbooks' attention to the Arab world context and the inclusion of social and economic themes were steps in the right direction, but the new books simply substituted one set of patriotic myths and ideological slogans for another'.[156] As noted by Abdel-Malek among others, no socialist or Marxist thinkers were consulted on this material, despite claims to represent Arab socialist thought.[157] Universities as well as schools and cultural institutions were also brought under intensive state surveillance. A major aspect of this was the attempt to produce and disseminate a certain historical narrative. This met fierce criticism from scholar like Louis Awad and Taha Husayn, who defended the university as a space of liberalism.[158] Another aspect was to stifle and control debates happening in educational spaces, which are often highly politicized.

Ideologically, these shifts in education were to have major effects. One sign of this was the institutionalization of nationalism in education curricula, and by extension support of the new ruling class. Student textbooks, for example, repeatedly extolled the virtues of nationalism, pan-Arabism, socialism and Islam: 'Textbooks are full of stories about the glory of medieval Islamic heroes and the great Arab nationalist struggle against colonialism and other political and socioeconomic injustices that culminated in the 1952 revolution. Many pages are given over to Qur'anic passages and sayings of the prophet on ethics. This overt and general pattern of socialization might on frequent occasions take the form of celebrating Port Said Day (the evacuation of the British and French troops in 1956), or Palestine Refugee Day, or any other nationalistic event'.[159] Faksh goes on to reflect on his own personal experiences in such an educational system:

---

[155] Abdallah, cited in Mossallam 2012, 117.   [156] Ibid., 205.   [157] Ibid., 206.
[158] This should be placed within the particular history of Cairo University – for more, see Reid 2002.
[159] Ibid., 52.

'Workers, Peasants, Soldiers, and Nationalist Capitalists'

Based on my own experience, it would be safe to assume that such ceaseless efforts to bring about an identification with the regime have been somewhat successful. My classmates and I developed a strong sense of identification and pride with Arabism, anti-colonialism, and nationalist leaders of Nasser's calibre.[160]

At the various universities, students had to take courses on the 23 July revolution, socialism, and nationalism.[161] The socializing effects of education cannot be underestimated. Not only did Nasser open up education – and the social mobility that comes with it – to many, but the material in curricula also aimed at solidifying the nationalist project of the new historical bloc. These spaces, however, also became central nodes of activism. The Faculty of Economics and Political Science at Cairo University, for example, became infamous for the debates around the National Charter, as well as being home to major intellectuals such as Anouar Abdel-Malek, Boutros Boutros Ghali, and Abdel Aziz 'Izzat.

This also had the effect of decreasing the social power held by graduates of foreign schools in Egypt. Under the British occupation and Egyptian monarchy, foreign schools proliferated rapidly and quickly become key sites of socialization for Egypt's future elite. Graduates from these schools were able to exercise immense power within society, and the financial barriers preventing most Egyptians from accessing these schools were considerable. During Nasser's wave of nationalizations, many of these schools and universities were either nationalized or brought under the control of the state.[162] Because Egyptians could now access university education for free, the social classes represented in educational institutions expanded. This in turn produced a technocratic elite – central to Nasser's historical bloc – that came from largely from this new and expanding middle class.

It is difficult not to compare this to contemporary Egypt, where foreign schools have one again become top tier destinations for Egypt's future elite, where socialization into foreign languages, norms, and values is emphasized. These schools and universities are inaccessible to the majority of the population because of financial barriers, and the networks and opportunities offered to graduates are

---

[160] 1976a, 236.   [161] Ibid.   [162] Ibid., 240.

128   *Hegemony in Egypt*

unparalleled. Public schools and universities are sites of constant budget cuts and worsening quality, leading directly to class inequality of worrying proportions. It is therefore not difficult to understand the intersections between public education, nationalism, and social equality, and how and why Nasser was able to mobilize these so effectively just decades ago.

The Arab Socialist Union

Made up of the same alliance of popular forces that underpinned the project as a whole – workers, peasants, soldiers, and nationalist capitalists – origins and trajectory of the Arab Socialist Union (ASU) provide a fascinating glimpse into how Nasser and the officers understood the nature of political rule. Initially started as the Liberation Rally[163] (1953–8) and then the National Union (1958–61), the ASU was created only in 1961, and lasted until 1976. The different moments during which these three organizations were founded reveal the different stages of the production of hegemony. The Liberation Rally was meant as a replacement for prerevolutionary political parties and to mobilize support for Nasser against Mohamed Naguib. The National Union was created after the nationalization of the Suez Canal and the tripartite attack, to galvanize support for the ruling class. Finally, the ASU represented the most mature stage of the revolution, during which Arab socialism had been officially adopted.

The Liberation Rally, which can be understood as testing the waters, was ineffective as an organization for creating consent. It lacked a clear leadership, cadres, an efficient organizational structure, and a clear ideology.[164] The National Union was more organized, and more attention was paid to the role of structure. A Higher Executive Committee was appointed by Nasser, and while all Egyptians were considered potential members, only active members were elected to

---

[163] The aim of the LR was announced in very general terms: the withdrawal of British troops; a new constitution expressing the fundamental aspirations of the Egyptian people; an "equitable" social system; a "fair" economy; an undefined political system; and friendly relations with all friendly powers (Arafat 2011, 189).

[164] Ibid.

committees at village or town level. However, the National Union ended up replicating older power structures, especially in villages where powerful families continued to dominate – precisely the families that Nasser was trying to disempower. For this reason, the Union was dismantled, and the ASU was created.

Where the Liberation Rally and National Union had acted more as networks – with limited capacity for ideological mobilization – the ASU instead had its goal as consent creation from the very start. As Hazem Kandil notes, 'the ASU was the seat of political power. Nasser's ruling organization was supposed to act as a popular vanguard'.[165] In a meeting with the ASU executive in 1966, Nasser highlighted the role of consent in political rule: 'We cannot succeed unless we understand the masses. We must take their ideas and opinions, study it, organize it, reflect it back to them, and then point them in the right direction'.[166] A Higher Executive Committee and a General-Secretariat – around forty individuals – ran the ASU, with a core formed of Nasser, Ali Sabri, Muhammad Hassanein Haikal, and Sami Sharaf; this was modelled on the Communist League within the Yugoslav Socialist Union.[167] In the Secretariat, Nasser appointed a secretary general who, in consultation with the president, recruited a group of less than thirty individuals to perform specialized party functions.

Having learned the lesson of the organizations that came before it, the ASU focused explicitly on ideology right from the start. In a fascinating process that deserves much more study, much time was spent throughout the 1960s defining 'the people' as well as various social forces, especially the workers and peasants, for the purposes of representation.[168] The Committee's debates around who should be included were aired on national television, and eventually all those affected negatively by land reform, nationalization, or sequestration were barred from joining, as well as anyone found guilty of exploiting public office. In the end, it was supposedly a group's demographic weight and contribution to national income that was taken into account; in practice, workers and peasants were under-represented and national capitalists, academics, and professional syndicalists were over-represented.[169]

[165] 2012, 252.   [166] Ibid.   [167] Ayubi 1996, 210.   [168] Ibid., 209.
[169] Beattie 1994, 163.

In 1962, the National Charter was revealed, including the formula that was created to ensure that the ASU represented a balanced mixture of the nation. 375 seats went to peasants; 300 to workers; 105 to national capitalists; 100 to public functionaries; 105 for members of professional unions; and 105 to lecturers and students. The National Charter, once created, was spread throughout the country through ministers. The Charter set wide parameters because it wanted to include as many Egyptians as possible, while still maintaining a clear ideological project: socialism. Under the surface, there were inevitable disagreements about what socialism meant, and whether the Charter referred to scientific socialism, Arab socialism, Islamic socialism, and so on. Scientific socialism referred to the idea that socialism is universal but that each nation had its own unique socialist path, and was radical in its understanding that power should be transferred to workers; Arab socialism tended to be anti-Marxist and argue that Arab nations had their own unique path and was less radical in that if often respected private property and national capital; and Islamic socialism emphasized Islam's 'socialist character'.[170] Despite this, soon after its establishment, it was reported that the membership had reached 6 million.[171]

Nasser also set up the Youth Organisation (YO), whose goal was to reach Egyptian youth and pass on the revolutionary ideals to future generations. The YO was envisioned more as a traditional political party, and was characterized by its massive organization capacity as well as major recruitment drives. Its aim was to 'harness the youth's selfless, boundless energy and nationalistic exuberance and directing them in ways that aided regime development policies: clearing ponds, setting up medical care units, services in rural areas, etc.'.[172] Alongside this, Nasser established the Higher Institute for Social Studies, which was explicitly meant to create a class of elites with a socialist belief system – cadres who would form a 'leftist force'.[173] It opened in the Cairo suburb of Heliopolis in 1965, and seven highly respected leftist academics taught a variety of courses on socialism, Egyptian history, Marxism, and so on. These students were then to return to their basic units and politically educate other members.

Related to the ASU was the Egyptian Trade Union Federation (ETUF) which was founded in 1957. Trade unions were now organized

[170] Ibid.   [171] Ibid., 166.   [172] Ibid., 179.   [173] Ibid.

'*Workers, Peasants, Soldiers, and Nationalist Capitalists*'

according to activity, and had to belong to this umbrella federation that was part and parcel of the state because of its affiliation to the ASU. Trade unions were thus now supposedly in support of the state, and this eventually created a relationship of dependency and co-optation that was to continue until 2011, after which hundreds of independent trade unions were created. The creation of the ETUF similarly resulted from a need to absorb and co-opt the energy of workers into the broader national project. Workers, after all, had already formed their own unions: in 1900, 'the league of cigarette makers' was formed, and in 1921, ninety trade unions came together to form the National Federation of Egyptian Workers.[174] This was dissolved in 1924 because of how active it was against the British imperial presence. Undeterred, workers continued organizing, and by the end of the 1940s there were over 500 unions. Under Nasser, 'there is general agreement that a large part of the labour movement was brought into a new relationship with the state, where the trade unions' independence was sharply restricted and they were eventually incorporated into a project of national development'.[175] This had the effect of discouraging workers' self-organization, and instead channelling their activities into the broader nationalist project.

The workings of coercion were never far from the scene in any of these mass organizations. Nasser often used these as a means of identifying and expelling or detaining political opponents, or those more generally against the political aims of the new bloc. The ETUF, like the ASU, was a hierarchical organization with a leadership, twenty-one unions, and at the bottom the units of these various unions. This undemocratic structure precluded the ability of workers to control their own units. Moreover, the ASU ended up replicating the same problem of the National Union; because of its top-down leadership, landed elites from older traditional bases of power were able to infiltrate.[176] This lack of grassroots mobilization within the ASU was clearly one of the reasons it eventually faltered. This was despite the effort put into mobilizing the grassroots in order to eliminate the power of the landed elite; an elite that somehow managed to consistently maintain power in one way or another.

Kirk Beattie has suggested that Nasser was preparing the ASU for a 'Gramscian war of position'[177] and that the aim of these organizations

---

[174] https://solidarity-us.org/atc/142/p2385/   [175] Alexander 2010.   [176] Ibid.
[177] Ibid.

132   *Hegemony in Egypt*

was to change the historical consciousness of the people.[178] While the weaknesses and problems of these organizations became clear over time, at that particular moment they functioned as attempts to bring together as many citizens a possible under the same ideological umbrella. The ASU had a clear socialist stance, with all of the contradictions this entailed. It was able to mobilize large numbers of people in favour of this ideology in ways that previous political parties – and future political parties – were unable to do. The idea of the mass organization, with its roots in the Soviet era, functioned as a key site of consent-making. The planning and thought that went into the structure, organization and outreach of organizations such as the ASU show some attention to consent on the part of the Nasserist ruling class.

Beyond Empty Rhetoric: Materiality and Ideology

I want to conclude this section by returning to the complicated notion of consent and its relation to agency. The Nasserist project, ironically, was successful in large part because it was not entirely new: it mobilized ideas, goals, hopes, and sentiments that were already deeply entrenched in a country that had been under foreign occupation for quite some time. If we think of the key ideological pillars of Nasserism – anticolonial nationalism and independent economic development – it becomes clear that these intersected with many social movements active pre-1952, and that they had large popular support more broadly within Egyptian society (and indeed the rest of the Middle East). Ethnographic work documents this,[179] showing how ordinary Egyptians saw themselves, their hopes, and their futures in the project the Nasserist bloc presented. Because of this, they were very much involved in the materialization of this project.

Alia Mossallam's rich ethnography of the workers that built the Aswan Dam – one of Nasser's major infrastructural projects – unpacks the complexity underlying the politics of consent under Nasser. Underlining the presence of a nationalist and anticolonial movement in Egypt before 1952, she writes: 'Their (the people's) "belief" in the ideology propagated by the state and their willingness to make sacrifices for it contributed to its successes, and their championing of the Revolution's ideology is what has it linger in popular Egyptian memory

---

[178] Crabbs 1975, 393.   [179] Mossallam 2012; Harik 1974.

'Workers, Peasants, Soldiers, and Nationalist Capitalists'

and politics until this very day'.[180] She points out that to understand hegemony under Nasser we should focus on a popular history of Egypt and the ways in which people were willing to sacrifice for a project they believed in. In other words, oppression and coercion alone cannot explain politics under Nasser:

I emphasize that these builders had a strong sense of ownership and agency in their building the Dam. They were mobilized by the idea of the Dam and how it was propagated, and they participated despite the odds. They were driven by the masculine ideas of honour and physical strength, but also by their conviction that they made of it the historic epic it became. This very sense of agency, however, allowed for a critical consciousness of both the hegemonic project, and those behind it.[181]

This view is echoed in other studies of popular mobilizations during the 1950s and 1960s. In an illustrious study of a Delta village in Egypt's countryside (Shubra el-Gedida), Iliya Harik traces some of the changes that came about following the 1952 revolution and in particular the land reforms.[182] The spread of agricultural cooperatives (to replace money-lenders), the overthrowing of the landed aristocracy, and the involvement in politics on the part of ordinary peasants all dramatically shifted the configurations of social life in the countryside. Despite valid criticisms of the land reform programme, which ultimately did not deliver much of what it promised, in places like Shubra el-Gedida changes were already beginning to show by the early 1960s. For example, no one person held more than sixty feddans and over two-thirds of all the land in the village was held in small parcels by over 93 per cent of families. This had dramatic effects on power relations within the village, most notably the burst of political participation that followed:

Village residents found local problems and organized to solve them. Co-operative labor macadamized the feeder from the village to the main road so that the provincial capital of Damanhur came within easy reach. The young men opened a butcher shop to competitively drive down the price of meat which they felt was artificially pegged. The price came down. Mass membership in the cooperative freed all from usury.[183]

---

[180] 2012, 14.   [181] Ibid., 139.   [182] 1974.
[183] Abu Lughod, cited in Harik 1974, 293.

134 *Hegemony in Egypt*

Despite this, the legal changes that were meant to bring about land reforms not only failed to deliver much under Nasser, but were eventually reversed by Sadat and, later, Mubarak. Nevertheless, what is striking about the story of this village is how dramatically political and social life changed after the institution of land reform. What Harik illustrates throughout the book is that the lives of villagers changed materially, and that this was the springboard from which other political and social changes happened. Material changes such as land reform, educational access, free health care, and guaranteed employment must be taken seriously as part and parcel of the Nasserist project; they were not simple by-products but rather were precisely the reason why the project was able to become hegemonic.

Related to these material changes are emotive attachments people had to the 'new Egypt'. This broader notion of how Egyptians *felt* about the revolution is key; it was the connection between sentiment and the new project that very much explains why so many people assented to it. Moreover, this process of ownership and agency did not mean a *carte blanche* for the contradictory elements of Nasserism:

Many people *did* feel a high level of ownership, engagement and agency during the revolution. This was despite the circumstances that they may have suffered on account of its deficiencies. People were conscious of the silences of the regime, both in mythologizing the Port Said struggle and in not taking responsibility for the army's absence. Similarly in Suez after the *naksa* in 1967, people were critical of Nasser for not seriously punishing the military.[184]

Mossallam notes how poetry and songs in support of Nasser and the revolution that were created and shared by people during this period cannot be understood straightforwardly as propaganda, as this would assume that people were simply manipulated. Rather, people engaged with and critiqued these cultural forms, and because people related to the broader struggle, they were willing to sacrifice for it.[185] Workers essentially rearticulated the values put forward by the hegemonic project and through this process made them their own.[186] In building the dam, workers were aware of the stakes: this was a nationalist project that was central to how Egypt would be perceived globally: 'International politics became a realm of the everyday. In working on

[184] Mossallam 2012, 72. [185] Ibid. [186] Ibid., 130.

'Workers, Peasants, Soldiers, and Nationalist Capitalists'

the dam, its builders believed they were chipping away at imperialism, building the history of a new nation and inscribing themselves into it'.[187] Workers described themselves as having been mobilized – not conscripted – precisely because they wanted to feel part of this new project, and new country.[188] The Aswan Dam was theirs, it belonged to them.[189]

This is particularly interesting in light of the massive toll the dam took on both workers and the Nubian community that was displaced in order to construct it: 'For the story of the building of the dam could not be told without the stories of those who consciously made the greatest sacrifice for its construction – their own homes and livelihoods'.[190] Mossallam notes that everyone she interviewed was aware of this toll, and that people kept repeating 'thousands died'; and yet this coexisted with immense pride in the dam itself, and what it represented.[191] The Nubians she spoke to similarly still saw the project as having been necessary, despite the displacement it caused them.

One of my central claims is that the Nasserist project could not have become hegemonic simply by repeating empty rhetorical slogans year after year. Tracing the use of ideas and discourses during this period is important, but what is equally important is acknowledging that these ideas appealed to many Egyptians; that they were already embedded within the aspirations Egyptians had for the future. As Mossallam writes, 'Nasser's ideas were hegemonic because people could relate to them and they answered a desire for freedom and growth'.[192] While this risks an over-generalization of who 'Egyptians' are, it also assumes that anti-colonial nationalism was a unifying ideology that could be found across large segments of society. This does not render it homogenous, but rather points to the political work anti-colonialism did in tying together disparate understandings of 'us', 'the future', 'nation', and 'freedom'. It was the mobilization of these understandings that was the key to success for the new bloc. Equally important to the creation of hegemony, however, is the material basis many of these ideological claims had. These were not mere rhetorical schemes precisely because of the

---

[187] Ibid., 131. [188] Ibid., 143. [189] Ibid., 149. [190] Ibid., 173.
[191] Ibid., 159. [192] 2012, 170.

136 *Hegemony in Egypt*

significant changes the Nasserist bloc made to Egypt's political economy. It is this I turn to next.

A Hegemonic Project

The consent outlined in the previous section was a result not only of the ability of the Nasserist project to mobilize popular ideological sentiments such as anticolonial nationalism, but also of the material changes that began to take shape after the bloc came to power. It was this interplay of the ideological and the material that allowed for hegemony. Here I explore both the ideological and material contours of the Nasserist project, to highlight some of the pillars on which it rested. In particular, through the prism of major events such as the nationalization of the Suez Canal and the building of the High Dam in Aswan, I want to unpack features such as internationalism, nationalization, industrialization, Arab socialism, and anticolonial nationalism in order to highlight how the bloc articulated these various elements through the lens of the nation. Ultimately, it was the strength and popularity of these various parts of the project as well as the particular historical moment during which they came together that cemented Nasserism as hegemonic.

The 'Lifeline of the British Empire': Suez as a Defining Moment of Decolonization

Perhaps nothing illustrates the coming together of particular historical conditions and the assumptions underpinning the Nasserist project more than the nationalization of the Suez Canal – referred to as the 'lifeline of the British Empire'[193] – and the building of the High Dam in Aswan, the two major and connected infrastructural projects that emerged in the 1950s and 1960s. These two projects illustrate some of the major pillars of Nasserism, particularly independent economic development, nationalization, and industrialization. The nationalization of the Canal in particular was an event of global significance, and a central part of the anticolonial nationalist project in place. The building of the High Dam, the financing for which came from the nationalization of the Canal, was similarly connected to

---

[193] Tignor 2015, 171.

A Hegemonic Project

global debates around industry and self-sufficiency, and was a pivotal moment of decolonization, symbolizing both the end of Britain's global influence and the emergence of Nasser as the leader of Arab nationalism. By the end of the Suez saga, Britain and France were no longer major players in the Middle East; the Arab world had united behind Egypt and Nasser; Egypt had begun on its path of non-alignment with the 1955 Czech arms deal; and a new global hegemon had clearly emerged in the form of the US.

In an article on the Suez Canal Company, Tal'at Harb – a prominent Egyptian nationalist and the founder of Bank Misr, Egypt's first national bank – discussed European financial imperialism and the domination of foreign capital over Egypt's economy, calling on the Egyptian state to insist on Egyptian membership on the board of directors, a percentage of the Canal's profits, and that the company would revert to Egyptian ownership once the concession expired. For Tal'at Harb, the Suez Canal Company (SCC) was an 'egregious example of rapacious and exploitative European capitalism', leading him to call for limits to be placed on its freedom of operation.[194] The SCC was an Egyptian firm, but its capital and managers were completely foreign. Egyptians held 0.2 per cent of shares in the company and the board of directors included only two Egyptians out of a total of thirty-two. Following the British occupation of Egypt, the SCC opened an office in London, and the number of British directors increased from three to ten. Britain was the largest user of the canal and thus British shipping was given preferential treatment.[195] 'In Egypt the company behaved as a state within a state. It considered itself immune from Egyptian law and in the canal towns behaved as if it, and not the Egyptian government, were the real authority'.[196] It was only in 1936, after the Anglo-Egyptian Treaty was signed, that two Egyptian directors were added to the board. Following mounting Egyptian pressure to 'Egyptianize' the company, Britain and the US had suggested that the canal be 'internationalized' – in other words, brought under international rather than Egyptian control.

Debates around the financing of the High Dam in Aswan set the scene for the nationalization of the canal. The High Dam was seen as part of Egypt's industrialization project, as controlling floods would provide

---

[194] Tignor 1977, 164.   [195] Heikal 1986, 22.   [196] Ibid., 23.

water for irrigation and generate electricity as well as benefit Egypt's farmland. The Egyptians preferred European private capital to American or World Bank financing. However English Electric – the main firm involved – threatened to back out of the deal if the World Bank was not included.[197] An arms deal with the Czechs that year, as well as Egypt's increasingly warm overtures to the Soviets, added more tension to already-fraught negotiations. The eventual decision by the British and US governments not to finance the dam was a culmination of growing tensions over the politicized nature of conditionalities attached to loans from the World Bank as well as Nasser's emerging non-aligned position.[198] Despite this, the decision to withdraw foreign funding still came as a shock to Nasser.[199] His response was swift, and shocked the world: on 26 July 1956, in a speech he gave to the Egyptian public, he announced the full nationalization of the Suez Canal Company. According to Heikal, 'nobody in Egypt slept much that night'.[200]

The response from the SCC was to push for total warfare, while calling for an international organization that would take over the assets of the SCC and manage the canal.[201] Following a build-up of tension that predated Nasser's announcement, Britain, France, and Israel attacked Egypt in what became known as the tripartite aggression. This soon came to an abrupt halt following a global outcry as well as the refusal of the US to support the invasion. Although the aim of the attack had been to discredit and remove Nasser, he not only emerged as a major figure of Arab and postcolonial politics, it also largely discredited the French and the British.

The nationalization of Suez marked a turning point in global politics. Internationally, it led to a powerful wave of Arab support for Nasser, including from countries that had given him a lukewarm reception just a few years earlier and that were pro-West in orientation, such as Iraq and Jordan. As Rashid Khalidi writes, this event not only united Arabs behind Egypt and Nasser, it also gave a 'final push to the tottering hegemony of Britain and France'.[202] After Suez, it was Nasser who would be seen as the leader of Arab nationalism. Suez was also what cemented Egypt's role in Non-Aligned Movement. There could be no more talk about eliminating Nasser on the part of the British and the Americans.

---

[197] Ibid., 105.
[198] Ultimately, Egypt was to turn to local capital to finance the dam.
[199] Heikal 1986, 74.   [200] Ibid., 127.   [201] Ibid., 122.   [202] Ibid.

A Hegemonic Project   139

Domestically, the repercussions were just as significant. The nationalization of the Canal was aimed at weakening foreign capital in Egypt, as well as targeting an important symbol of British and European imperialism. This was compounded by the increasing tension between Western powers and Egypt, particularly after the tripartite aggression which severed most links between Egypt and France and Britain; following this many foreign nationals began leaving Egypt and the assets they owned were sequestered. As noted by Robert Tignor, the invasion was what led to the dissolution of the long-standing British and French economic presence in Egypt. 'By viewing the evolution of the government's relationship towards foreign capital during this period of acute strain, it is possible to see how the regime, so conflicted on the issue of foreign capital and the private sector, took its first decisive steps to undercut the power of foreign capital'.[203]

Nationalizing the Canal was symbolic of the new direction Egypt was to move in, and illuminates the centrality of infrastructure to the broader project of independence, nationalism, and sovereignty.[204] Debates around nationalizing the Canal make visible both the racialized assumptions held by colonial officers (Egyptians cannot run the Canal, thus it must be under international control) as well as the nationalist ones held by Nasser and the officers (full sovereignty includes full ownership over Egyptian land and control over all sources of revenue). The nationalization of the Canal was very much the moment during which Nasser cemented his hegemony, underlining the importance of infrastructure to anticolonial nationalism. Moving beyond concerns about the revenue of the Canal (although this may have been the initial rationale), the nationalization came to symbolize an attempt by a postcolonial nation to assert sovereignty, economically and politically.

Recalling Jabri, who argued that the nationalization of the Suez Canal represents a paradigmatic moment in postcolonial resistance, it is crucial to contextualize it within the broader moves to decolonize the international:

In this moment was contained not simply the desire to reclaim a valuable resource for the nation, but to constitute the nation as

---

[203] Tignor 2015, 128.
[204] For a study on the role of infrastructure and technology in nationalist projects, see Nye 1996.

a viable political community with a right of access to the realm of the international.[205]

Suez marked a moment of resistance; a moment during which, with massive popular support, the 'lifeline of the British Empire' was swiftly decolonized. Nationalization can thus be read as an act of sovereignty; an attempt to access the international on Egypt's own terms. It was not simply about finding capital to finance the building of the High Dam; it was also about making a claim to Egyptian national resources and their place within the international political economy. It is pertinent to recall the push by Britain and the US to 'internationalize' the Suez Canal, thereby bringing it under international protection; the underlying assumption being that Egyptians could not run the canal alone. Nasser's nationalization moved beyond this form of 'internationalization' and instead made a very different claim, one that was widely supported by other Arab states as well as the broader postcolonial world.

Perhaps nothing highlights this more than the massive sacrifices that were required from Egyptian workers – and Egyptians more broadly – in the building of Nasser's infrastructural projects. Although we don't have much in the way of specific details around deaths, injuries, or displacement, we do know that the building of the High Dam at Aswan was staggering in the life it claimed. The displacement of Nubians from their ancestral land, followed by the massive numbers of workers killed or injured during the building of the Dam stand as twin testaments to the high price paid for 'independence' through infrastructure. While it is true that both of these communities saw the Dam as essential to the goals of the revolution, that they felt strong ownership over it, and that they fully supported the view that infrastructure was key to decolonization and independence,[206] Fanon's prophetic words about 'keeping the people out' cannot help but trouble this neat picture, revealing the contradictions underlying the move to decolonize infrastructure in an attempt to establish full sovereignty – still on terms set by centuries of colonial rule.

By arguing that the Suez Canal was Egyptian and that Egypt as a sovereign state had the right to nationalize it, Nasser was re-scripting sovereignty in an attempt to expand the circle of nations who should be thought of as sovereign. And yet, in this inscription of sovereignty, we begin to see the contradictions of anticolonial nationalism and state-led capitalism. Following Julietta Singh, we can see in this instance a clear

[205] Jabri 2012, 103.   [206] Mossallam 2012.

A Hegemonic Project

141

manifestation of 'mastery': over nature, over people, and over territory. In attempting to become sovereign, Egypt in turn reproduced a problematic understanding of what sovereignty was. The displacement of Nubians, the exploitation of workers, and political act of mastering nature all betray an allegiance to a reproduction of colonial forms of developmnet. Similarly, the centrality of mastering "the masses" also betrays a colonial understanding of nation-building. As Omnia El Shakry writes, 'Anticolonial nationalists claimed the moral and material improvement of the demographic masses as their primary object.'[207] What shifted, then, is who is asserting the claim to sovereignty, not what sovereignty itself means. Nevertheless, this assertion was essential to the politics of decolonization at that particular moment; the alternative to it was colonial sovereignty.

Industrialization as Nationalization

The High Dam in Aswan represents Nasser's most ambitious infrastructural project, one very much connected to the bloc's broader project of industrialization. Figure 2.3 represents the grand scale of this infrastructural project, and the immense amount of labour that went into it. In many ways, it symbolised what Singh calls the 'mastery' embedded within postcolonial projects that depended on mastering nature, people, and the future.[208] Nasser was not the first Egyptian leader to see industrialization as central to breaking the dependency between Egypt and global capitalism; in the previous chapter, I touched on Bank Misr as an earlier attempt at independent industrial development, one that eventually failed in its attempt at replacing foreign capital with local financing. Here I focus on Nasser's project and its attempt to transform Egypt's economy and dependency on global capital through independent industrialization.

One of the new bloc's first political decisions was to reduce the power of the landowning elite and redirect capital investment towards industry through the creation of a new social force made up of industrial capitalists, bureaucrats, and technocrats, who also made up the newly expanded public sector. Duties paid on imported industrial commodities were increased, and duties on imported material inputs were

[207] 2007, 5.   [208] 2017.

Figure 2.3 Construction of Aswan High Dam. Credit: Dmitri Kessel / The LIFE Picture Collection / Getty Images.

decreased in order to develop Egyptian industry. New companies did not have to pay taxes on profits for their first five years, and tariffs on luxury imports were raised.[209] It soon became clear that the aim was not to displace private investment in the economy, but to shift it from agriculture to industry. This was part and parcel of the new bloc's attempt to re-articulate Egypt's capitalist trajectory rather than dismantle it. At the same time, the new ruling class restricted foreign capital, pushed through import substitution industrialization, and invested heavily in infrastructure.[210] Nasser described these moves as the creation of a 'controlled capitalistic economy.' As noted by Omnia El Shakry, economic nationalism under Nasser aimed to place Egypt 'on the path to a successful and indigenous modernization, through an ideology of self-reliance.'[211]

Nevertheless, there were numerous tensions within this new configuration. The project of the new bloc, which centred on minimizing the power of foreign and private capital, was not always the main priority of these new fractions. Nasser's nationalization of major enterprises was a key

[209] Aoude 1994, 6.   [210] Ibid.   [211] 2007, 181.

A Hegemonic Project

source of tension within the historical bloc given that it removed control of these enterprises from the very capitalists it sought support from. Take for example the sequestering of Ahmed Abboud's sugar company in 1952 – then one of the largest privately owned companies in Egypt – although it owed the government over 5 million pounds in payment. Targeting this one company was a threat to Abboud's entire economic empire, built on many different companies and investments.[212] Following the sequestration, the government became the major shareholder in the sugar company and paid off the French investors who dominated the company's board. This move was read as a warning signal to the capitalist class in Egypt, who were worried that it would set a precedent. The move itself, however, was a clear indication of what the bloc wanted: to divest companies of foreign control; to shift ownership to the state; and to encourage continued economic investment within this new paradigm. Nasser needed the state to control production and accumulation, in order to direct it towards national development.

This tension around what the goals of capital accumulation should be was what defined this moment. Tignor notes that businessmen used the 'traditional criteria of profitability and safety to decide on their investments and shied away from many of the large-scale projects that were close to the heart of Egyptian rulers'.[213] However, Nasser needed these projects, not least for the legitimacy they provided. For many within the ruling class, profitability was the driving force determining where capital investments went. The aim of the bloc was not necessarily to disrupt profit making but rather to divert some of this profit to the development of large-scale projects that pushed forward national development. This was their criteria, and it was here that the tension was located. Moreover, there was the additional problem that certain sectors have historically been more profitable than others: investment in agriculture, land and real estate is less 'risky' than in industry.[214] The aim of the new bloc was to re-articulate Egypt's position vis-à-vis capitalist development, and to do this required changing the direction of Egypt's development and the ways in which capital was invested. These large-scale projects were therefore necessary, alongside the nationalization of key enterprises. In other words, nationalization should be understood within the framework of the new direction of the bloc rather than simply as a means of amassing power.

[212] Ibid., 112.   [213] 2015, 113.   [214] Mabro and Radwan 1976, 24.

144   *Hegemony in Egypt*

These moves to redirect capital towards industry were thus the first step in independent industrialization; radically shifting the balance of power between the private and public sector was another. Private ownership was limited to the sectors of construction, land, and industry; land reform, rent controls, and new taxation rules were implemented; and social welfare benefits such as education, health care, and a minimum wage were ensured.[215] This was soon followed by a wave of nationalizations. In the 1960s, the National Bank of Egypt and Bank Misr were nationalized. This was followed by all insurance companies and banks, fifty industrial and shipping companies, and most of the financial and manufacturing sectors.[216] The 1962 National Charter allowed the state to nationalize any company owned jointly with the private sector, and large companies owned by private individuals were also nationalized.[217] Nationalization laws 117 and 118 were implemented, in order to create a public sector and, by extension, make the state the central actor in production.[218] This is where we begin to see a particular relation between the state and capitalist development, one brought about by the particular conditions of the Nasserist bloc. By the end of the first five-year plan, the public sector represented 90 per cent of total investment, leading some to argue that state capitalism had successfully eliminated foreign control of Egypt's economy.[219]

These moves to weaken the private sector should be contextualized within broader debates happening at the time. As Robert Tignor notes, 'not only had the private sector failed to be a powerful engine of economic development, but in the period leading up to the military coup in 1952 it came under intense scrutiny from many segments of Egyptian society'.[220] Egyptians had come to question the private sector not only from the perspective of economic profitability, but from the perspective of what kind of society a strong private sector led to and whether such a society was the ideal form. This eventually led many to call for stronger state intervention in order to promote social and economic institutions that were more socially conscious.[221] Tignor puts this in a broader context:

The debate over social questions elevated certain words to almost liturgical prominence. Education, health services, wealth redistribution, and economic development were the keys to a just and happy society. Two other words figured prominently in the political vocabulary: *islah* (reform) and *ishtirakiya*

---

[215] Aoude 1994, 8.   [216] Beattie 1994, 155–6.   [217] Ibid.   [218] Ibid.
[219] Ibid.   [220] 2015, 30.   [221] Ibid.

A Hegemonic Project

(socialism). Although true socialists were in a small minority, even the politicians of the established parties were fond of characterizing themselves as socialists.[222]

The distinct roles to be played by the private and public sectors were clearly set out in the Free Officers' National Charter. It limited private ownership to the sectors of construction, land, and industry; and made exploitation less likely by implementing land reform, rent controls, and new taxation rules. The Charter guaranteed social welfare benefits such as education, health care, and a minimum wage,[223] thereby changing the role of state capitalism: it was now focused on either the public sector or joint projects between the state and the private sector. The declining role of British capital and the focus on industrialization both played a role in prompting the state to expand its role in production. The shift became apparent with realignments happening at the government level. Before the nationalization of the Suez Canal, for example, the government divided the Ministry of Commerce and Industry into two separate ministries. Aziz Sidqi, who was an advocate of state planning and industrialization, was named the head of the Ministry of Commerce.

Both the mechanics of nationalization and the move to limit foreign capital and encourage the development of the public sector ultimately worked to create a new of social force. While the specific relationship between the public and private sectors was not defined clearly, it was clear that the public sector was to play the dominant role in economic development. The new laws ensured that the public sector owned companies in key sectors such as banking, insurance, and industry, as well as varying degrees of ownership in other sectors. Top positions in these companies were filled by public agency employees, consolidating the emergence of a new technocratic class. By 1961, the boards of 238 newly nationalized companies consisted of one-third engineers and scientists, while the rest were made up of lawyers, business graduates, judges, and councillors.[224] The middle ranks of management within these companies were also transformed as more students were admitted into universities and technical institutes. From 1964 to 1965, for example, skilled workers increased by more than 1 million.[225] This ultimately led to the creation of a new social category – the technocratic class – as intended by the new ruling class.[226]

---

[222] Ibid., 32. [223] Aoude 1994, 8. [224] Ibid., 176. [225] Ibid., 177.
[226] Ibid.

By the early 1960s, Egypt's economy had both changed and remained the same. Abdel-Malek, writing of this period, states:

> The Egyptian economy appears to be a mixed economy. It is still capitalistic in many ways: the land remains nearly untouched by nationalisation; the public sector, though under the direction of technocrats, is still regulated by market demands and profit incentive; planning, and foreign aid in particular, tend to strengthen this pattern. It is a relatively fast-growing economy with a central state-capitalistic sector of unusual proportions, but although every new wave of nationalization (sic) weakens the power of private capital, it only provides more solidly entrenched power to the technocrats.[227]

Ultimately, like those before it, the Nasserist project was unsuccessful at developing a strong industrial sector. The capital needed for significant investments belonged to a very small circle of capitalists who saw Nasser's land reforms as too drastic, and were thus unwilling to invest in associated projects.[228] The regime's dismantling of the old political parties also eliminated the avenues of influence this circle of elites used, further estranging them from the new government.[229] Class tensions played a role here, as the old elite often looked down on the new class of officers who they saw as less sophisticated.[230] While there was support for industrialization from the rural middle class, they did not have the capital needed for this diversification.[231] What this ultimately meant was that state actors became, by default, the principle economic actor while – as Beattie puts it – 'capitalists were left holding the short end of the stick'.[232]

The 1960s saw a deepening economic crisis in Egypt. Fiscal crisis, trade deficits, and regional inequalities slowed down the import substitution industrialization (ISI) approach.[233] Even before the 1967 war, protests, strikes and forms of resistance were breaking out across Egypt. The economic crisis hit rural Egypt in particular, and massive unrest built up in from the mid-1960s.[234] The 1967 war with Israel signalled the official death of the Nasserist project – albeit not of Nasserism – and the start of Egypt's neoliberal transformation.[235] The power to control the economy had shifted from one social force to another, and this had wider ramifications than simply being a transfer of power. The shift to the public sector meant a shift in who had access to the economy. Those who accumulated

---

[227] Ibid., 35.   [228] Beattie 1994, 144.   [229] Ibid.   [230] Ibid.
[231] Ibid., 147.   [232] Ibid.   [233] Pratt 2007, 61.
[234] See Mitchell 2002 – chapter five.
[235] The crisis, as Sherif Younes argues, began with the failed union with Syria.

Hegemony in Egypt

through the new and expanding public sector were not only often middle-class and thus able to achieve social mobility, but they were also part of a public sector whose modus operandi was the provision of social welfare. Industrialization and its focus on national development questioned inequality at the global level by asserting Egypt's sovereign right to control its own economy. Despite this, and because of other weaknesses in the project itself, the colonial international was to re-emerge in the 1970s with the global neoliberal project and an increasing turn away from development to dependency.

In the final chapter, I use the notion of *haunting* to trace the ways in which Nasserism lived on as an afterlife of hegemony. In some senses, what ended in 1967 was not the hegemony of Nasserism as an idea or a promise, but rather the hegemony of the Free Officers and the ruling class that had coalesced around Nasser. Nasserism as a promise continued, in some ways, to be hegemonic decades into the future, in that it continued to act as a possibility and a benchmark of what a nationalist project could look like. This form of living on in the afterlife of hegemony – what I refer to as haunting – serves as an indication of just how powerful and contradictory a project it was in the broader public imagination.

Hegemony in Egypt: Arab Socialism and Its Discontents

Nasser's funeral drew millions of Egyptians (Figure 2.4), despite the setbacks the project faced in the late 1960s, including rising public discontent and demonstrations. The funeral symbolised the end of an era, as well as the start of a period of uncertainty. If we measure the resistance of the postcolonial state in terms of its relation to the constraints of the international, as Vivienne Jabri suggests, then the nationalization of the Suez Canal marked a moment of resistance, whereas the opening of Egypt's economy in the 1970s marked a moment of capitulation. Both moments trace a particular relationship between Egypt and the international; but in both instances, the international remains very much colonial in its articulation of global inequality. Under Nasser, industrialization and nationalization were implemented in opposition to the constraints of the international. Resources were no longer available to be exploited by colonial rulers, but were to become the property of a new and sovereign nation on the path to modernization. Postcolonial states thus had two projects: one political and one social. As Omnia El Shakry notes, quoting Nasser, the challenge was always to carry out both a political revolution of

Figure 2.4 President Nasser's funeral procession. Credit: Express / Archive Photos / Getty Images.

self-determination, as well as a social revolution.[236] It was the assumptions underpinning the social revolution that reveal the type of project the Nasserist regime envisioned. The nationalization of the Suez Canal in particular highlights these two projects: 'In this moment was contained not simply the desire to reclaim a valuable resource for the nation, but to constitute the nation as a viable political community with a right of access to the realm of the international'.[237]

Despite these attempts at decolonization, these projects ultimately embodied severe internal contradictions. The fact remains that Egypt had a chance of independence in a meaningful or radical sense during these moments; this alone suggests a productive rethinking of this juncture is pertinent. I conclude here by reviewing the Nasserist reproduction of nation, nationalism and capitalist development, and how this served to contradict the radical anticolonial moment. If we take seriously the vast potential that existed in the lead-up to 1952 and the futures that were imagined and fought for, we begin to see the limitations of statist projects of independence and postcoloniality. Rather than hold Nasserism to account

[236] 2007, 207 [237] Jabri 2012, 103.

Hegemony in Egypt

in comparison to other state-based projects of modernity or nationhood, it is perhaps more pertinent to hold Nasserism to account vis-à-vis the radical energies it built on and then demobilized.

Chatterjee's famous distinction between the material and the spiritual asserts that postcolonial elites were willing to adopt Western technology and science in order to advance economically – given the clear advantage Western nations had in those areas – but that they needed at the same time to preserve culture and nationalism as authentic domains that were to remain untouched by Westernization. In other words, the adoption of nationalism and the nation-state meant that postcolonial elites had to both modernize in terms of the economy, and assert itself as national and anti-colonial.[238] Building on this, Joseph Massad writes: 'National time is double time. The nation's commitment to the preservation of a traditional national culture carried through from the past and its project of technological modernization as the present goal to be achieved in the future place the nation on a synchronic temporal continuum, whereby the nation simultaneously lives its traditional past, its present emergence, and its future modernity as one unmediated moment'.[239]

The problem is not so much the adoption of nationalism in order to fight colonialism – an adoption that was rendered necessary and was often the only option for many postcolonial nations. The problem is that these leaders did not see the dangers of *believing* that this adoption was more than simply strategic. In an excerpt that deserves to be quoted in full, Massad lays bare both the power and pitfalls of anticolonial nationalism:

Perhaps anticolonial nationalism's main manifestation of its agency was its opposition to colonial rule and colonial racial hierarchies that denied the colonized their agency. However, the ontological status of anticolonial nationalism changes with the historical moment. By appropriating colonial discourse, anticolonial nationalism was able to subvert it and resist it, leading to the end of colonial rule. Its subsequent refusal, however, to question colonial modes of governance and the very precepts of colonial epistemology, except for its place in them, meant its abdication of agency to colonial law and discipline. Instead of understanding their anticolonial nationalism as

---

[238] Massad (2001, 6) writes: 'Here nationalism launches its most powerful, creative and historically significant project: to fashion a "modern" national culture that is nevertheless not Western. If the nation is an imagined community, then this is where it is brought into being'.

[239] Ibid., 25.

150 *Hegemony in Egypt*

a *strategic* essentialism to fight colonial power, anticolonial nationalists mistook their nationalism for an absolute essence.[240]

Massad's book focuses on the law and the military as two spaces in which colonial epistemology is embedded and thus the adoption of these institutions by nationalist elites merely ensured the perpetuation of colonial modes of governance – even if these more momentarily subverted to gain independence. I turn now to the space of economic development to show that in the case of Nasserist Egypt, the decision to use state-led capitalist development was perhaps an even more consequential continuation of colonial epistemology.

When the Free Officers came to power, the dominant national social force was the landed elite, and foreign capital was a major player in the Egyptian economy, represented mainly through British interests. Following 1952, a new social force that would drive forward industrialization – the centrepiece of the new hegemonic project – was cultivated, and the balance between the public and private sector changed radically. Whether this represented a departure from the capitalist mode of production is doubtful, however, suggesting we should be sceptical of labelling the Nasserist project a socialist one. By probing the debate around Nasser's Arab 'socialism' I explore the disjuncture between what Nasserism claimed it *was* on the one hand, and on the other hand, what political work the Nasserist project did.

In his pivotal work *Overstating the Arab State*, Nazih Ayubi posits that Nasser did not initiate anything resembling a socialist economy: 'It is not sound to call a system socialist simply because its leaders happen, at a particular political juncture, to raise socialist banners and to use socialist terminology'.[241] Ayubi goes on to point out that socialism refers to the popular control of and participation in the economic and political affairs of a country on the part of all classes. In Egypt, however, socialism developed as part and parcel of the nationalist project and its programme for the economy of the country. It also served as a means of mobilizing Egyptians as well as controlling the public sphere: 'The norm was a military coup or a "palace coup", and although this sometimes proceeded to build up a single political organization that eventually adopted some "socialist" objectives, this was done from a position of authority and was often aimed at installing "socialism without socialists", as a familiar Arab phrase describes it'.[242]

[240] Ibid., 277–8.   [241] 1996, 92.   [242] Ibid., 94.

Hegemony in Egypt

Partly, this is because the main goals of postcolonial states have been political – as Nkrumah put it, 'seek ye first the political kingdom'.[243] Socialism was not the base from which these states started from; as Ayubi suggests, 'it crept, gradually and piecemeal, into the ideologies of such regimes, juxtaposed on to other more important 'nationalistic' or 'modernising' concepts; they were basically technocrats interested in modernisation through industrialisation, rather than ideologues or militants striving to install the rule of the working classes'.[244] Alongside Ayubi, several other scholars of the Nasser period have argued that the new ruling class had never intended to transition to socialism or to restructure the economy in order to allow for mass participation. The aim, rather, had always been to take control of the economy. Mahmoud Hussein, for example, has argued: 'Egyptian "socialism" was a cover up for the domination of the major levers of the production process by the Egyptian state bourgeoisie and for the systematic removal of the working masses from any real responsibility in that process'.[245] Following this, the control over the means of production shifted from one social force to another, but did not become accessible to a wider base of Egyptians. Ibrahim Aoudé has similarly argued that Nasser's regime developed a state form of capitalism that had nationalist underpinnings. Equally pertinent is Omnia El Shakry's point that Nasserism did not radically dismantle class relations and power structures. Citing Chatterjee, she writes: 'The postcolonial state achieves a synthetic form of hegemony…the reification of the nation in the body of the state becomes the means for constructing this hegemonic structure, and the extent of control over the new state apparatus becomes a precondition for further capitalist development.'[246] This is precisely what we see with Nasserism: a continuation of capitalist development made possible through the coming together of nation and state through anticolonial nationalism.[247]

The decision by the new bloc to limit rather than eliminate capitalist forms of economic development meant that Egypt's integration into the capitalist world market – its organic dependence on it – was reinforced rather than broken.[248] Given the difficulty in separating capitalism from European imperialism, because of the enabling role they played in one another's expansion, the decision to adopt state-led capitalist development cannot be seen as anything but a continuation of colonial domination by

---

[243] 1965. [244] Ibid., 200. [245] 1973, 172. [246] 2007, 203. [247] 1994, 2.
[248] Hussein 1973, 206.

other means. Industrialization was based on notions of scientific progress, modern planning, and centring the state within capitalist production. Even if we locate this within Soviet understandings of economic development, it is difficult to escape the modern telos underwriting industrialization-as-development. As Nicola Pratt notes, Nasserist hegemony was built on the idea of national modernization – both embedded within colonial norms of governing.[249] Restructuring the economy through five-year plans and notions of scientific accuracy, on the one hand, and imposing strict discipline on workers, on the other, both demonstrate the problems with the Nasserist project's attempt to gain independence. While under Nasser investment was to be concentrated in industry, making it a key locus of the extraction of surplus value as opposed to agriculture, this did not represent a departure from the capitalist mode of production. It is perhaps only by rejecting this mode altogether that true independence could have been achieved, for can we not understand capitalism as the ultimate colonial mode of expansion?

This becomes more acute when we look at the fate of workers under Nasserism. As Adam Hanieh and others have noted, perhaps nothing indicated the problems with the Nasserist project more than its decision to exclude labour from the centres of power.[250] On the one hand, the co-optation of labour's struggles rather than the centring of these struggles meant that the Nasserist project could only go so far in challenging global capitalism. On the other hand, while it is true that under Nasser investment was to be concentrated in industry, making it a key locus of the extraction of surplus value as opposed to agriculture, this did not represent a departure from the capitalist mode of production. Even if Nasserism had not excluded workers, the attempt to develop economically through ISI meant that massive amounts of capital had to be committed to modernizing industry. Without turning this into an export-led growth path, as De Smet notes, the state would soon face a balance-of-payments crisis – and indeed it did. For such a strategy to have been profitable for Egypt, competitive industries would have had to be developed, which meant the disciplining of labour in order to achieve high productivity and maintain low wages.[251] This clearly contradicted the demands of workers, and indeed the ideological basis of the Nasserist project itself. By the mid 1960s, these contradictions were clear: capital-intensive industrialization and high levels of consumption were incompatible.[252] In addition to this,

[249] Pratt 2007, 14.   [250] 2013.   [251] 2016, 159.   [252] Ibid.

Hegemony in Egypt

De Smet shows that because nationalization did not target the entire Egyptian economy, pockets of private accumulation continued to exist, which meant that the agrarian bourgeoisie was able to gradually strengthen itself.[253] Finally, the costly military intervention in Yemen from 1963 to 1967, as well as the 1967 defeat to Israel both drained public resources.

Fanon discusses this tension between capitalism and socialism, reading them as representatives of colonialism and anti-colonialism, respectively:

> Of course we know that the capitalist regime, in so far as it is a way of life, cannot leave us free to perform our work at home, nor our duty in the world. Capitalist exploitation and cartels and monopolies are the enemies of underdeveloped countries. On the other hand the choice of a socialist regime, a regime which is completely oriented towards the people as a whole and based on the principle that man is the most precious of all possessions will allow us to go forward more quickly and more harmoniously, and thus make impossible that caricature of society where all economic and political power is held in the hands of a few who regard the nation as a whole with scorn and contempt.[254]

For Fanon, socialism is in and of itself democratic. Democracy here takes on a different meaning from civil institutions, civil liberties, and the protection of liberal freedoms; rather for Fanon democracy refers to the redistribution of wealth across the nation. This wealth does not refer only to wealth within the nation, but also imperial wealth: 'We are not blinded by the moral reparation of national independence; nor are we fed by it. The wealth of the imperial countries is our wealth too'.[255] Yet it is its redistribution that is key: the wealth of the nation belongs to all of us within the nation. Indeed much of Fanon's work has looked at the exclusions within the nation, most prominently the exclusion of the peasantry. For him, real decolonization takes place once everyone within the nation is able to access this wealth. As El Shakry and Chatterjee both note, the postcolonial state s distinguished by its concern for developing the nation, as distinct from the colonial state's concern for exploiting resources.[256] Following Fanon, however, under Nasserism these two concerns became blurry at times. While nationalizing industries is important, the bigger question is who is allowed to partake in this process of nationalizing. In a strong condemnation of nationalist elites, he writes: 'For if you think you can manage a country without letting the people interfere, if you think that the people upset the game by their mere presence, whether they slow it

---

[253] Ibid.　[254] 1963, 78.　[255] Ibid., 81.　[256] 2007, 207.

down or whether by their natural ignorance they sabotage it, then you must have no hesitation: you must keep the people out'.[257]

It is in this bringing together of economic independence and a deep-seated notion of democracy that we more clearly see the flaws of the Nasserist project. The project did redirect Egypt's trajectory: capital was accumulated for national development, and indeed by 1961 the state accounted for 90 per cent of total investment. Reducing the influence of large-scale capitalists, monopolies, and private sector domination; initiating land reforms; opening up the education and health care systems as well as the employment market; and promoting political stances of neutrality and anti-imperialism all served to dismantle many of the relations of production in place before 1952. This bloc may have continued along the path of capitalist development, but the articulations shifted to a state-led form of development, where accumulation was diverted to nationalist projects and new and emerging social forces connected to these projects. This is a far cry from Egypt before 1952, where accumulation was controlled by foreign interests alongside an agrarian bourgeoisie that accumulated through exploitation, dispossession, and dependency. Nevertheless, coming back to Fanon, the exclusion of 'the people' from the project of decolonization meant that the Nasserist bloc was unable to centre class struggle and fully liberate itself from the colonial international. As Fanon noted, the national government should always *cede its power back to the people*. It should, in effect, *dissolve itself*. Because nationalist consciousness during the anticolonial moment comes from the people, this is where it should reside.

In the final chapter, I draw on Julietta Singh's book *Unthinking Mastery*, to probe deeper into the notions of sovereignty and mastery that seeped through the Nasserist project and without which hegemony would have been unthinkable. Singh explores the ways in which postcolonial thinkers – even as they criticized the colonial project – reproduced elements of it in their envisioning of a future beyond empire.[258] If we

---

[257] Ibid., 152. Fanon added: 'Yet the national middle class constantly demands the nationalisation of the economy and of the trading sectors. This is because, from their point of view, nationalisation does not mean placing the whole economy at the service of the nation. For them, nationalisation does not mean governing the state with regard to the new social relations whose growth it has been decided to encourage. To them, nationalisation quite simply means the transfer into native hands of those unfair advantages which are a legacy of the colonial period' (ibid., 122).

[258] Singh 2018.

Hegemony in Egypt

follow Gramsci, we must accept that hegemony requires mastery; indeed, one could even suggest that hegemony *is* mastery. But to what ends? And for how long? To adopt mastery as the means of thinking a new future beyond empire was to adopt colonial ways of relating to the world; and thus to embed the impossibility of full decolonization within the project of decolonization itself. The trinity of capitalist development, the military, and nationalism – brought together under Nasserism and solidified through the hegemonic nature of the Nasserist project – would continue to haunt Egypt in the decades to come. It is difficult to imagine the events of 2011 and 2013 outside of this trinity, and therefore to imagine these events as unconnected to the historical trajectory set in place by the Nasserist project. This brings us back to the question of historical and political necessity: to what extent could anti-imperialism have succeeded without counter-mastery? As Getachew has argued, anticolonial nationalists saw sovereignty as only the first step in a broader project of world-making, a project that – if it had been allowed to continue – would likely have reconfigured the colonial assumptions of sovereignty itself.[259] She also makes the point that sovereignty was necessary, and it is this that I want to underline in relation to Nasserism; the choice of Egyptian sovereignty was made in a context of colonial rule and the continuation of the colonial international; the 'limits of the possible', as Gramsci might say. Given these conditions, one could ask whether anticolonial nationalism, Egyptian sovereignty, and modernist development were a response – perhaps the only realistic response – to a postcolonial world gathering itself after the violence of empire.

[259] 2019.

PART II

Hegemony and Its Afterlives

3 Laying Neoliberal Foundations
Infitah and a New Egypt

The capitalist dream that had seemed almost attainable under the socialism of Abdel Nasser had, amazingly enough, become impossible during the capitalist era of Sadat.

Sonallah Ibrahim[1]

Russians can give you arms but only the United States can give you a solution.

Anwar el Sadat

Nothing about this free market was free, of course. It was built on coercion and enforced hardship barely concealed by the thin veil of national sovereignty.

Arwa Salih[2]

The joke was that at the crossroads the driver would ask Sadat whether to go left or right. Sadat would ask the driver which way Nasser had gone. He would reply that he had turned left, so Sadat would tell him to signal left but turn right.

Mohamed Berrada, *Like a Summer Never to Be Repeated*[3]

With every step I take, my eyes are dazzled by the glitter of the open door policy. I need only walk into any grocery store to breathe a sigh of relief and to thank God that he has compensated us so well for the long period of frustration and deprivation.

Lutfy Adul Azim[4]

Egyptian film and literature are full of references to the 1970s and 1980s and the rapid transformation of society that took place at this time. This particular era was marked by the rise of a new group of businessmen, who, along with their families and social circles, are

---

[1] Ibrahim 2005, 14.   [2] 2018, 34.   [3] Mehrez 2011, 155.
[4] Quoted in Baker 1990, 380.

160   *Laying Neoliberal Foundations*

often shown as rich beyond imagination, decadent, Westernized, and extremely conscious of their (newly achieved, in a very short amount of time) heightened positioned in society. Many are portrayed as corrupt businessmen or drug dealers who managed to make millions quickly, and whose culture and values did not transform fast enough to 'keep up' with their material gain and concurrent rise in society. Labelled the *nouveau riche,* this new class was seen as distinct from 'old money' in terms of being less refined. These differences point to major transformations in Egyptian society and economy during the post-1967 era, key among them the rise of a new ruling class. This new class is distinctive not only in terms of how it accumulated wealth or its norms and values, but also in its failure to create a hegemonic project. The central argument of this chapter, then, is that while we see the beginnings of a historical bloc emerge during this period, with Anwar el Sadat at its helm, and while we also see the emerging contours of a hegemonic project, ultimately this class failed to create hegemony in the way the Nasserist bloc had just decades before.

I read this failure through Gramsci's notion of an *interregnum,* a period during which things are shifting rather than stable, which he captures through his famous quote 'the crisis consists precisely in the fact that the old is dying and the new cannot be born; in this interregnum a great variety of morbid symptoms appear'.[5] This period between one ruling class and another, or one project and another, can be understood as a time-lag of sorts. It is a form of time that is experienced as both a rupture and as setting of the stage for what is to come next. Broadly, I refer to the period between 1967 and 2011 as the *afterlife of hegemony,* signifying that these decades should be understood as part of a single time frame marked by the absence of hegemony, the absence of a historical bloc, the increasing disembedding of consent from coercion, and Egypt's re-insertion into the colonial international. One way of making the events taking place during these decades legible is through placing them within the trajectory laid out by Egypt's first and last hegemonic project; to put it crudely, where Nasserism was the rise of a hegemonic project, the projects that came after were connected to the fall of that same project. Understanding it as a unified afterlife of hegemony allows

---

[5] 1992, 32.

Laying Neoliberal Foundations

for an analysis that sees ruptures and continuities that do not map neatly onto the conventional split between the presidencies of Sadat and Mubarak.

This chapter looks at the first part of this afterlife – 1967 to the mid 1990s – and the next chapter looks at the mid 1990s to 2011. While the late 1960s to late 1970s can be seen as a pause, during which various social forces recalibrated around the project of infitah, the 1980s to mid 1990s can instead be seen as 'empty time', during we do not see the cultivation of a new hegemonic project. From the mid 1990s, we see a dramatic acceleration, suddenly, of neoliberal restructuring, characterized by the rise of a new ruling class. We can therefore see different movements and tempos within this afterlife; but not the presence of different projects, nor the creation of hegemony. Following a reading by Zygmunt Bauman of Gramsci's interregnum in which states 'he attached it to the extraordinary situations in which the extant legal frame of social order loses its grip and can hold no longer, whereas a new frame, made to the measure of newly emerged conditions responsible for making the old frame useless, is still at the designing stage, has not yet been fully assembled, or is not strong enough to be put in its place',[6] I look at the post-1967 moment as one during which the old was indeed dying. And yet, this did not herald a clear shift towards a new form of hegemony; in other words, the new could not be born yet. An interregnum, then, is a time of uncertainty during which political changes occur but during which a new ruling class is never quite able to create hegemony.

I begin with the formative moment of 1967, during which the entire Middle East instantly changed, tracing the ways in which 1967 was symbolic of the broader collapse of anticolonial nationalism across the region, setting the scene for the neoliberal transformation that began in the early 1970s. I then trace the emergence of a new ruling class, arguing that the basis for this class – which never quite coalesced into a bloc – should be traced back to the mid 1960s rather than 1972 as is commonly assumed. I explore the contours of this bloc by looking first at the decline of Nasserism as a hegemonic project, particularly through the lens of the 1967 and 1973 wars and the battle between leftist and Islamist forces; and second at the

---

[6] 2012, 49.

emergence of what Fanon called a 'dependent national middle class'. This social force, which Fanon predicted would emerge across the postcolonial world, is distinctive in three ways: its reliance on transnational capitalist forces, the over-representation of businessmen within its ranks, and the lack of internal consent it produced within society. The ruling class that emerged post-Nasser very much fit Fanon's dependent bourgeoisie, suggesting that this era should be understood through Gramsci's concept of interregnum rather than hegemony.

1967: The Year That Changed the Arab World

It is difficult to overstate just how momentous the 1967 defeat to Israel was for the Arab world. Referred to as both the *naksa* and the *nakba*, it was a moment in which entire nations' hopes and dreams were shattered. It was the official death knell for pan-Arab nationalism as well as the end of the various anticolonial nationalist projects still active in the region. The year 1967 was especially momentous for Palestinians, as it brought home the reality that Palestinian liberation would not be won through pan-Arab solidarity. Aside from the astounding, if not surprising, military defeat, what was even more tragic was the death of the hope and optimism that had coloured the decades since independence. It symbolized the symbolic death of independence and the many promises that had been made by leaders like Nasser. If anything characterizes the post-1967 period, it is a sense of confusion, soul-searching, and profound loss.

The Six-Day War, also known as the June War or the 1967 Arab-Israeli War, was fought between 5 and 10 June 1967, and involved Israel, Egypt, Jordan, and Syria. The war resulted from a build-up of tension, primarily around Nasser's decision to close the straits of Tiran to Israeli ships. On 5 June, Israel launched pre-emptive air-strikes on Egyptian airfields, resulting in the destruction of almost the entire Egyptian air force. At the same time, the Israelis launched a ground offensive into the Gaza Strip and Sinai, forcing Nasser to order the evacuation of Sinai. Israeli forces pushed through Sinai, capturing it and leaving a trail of heavy losses in its wake. Israel also captured the Syrian Golan Heights as well as the Jordan-controlled West Bank, both of which it holds until today. On 11 June, a ceasefire

1967: The Year That Changed the Arab World 163

was signed. It was clear that Israel had defeated not only the Egyptian army – largely because they were caught by surprise – but also the Jordanian and Syrian armies. The defeat was overwhelming not only because of how fast it had occurred but because of what it symbolized for Palestine and Palestinians, and because of how much land Arab states had lost.

These dramatic effects played out just as intensely in Egypt, a nation reeling from a short but devastating six days of war. It would soon emerge that Egypt's leaders, as well as their various organs of mass media, had lied to Egyptians about the state of the war, reportedly claiming to be advancing against Israel when in fact they were being swiftly defeated from all sides. The loss of life, of infrastructure, and of dignity was felt even more intensely precisely because Egyptians had believed themselves to be winning, to be close to victory over Israel; the truth is somewhat easier to swallow when you have been expecting it. When defeat had become undeniable, a visibly shaken Nasser appeared on national television to take responsibility and announce his resignation. Egyptians flooded the streets, weeping or shouting, in a communal expression of emotion.

In Egypt, the role of the army in the defeat became a central point of contention. Abdel Hakim Amer and Nasser had made the decision to go to war knowing that Egypt was not fully prepared. In December 1966 Amer received a report by the military's high command advising against any confrontation with Israel. Because of Egypt's disastrous experience in Yemen – known as the region's 'Vietnam' – the army was already suffering from shortages in both manpower and weaponry.[7] Around dawn, an Israeli armada of 196 fighter- bombers (approximately 95 per cent of the Israeli Air Force) headed towards Egypt. Before noon, 85 per cent of the Egyptian air force (304 planes) was destroyed. Over the next six days, Egypt lost 700 tanks, 450 field guns, and 17 500 soldiers (11 500 killed and the

---

[7] Kandil 2012, 258. Kandil continues: 'By May 1967 – the month Amer began to agitate for war – the army suffered a 37 percent shortage in manpower, 30 percent shortage in small arms, 24 percent in artillery, 45 percent in tanks, and 70 percent in armored vehicles; and trained pilots were fewer than the available aircraft. Another report described 1966– 1967 as the worse training year in the army's history'.

rest injured or captured), and out of its 300 000 men in arms, only half remained in formation.[8]

Unsurprisingly, 1967 led to what Gramsci would call an 'organic crisis' within Egypt's historical bloc. The war was not solely to blame for this; an intensifying economic crisis and growing resistance from groups within the historical bloc – particularly labour both in the cities and countryside – meant that there was increasing pressure on Nasser and the Free Officers. As I show, questions were being raised about Nasser's hegemonic project, and whether it was sustainable in the long term or even whether it had produced the results it had so clearly promised. Nasser had already begun to respond to some of these criticisms, primarily by appointing free market–oriented ministers to key posts as early as the mid 1960s. For instance, Zakaria Mohieddin, who was in favour of a free market economy, was appointed prime minister in 1965 and although he was swiftly removed following resistance to his appointment, it suggests that Nasser was thinking about possibly moving towards a mixture between Arab socialist policies and a free market economy. 1965 saw prices on general goods and taxes being raised, and subsidies being lowered. Private investment was encouraged and efforts were made to reduce imports.[9] The 1960s also saw a growing reliance on foreign aid, primarily from Western countries.[10]

In fact, we can already see the outlines of a new ruling class emerging in the mid 1960s because of the very changes Nasser put in place in an attempt to address a growing economic crisis. Although historiographical accounts of the transition from Nasser to Sadat commonly see the Sadat era as marking the official beginning of Egypt's free market experiment, this shift began much earlier. The changes being made under the Nasserist bloc should be seen as laying the groundwork for the coming ruling class whose project would be defined by free market capitalism. What brought these tensions to the surface was the defeat of 1967. The defeat led to a complete rebalancing of social forces, and it is at this precise moment that we see the emergence of a new project.

1967 was not Egypt's last war with Israel; there would be another one in 1973; indeed it makes sense to think of these two wars together, since one was arguably an attempt to finish the other.[11] The 1973 War – also

---

[8] Ibid., 264.   [9] Abdel-Malek 1968, 311.   [10] Hussein 1973, 221.
[11] 2017, 293.

known as the Yom Kippur War, the Ramadan War, and the October War – was fought between 6 and 25 October 1973. Egypt's goal was to recapture Sinai, which was still held by Israel. The war was started by a surprise joint Arab attack on Israel on 6 October, with Egypt successfully crossing the Suez Canal and advancing into the Sinai Peninsula. Three days later, Israel managed to stop the Egyptian offensive, resulting in a stalemate. Syrian forces had advanced into the Golan Heights, only to be repelled; Israel then launched a counter-offensive that went deep into Syria, almost reaching Damascus. Israel also counter-attacked on the Egyptian side, managing to cross the Suez Canal into Egypt and advance towards Suez. A first ceasefire on 22 October failed, but a second one on 25 October held.

Like 1967, this war had major ramifications throughout the region. Seen largely as a victory by Arab states, it went some way in lifting the burden of defeat experienced six years earlier: where 1967 was a quick, clear and utter defeat, 1973 was more complicated. 1973 also created the conditions for the 1978 Camp David Accords, during which Sadat normalized Egypt's relations with Israel, receiving Sinai in return (see Figure 3.1). Scholars like Hazem Kandil have argued that Sadat used

Figure 3.1 Egyptian President Anwar Sadat, US President Jimmy Carter, and Israeli Prime Minister Menachem Begin. Credit: Photo12 / Universal Images Group / Getty Images.

1973 as a chance to fully delegitimize the Egyptian military and gain favour with the Americans. Through giving them a series of concessions during the Israel-Egypt conflict, Egypt was eventually defeated and forced to sign the Camp David Accords.[12] Kandil demonstrates that a defeat for Egypt was far from inevitable, and that it was Sadat's decisions throughout the war that had made it the only possible outcome. 'The president's plan had been to wage limited war, which was only meant to act as a catalyst for political settlement'.[13] Saad el Shazli, an incredibly popular military officer whom Sadat had removed, was to write in this memoir that the 1973 defeat had not been due to military incompetence: 'Egypt's soldiers and Egypt's commanders were of a high standard and they fought well, but they were let down by their political leaders'.[14]

On the other hand, to many 1973 was seen as a victory rather than a second defeat. After all, the aim of the war had been to regain Sinai, which Sadat ultimately managed to do. One can always ask the question: at what expense?; what I am more interested in here is the how the 1967 and 1973 wars represented very different moments, despite being just six years apart. 1967 and 1973 are symbolic of the fall and rise of two very different ruling classes and projects. 1967 was symbolic of the defeat of Nasserist hegemony, of pan-Arabism, of anticolonial nationalism, and of independent economic development. 1973, on the other hand, was symbolic of a new Egypt that was now open to the world, economically, culturally and politically; it was also symbolic of the rise of Sadat. Indeed 1973 would be Sadat's main attempt at creating consent around his project and producing the kind of stature for himself that Nasser had enjoyed.

Nasserist social forces that supported state-led capitalist development, industrialization, and a strong public sector had dominated for over fifteen years. These forces had succeeded in strengthening the public sector, undercutting the power of the landowning bourgeoisie, reducing the influence of foreign capital, and pushing for industrialization based on an ideology of national capital. However, by the late 1960s the structural constraints facing Egypt and contradictions within the bloc revealed that development along the lines envisioned by the Nasserist bloc was impossible. The very mechanisms new postcolonial nations were trying to reverse in order to gain economic independence

---

[12] 2012. [13] Ibid., 235. [14] Ibid.

An Egyptian Free Market

and forge a new international order eventually ended up defeating them and reasserting colonial era forms of inequality. Egypt's debt had risen tremendously, economic growth had slowed, and the Israeli defeat was a major social, political, and economic shock to the nation. It was only after this defeat that Nasser was to experience low levels of public support. The war was not only a blow to Nasser's popularity, but to the Nasserist project and bloc as a whole. The question of how Egypt should move forward – a question the Free Officers had so successfully answered a mere fifteen years ago – now brought up a range of answers from new social forces. One social force in particular – who favoured free market capitalism as a solution – was to gain enough momentum to forge its own project.

An Egyptian Free Market: The Emergence of a New Project

Frantz Fanon wrote extensively about what he saw as the biggest threat facing African countries after independence: the emergence of a national middle class that was dependent on global capital. Fanon's dependent national middle class was antithetical to the project of anticolonial nationalism, and in many ways represented the demise of the independence spirit. Fanon predicted that this class would emerge at the time of independence, working to destroy the spirit of revolution and progress that had fought for independence up until that moment. Following this, Nasser and the Free Officers could be read as an iteration of Fanon's dependent class, alongside the governments of Kwame Nkrumah, Jomo Kenyatta, Kenneth Kaunda, Julius Nyerere, and others across the continent. I want to suggest, however, that while some of these instances certainly represented a dependent class, many of them were far more complex and contradictory in their effects. In the specific case of Egypt, I posit that the Nasserist bloc in effect delayed the emergence of Fanon's dependent national middle class, which in reality emerged after 1967. It is this class that made up the post-1967 ruling class.

Fanon's aim in tracing the emergence and characteristics of the national middle class was to show how a relation of structural dependency between colonizer and formerly colonized was maintained, even after independence. This allows for a deeper theorization of capitalism in postcolonial contexts, particularly in terms of how capitalism is reproduced before and after colonial rule. This class was not simply a natural by-product of capitalism that evolved organically in these contexts, but a result of the colonial process itself. Fanon's conception of a dependent class not only manifests itself most clearly with the new post-1967 project, but also provides a way of connecting the transnational to the national at the moment of neoliberal emergence.

Fanon's attempts at deepening the Marxist notion of a ruling class resulted from his understanding of the different relationship between base and superstructure in the colonial context. In *The Wretched of the Earth*, Fanon argues that the national middle class that took power in most African countries after independence failed in its task of rejecting neocolonialism and pursuing independent economic development. Instead, it sought to connect itself to the capitalist core and further impoverish countries yet to recover from the colonial experience. By failing to become a bourgeoisie – as happened in Europe – this middle class ended up using nationalism in the worst way possible. Westernized and speaking a different language, this class had become detached from the rest of the country, unable to lead it. Fanon's harsh assessment of this class is often connected to the class structure in colonial contexts:

The national bourgeoisie, which takes over power at the end of the colonial regime, is an underdeveloped bourgeoisie. The national bourgeoisie is not geared to production, invention, creation, or work. All its energy is channeled into intermediary activities. Networking and scheming seem to be its underlying vocation. The national bourgeoisie has the psychology of a businessman, not that of a captain of industry.[15]

The extraction of natural resources and the setting up of an entire infrastructure solely geared towards exporting these resources to the colonial metropolis – to meet their industrial needs – is the initial moment when African countries are drawn into the global capitalist system. This infrastructure did not simply disappear at the moment of independence; it continued to structure relations between industrialized and dependent countries.

As I argued in the last chapter, the Nasserist project attempted to break with this infrastructure of domination. This project represented a change in production that is out of line with Fanon's description. The Nasserist

[15] 1963, 98.

An Egyptian Free Market

project was about industry as the basis of production, and a new social force was cultivated that was to be a central locus of capital accumulation: the public sector, managed by a new technocratic/bureaucratic class. This social force was not directly connected to an independent source of capital or wealth, such as land or industry, but they were connected to the state and the Free Officers. While this social force did not have the material means to organize production according to their own interests, the state did. The various changes put in place by the Free Officers did not eliminate the foundation of capitalism in Egypt, but did restrict the space within which capitalists could operate, especially with regard to foreign investment. It was this space that expanded once again during the shift to the new project. This new project was very much articulated opposition to the project it was trying to displace: Nasserism.

The Sadat years (see Figure 3.2) are known for *infitah*, the opening of both Egypt's markets and Egypt more broadly, to the rest of the world. One could ask what this commonly heard phrase means, since Egypt had been open to much of the world for decades; anticolonialism was anything but parochial. Perhaps a more accurate description is that Egypt under infitah was finally open to the West – in particular Western capital – and

Figure 3.2 Anwar Al-Sadat. Credit: Evening Standard / Getty Images.

that Egypt's markets were open to the new emerging common sense around neoliberal economics. Despite the crisis of hegemony Egypt's ruling class had been facing since the mid 1960s, the emerging social force attempted to resolve this political crisis in two ways: through highlighting the failure of the Nasserist historical bloc and discrediting the project Nasser had symbolized; and through a transnational re-positioning that gained Sadat much-needed Western support. Fanon's insight that postcolonial nations can rule for a limited time by relying on transnational forces is central to understanding the ruling class around infitah. The infitah ruling class was able to rule not because they built high levels of consent inside Egypt (as the Nasserist bloc had) but because they were able to capitalize on a growing global consensus around neoliberalism as well as to rely on the US and other Western powers for both material and ideological support.

Perhaps one of the glaring contradictions of the 1970s and 1980s is that despite the absence of hegemony, the new ruling class ruled over one of the biggest transitions in modern Egyptian history. The new social force that came together around free market economics is infamous for its rapid rise to riches through new forms of accumulation, as well as the new norms and values it embodied and spread. It is also known for facilitating the rise of corruption at the level of business and politics, which intensified with the financialization of the Egyptian economy in the late 1990s. While Egypt's process of neoliberalization only took off in the early 1990s – ironically after the rise of a new ruling class – the foundations of a free market project were laid post-1967. As I noted, the shift towards a new project began while Nasserism was still very much alive; the social forces that made up the infitah ruling class gained momentum after the 1967 defeat and were able to push forward their solution of free market economics.

The economic, political and social chaos that followed the defeat opened up the necessary space for the long-brewing tension between state-led capitalist development and free market economics to explode through the surface. It is not that there was no support left for state-led capitalist development, or continuing along the path that had been set since 1952; there were still those who saw it as the best way forward, in spite of the economic crisis Egypt was in. But this crisis, combined with the shock of the defeat, meant that Egyptians were looking for something different. Sensing this, those in support of the free market transition made their case: the only way forward was to try something radically different. A free market meant not only a shift in economic

An Egyptian Free Market

direction, but also a move towards liberalism, towards a different political system. Given the extremely low levels of support Nasser was experiencing at this particular moment, it is no surprise that people began to imagine the possibility of a different way of doing politics.

These low levels of support didn't last long, since we know that there was widespread opposition to Nasser's resignation, as well as the massive outpouring of grief that erupted when he died. And yet this moment is important because it was the beginning of the demise of the Nasserist bloc, even while Nasser was still in power – and even then, Nasserism as a project of the imagination was to live on for a very long time. The shift from one project to another was therefore larger than a simple transition of authority or a change in political authority.[16] Ibrahim Aoudé has argued that the structural changes that took place under Nasser marked the beginning of capitalist development in Egypt and that Sadat merely continued this under new conditions.[17] For him, the 1967 defeat marked a turning point after which the same class fractions involved in national capitalist development decided structural changes were necessary, a decision that ultimately reinvigorated a seemingly dormant social force that pushed for Egypt to be integrated into the global economy. This shift was what ultimately provided the momentum to a new social force, one that had already started pushing back against some of the Nasserist bloc's economic policies. 1967 represented a moment during which they could re-exert control over the economy.[18] It was this social force that came to dominate under Sadat.

The Decline of the Nasserist Bloc

Anwar el Sadat officially came to power on 15 October 1970, after Nasser passed away from a heart attack. One month into his presidency, Sadat outlined the main elements of his political and economic programme in a statement to the National Assembly. These included: completing the base of a heavy industry in Egypt in order to guarantee that the economy would

---

[16] Ayubi 1982, 280.

[17] 1994, 1. I would disagree and instead posit that the beginning of capitalist development in Egypt can be traced back much further, at least to the reign of Ismail Pasha.

[18] I use the term *re-exert* here because this social force was not new in any sense but rather can be traced back to the social forces that dominated Egypt pre-1952, made up largely of agrarian interests and businessmen with close ties to foreign capital.

be an industrial one; transforming scientific agriculture and achieving self-sufficiency; freeing the Arab lands that had been conquered by Israel in 1967; achieving socialism; acting as part of the non-aligned and liberation movements across the postcolonial world; and finally, consolidating Egypt's support for the Soviet Union. Anti-imperialism and attacks against both Israel and the US were made in strongly worded terms.

It is these themes that mark most of Sadat's early speeches, and indeed it is difficult to differentiate them from Nasser's speeches and the broader political and economic programme put forward by the Nasserist bloc. If anything, it seems like a replica of it. This supposed continuity between Nasser and Sadat was soon broken, however, and we see the emergence of a new ruling class, a new project, and a new set of ideological justifications. Alongside this was the simultaneous move to discredit the Nasserist project, to render it a failure in order to justify the need for something new. Here I focus on two particular ways in which this new ruling class performed this rupture with the Nasserist project. The first rupture was a primarily material one: the depoliticization of the military, and the replacement of military men with economists, businessmen, and technocrats. The second rupture was an ideological one: the re-representation of the public sector as a barrier to economic growth.

Before exploring these ruptures, I want to touch on Sadat's 'corrective revolution' Although Nasserism can be understood as an instance of a *hegemonic* passive revolution, the project of infitah seems to be a more straightforward instance of 'revolution from above' or 'revolution without a revolution'. A passive revolution happens when the ruling class is able to gather power into its own hands; it is a project focused on prevention – preventing alternative projects from emerging, which could potentially be hegemonic – and not creation. Under infitah we do not see a hegemonic project emerge; but we do see clear attempts at dismantling Nasserism and expanding control over subaltern forces such as students and workers. This began with his corrective revolution, launched in May 1971, which demilitarized the Egyptian cabinet and other political institutions, and purged both the Nasserist elite as well as supporters of Nasserism in various positions of power.[19]

In particular, Sadat targeted Ali Sabri and his group of loyalists, who represented a continuation of Nasserism into the 1970s.[20] The Socialist Vanguard – Sabri's 'special apparatus' – was shut down, and membership

[19] Cooper 1979, 205; Aoudé 2004, 11.   [20] Arafat 2011, 10.

An Egyptian Free Market

in the ASU was opened up to all citizens.[21] Much later, the ASU was dismantled entirely, and both the Misr Party (also known as the Arab Socialist Party of Egypt) and the National Democratic Party (NDP) were formed. This initial defeat of Sabri was important in performing a rupture with the Nasserist project. Replacing Nasserist, leftist and military men were lawyers, economists, and businessmen.[22] The posts occupied by military officers were dramatically reduced, and were to be given only in areas directly related to military expertise. Sadat broke the trend of deputy premiers coming from the military when he appointed Mahmoud Fawzy – a diplomat – in the November 1970 cabinet and Abdel Aziz Higazy – a British-trained economist – in the 1974 cabinet. From 1972, two of the most important ministries – Local Government and People's Assembly Affairs – were demilitarized.[23] Although the post of vice president continued to be given to a military officer – Hosni Mubarak – overall there was a dramatic reduction in the political power wielded by the military under this ruling class.

In the October Paper of 1974, Sadat explicitly blamed the military not only for Egypt's recent military defeat but also for ongoing economic problems, hinting at his intention to open up the economy and in particular reach out to American investors.[24] Much of the tension between the Nasserist and infitah projects was very much centred on the position of the military. The military had already tried to organize a coup against Sadat to prevent him from coming to power, and Sadat in turn quickly removed influential military officers from their posts.[25] This was not necessarily because of a conviction that the military should not be involved in politics; rather it was a question of what kind of politics the military favoured. The military had been part and parcel of Nasser's bloc and were the central proponents and beneficiaries of the state-led capitalist development project. For many military men, a move towards free market capitalism was not – at that time – in their interest.[26]

In the battle between the new social force and the military, it was ultimately the military that lost. Sadat successfully removed them from

---

[21] Ibid.   [22] Ibid., 11.

[23] The 1973 cabinet was an exception – with a large number of military officers – but this can be explained by the October War. Soon after the war ended, key posts were returned to civilian politicians.

[24] Ibid., 261.   [25] Bou Nassif 2013, 510.

[26] Indeed, large numbers of military officers had resigned as a protest against Infitah, and the anti-Communist role now assigned to the military was not well received (Dekmejian 1982).

political posts and redirected military energies towards economic investment. The military were still a part of Egypt's ruling class; this has not changed since 1952. What has changed is the power they have wielded within successive ruling classes; in other words, their *position* within the ruling class. During the Nasserist bloc they were the centre of the ruling class alongside the public sector elite, exercising both political and economic power; under the new infitah ruling class they were mainly able to exercise economic power. As opposed to Nasser, Sadat instead aimed to depoliticize the military entirely and redirect them towards the types of economic investments available under infitah.

The military's economic empire very much depended on another major shift that took place under infitah: the expansion of the private sector. This is the second major rupture performed vis-à-vis the Nasserist bloc, given how central it was to drawing the lines around the new project. It was the public sector in particular that was to come under attack in a broader attempt to discredit state-led capitalist development. By the late 1960s, the dominant narrative was that the public sector was experiencing a crisis.[27] The problem, it was understood, was that the Nasserist bloc had not seriously reformed the structure of the public sector, making it unable to deliver on promises the bloc made such as the provision of full employment to all university graduates. Such complaints were used to push for a strong private sector that would replace the 'failing' public sector. But was the public sector actually failing?

In a detailed exploration of Egypt's public sector, Nazih Ayubi shows that most public sector firms at the end of the 1960s were neither inefficient nor performing as badly as assumed.[28] The public sector was not 'failing' in any sense. Similarly, Hazem Kandil argues that despite the conventional account which emphasized that Egypt could no longer afford the losses generated by its failed public sector, at the start of the International Monetary Fund (IMF) programme, 260 out of the 314 state-owned companies were profitable, 54 were suffering losses, and the rest were breaking even.[29] Looking at the specific question of whether the public sector was losing money, Timothy Mitchell also argues that it was simply not the case, citing the year 1989/1990, during

---

[27] Ayubi 1980, 280.   [28] Ibid., 282.   [29] 2012, 352.

An Egyptian Free Market 175

which 260 out of 314 non-financial state-owned companies were profitable.[30] Rather than having any basis in how the public sector was actually functioning, the need to represent it as having failed should be understood as part of a shift towards a strong private sector – a key element of the new infitah project. The material shift from investing in a public sector to instead investing in a private one necessitated the reframing of the public sector as having failed. This in turn was linked to a broader failure: that of the Nasserist bloc's entire project.

Recalling the centrality of state-led capitalist development through industrialization, it makes ideological sense for the public sector to have come under attack. The public sector was very much the symbol of independent industrialization, for not only had it been expanded under Nasser, this happened at the expense of the private sector. The shift to neoliberalism necessitated a reversal of this dynamic, with the private sector coming to dominate. This touches on a broader point, namely the resistance of Sadat and future ruling classes to making industry the basis of the Egyptian economy. The international project of neoliberalism was very much based on retaining the colonial dynamic whereby the industrialized West added value to products exported from the postcolonial world, in particular Africa. Central neoliberal reforms such as privatizing social services hit Africa and the rest of the postcolonial world first, and free trade (free within certain limits) meant that many postcolonial countries could not protect their industries and had to become increasingly dependent on foreign capital. The private sector was the mechanism through which this process largely took place.

It was not enough to represent the Egyptian public sector as having failed; the private sector – strictly controlled by the Nasserist bloc – also had to be constructed as a worthy alternative. Here the idea of efficiency was key; an idea that slowly made its way into the restructuring of many companies. Take the example of a specialized company for hard currency foreign transactions that was set up in 1971. Workers in the already-existing trade company complained to the Arab Socialist Union about a company being set up solely for this purpose, and a debate began in the National Assembly.[31] In one example, a minister claimed that a specific company had gone into a deficit when it tried to

---

[30] 1999, 11.   [31] Cooper 1979, 488.

176 *Laying Neoliberal Foundations*

assume free currency operations, and that there was a need to create a new, more efficient company to replace it.[32] Workers in the old company argued against this, claiming that 'tying income to "work" and "productivity", imposing economic criteria, would damage their interests in the structure'.[33] Both the language used by the minister and the response by the workers hint at a changing landscape; the 'practice of free market activity' was now a priority.

The notion of efficiency was important in this attempt to make the private sector central to accumulation, and this case shows how it was used by the new ruling class while also being resisted by labour who saw through the language of productivity. As Frederick Cooper notes, 'This policy of liberalisation, when it impinged on the public sector, meant change in the distribution of resources – either between the public and private sectors, or among units within the public sector – and immediately raised political temperatures'.[34] It was politically controversial, especially for Egyptian labour, because any limitations put on the public sector were seen as an attack on the socialist nature of Egypt's economy, and thereby an attack on Nasserism. Interestingly, calls for regulating the public sector during this period were often made using the language of science and scientific management.[35] This is a marked departure from the common usage of scientific management under the Nasserist bloc as a means of achieving Arab socialism. We can see here again how this new ruling class used familiar terms that had initially been given meaning by Nasser in order to capitalize on their popular currency, even as over time the terms started to take on new meanings: 'There was a particular emphasis on the theme of continuity with the principles of the 1952 revolution: that infitah is not a retreat from socialism but rather a policy for achieving the same goals'.[36]

The shift to making the private sector central to accumulation necessitated a whole range of institutional changes, key among these changes to Egypt's legal system. Attracting foreign investment meant that Egypt needed independent courts that could guarantee foreign companies legal protection, especially given Nasser's move to sequester foreign companies. It was for this very reason that an independent constitutional court was established: the Supreme Constitutional Court. Nasser's nationalizations in particular had shaken investor confidence, and thus ensuring property

---

[32] Ibid., 489.   [33] Ibid.   [34] Ibid., 488.   [35] See Sidqi, in Cooper 1979, 492.
[36] Dessouki 1981, 410.

Infitah   177

rights was imperative in order to attract foreign investment. These legal changes encapsulate the priorities of the infitah ruling class, which by now had performed a rupture with the Nasserist bloc and project through a series of moves, from depoliticizing the military to changing Egypt's laws around foreign investment. Interestingly, the public sector did not decrease in shape, size, or form in any significant way during this shift; what changed was the expansion of the private sector. A booming consumer market, the rise of a class of Egyptians who wanted to buy luxury imported goods, and the rapid increase in rents and real estate speculation all marked this expansion. These changes also served to underline the differences between one project and the other; but there were to be two more pivotal events that consolidated the infitah ruling class and project: their use of Islamist groups to defeat leftist forces, and the 1973 war.

Infitah

In some ways, Egypt was quite unique within the postcolonial world for the extent to which it embraced both US hegemony and the new neoliberal order. Egypt was the first Arab country to make peace with Israel, and Sadat the first Arab leader to visit Jerusalem. Egypt was also one of the pioneers of the neoliberal shift itself across the postcolonial world. These two transformations – one economic, the other geopolitical – cannot be overstated in their global and national impact, and the new ruling class could not have chosen to signify Egypt's departure from Nasserism any more clearly.

While Egypt was perhaps at the forefront of liberalization in the postcolonial world, it was by no means alone. The government's role as director of the national economy came under attack, and deregulation, reliance on market forces, and disinvestiture became widespread. This dealt a major blow to the provision of welfare, particularly after many countries began signing IMF structural adjustment deals.[37] Alongside these economic changes was an ideology of political liberalism, which references participatory and liberal democratic systems of governance.[38] Moves to privatize, devalue local currency, rejuvenate capital markets, reduce subsidies, and strengthen the private sector

[37] Tschirgi 1996, 9.
[38] For a proponent of this view, see Springborg 1999. He outlines how the literature views liberalization with regard to the Middle East: politically, free elections, less media censorship, associational organizations and the lack of one-

were supported by a growing international consensus that saw development and economic growth as being achievable only through integration into the global capitalist economy.[39] A new common sense had emerged.

In 1974, Law 43 was passed, widely known as the October Paper. This was the legislative basis for infitah. Law 43 created free zone areas in Port Said and other Suez Canal cities, legislated for the relaxation of exchange laws and the facilitation of the repatriation of profits, allowed the private sector access to the parallel market, and curtailed the state monopoly of foreign trade.[40] Combined with Law 32 of 1977, the aim was to redefine the role of the private sector and regulate the public sector through principles of profitability. Over 100 laws were drafted in total, targeting almost all sectors of Egyptian political and economic life.[41] Law 65 of 1971 allowed foreign capital to invest in an extensive number of areas that had previously been off-limits.[42] In 1972, a preferential trade agreement was signed between Egypt and the European Economic Community. Soviet military advisers were ordered to leave Egypt, and diplomatic relations with West Germany were resumed. In 1973, the term *open door policy* was used for the first time in an official government statement.[43]

Infitah itself, then, was a project of refocusing Egypt's economic priorities and shifting the class basis of capitalist power. This involved opening up to foreign direct investment and foreign capital more generally, which in turn involved legal, political, and social shifts. It also involved strengthening the private sector, encouraging foreign banks and businesses through reducing taxes and import tariffs, investing in sectors of the economy such as real estate, construction, and import/export, as well as shifting the focus from industry to other forms of capital accumulation. Peace with Israel, a break with Soviet Russia, and an alignment with the US were also part and parcel of infitah. Infitah should therefore be understood as a holistic project that was not only

---

party rules are what demonstrate that a country is liberalizing. Economically, privatization, currency devaluations, partial flotations, rejuvenation of capital markets and the reduction of subsidies on basic consumer goods are indications of liberalization. In the same article, Springborg goes on to lament that Arab countries would not undergo a 'thorough liberal transformation' engineered by an entrepreneurial bourgeoisie – as happened in Europe. Thus the teleology is made clear, as well as the assumption that Arab countries should follow the path Europe followed in the eighteenth century.

[39] Springborg 1989, 3.   [40] Hamed 1981, 3.   [41] Ayubi 1980, 281.   [42] Ibid.
[43] Ibid.

Infitah 179

material but also ideological; its aim was to transform the economic, political, and social fabric of Egypt.

The shift in economic priorities was swift. On 27 March 1977, the newly created Investment Authority approved 102 projects in five hours.[44] Eighty-one per cent of these were directed to non-industrial sectors such as services and tourism and there was a growth in traded good and services at the expense of traded commodities.[45] One year later, in 1978, 591 enterprises and 312 free zones were approved as part of the infitah project, and the total capital involved amounted to many millions of Egyptian pounds. Foreign investors were guaranteed that their businesses would not be confiscated and did not have to pay income taxes for the first five years.[46] Investment in industry decreased significantly, unsurprising given that the state was no longer actively encouraging investment in industrialization, and that the political stability encouraging investments with long-term pay-offs was missing during infitah.[47] Additionally, foreign investment was now the state's priority; Egyptian investors without foreign capital were at a disadvantage, and in any case, foreign investors were more likely to invest in projects with a quick profit trajectory – naturally excluding major industrial projects.[48]

---

[44] Waterbury 2014, 145. [45] Soliman 2011, 13. [46] Dessouki 1981, 411.
[47] Ibid.
[48] See Zaalouk 1989. Despite this, Soliman goes on to argue that Egypt did experience accelerated industrialization in the latter part of infitah, a process that continued throughout the 1980s and 1990s: the share of industry in GDP increased, and the rate of growth of industry also increased and was above that of numerous other sectors (2011, 16–17). The reasons behind this acceleration were the private sector and the investments made by industrial capitalists. The share of the private sector in industry rose from 36.9 per cent to 55.6 per cent in 1989/1990 (although this was also due to increased privatization of public sector companies) (ibid., 21). Industrialization began to slow down following the IMF's structural adjustment program in 1992. However, it is important to point out that this industrialization process relied on foreign goods and capital in several ways. For example, whenever foreign exchange reserves were low, it became difficult to import needed materials. This was a problem because, as Soliman notes, Egyptian industry was highly dependent on imported machines and equipment (ibid., 23). Another example is the production of motor vehicles. During the 1960s, there was one national company producing cars in Egypt. During the 1980s and 1990s, there were thirteen *foreign* companies producing cars in Egypt. While it is true that they used locally produced components and created local jobs and that local businessmen provided 50 per cent of the capital, the fact that they were foreign is a notable shift from the Nasser period (ibid., 28).

By the mid 1970s, liberalization was an inevitable reality that had set in motion a whole host of economic, political, and societal transformations. The question was no longer whether Egypt should liberalize, but how *much*. Some argued that international capital should dictate all sectors of the economy, including subsidies. This would force public sector companies to operate according to the laws of profitability and would ensure that the state would no longer offer subsidies on a large scale. Others argued that this was too drastic and that it would create deep class tensions. As pressure from transnational actors, including the IMF, pressed Egypt to remove subsidies and float the pound, the ruling class began to experience tensions over how to deal with the liberalization of the economy. Those who resisted the pressure to liberalize completely were dismissed from their positions.[49] By 1976, both the Minister of Economy (Hamid Sayeh) and the Minister of Finance (Muhammad Hamid) were both major supporters of Egypt's drive to liberalize the economy.

One immediate ramification of the new infitah project was the new range of social forces it empowered. One of these, to be discussed further on, was the Muslim Brotherhood; another was the old landed elite that the Nasserist project had attempted to dismantle just decades earlier. Already by 1970, Sadat had formed a committee to address the 'past injustices of land dispossession'. A new law was introduced to regulate landlord–tenant relations, which gave numerous rights back to the landlord that Nasser's reforms had previously taken away, including amendments allowing landlords to evict tenants (following a compensation payment of 10 per cent of the land's market value), limits to the inheritance of rental contracts, and stipulations allowing rent increases of over 100 per cent in some cases.[50] This is not surprising considering the central role land speculation was to play within broader capitalist accumulation during this period; land speculation was a key factor in the rapid increase in the number of Egyptian millionaires which went from zero in 1970 to 17 000 in 1980.[51] Over 90 per cent of building construction during the 1970s went towards luxury villas, apartments, and holiday homes.[52]

The landed elite, then, returned to haunt the 1970s, but not in the same form it had existed under British colonial rule. New investment opportunities allowed for new ways of accumulating capital, and this

---

[49] Ibid., 456.　　[50] Springborg 1990, 449.　　[51] Kandil 2012, 292.　　[52] Ibid.

Infitah 181

in turn transformed and expanded this social force. Many businessmen who accumulated vast amounts of capital during this period were able to draw on power bases outside of the public bureaucracy, such as land. Take Sayyid Marei, for example, who came from an old landed family and who rose to prominence during infitah to become the People's Assembly Speaker. They used this alternate power base to then expand their investment in finance capital, speculation and the import/export of luxury goods, as well as expand their political power.[53] Marei, for instance, was heavily involved in agrarian policy-making, and supported infitah as a means of speeding up production.[54] He pushed for more power for landed families, claiming this was necessary if the state wanted growth in the agricultural sector.[55]

Infitah also placed Egypt on a completely different geopolitical trajectory. Here the porous boundaries between the political and economic reveal themselves; support for US hegemony went beyond mere politics and was very much connected to neoliberal expansion. The USAID programme, set up as infitah was unfolding, insisted on the right to determine Egypt's investment priorities.[56] The US government, claiming that Egyptian debt was a result of Egypt's mismanagement of the national economy, set up an entire programme that served to bolster US capital. US corporations received the bulk of this money, with more than half of the aid package spent on US goods, primarily grain.[57] This quickly created a dependency on importing US food products and equipment, and led to the accumulation of massive amounts of debt.[58] Recalling Timothy Mitchell: 'USAID operates as a form of state support to the American private sector, while working in Egypt to dismantle state supports. None of this is explained in the discourse of USAID itself, which pretends to stand outside Egyptian politics, conducting merely a "dialogue" at the rational, detached level of "policy"'.[59]

International financial institutions similarly began to exert increasing pressure on Egypt's economy and political sphere. The IMF began approaching Egypt as early as 1975, and after one of their initial meetings with the government, they released the following statement:

---

[53] This is a major distinction from the Nasserist bloc, where, because of the dismantling of the agrarian fraction, there was little outside of the state and public bureaucracy from which individuals could draw on as a power base.

[54] Springborg 1979, 54. [55] Ibid., 54. [56] Handoussa 1990, 110.

[57] Mitchell 1991a, 30. [58] Ibid., 31. [59] Ibid.

The Egyptian authorities have reaffirmed their commitment to the 'open door' policy. Domestically, subsidization needs to be sharply reduced to ease the budget deficit and release resources for investment. The structural imbalances in the Egyptian economy are particularly severe in the external sector. To correct these imbalances, it is essential to make appropriate adjustments in exchange rate policies.[60]

These structural imbalances and what the IMF saw as Egypt's extremely slow liberalization process led them to increasingly pressure Egypt into signing a structural adjustment deal, which it did in 1977.

The major aspect of this deal was Sadat's promise to cut subsidies and reduce government spending for public services. This led to the first organic crisis the infitah project faced, one that would be repeated several times in the build-up to 2011. Soon after the announcement was made that subsidies would be cut, riots erupted all over the country, later becoming known as the 'bread riots'. Egyptian labour also participated in these riots, which encompassed many segments of Egyptian society.[61] This was the first indication of the power of the workers' movement in its challenge towards neoliberalization. Privatization and liberalization, key policies of the new infitah project, were to hit workers first and hardest.[62] This led to a process of de-industrialization which increased unemployment and decreased wages.[63] Moreover, while workers had had a tenuous relationship with the Nasserist project, this was not the case with the infitah project, which many were more likely to see as especially detrimental to their own futures.[64]

The new ruling class had not, however, predicted the extent of anger and resistance that erupted with the bread riots. The riots left 800 injured, and more than 1200 were arrested. The military had to be called in to bring back public order, following the failure of the police to diffuse public anger. Subsidies were swiftly reinstated. Sadat promptly attempted to blame leftist forces for what was clearly a spontaneous event. Once the streets were back under control, all leftist newspapers were shut down and leaders seen to have socialist, communist, or Nasserist ties were imprisoned.[65] This did not detract

---

[60] IMF 1976, 16–17. [61] De Smet 2016, 166. [62] Ibid., 165.
[63] Kandil 2012, 161.
[64] Sadat, to some extent, had foreseen this and suggested that workers be allowed to buy shares in companies set to be privatized.
[65] Posusney 1997, 237.

Infitah 183

away from the gravity of the situation; these riots were a clear signal to the new ruling class – only three years after infitah had officially been launched – that consent for the direction this new project was taking Egypt in simply did not exist in any meaningful way.

I want to underline the gravity of the bread riots because they were a clear indication of the failure to build hegemony early in the infitah project. The riots signalled the weakness of relying on transnational finance – such as the IMF – at the expense of internal consent. Moreover, it is no small fact that the riots were connected to subsidies and social services. Here the legacies of Nasserism became visible, a project very much centred on the provision of welfare. Attempts to discipline workers and Egyptian society more generally through the withdrawal of subsidies – a form of coercion – simply would not hold if they were not justified or legitimized through some level of consent. What is even more interesting is the inability of coercion to control the crisis once it erupted: the fact that police forces could not bring back public order highlights the limits of coercion. There were many lessons here, perhaps the most pertinent one the need for internal consent if a ruling class wanted to avoid major organic crises that challenged their position. In the end, though, only one lesson was learned from this: the need to bolster security forces in order to make coercion more effective. The 1990s and 2000s saw a massive expansion of security forces, making it no surprise that the first day of the 2011 revolution – 25 January – was held on a day meant to celebrate the police.

Sadat's decision to reinstate subsidies is also no small part of this story. Ultimately his attempt to accelerate neoliberalization failed, because of a massive act of resistance on the part of Egyptians. This would play out across the postcolonial world, where protests, demonstrations, and strikes erupted in response to IMF structural adjustment deals. The bread riots were symbolic of the struggle Egypt's elites were to face until 2011: how to balance the narrow interests of the ruling class to accumulate capital through free market reforms on the one hand, and the need to create some level of consent to maintain political stability on the other. The public response to the cuts was colossal, and while it was not enough to dislodge this ruling class or the infitah project more broadly, it did signal the absence of widespread support for Egypt's free market reforms. Yet this project continued unabated for forty years to come. What was it about this project that allowed it to survive such a massive political crisis? The answer, I suggest, lies in its reliance on external forces to construct and defend its implementation. Further on in the chapter, I turn once again to the question of the international – one that was still very much colonial, despite the challenge anticolonial nationalism had posed. The next section charts the relationship between the new ruling class and its significant domestic friends and enemies.

Sadat, the Students, and the Islamists: From Left to Right

A central argument of this chapter is that Sadat was unable to create hegemony in the way Nasser had just decades before. Here I touch on two shifts that took place in the 1970s and 1980s that suggest the absence rather than presence of hegemony: the brute coercion used to deal with the student movement on the one hand, and the transformation of the Muslim Brotherhood into a central pillar of neoliberal accumulation on the other. Both the student movement and the Brotherhood represented trends within society that called for political change. The student movement, which arguably had a more comprehensive programme, managed to mobilize public support in the years after the 1967 defeat and call for structural political transformations. In response, Sadat employed both manipulation and coercion to completely demobilize the movement; this is in comparison to Nasser who instead had made use of both coercion and consent. The Brotherhood, on the other hand, were used by the new ruling class as a counterbalance to leftist forces; indeed as the Brotherhood were let out of jail, many leftists took their places (again). The use of the Brotherhood as a counterforce to leftists not only worked to co-opt the Brotherhood and destroy what was left of the left after Nasserism, but also contributed to the economic empire the Brotherhood would acquire during infitah.

Taken together, these two moments under the new ruling class suggest the absence rather than presence of hegemony. The decision to use coercion alone to deal with the student movement as well as the incorporation of the Brotherhood through financial incentives rather than ideological commitments both differentiate the infitah project from the Nasserist one. While one could argue that the Brotherhood accepted the legitimacy of the new neoliberal turn, and indeed were one of its major beneficiaries, this did not neatly translate into broader support for the new infitah project as a whole.

Sadat, the Students, and the Islamists

By the end of the 1970s, the student movement had been demobilized, leftists were in prison, and the Brotherhood had become a central player within Egypt's new economic empire – alongside, ironically, the military. Nasserism created a historical bloc by including students through ideological consent mixed with forms of coercion, and excluded the Brotherhood using coercion; Sadat likewise excluded certain groups through coercion – such as students – but had not managed to include groups such as the Brotherhood through ideological commitment. It is precisely because of this that we can pick out the absence of consent, or, further on, hegemony.

The (Second) Demise of the Left and the Return of the Brotherhood

It is commonly held that the Muslim Brotherhood made their comeback during the 1970s and 1980s, not least because of Sadat's decision to use them as a counterweight to leftist forces. Many Muslim Brotherhood members were released from jail, and replaced with the Nasserists and leftists whom Sadat saw as the biggest threat to his project. This heralded a new era during which Islamist influence over society and the economy spread; culminating in their success in various elections throughout the 2000s. In this section I look at the Muslim Brotherhood in particular, tracing their re-emergence after 1967 as well as their expanding economic empire that very much depended on infitah and the changes it brought about. I conclude by exploring the relationship between the Muslim Brotherhood and hegemony, given that they are often thought to be a social force that could, in theory, produce the type of consent needed for a historical bloc and hegemonic project. Yet this has never quite materialized, whether because they were excluded and repressed under the Nasserist project, or because they were deeply implicated in the infitah project.

One of the major beneficiaries of infitah were undoubtedly businessmen of various Islamist stripes who were able to amass vast amounts of wealth during these decades. An archetypical example is Khairat al-Shatir, who was born in the Nile Delta town of Mansoura. He was involved in the socialist Vanguard Organisation, and took part in the student protests of the late 1960s. He later joined the Muslim Brotherhood, moving to Saudi Arabia, and then later Jordan, Yemen, and England. By 1987 he had returned to Egypt, after losing a lot of money in a currency exchange business. Then his luck changed: he partnered with Hassan Malik, a wealthy Brotherhood member, and launched a computer technology company called Salsabil. In 1995 he was put in charge of Brotherhood finances, and soon opened in businesses in a variety of fields, from tourism to pharmaceuticals. After serving a prison term for funding the Brotherhood, he became deputy General Guide before serving a second sentence in 2006.[66]

Similarly, several Brotherhood businessmen 'made' themselves through the burgeoning field of Islamic finance and banking in the 1970s and 1980s. Another prominent example is Youssef Nada, who pioneered modern Islamic finance in Egypt alongside building an empire in trade, construction, and transport. Appointed as the Brotherhood's foreign minister, he negotiated with Khomeini and his successor, Saddam Hussein, the al-Saud family, the rulers of Qatar and Yemen, and the various Afghani warlords, and liaised with Islamist movements, including the Tunisian al-Nahda.[67] What is notable is the major role businessmen like Shatir and Nada played in the organization, and the immense power they held. As noted by Beinin, 'The leadership of the Muslim Brothers in the 1970s and 1980s was associated with old-money and landed families, a tendency that began when Hasan al-Hudaybi became General Guide in 1953. The family of his successor, 'Umar al-Tilmisani, owned 300 feddans (acres) and seven houses. Al-Tilmisani's deputy and eventual successor as General Guide, Mustafa Mashhur, came from a wealthy land-owning family in Sharqiyya province'.[68]

A large class of Islamist businessmen was thus created, who took advantage of the proliferating business opportunities arising from infitah. The gradual withdrawal of the state from providing social services also created new spaces in which Islamists were able to expand their influence through providing these services, and charitable associations became a central aspect of Islamist businessmen's prominence in many parts of Egyptian society. What is notable here is that it was the money made from investments following infitah that allowed Islamist businessmen to invest in these social services that in turn gave them political power.[69] In a monthly publication supported by some of these businessmen, Nasserist policies such as land reform and nationalizations were

---

[66] Kandil 2015, 78–9. [67] Ibid., 79–80. [68] 2005a, 12.
[69] For an important text on this, see Hanieh 2016.

Sadat, the Students, and the Islamists 187

severely criticized, and neoliberal policies were presented as desirable.[70] By the 1980s, eight of the eighteen families that controlled the private sector were connected to the Muslim Brotherhood.[71]

Sadat eventually cracked down on more extreme Islamist groups such as al-Jama'a al-Islamiyya, which led to his assassination by splinter group Jihad in 1981. Both of these groups were pursued by the state following this assassination, only to re-emerge in the 1990s and carry out a series of deadly attacks on Copts and tourists, most notably the Luxor attack in 1997 which killed more than sixty people. These violent attacks alienated the majority of Egypt's population, and played a role in the inability of these groups to develop a large social base.[72] These attacks mirrored earlier ones such as an attempted assassination on Hosni Mubarak during a trip to Ethiopia as well as the assassination of secular journalist Farag Fouda in 1992.

Hazem Kandil has made the interesting observation that the Muslim Brotherhood was an unusual phenomenon because it was essentially an ideology without intellectuals. Although it positioned itself – and was positioned by history – as the only viable alternative after the defeat of anticolonial nationalism – it did not necessarily have a solid project that could *act* as an alternative. In other words, the Brotherhood did not have the organic intellectuals who needed to do the work of spreading a new project that could ultimately become hegemonic. Take for example a comment given by one of the group's leading businessmen after 2013 stating that there was nothing unsound about Mubarak's economic programme – it had simply been undermined by monopolies and corruption; the Muslim Brotherhood would thus leave these policies in place and instead focus on corruption.[73]

At the same time, Kandil suggests that despite the lack of new ideas put forward by the Brotherhood, their move to ask Muslims to reflect on the discrepancy between what Islam asks for and what Muslims today are doing represents a 'Gramscian strategy par excellence'[74] because any counter-hegemonic movement must push people to reflect on the contrast between two conceptions of the world, one imagined and one in action. While this is true, it can only exist as a first step on the path to hegemony. For hegemony to be achieved, there must also exist an actual hegemonic project that includes political, economic, and

[70] Kandil 2012, 163. [71] Ibid. [72] Gerges 2000, 593. [73] Kandil 2014, 46. [74] Ibid., 51.

social strategizing. While this existed within the Brotherhood itself, at no point was there a strong enough project that could spread through society and create a Brotherhood-led hegemony. Similarly, Chalcraft argues that the Muslim Brotherhood *sought* to achieve its goals through a war of position in the Gramscian sense, first by calling for the moral reform of individual Muslims; second through organizational development; and third through acquiring state power.[75] He goes on to note that the Muslim Brotherhood achieved the first two steps, but not the third, precluding the possibility of hegemony.

There was one moment, however, during which the seeds of hegemony appeared to be sprouting: 1967. One of the consequences of the defeat of 1967 was the rapid spread in popularity of the Brotherhood across various parts of Egyptian society. Nazih Ayubi notes that there were three responses to the question Egyptians asked themselves in 1967 – 'Why were we so utterly defeated?' – a social explanation that blamed the bureaucratic army and the lack of popular participation in society; a technological explanation that blamed underdevelopment and called for modernization; and a religious explanation that blamed the lack of piety on the part of Egyptians.[76] It was this religious explanation that was to be the basis of the Brotherhood's resurgence. At a deeper level, the defeat of one project – anticolonial nationalism – which I argue was hegemonic – led to the search for an alternative project; one of these alternatives ended up being an Islamic-oriented one. This does not mean, however, that this alternative was hegemonic; as we will see, it failed to create hegemony.

Where 1967 became symbolic of the defeat of anticolonial nationalism, 1973 was seen as symbolic of the victory of Islam.[77] It was after 1973 that we see the spread of Islamic political ideas throughout society. One sign of this is the tremendous success the Brotherhood had in taking over student organizations and professional syndicates from the 1970s onwards. Twenty-one syndicates – including more than 2.5 million members – came under Brotherhood control, including the secular Lawyer's Syndicate in 1992. This dislodged the more critical student movement led by Nasserists and Marxists that had been critical of Sadat's failure to regain Sinai from Israel. According to some, Sadat called on Muhammad Osman Isma'il to 'encourage the formation of Islamic student groups on university campuses'.[78] It was this group of

---

[75] 2016, 293 (italics mine).   [76] 1980, 489.   [77] Ibid., 491.   [78] Ibid., 10.

Sadat, the Students, and the Islamists   189

student organizations that displaced the leftist ones that had dominated until then, and that began to win landslide elections in various student groups as well as the student union.

Alongside these victories, society underwent a transformation vis-à-vis Islam. Symbols, discourses, and ideas changed, following a more conservative brand of public Islamic piety. There is little doubt that specific elements of Brotherhood influence did become hegemonic, at least culturally. This is particularly in relation to understandings of Islam, what it means to be Muslim, and societal norms and values. The 1970s and 1980s saw dramatic transformations of Egyptian society that were visible in people's dress, public morality codes, and gender norms. This also expressed itself in increased – although not novel – antagonisms towards Egyptian Copts. One sign of this new cultural hegemony was the increasing turn to Islam in political discourse, by both Sadat and Mubarak.[79] Another was the introduction of informal segregation in universities as well as the increasing visible presence of women wearing the veil or face-veil. Yet another was the control exercised by the Islamists in neighbourhoods such as Imbaba, which became known as the 'Islamic Republic of Imbaba'. Beinin has noted that these victories – especially within professional associations suggested the hegemony of Islamism in public culture.[80]

Despite these successes, I argue that the Brotherhood never had a comprehensive project that would have been able to vie for hegemony. To say that the Brotherhood did not create hegemony is not, therefore, to ignore that elements of their ideology did become widespread; rather it is to note that this, in and of itself, was not enough. Firstly, they faced numerous crises that raised questions about their general project. One of the first was the extreme repression they faced in response to the assassination attempt on Nasser; the arrest of most of the organization after its failed 1965 insurgency; the repression they faced by Mubarak in the 1990s; and more recently, the massacre at Raba'a al'Adawiyya mosque in 2013. Internal tensions within the Islamist trend also posed a challenge to the Brotherhood, most notably how to absorb the Salafis, who largely functioned within an organization called the Islamic Group.

[79] Gerges 2000, 604.   [80] Beinin 2005a.

Secondly, their paradoxical positioning as both opposition and supporter of various regimes raises questions around seeing them as 'counter' hegemonic. A particularly turbulent moment came when the Brotherhood endorsed Gamal Mubarak for president, signalling their support for the Mubarak regime. This led to vocal criticism of the Brotherhood from within its ranks, especially from younger members such as Ibrahim al-Hudaybi and Ahmed Samir.[81] This criticism did not lead to significant changes, and thus they ended up joining forces with groups such as 6 April instead. As Joel Beinin notes, Islamism appears to appeal to both the losers and the winners of global neoliberal economic restructuring.[82] This does not, however, detract from the reality that its leadership has generally benefitted from and thus supported this neoliberal restructuring, which, in places like Egypt was very much characterized by an alliance between the state and Islamists against the left. This, in turn, allowed Islamists to create the networks of social welfare for which they are famous and which some claim is the key to their success, as it enabled them to 'speak in the name of resistance to foreign domination and exploitation of "the people"'.[83]

Thirdly, and perhaps most significantly, the Brotherhood's economic approach drew very much from the economic projects in place, rather than formulate a new or critical approach to social justice. In particular, the support the Brotherhood gave Sadat's ruling class and their project of infitah, suggests that their priority is political advancement rather than the articulation of a solid economic project. As noted earlier, much of the current Brotherhood leadership is made up of wealthy businessmen who made their fortunes during infitah as well as their connections to Gulf capital. In some ways, Beinin was correct in noting that political Islam can, and has, served as a cultural framework for capital accumulation.[84]

Finally, the power held by the Brotherhood can often be overemphasized because of a tendency to view them through the prism of the symbolic. The language, ideology, and symbols that they use, as well as the focus on their ideas and how they articulate them,[85] mean that they can often appear to have compelling ideological pronouncements that many Egyptians can relate to, but this does not necessarily translate into the type of consent needed for a hegemonic project. No doubt these ideas are important, but equally significant are the political, economic,

[81] Kandil 2014, 136.   [82] 2005.   [83] Ibid., 7.   [84] 2004, 4.   [85] Ibid., 3.

Sadat, the Students, and the Islamists

and social policies and material changes put in place. In other words, hegemony is not just ideology: it is the co-constitution of the material and the ideational. As such, the Brotherhood can be said to have a *response* to particular historical events such as British colonial rule or the 1967 defeat. As Fawaz Gerges notes, 'Islamism represents less of a coherent ideology and more of a historic reaction and a protest movement against the inadequacies of the two powerful doctrines that shaped the world in the last several decades, namely market capitalism and Soviet communism'.[86] Similarly, Adam Hanieh sees the Muslim Brotherhood in particular as a fraction within the Egyptian capitalist class, rather than as a subaltern force,[87] while Ayubi, reading Islamism through a material lens, argues that 'a discourse like that of the Islamists does not seem to carry much by way of a clear class content. Being essentially an anti-state discourse it often manages to interpellate different or even contradictory classes and forces which may eventually form a power bloc united in its opposition to the state'.[88] In many ways, the Muslim Brotherhood in particular benefitted greatly from neoliberal restructuring, thus enabling them to mobilize business interests in 2012 during Morsi's presidency. It is therefore more accurate to position them as a member of various ruling classes from the time of infitah onwards, who mobilize certain social bases but who ultimately should be analysed as part of the capitalist class.

In spite of the failure of the Brotherhood to create a historical bloc or hegemony, it is clear that the ups and downs experienced by them are very much connected to the rise and fall of various Egyptian projects. Falling out of favour with Nasser and the Officers; being revived by Sadat and infitah; and more recently their precarious situation under Mubarak and post-2013. Similarly, the evolution of the Brotherhood should be placed within a global context: their creation in the 1920s as a response to colonial modernization; their revival after the defeat of anticolonial nationalism in 1967; and the reality that they are a quintessentially modern phenomenon, despite claims to the contrary.[89] There is little doubt that the Brotherhood have experienced repeated bouts of repression, and that this plays a role in the downturn of political Islam; however, as Asef Bayat notes, this is not the whole story. Just as responsible for this downturn is their inability to create sustainable public support, or to formulate a hegemonic project.

[86] 2000, 603.   [87] Hanieh 2013, 171.   [88] 1996, 28.   [89] See Aydin 2017.

1973 and the Student Movement

1972 and 1973 saw the eruption of a major student uprising across Egyptian universities. The student movement emerged at a time of great transition in Egyptian politics, a time during which many were grappling with the disappointment of the failed revolution as well as the after-effects of the 1967 defeat. The student movement represented much more than just the demands of students. As Arwa Salih notes, 'The student groups vigorously channelled the energy of the street to organise and lead the protests in the name of an insurgent dream: to change the future of the nation, to save it'.[90] In particular, the over-arching demand of most Egyptians at this moment was the recovery of national sovereignty – sovereignty it had only briefly held, and that had now been nearly taken away again.

This section traces some of the historical lineages of student activism in Egypt, before showing how 1967 was central to a reawakening of student activism and resistance across Egyptian universities and schools. Students were perhaps the most vocal in challenging Sadat to take back the land Egypt had lost in 1967, as well as calling for broader political and economic changes. Sadat responded to these challenges primarily through coercion, again in distinction to the Nasserist approach to student activism which made use of both coercion and consent. Ultimately, this use of coercion as well as the amount of public support students received were signs that the new infitah project was not as stable as it needed to be in order to become hegemonic.

Student activism was one of the main currents against British colonial rule in the early twentieth century, bringing together far-reaching demands around progressive education, democratic universities, and nationalism. As a movement, it was split between different trends, the most prominent being the Communists, Muslim Brotherhood, and Young Egypt.[91] There were multiple student uprisings before 1952, including two prominent ones in 1935–6 and in 1946. As with other movements, including those led by feminists and workers, students very much understood nationalism and anti-colonialism to be central to their struggle. The first and foremost goal was to liberate Egypt, after which would come particular negotiations around what Egypt would look like.

[90] 2018, 18.   [91] Abdalla 2008, 21.

Sadat, the Students, and the Islamists 193

As I noted in the last chapter, Nasserism as a project paid a lot of attention to education. School and university fees were eliminated, foreign schools were nationalized, technical and vocational education was made widespread, and higher education was massively expanded. New regional universities were built, and student hostels at a low cost and financial assistance were made widely available.[92] In effect, as Ahmed Abdalla points out, this allowed students to move into, or solidify their position within, the middle class with more ease.[93] This to some extent meant that students largely supported the Nasserist project ideologically, at least at the start, given its focus on social welfare as well as its delivery of these social services. As Abdalla notes, 'government control of the student body was not based on coercion alone; it depended also on the wider social and political achievements of the revolution and responded to the government's offer of wider educational opportunities and guaranteed employment upon graduation'.[94]

And yet coercion played no small part in what can only be called the demobilization of the student movement under Nasserism. One contentious issue was the question of democracy: for students, who initially supported the Nasserist bloc and project, the closing down of political space was a worrying development that raised warning signals about the direction of the new ruling class. After several confrontations around this issue, Nasser tried to either channel student energy into official organizations such as the Socialist Youth Organisation or the Liberation Rally – which had a youth section (the Youth Bureau) – or coerce students into silence. This was primarily through expansive control of universities: a military figure was appointed general secretary of university administrations, faculty deans were to be appointed rather than elected; political activity among students was prohibited, and surveillance of security agents who were placed on campuses was extensive.[95] As Reid notes, professors and students were to feel much freer under Sadat than under Nasser.[96]

The picture of student activism under Nasserism is thus complicated, mirroring the experience many other radical movements had with Nasserist hegemony. Reading through the demands students made, over and over again, it is difficult not to feel a great sense of loss at what could have been. Profound demands such as free education, anti-

---

[92] Ibid., 105.   [93] Ibid.   [94] Ibid., 137.   [95] Ibid., 124.   [96] 2002, 218.

imperialist forms of knowledge production, social justice, and universities as spaces of democracy and debate, were made repeatedly throughout the twentieth century by young students who constantly found themselves in confined political spaces and within failing educational infrastructures. As Malcolm Kerr notes, 'they were a generation of students who had the achievements in their memory and lived the defeat in reality'.[97]

The defeat of 1967 changed all of this, because one of its major effects was to re-radicalize the student movement and bring student demands back to the centre of public debate. Students were the most vocal in demanding retribution for the defeat, alongside workers. When the military court announced its verdict on the charges of negligence brought against leaders of the air force – widely seen as responsible for the defeat – demonstrations broke out in Helwan that quickly spread to universities. This wave of uprisings – in 1968 – was taken seriously by the Nasserist bloc given the public sympathy students tended to draw as well as the vulnerability of the ruling class as a whole right after the defeat. Students did not only call for a guilty verdict, but also pushed for more freedom of expression for the press, a representative parliament, the withdrawal of intelligence from university campuses, and laws establishing political freedom.[98] In these demands we can see the clear weakening of Nasserist hegemony; students realized – and emphasized – that the defeat was not solely a military defeat, it was also a political defeat. In other words, questions were being asked about the Nasserist project and the way it had played out politically.

The scale of the 1968 uprising was too big to contain, and the lesson learned from this was that riot police needed to be more prepared in the future; it was specifically after this uprising that the Central Security Forces were created. However, certain university restrictions were lifted, allowing students more space to organize politically. By the time Sadat came to power, the student movement was a major locus of resistance, setting the scene for the 1972–3 uprisings. By this point, the main aims were freeing the occupied territories (both in Egypt and Palestine), and democratizing the political system.[99] The wave of student mobilizations had numerous highs and lows; throughout these they enjoyed widespread public support – including from professional

[97] Ibid., 137.   [98] Ibid., 152.   [99] Ibid., 159.

Sadat, the Students, and the Islamists

syndicates, the intelligentsia, and society more broadly. The ruling class met with student representatives several times, including in parliament, but consistently went back on their word to give in to some of the demands. In a troubling pattern, members of parliament would make agreements with students in order to demobilize them, only to arrest or violently disperse them just hours later.[100]

Sadat realized that public support for the student movement indicated something more than just sympathy; in a special session of the National Congress of the ASU, he made a somewhat conciliatory speech: 'The discontent expressed by the Egyptian youth movement has echoed the general atmosphere of impatience in the country at large. It was only natural that this impatience should surface first among the youth ... I have no wish to contain, isolate or crush the youth movement'.[101] It is precisely the discontent and impatience in society as a whole that provided students with much of their support; they had clearly touched a nerve by centring questions of political and economic legitimacy. Indeed by this point, their demands stretched beyond democratizing politics and regaining Egyptian land and included transforming Egypt's economic structure to make it more equal, which included demands such as ensuring the highest income is never more than ten times the lowest income and that Egypt not link its economy with imperialist nations through free trade zones.[102]

The culmination of this wave of uprisings was the arrest of student movement leaders at the end of 1973. This did not, however, solve the core problem Sadat and the infitah project more broadly now faced, the absence of legitimacy and therefore hegemony:

The political reality of Egyptian student action after 1967 was that it formed a representative movement acting on behalf of a wide range of national forces in the face of territorial dismemberment and humiliating defeat, as well as acting on its own behalf to realise the more typically middle class ambitions for political expression and participation. They were the organised vanguard, not just the youth of the university.[103]

Many of the changes that were yet to come following the official implementation of infitah would affect students in particular. The decision to promote private education meant the proliferation of private nurseries, schools, and universities that cater almost exclusively to

---

[100] Ibid., 188.   [101] Ibid.   [102] Ibid., 190.   [103] Ibid., 215.

Egypt's elite or aspiring elite. An even graver change has been the increasing deterioration of the public sector; although some students benefitted from infitah, the majority continued to rely on employment in the public sector after graduation. As this became increasingly impossible, many turned to immigration instead, primarily to the Gulf states. The reality was that the promises of infitah reached very few.

Alongside changes in Egypt's economic and class structure, other elements of the infitah project were also opposed by the student movement, including its pro-US foreign policy orientation. The student movement continued to be active after 1973, but came to an abrupt end in 1977, following the bread riots. Sadat blamed students for the outbreak of the riots, claiming their political agitation was indirectly responsible.[104] Censorship on campuses, as well as the return of surveillance were instituted immediately, with detrimental effects on the active and energetic movement going into its tenth year.

Gramsci's Interregnum and Fanon's Dependent Bourgeoisie

The infitah project can be characterized by two connected phenomena: Gramsci's interregnum and Fanon's dependent bourgeoisie. A time of interregnum is a time of fluidity and movement; nothing is stable, and so nothing is fixed. Recall Bauman, who wrote that an interregnum is when the frame of a social order loses its grip and can no longer hold, but during which a new frame is not quite able to take its place, because it is not yet strong enough.[105] The infitah project, I have argued, was a frame that was not strong enough to hold, and so society continued to experience a constantly shifting rather than solid social frame. In contrast to the Nasserist project, which was hegemonic and therefore in some ways fixed, the infitah project was constantly in search of hegemony without ever quite finding it. Yet this fluidity and change also produced something tangible which was to have major after-effects across Egyptian society for decades to come: a dependent bourgeoisie. Here I return to Fanon's diagnosis of postcolonial dependency, before concluding with the notion of an interregnum.

I have argued in this book that Fanon's move to trace colonialism's creation of a 'native' or 'dependent' bourgeoisie that reproduced the

---

[104] Ibid., 229.   [105] 2012, 49.

Gramsci's Interregnum and Fanon's Dependent Bourgeoisie   197

relation of structural dependency between colonizer and formerly colonized provides a deeper theorization of capitalism in postcolonial contexts. Fanon's conception of a native bourgeoisie allows for an analysis of capitalist expansion during the new infitah ruling class that connects the national to the transnational at the moment of neoliberal emergence. In this sense, Fanon provides a more expansive version of the Marxist notion of a ruling class. For Fanon, these attempts to criticize and deepen Marxist analysis result from his understanding of the different relationship between base and superstructure in the colonial context. Tracing the emergence of a dependent bourgeoisie under Sadat is partly an exercise in understanding why this dependent bourgeoisie hadn't emerged under Nasser – which is, after all, when Fanon predicted it to emerge.

When the Nasserist ruling class came to power, they addressed the dominance of the private sector by weakening the power of the agrarian faction that dominated it, which was tied to foreign capital and institutions. The aim, however, had not been to eliminate private property itself – which would indicate a stronger socialist transition – nor to institute new relations that would bring back a conceptualization of land as communal; but rather to dismantle feudalism and the agrarian fraction that benefitted from it and replace it with new fractions that would develop the new ruling class's drive towards state-led capitalist development through industrialization. The agrarian law of 1952 that limited personal ownership of land not only weakened the agrarian fraction that accumulated capital through the land, but also affected flows of capital by favouring a new industrial fraction.[106] There were also restrictions placed on foreign capital. These changes significantly affected the space within which capitalists could operate, particularly in regard to foreign investment in Egypt. It was this space that changed during the shift to infitah, as highlight by Sadat's new relationship with capitalists such as Henry Ford (Figure 3.3).

To draw out this shift and the changes it brought about, I focus on the particular case of Osman Ahmed Osman. He is an interesting figure because although he was successful under both Nasser and Sadat, the form this success took varied greatly. Osman rose to prominence under Nasser, and eventually won the tender to build the High Dam. This happened because of the position the Free Officers took vis-à-vis

---

[106] Aoude 1994, 2.

Figure 3.3 Meeting of Henry Ford with Mohammed Anwar Sadat. Credit: Imagno / Hulton Archive / Getty Images.

foreign capital: Nasser had rejected offers from foreign capital to build the Damn because of the conditionalities attached. Instead he turned to Egyptian capitalists and national capital, eventually choosing Osman's company. Osman already enjoyed some special privileges during the Nasser era because of his friendship with Amer: he did not have any workers on his board, for example, in distinction to other companies. Beyond this, Osman kept his distance from politics, seeing Nasser's socialist policies as destructive to the private sector.

It was under infitah that Osman both expanded his economic empire and became involved in overt political life. Sadat's rise to power was supported by Osman, a close friend whose children had intermarried, and soon after Sadat became president Osman became the most prominent businessman in the country, representing the non-agricultural fraction of capital. Altogether, he and his sons founded twenty-six companies.[107] He accepted numerous influential government positions, including minister of reconstruction, deputy prime minister of popular development, and head of the Engineer's Syndicate. Over time, he built an extensive business empire of diversified holdings in the area of construction, including everything from trucking to banking.[108]

[107] Baker 1990, 27. [108] Arafat 2011, 64.

Gramsci's Interregnum and Fanon's Dependent Bourgeoisie 199

Osman was a strong supporter of free market principles and expanding the private sector. Indeed it was his firm belief in these principles that guided his work as a minister in Sadat's cabinet: 'I became convinced that I could serve a useful purpose as a government minister only after I saw [that] Sadat's goals coincided with mine to end the public sector's stranglehold on our economy'.[109] For Osman, freedom under Sadat was different from the 'bread of the socialist era'; the idea of freedom now was about opportunity through hard work and individual effort.[110] He believed that by dismantling Nasser's 'oppressive structures', Sadat was creating opportunities for all Egyptians.[111]

Osman saw private property as essential to the 'new Egypt' and argued that nationalization had had an extremely negative effect on the country. Although he remained firmly against the idea that foreign capital should dominate Egypt, and was also wary of the increasing consumerism among the new generation who were benefitting from the new economic policies, Osman's case suggests that the line between business and politics became exceedingly thin after infitah. Under Nasser, Osman did not exercise the type of political power he had under Sadat. Even more telling, he did not have the ability to determine economic policies and goals under Nasser, despite his significant investments in the Egyptian economy. This highlights the shift from a strong state-led form of development to development based on the market.

In 1963, Fanon wrote:

A bourgeoisie similar to that which developed in Europe is able to elaborate an ideology and at the same time strengthen its own power. Such a bourgeoisie, dynamic, educated and secular, has fully succeeded in its undertaking of the accumulation of capital and has given to the nation a minimum of prosperity. In under-developed countries, we have seen that no true bourgeoisie exists ... This get-rich-quick middle class shows itself incapable of great ideas or of inventiveness. It remembers what it has read in European textbooks and imperceptibly it becomes not even the replica of Europe, but its caricature.[112]

What happened under Sadat is that capital was once again redirected from one place to another. Under Nasser, capital had been redirected away from an agrarian fraction of capital towards industrialization and the public sector. Under Sadat, capital was redirected away from the public sector and towards the private sector. The state was still

[109] Ibid., 25.　[110] Ibid., 26.　[111] Ibid.　[112] 1963, 175.

central; indeed it was the state that redirected investments away from social services and the public sector. As Mitchell notes, 'The reform program did not remove the state from the market or eliminate profligate public subsidies. Its main impact was to concentrate public funds into different hands, and many fewer. The state turned resources away from agriculture and industry. It now subsidized financiers instead of factories, cement kilns instead of bakeries, speculators instead of schools'.[113] Moreover, this arrangement encouraged many within the public sector to grasp the new opportunities infitah brought about for individual gain. The 1990s and 2000s were to follow this trajectory, with finance capital eventually dominating productive capital.[114]

This was the bigger shift between the two eras: the transformation of the economic infrastructure itself, and in particular the role of productive versus finance capital. What Fanon seems to read as a progressive economic project assumes the state and bourgeoisie as relying ultimately on productive capital. Under Nasser, the aim had been to make the public sector the base of the economy, predicated on investment in industry. Under Sadat, we see a reversal of that, with financial speculation – based primarily on land – becoming the main form of capital generation, as well as import and export. This is not new, however, as it reproduces – or rather, returns to – the arrangement in place pre-independence. Capital as unproductive means that land and money were relied on to generate capital, rather than being invested in industry, trade, or other long-term projects.[115]

This has had a dramatic impact, in particular, on the public sector: once the harbinger of development, it has slowly degenerated to its current condition, where it is racked by corruption. Ironically, the criticisms of the Nasserist public sector – that it was unproductive, corrupt, and inefficient – became more pronounced after the shift to a free market system. As Fanon noted, the native bourgeoisie would elaborate an ideology that would strengthen its position in power, and this we saw with both Nasser and Sadat. However, it is only under Sadat that we see the native bourgeoisie as dependent in the Fanonian

[113] 2002, 276.

[114] The argument that capitalism today is marked by prioritizing financialized activities over productive ones has been made by a variety of scholars, including Thomas Piketty (2014), David Harvey (2009), and Adam Hanieh (2013, 2018).

[115] Piketty 2014; Harvey 2009; Hanieh 2013, 2018.

Gramsci's Interregnum and Fanon's Dependent Bourgeoisie   201

sense. Recall the beginning of this chapter and my descriptions of how Egyptian popular culture has represented the Sadat ruling class; it mirrors exactly the terms Fanon uses to describe the dependent bourgeoisie: get-rich-quick, incapable of great ideas or direction, and ultimately nothing more than a caricature of the global Western elite.

I am not suggesting that infitah was the first time we see a dependent bourgeoisie in Egypt. The agrarian bourgeoisie we see in the late 1800s and early 1900s is perhaps the clearest example of one that had come before, given its formation as a class whose sole objective was to profit from Egypt's subservient position within the global political economy. However, Fanon's point is that under colonialism, dependent bourgeoisies are an inevitability; his interest is thus in the postcolonial, precisely because decolonization is meant to signify – at the very least – a break with dependency.

Returning to the discussion about hegemony in the first chapter, I have shown that Fanon's understanding of how a dependent bourgeoisie reproduces itself is an important intervention in Marxist and Gramscian understandings of hegemony. A ruling class in the postcolony does not always need hegemony to rule; it does not always need to universalize its interests successfully. If it can rely on transnational forces and transnational capital, this can make up for a lack of internal consent, as we have seen with the case of the infitah ruling class. While this comes at a price – as it produces an unstable situation and only lasts for a limited time – it does allow ruling classes to forego the problem of legitimacy by instead getting ideological and material support from transnational actors. This, as I show now, reiterates the importance of understanding the international and its colonial nature.

This brings us, finally, to Gramsci's interregnum. An interregnum is a time of uncertainty during which political changes occur but during which a new ruling class is never quite able to create hegemony. Bauman convincingly reads Gramsci's use of the *interregnum* in the following way:

He attached it to the extraordinary situations in which the extant legal frame of social order loses its grip and can hold no longer, whereas a new frame, made to the measure of newly emerged conditions responsible for making the old frame useless, is still at the designing stage, has not yet been fully assembled, or is not strong enough to be put in its place.[116]

---

[116] 2012, 49.

By the defeat of 1967, it was clear that the old was dying. The defeat marked the end of the Nasserist project and bloc, both of which had already experienced several defeats by the time the war with Israel began. And yet, this did not herald a clear shift towards a new form of hegemony; in other words, the new could not be born yet. The conditions that would allow Sadat and a whole host of new social forces to establish a bloc and hegemony simply did not exist.

The project of liberalization that defined the infitah project had economic, political, social, and moral effects that restructured much of Egyptian society. The project imagined a new type of citizen, one that defined himself or herself through social mobility, consumerism, and individualism. Where social mobility during the Nasserist bloc was mobilized in order to modernize the nation, the infitah project mobilized social mobility to create individual wealth. The shift to citizenship-as-consumption was neither accidental not inevitable, but a result of this new project whose material underpinnings were based on import/export, luxury items, rents, and real estate.

It is these realities that made it impossible for the infitah ruling class to create the type of hegemony the Nasserist bloc had created, and that mark this era as the beginning of an interregnum. If the key to creating hegemony is universalizing the narrow interests of one social force and making them seem to be in everyone's benefit, then it is no wonder that this ruling class could not create hegemony by relying on internal consent. It did not take long for many in Egypt to see that this project's ideology of national development did not mean development for the nation nor development for all Egyptians. It is not that the ruling class did not have the material power to spread its ideologies, but rather that they could not create enough legitimacy around them to pierce society the way Nasserist ideologies had just decades before. What *was* different, however, was that they had geopolitics on their side: through forming alliances with Western capital and the US in particular, Sadat took the chance that this would be enough to rule Egypt without rebellion. As I have shown, he was wrong: the bread riots, the riots by security forces, and his assassination all point to the failure of international support in making up for a lack of internal consent. It is here that Fanon's intervention is important for Marxist theory. Ruling classes in the postcolony can rule through international support for a certain amount of time. However, this can never be a long-lasting solution:

at one point or another, the house of cards will fall. For Sadat, this happened with his assassination.

The Return of the Colonial International

The transition from anticolonial nationalism, with its many flaws and pitfalls, to neoliberalism, is a sobering reminder of how difficult the process of decolonization has been. Timothy Mitchell writes:

Neoliberalism is a success of the political imagination. Its achievement is a double one. It makes the window of political debate uncommonly narrow and at the same time promises from this window a prospect without limits. On the one hand it frames public discussion within the elliptic language of neoclassical economics. The condition of the nation and its collective well-being are pictured only in terms of how it is adjusted in gross to the disciple of monetary and fiscal balance sheets. On the other, neglecting the actual concerns of any concrete local or collective community, it encourages the most exuberant dreams of private accumulation – and a chaotic reallocation of collective resources.[117]

What came after this failure was a shift to free market capitalism, also put forward in nationalist terms, albeit no longer of the anticolonial variety. The project of neoliberal restructuring was accelerated soon after, culminating in the 2011 revolution.

If what set the Nasserist project apart was its understanding of the need to re-articulate Egypt's relationship to the international as well as to change the nature of the international itself, then what characterizes the infitah project was precisely that it did not take seriously the dangers of a highly unequal international system. Sadat made a bet that this system would protect him, a bet he ultimately lost. Vivienne Jabri's naming of the 'postcolonial' international as reproducing colonial dynamics is instructive here.[118] I argued in the previous chapter that the Nasserist bloc recognized the colonial nature of the international and that many of its decisions can be understood as attempts to resist its position within this international, a position that was a legacy of British colonial rule. The new ruling class that emerged in the late 1960s, however, chose to reintegrate Egypt into this international order. From the Camp David Accords to infitah itself, the decisions made under this historical bloc brought Egypt back into what was still

[117] 1999, 5. [118] 2012, 103.

a colonial international. What had characterized the Egyptian economy before 1952 returned: a dominant private sector, an emphasis on foreign capital, prioritizing imports over industrial production, and norms and values that saw Westernization as modernization. This was Nasser's greatest fear: 'As he one day told the director of the International Monetary Fund, Nasser was sure a state that basically provides raw materials and services to the industrialized world, and whose economic elite are largely merchants and speculators, rather than industrialists, will shortly become the victim of an unpatriotic, corrupted wealthy class'.[119]

If, as Jabri suggests, the resistance of the postcolonial state should be measured in terms of its relation to the constraints of the international, then there is a sea of difference between Nasser and Sadat. The nationalization of the Suez Canal marked a moment of resistance, whereas the opening of Egypt's economy marked a moment of convergence. Both moments trace a particular relationship between Egypt and the international; but in both instances, the international remains very much colonial in its articulation of global inequality.

The failure to establish hegemony by the infitah ruling class marks this period as the start of an interregnum; a time of uncertainty where the old is dying but the new cannot be born. Although much changed under the infitah project, and although new paths were charted, this did not ultimately lead to hegemony. The 1950s and 1960s in Egypt show a complicated picture: to some extent, much capital and expertise was put at the disposal of the people, in the form of education, employment, and other social benefits. On the other hand, this process was not completed, and the state did not pursue anti-capitalism as a path towards social justice. It was not the people who decided how capital and resources were to be used; it was the new ruling class and the state. By the 1970s, the picture was much less complicated, for it is here when we see the emergence of Fanon's dependent, anti-national bourgeoisie.

Although Fanon was right in his prediction that colonialism would produce a dependent ruling class across Africa, what differs is the temporal emergence of this class. Whereas in some places we see it emerge at the moment of independence, in others – like Egypt – it instead comes later, decades into the postcolonial moment. Egypt's instantiation of the dependent ruling class a la Fanon marks the rise

[119] Kandil 2012, 296.

of infitah as the political project that would dethrone Nasserism, even as it failed to become hegemonic in the same way. The 1960s and 1970s were a time of shifting national energies, and the rise and fall of various social forces, culminating in the decision to open Egypt up to the West. I have read these decades through Gramsci's *interregnum*, to highlight the movement that characterized this period and to reject any notion of fixity or stability. By the time Sadat was assassinated, the infitah project was in place, although not as securely in place as Nasserism had been. Indeed to keep it in place, we see Mubarak and later his son turn increasingly to coercion, moving further and further away from hegemony.

4 | *Finance Capital and Empty Time*

So here was a historic reversal of the revolutionary project, a new historical conjuncture, a moment when all the reference points, the predictions, have been shot to bits. The political universe, as you have come to inhabit it, collapses.

Stuart Hall[1]

If the ruling class has lost consensus, that is, if it no longer 'leads' but only 'rules' – it possesses sheer coercive power – this actually means that the great masses have become detached from traditional ideologies, they no longer believe what they previously used to believe.

Antonio Gramsci[2]

Egypt can be said in a certain sense to be the 'mother of Arab liberalisations'.

Nazih Ayubi[3]

For violence to be seen as acceptable, it must be measured and infrequent.

Farha Ghannam[4]

Mubarak is an accidental president. Even he did not expect to be president of Egypt, thinking Sadat would make him head of Egypt Air or perhaps ambassador to London. Many consider him an unremarkable leader – an administrator more than a politician. He lacks Gamal Abdel-Nasser's charisma or Anwar Sadat's dynamism. Mubarak is stolid, conservative, and predictable.

Alaa al-Din Arafat[5]

---

[1] 2017. [2] 1992, 32. [3] 1996, 339.
[4] Connecting violence and masculinity in particular, she writes: 'Knowing when to use or avoid violence, the right context for its use or avoidance, and amount of violence to use is an important skill that is not mastered by all men' (2013, 120).
[5] 2011, 134.

Finance Capital and Empty Time

Time and the way it is arranged and represented can tell us a lot about the types of political stories we are supposed to know.[6] This chapter traces the ways in which Egypt's postcolonial era is cut up into different parts, and what this 'cutting up' reveals about how we understand modern Egyptian history. In particular, I make two arguments. First, as I noted in the last chapter, we should understand the years between 1967 and 2011 – which saw periods of dramatic change and periods of empty time – as united within a single time frame. Second, I posit that we should understand this period as an 'afterlife' of hegemony, made up of different tempos rather than clearly differentiated projects. While the late 1960s to late 1970s can be seen as a pause, or an interregnum, during which various social forces recalibrated around the project of infitah, the 1980s to mid 1990s can instead be seen as empty time, during which little changed. I imagine this period through the visual of a boat that has just had its engine turned off and is now drifting or moving along with the water. Empty time does not suggest that nothing took place at all but rather that we do not see attempts at creating a political project. I show that when we interrogate the rupture between Sadat and Mubarak, we find that it does not fully exist, since Mubarak's presidency was very much a continuation of the infitah project. This changes from the mid 1990s, when we see a dramatic acceleration of neoliberal restructuring, and the emergence of finance capital along with a new class of businessmen; this attempt was to create the immediate conditions for the 2011 revolution. We can consequently see different movements and tempos within the afterlife of hegemony; but not the presence of different projects, nor the creation of another hegemonic project.

I pick up on the last chapter's discussion of Fanon's dependent bourgeoisie, deepening my exploration of how to 'stretch' Marxism in the postcolony through analysing both dependency and the changing *tempo* of decolonization. Taking seriously the claim that capitalism is intrinsically different in the colonial context, by extension we can assume that the pace at which capitalist time unfolds in the postcolony takes on a different form. This changing tempo is linked

---

[6] See Barak 2013; Hanna 2011.

to both the particularity of capitalism in the postcolony, as well as the afterlife of hegemony; time slowed down, or was empty, because of the emergence of Fanon's dependent bourgeoisie and its inability to form a hegemonic project.

I am especially interested in Fanon's understanding of what a 'real' bourgeoisie ought to do, and the parallels this has with Gramsci's understanding of hegemony. For Gramsci, a class that successfully creates hegemony must be able to maintain a balance between consent and coercion, but also between narrow interests and universalizing reforms. Any successful hegemonic class has to be able to universalize their own interests, both through ideology and through material reforms, in order to rule any given society. If a class is seen as being for itself, it is unlikely to be able to create a historical bloc or hegemony. Gramsci wrote of this balance in relation to Italy; Fanon wrote of this balance in relation to the difference between European and (post)colonial ruling classes. As I have shown, in Egypt the Nasserist bloc realized the form of entrapment this colonial binary entailed, and thereby tried to subvert it by challenging the space in which this binary was produced and reproduced: the international.

Where the infitah ruling class was unable to create hegemony internally and had to draw on transnational forces and a growing consensus around neoliberalism to rule, the financial ruling class that emerges in the 1990s were produced at a historical moment during which even transnational support could not compensate for the lack of hegemony. This historical moment and the shift in tempo that characterizes it – marked by acceleration – ultimately was what destroyed the balance both Gramsci and Fanon spoke of as being integral to hegemony. The acceleration of neoliberal restructuring throughout the 1990s and 2000s swung the pendulum towards coercion and let go of any attempts to represent the new ruling class as anything but a class for itself. Coercion became completely detached from consent, revealing itself for what it was.

In what follows, I outline the attempts by Hosni Mubarak to save the infitah project through the 1980s and 1990s – characterized as *empty time* – before turning to the emergence of a new cabinet that was elected in Egypt in 2004, a cabinet that informally came to be known as the 'cabinet of businessmen'. It was this cabinet that signalled a change in tempo, characterized by the absence, not presence, of a historical bloc, ensuring that these decades were therefore decades without hegemony. Where the infitah ruling class had realized the dangers of drastic economic and political changes without any level of consent – a lesson they learned from the 1977 bread riots – this ruling class paid little attention to the dangers of policies that were seen as illegitimate. This failure highlights the limits of any type of hegemony in the postcolony that does not take internal consent seriously. Transnational forces may sustain a ruling class for a limited amount of time, but this recipe eventually falls apart – precisely what happened in the late 1970s and again in 2011. This chapter is therefore the story of the ruling class that made the 2011 revolution an inevitability.

Empty Time

Hosni Mubarak (Figure 4.1) became president of Egypt in 1981, signalling a new era in Egyptian politics. However, just as the decline of the Nasserist project did not happen with the death of Nasser himself, the decline of the infitah project was not directly related to the death of Sadat. The infitah project continued well into the presidency of Mubarak; its real decline came about in the mid 1990s, by which time Mubarak had already been in power for over a decade and a half. Although the tendency has been to understand modern Egyptian history chronologically through the rise and fall of these various individual leaders, I suggest that this period in particular shows why tracing hegemony and attempts at hegemony prompts us to think of alternate chronologies. This section brings together the idea of *empty time* and Gramsci's concept of *transformismo* – 'damage control' – to read the years between Sadat's assassination and the rise of a new ruling class in the mid 1990s. *Transformismo* refers to an attempt to co-opt rising challenges in order to maintain both the state of consensus and the power and dominance of the ruling social force. The early years of Mubarak's reign can be read as a period of damage control, during which he recognized the need to make a series of changes in order to alleviate some political, social, and economic pressure.

Accounts of Mubarak often describe him through what he lacks: charisma, dynamism, ideology, and a political project; this telling

Figure 4.1 President Mubarak. Credit: Central Press / Stringer / Hulton Archive / Getty Images.

of his story through what he lacks is interesting in light of my designation of this period as *empty* time. It is precisely his lack of an ideological project more broadly that constructs his first fifteen years in power as empty time; political, economic, and social changes were happening, but these were not gathered together under a project in the way we could see under Nasser and Sadat. In other words, from the viewpoint of hegemony, these years were perhaps the clearest point post-1952 during which we see political change happening as a reaction and response rather than as an attempt to produce something new. These years can be read as stable; they can also be read as stagnant, begging the question: what happens when time stops?[7] By reading Hosni Mubarak's first decade and a half in power through the lens of *transformismo*, or damage control, I show that Mubarak did not create a new project, nor did he produce or work with a clear social force that had its own project. Instead, Mubarak's goal was to deal with rising discontent from various sections of society towards the infitah

---

[7] Osama Ghazali Harb, an academic, editor and Shura Council member, once said, 'We have not suffered from stability. We've suffered from total stagnation, total stagnation from 1980 until now' (Arafat 2011, 167).

Empty Time   211

project, a project he more or less continued. This move towards damage control, however, also laid the ground for a new social force to emerge halfway through his reign, one I refer to as the financial class. Through IMF-led structural adjustment in particular – a direct attempt at mediating the problems facing Egypt's economy – Mubarak set the scene for the acceleration of privatization that was to mark the new social force and its overall project of accelerated neoliberal restructuring.

When Hosni Mubarak became president, Egypt was once again experiencing a period of economic crisis. Challenges to the social order from the rise of new social forces as well as new ideas need to be co-opted and absorbed for hegemony and the historical bloc to stay in place.[8] This has been one of the historical forms of 'passive revolution' – or revolution without revolutionary change.[9] Some of the moves Mubarak initially made upon coming to power demonstrate an awareness among some within the ruling class that the imbalance between coercion and consent was dangerous. Mubarak is known for his overtures to the media, allowing them new freedoms, as well as for releasing political prisoners during the 1980s. Mubarak increased Egypt's production of housing and medicine, and indicated he would be less open to Israeli cooperation than Sadat had been. Notably, he did not fully support the complete withdrawal of the state from providing subsidies.[10] Having learned the lessons of the 1977 bread riots, he clearly saw the need to undo some of the damage that had been done by Sadat's coercive policies. Despite this, two major developments took place during the 1980s and 1990s that deepened neoliberal restructuring without necessarily changing the pace at which it had been happening, thereby weakening consent even further. The first is the IMF deal and its devastating effects; and the second is the increasing dominance of the military within the Egyptian economy.

Structural Adjustment and Privatization

Structural adjustment – put forward by the IMF and World Bank – has been a central mechanism in deepening privatization across the

---

[8] Gramsci 1971, 157.   [9] See Sassoon 2001 on passive revolution.
[10] Abul-Magd 2017, 93.

212   *Finance Capital and Empty Time*

postcolonial world. Targeting primarily social services provided by the state, structural adjustment has weakened the ability of the public sector to provide education, health care, and employment on the one hand, while leading to the dramatic increase in privatized services that benefit an increasingly small group on the other. Egypt's structural adjustment programme was implemented under Hosni Mubarak, and very much laid the ground for the new ruling class that would emerge in the mid 1990s. Through its insistence on Egypt's need to speed up its privatization programme, the IMF and World Bank contributed directly to the emergence of this ruling class, whose acceleration of neoliberal restructuring would lay the immediate foundations of the 2011 revolution. In this section, I trace the emergence of Egypt's structural adjustment programme, before turning to the role of the military in this broader project of privatization in the next section.

Like Sadat, Mubarak inherited a country full of economic problems. In particular, the activities around foreign capital investment were proving costly, notably speculation and short-term ventures of investors and their foreign partners.[11] On top of this, the consumption tendencies directed towards imported luxuries were the purview of a small elite, and yet had massive costs for the national economy.[12] The twin dominance of consumption and speculation meant that Egypt's productive industries were weak. Corruption had become endemic, primarily in the public sector, which could no longer produce the jobs needed. Foreign debt increased exponentially during the 1970s and 1980s, and by 1989 Egypt had to declare bankruptcy. In other words, the economic prosperity promised by the turn towards infitah did not materialize; instead, Egypt was once again in a deep economic crisis.

This crisis was one shared with other countries across the postcolonial world. In some ways, this crisis can be understood as a particular phase in the process of decolonization. The failure of projects around industrialization, state-led capitalist development and public sector expansion that emerged around the postcolonial world at independence quickly led to major budget deficits, balance-of-payments issues, illustrating the contours of a re-emergent colonial international. Moreover, the increase in oil prices that took place in the 1970s, as well as the drop in global demand intensified these economic crises. This prompted a turn towards neoliberal restructuring in countries such as Egypt, who assumed that

[11] Soliman 2005, 40.   [12] Ibid.

Empty Time   213

the new emerging global common sense around privatization and liberalization would solve the deep economic crisis. At the same time, increasing pressure from the IMF and World Bank attempted to accelerate these
transitions, which had to take place at a certain pace in order to avoid
massive resistance. Almost uniformly across the postcolonial world,
where IMF structural adjustment programmes were eventually implemented, protests, demonstrations, and strikes broke out in an effort to
reverse the tide of public sector cuts. The centrepieces of SAPs tended to
be health care, education, and employment – all provided by the public
sector – and all central to the reproduction of a middle class that had
emerged at decolonization.

Shifts during the 1970s had already set the scene for the deepening
of liberalization proposed by the IMF. In particular, the internationalization of capital through foreign direct investment, joint ventures,
listing companies on overseas stock markets, and the licensing of
brands and agency rights mean that countries across the postcolonial
world became part and parcel of global financial markets and international banking systems.[13] Neoliberalism, however, as I suggested in
the previous chapter, was more than just these economic policies; as
Adam Hanieh notes, following David Harvey, it is an attempt to 'recon-
stitute and strengthen class power in the favour of capital'.[14] The logic of
neoliberalization – now international – pierced all national formations in
order to integrate them into global circuits of capital: 'By speeding up the
rate at which capital moves across and through national spaces, and
widening the spheres of human activities subject to the imperatives of
accumulation, neoliberalism aimed to ensure the conditions for capitalist
reproduction at a global scale'.[15] This internationalization impacted the
Middle East in particular in the 1980s, and was driven by institutions
such as the IMF and World Bank, as well as the government of the US.

Mubarak initially tried to alleviate some of Egypt's financial problems by participating as a US ally in the 1991 invasion of Iraq. This
earned Egypt the cancellation of half of its debt, but ultimately was not
enough to relieve its economic crisis. Egypt also became a major beneficiary of US food aid, a tool of American neocolonialism. Food aid
not only allowed the US to get rid of its agricultural surplus, but more
specifically created a relationship of dependency between recipients
and the US.[16] This was already happening as early as 1961, by which

---

[13] Hanieh 2013, 5.   [14] Ibid.   [15] Ibid.   [16] Ibid., 45.

214   *Finance Capital and Empty Time*

time 77 per cent of Egyptian wheat imports and 38 per cent of total supply were coming in through US food aid programmes.[17] 'This aid was explicitly political in nature, with the US ambassador to Egypt noting that the intent was to establish a conscious association between Egyptian "policies and attitudes towards the United States and continuation of such [food] assistance in the future"'.[18] The amount of food aid Egypt accepted dropped in the 1960s, following the rise of Nasser's non-aligned position, but resumed in the early 1970s. Between 1973 and 1979, Egypt received one-fifth of all US food aid globally.[19]

These forms of indebtedness made Egypt increasingly reliant on the global market and global capital, particularly through foreign currency, which determined whether Egypt could meet its food needs.[20] Moreover, Egypt went even deeper into debt after the 1973 war, which cost over $40 billion. Sadat turned to the US and Europe, as well as the Gulf states, for loans, often on the condition that Egypt would cut ties with the Soviets and cede control of its economic reform programme to the US Treasury, IMF, and World Bank. In practice this meant the end of subsidies and the deregulation of the Egyptian pound.[21]

Egypt also began signing treaties that more formally integrated the country into the world market. In 1995, Egypt joined the World Trade Organization, and established an Association Agreement with the EU soon after.[22] Much of this depended on the logic of 'comparative advantage' which came to dominate the approach of international finance to the Middle East. The Middle East's 'comparative advantage' (outside of the Gulf states) was essentially its cheap labour. To profit off of this, tariffs were lifted and regulations reduced in order to attract foreign direct investment. Special economic zones were opened, and these became sites of hyper-exploitation, where minimal labour regulations were applied. This had the effect of 'feminizing' the labour force in these zones, in order to access even cheaper labour.[23] Adam Hanieh writes of the textile industry: 'Each country became essentially a platform for cheap labour, in which clothing was "cut, made, and trimmed" according to the specifications of international firms'.[24] The labour conditions that exist in these zones are generally very severe.

All of this set the scene for the crisis that emerged in the 1980s. By 1991, Egypt had no choice but to sign an IMF structural adjustment

[17] Ibid.   [18] Ibid.   [19] Ibid.   [20] Ibid., 47.   [21] Ibid., 48.   [22] Ibid., 100.
[23] Ibid.   [24] Ibid.

Empty Time 215

deal, known as the Economic Reform and Structural Adjustment Program (ERSAP). Like Sadat, who had realized the pitfalls of signing an IMF agreement and had only given in after mounting international pressure, Mubarak similarly attempted to resist the IMF's insistence and Egypt's negotiating team extended negotiations for quite some time. The IMF's call for shock therapy as the only solution to stabilizing Egypt's economy was rejected by the negotiating team, who no doubt had the very recent memories of the 1977 bread riots in mind.

The overarching goal of ERSAP was to transform the Egyptian economy into a market economy in order to fix the damage caused by state intervention in the economy.[25] Reforming the public sector, cutting subsidies, transforming investor policies, and monetary and fiscal reform are the various elements of this programme. More specifically, reform included: privatizing public assets to widen the influence of market forces; raising domestic savings rates and investment; increasing the flow of foreign exchange to pay for imports; streamlining the public sector – especially health and education – and raising taxes so that the budget deficit is contained.[26] Privatization in particular was delineated as the main goal under ERSAP. Government-owned enterprises were privatized through sale or rent, and the goal was to sell 85 of 300 public sector companies by 1997.[27] Although privatization had been a part of the infitah project from the very beginning, little progress was made on that front throughout the 1970s and 1980s. While the infitah ruling class had realized the importance of treading gently around the question of actually privatizing Egypt's expansive public sector, the new social force that was to emerge around Gamal Mubarak had no such foresight, as we will see.

Indeed privatization under structural adjustment travelled a similar path to the one under Sadat; a discourse of crisis was created, which then did the political work of legitimizing privatization. IMF and World Bank reports in particular consistently warned Egypt of the dramatic repercussions of not taking action, particularly in terms of unemployment, social unrest, and the growth of informality. As before, this story left out the colonial international:

This talk of crisis completely side-stepped the history of imperialist intervention. Two centuries of occupation and war, the forced dependency on external markets for food and technology, and the ongoing drain of wealth through

---

[25] For an excellent book on the free market and structural adjustment in Egypt through the lens of entrepreneurship, see Elyachar 2005.
[26] Bromley and Bush 1994, 204.   [27] Arafat 2011, 78.

debt and other capital flows were simply disappeared from the terms of the debate or posited as a consequence rather than as a cause of the region's predicament. But with the scale of the problem established and its framing nearly circumscribed, IFI's took the lead role in articulating a direction out of the potential crisis. Indeed, 'some kind of crisis' – as the World Bank noted in 2003 – was seen as very much an opportunity because it would help compel policy makers to make a 'firm commitment' to a new economic trajectory.[28]

The social impact of structural adjustment, following a global trend, is particularly disheartening.[29] Devaluation of the currency meant that the cost of living went up following increases in prices of transport, energy, and commodities; subsidies were removed; and indirect taxes were raised. Real incomes were reduced, and a reduction in government spending led to lower economic growth and a decrease in job creation.[30] Finally, social services such as education and health were drastically cut. All of these changes increased poverty among segments of Egyptian society who were already struggling. Reforms associated with structural adjustment also increased land rent, terminated the leases of small tenants, and led to an increase in rural poverty.[31]

This was to have very particular gendered effects. On the one hand, Nasserism's state-centric approach to gender equality, an approach built on the public sector and women's labour within it, was abandoned. On the other hand, the expansion of the private sector led to new opportunities for a small number of women. But even for those middle-class women for whom opportunities were now available, these often came at the price of an increased work load given the continuing presence of social reproductive work.[32] The benefits offered by the private sector did not match the ones the public sector had been able to provide, notably job security, long maternity leaves, and fixed working hours. Perhaps most importantly, however, infitah had the effect of feminizing a certain part of the labour force by pushing urban and rural working-class women into certain jobs: 'While most male workers were interested in the better paying jobs of the private sector and/or of the Gulf economies, in order to deal with spiralling prices, women workers preferred employment in the public sector because it offered such benefits as subsidized transportation, child care, and maternity leave'.[33]

The effects of structural adjustment across the postcolonial world have significantly challenged the neoliberal common sense pervasive

[28] Hanieh 2013, 89.   [29] Korayem 1997, 21.   [30] Ibid.   [31] Ibid., 23.
[32] Hatem 1992, 233.   [33] Ibid., 238.

Empty Time   217

throughout the 1980s. Rather than developing countries, structural adjustment has directly de-developed them by cutting social services, cutting subsidies, devaluing currencies, reducing real wages, and raising taxes. These changes are now taking place in Western nations as a response to austerity, despite their failure elsewhere. And yet the term *failure* brings up an interesting question: did structural adjustment fail? This depends on what its goals were and what was meant by 'development'. The goal of transforming economies across the postcolonial world into free market economies was in some senses successfully accomplished, although, as Julia Elyachar convincingly argues, we should always centre the ways in which resistance and other understandings of market relations existed alongside this.[34] Economic growth – at least for some time – was achieved; just one year before the 2011 Egyptian revolution Egypt was named a top reformer by the World Bank. The definition of development is more difficult to address; economic growth is one thing, but the social and political consequences suggest the reverse of national development took place following ERSAP.

Just a few years after the IMF deal was struck, 75 per cent of Egypt's subsidies had been cut and most public sector companies were being prepared for privatization. Egypt had privatized more public sector firms than any other country in the region and had made $15.7 billion from these.[35] As Hanieh notes, 'Unlike other states, in which just one or two deals made up the majority of privatisation receipts, Egypt's sell-off was very broad-based – covering flour mills, steel factories, real estate firms, banks, hotels, and telecommunication companies'.[36] It was 1995 and neoliberalism was finally under way.[37] Egypt's budget deficit was cut and the economy began to experience growth.[38] While some saw this as vindication of the IMF strategy, it is useful to recall

---

[34] 2005.   [35] Ibid.   [36] Ibid., 90.

[37] Members of government who were against privatization were side-lined during the 1990s, most notably Abdel Wahab, Minister of Industry. Ironically, he became chairman of a company that eventually benefitted greatly from privatization: the Arab Swiss Engineering Company (Kandil 2012, 94). By 1991, Law 203 was passed, which created the legal framework for privatization by dividing the public sector into holding companies that were allowed to put their components up for sale or liquidation. This law did not reduce the role of the public sector, but rather 'made it the agent of its own privatization' (Alexander and Bassiouny 2014, 47). Law 8, passed in 1997, prohibited the nationalization or sequestration of companies and prevented the interference of administrative authorities in pricing or regulating profits.

[38] Ibid., 350.

218   *Finance Capital and Empty Time*

Timothy Mitchell's dire assessment of the politics around structural adjustment: the reform programme did not 'remove the state' from the market; it mainly concentrated public funds into fewer hands.[39]

Following this, privatization was dramatically accelerated, and in 2005–6 the IMF commented that Nazif had already surpassed expectations.[40] Between 2004 and 2008 Egypt's privatization programme turned towards telecommunications, banking, and real estate, 'through direct offerings to potential investors, sometimes without even publicly announcing the sales of assets'.[41] Shockingly, many of these were sold far below market value. Egypt's total receipts from privatization between 2004 and 2008 constituted 70 per cent of all privatization revenues since the beginning of structural adjustment in 1991, earning Egypt the title of the 'region's top reformer' from the World Bank in 2006, 2007, *and* 2008. In 2008, Egypt was also crowned the world's top reformer.[42]

Finance capital was central to this, as Hanieh has argued, with the removal of government controls over credit, lending, and interest rates; the foreign investment in banking and privatization of state banks; and the introduction of non-bank financial markets such as stocks and insurance. These were all on the basis of IMF and World Bank conditionalities.[43] This financialization was what pushed forward investment in Egyptian real estate, especially through the creation of mortgage and bond markets.[44] It has also directly impacted agriculture, which has been a particular target of the World Bank and IMF. This has deepened the commodification of land, removed rent ceilings, and transformed state land into private land. In other words, it is a direct reversal of Nasser's land reform programme, leading to massive foreign investment in Egyptian agriculture, particularly from Gulf corporations.[45]

Although presented as an objective attempt to stabilize Egypt's economy, structural adjustment was underpinned by ideological assumptions tied to neoliberalism. The market can and should be free; the state is rent-seeking while the private sector is not; and social consequences are minimized in light of the preference given to economic reform. The centrality of privatization rests on the sacredness of private property, as well as the assumption that corruption can be found in the state but not

---

[39] 2002, 276.   [40] Hanieh 2013, 93.   [41] Ibid.   [42] Ibid., 95.
[43] Ibid., 140.   [44] Ibid.   [45] Ibid., 150.

Empty Time

the private sector. The market is also built on certain assumptions: 'It is the market of the neo-classical textbooks bereft of social actors which shape it and which is reified as the efficient allocator of resources to contrast with the inefficiencies of the state. It is an ahistorical abstract market'.[46] Throughout the 1990s Egypt saw worsening poverty, increasing inequality, a decline in public services, and an increase in economic growth. However recent history prompts us to continue to ask: growth for whom, and at what cost?

A Neoliberal Military?

One of the main economic beneficiaries of this era was the military. As we have seen, under the Nasserist bloc the Egyptian military came to occupy high-ranking positions and were key to decisions regarding production. Under infitah, the military was to lose its control over such positions, as Sadat's corrective revolution replaced military men with economists and other civilians. The 1967 and 1973 wars played a central role in weakening the military's power. Much of the military's attention was now to turn towards investing in the new economic opportunities available because of infitah.

The demilitarization of the army under the infitah ruling class should be seen as central to the changing position of the military in Egypt. The position of the state has always been key to accumulation and production, and therefore the removal of the military from state power – power they had previously monopolized – would clearly have an impact on the ability of the military to control the levers of production. This is not to say that the military did not have access to the economy or new investment opportunities – it is clear that under the infitah project they did; but having access is not the same as controlling the area, priorities, and extent of investment itself. I want to propose a way of bringing these two extreme positions on the military pre-2011 together. Understanding the military as part of the ruling class through each era allows us to trace the ways in which the military shifted in terms of other social forces within the ruling class. Under the Nasserist bloc it is clear that the military were the centre of the ruling class and historic bloc; there is little doubt that this shifted under the infitah ruling class and the financial ruling class. We can see that post-2013,

---

[46] Bromley and Bush 1994, 206.

the military has once again come to the centre. The ruling class is therefore never static, but always shifting, and indeed the changing position of the military has been one of the major measures with which the rise and fall of different ruling classes can be traced in Egypt.

Part of this shift has been the turn to neoliberal forms of accumulation. The process of demilitarizing political posts that was started during the infitah project had redirected military men towards economic investments, and in particular national development projects. Through organizations such as the National Service Projects Organisation and the Arab Industrial Organisation, manufacturing and construction became increasingly dominated by the military. While some scholars have argued that this turn towards economic investment meant that the military had been pushed out of power, others countered by pointing out that the military continued to wield tremendous power under Sadat and Mubarak.[47] Zeinab Abul-Magd argues that the 1980s and 1990s saw the emergence of a neoliberal army, whose officers took advantage of infitah and Egypt's opening markets.[48] Economically speaking, the military have several advantages: access to cheap or free labour through conscription, a budget that is hidden from official audits, and ownership of large swathes of public land.[49] The military are also exempted from customs and tariffs. Sadat's policy of demilitarizing the government and the emergence of influential officers such as Mohamed Abu Ghazala meant that the military began investing massively in Egypt's domestic market.

One of the main mechanisms through which the Egyptian military accumulates wealth is through the Arab Industrial Organisation, started in 1975 with the aim of building Egypt's military industrial power. The organization began with the production of rocket, military, and missile vehicles but soon became involved in manufacturing non-military goods as well.[50] The military has also created the National Service Projects Organisation, which established business enterprises and whose budget was independent from the Ministry of Defence.[51] Food, car manufacturing, construction, textiles, and other markets were widely infiltrated by military men. These organizations are examples of how the military became part and parcel of infitah by taking up

---

[47] Sayigh 2012; Abdelrahman 2014. Although both argue that the military were no longer the central decision makers under Sadat and Mubarak.
[48] 2017. [49] Ibid., 100–3. [50] Kandil 2012, 526. [51] Ibid., 81.

Empty Time 221

the new investment opportunities and simultaneously turning away from the Nasserist bloc's programme of national development. Moreover it was the military's investment in shopping centres that began the trend of American-style shopping malls that now dominate parts of Cairo, as that land was originally meant for military camps and bases.[52] The military also invested in factories that produced goods for less wealthy consumers, alongside the shopping malls, private hospitals, luxury private cars, and luxury real estate for the wealthy.

The only major confrontation Mubarak was to have with the military was when he faced competition from Major General Abd al-Halim Abu Ghazala, who, unlike Mubarak, had been a member of the Free Officers. Abu Ghazala was extremely popular within the military, not least because he raised wages, upgraded facilities, and was seen as a down to earth figure.[53] Importantly, Abu Ghazala oversaw a period under which the military became involved in manufacturing and food production on an unprecedented scale. By 1986, 18 per cent of food production was under the control of the National Services Projects Organization, run by the military.[54] His anti-communism meant that the US saw him as a potentially more useful ally than Mubarak, a point Mubarak was well aware of. Following a scandal over allegedly smuggled weaponry, Abu Ghazala was eventually demoted, but these events demonstrate the continuing threat posed by the military: as depoliticized as they may have been by the end of the 1980s, they still had a strong enough material and ideological basis from which to challenge other parts of the ruling class.

Because there is no historical bloc to speak of from the 1970s until 2011, the relationship between the military and other social forces within the ruling class was never as robust as it needed to be for a cohesive hegemonic project to materialize. The relationship between the military and the new financial ruling class in particular was tenuous at best, given the rapid privatization of the public sector which had historically been part of the military's economic investments. At the same time, as Abul-Magd shows, individuals within the military benefitted greatly from the acceleration of neoliberal restructuring. Abul-Magd argues that the military survived privatization, and even benefitted from it by transferring public companies that were supposed to be privatized into their ownership.[55] The question remains, however, of

[52] Ibid., 96.   [53] Kandil 2012, 413.   [54] Alexander and Bassiouny 2014, 55.
[55] Ibid., 126–31.

whether this gave the military equal economic and political power compared to the financial ruling class. Even as military officers were benefitting greatly from their investments in cement, steel, and so on, these industries remained – at least partially – under the control of members of the financial social force.

The military's intervention in the 2011 revolution suggests that this mutually beneficial relationship may not have been as mutual as it appeared. Because both social forces – financial and military – were part of the ruling class, there is no doubt that they both benefitted from the massive accumulation of wealth from the 1970s onwards. The political question around who was determining the accumulation strategy, however, remains key. Transformations within the military point to a more important shift. Particularly under the Nasserist bloc, the military had always represented productive and national capital, and industrialization and investment in infrastructure were key mechanisms through which they accumulated capital. However, while productive and national capital had been the basis of the Nasserist bloc, by the time we get to the 1990s and 2000s, financial capital had replaced national and productive capital. It is this displacement that is to the why the financial social force was unable to create hegemony.

A New Ruling Class: The Cabinet of Businessmen

Understanding the Mubarak years as one temporal whole risks missing the emergence of a new ruling class during this period, one that was central to the 2011 revolution. While Hosni Mubarak may have been invested in continuing the infitah project – with minor changes for damage control purposes – this was not the case for his son, Gamal. The new financial class that emerged in the mid 1990s around Gamal Mubarak did not differ substantively in ideology from the infitah ruling class; what changed was the speed at which neoliberal restructuring should, and did, take place. While the entire period 1967–2011 consisted of a propagation of neoliberal ideals, the speed at which this restructuring took place varied greatly, which in turn had extremely varied social, political, and economic effects.

By the time we see the rise of Gamal Mubarak and the 'cabinet of businessmen', a clear power struggle within the NDP itself had split the party in two. On the one hand, Youssef Wali, Kamal al Shazli, Safwat al Sharif, and Fathi Sorour made up what Arafat terms the 'Big Four' or

A New Ruling Class 223

the old guard. On the other hand, Gamal Mubarak, Ahmed Ezz, Hossam el Badrawi, Ali al Din Hilal, Mohamed Kamal, Mahmoud Mohie el Din, Mahmoud abou el Enein, and Youssef Boutross Ghali made up the 'Big Eight' – or what I call the new financial class. The old guard had been central to Hosni Mubarak's process of damage control and were part of the infitah project; the new guard emerged in the mid 1990s. Because of the NDP's disastrous performance in the 1990 elections, Gamal Mubarak was able to make a case for a radical restructuring of the party. This in turn also meant a radical restructuring of the NDP's political platform; in particular he called for increasing political and economic liberalization through private sector expansion. To carry all of this out, he created the Policies Committee, which was to become central to the new class and its accelerated form of capital accumulation.

The emergence of this new social force was partly a result of the broader shift in the Middle East and North Africa during the 1990s that saw finance become increasingly integral to economies as a result of deepening neoliberalization. In Egypt, government control of credit was liberalized in the early 1990s, making credit widely available to the private sector. In 2000, for instance, 42 per cent of the LE 206 billion lent to the private sector went to only 343 clients; by 2002, 18 per cent of loans went to 12 clients. This attracted a very particular group of businessmen, who eventually coalesced into what became commonly known as the cabinet of businessmen. They were connected to the Mubarak regime and by the 1990s the state was seen as essentially 'running a loan distribution network connecting public banks, businesses and the political system'.[56]

This group of businessmen were neither an inevitability nor an accident.[57] Rather they were a product of both the process of IMF-led neoliberal restructuring and the materialization of the infitah project. What distinguished them, however, was precisely that they were willing to carry out this restructuring at the pace the IMF wanted; it was the *accelerated* nature of their neoliberal restructuring that ultimately renders them a new social force separate from the infitah ruling

---

[56] Hanieh 2014, 82.

[57] As Sfakianakis (2004, 89) writes, 'the networks that elite businessmen put in place in the mid-1990s were not circumstantial. They were established as a result of the dwindling power of the public sector elite and the regime's intention to see businessmen replace the bosses of the state-owned enterprises'.

224 *Finance Capital and Empty Time*

class. Their reliance on finance capital on the one hand and their insistence on rapid privatization on the other served to construct them as a social force in their own right – one I call the financial class.

The cabinet of businessmen materialized first within the NDP itself. By the late 1990s, seven committees were dominated by businessmen, including housing and construction (Tal'at Mostafa, Mohamed Abu al-'Enein); economic affairs (Abdallah Tail); planning and budget (Ahmed 'Ezz); education and scientific research (Hosam Badrawi); youth affairs (Hossam Awad); complaints (Mohamed Geweily); and industry and energy (Amin Mubarak). Businessmen also held more than 40 per cent of committee chairmanships. The newly formed Policies Committee also became a space within which accelerated restructuring was incubated. The head of all of this, however, was clearly Gamal Mubarak.

Gamal Mubarak completed his education at the American University in Cairo, before working as an investment banker for Bank of America in Cairo and then in London. He returned to Egypt in the mid 1990s and became very active in the NDP as well as in public life more broadly, founding a financial advisory firm and an NGO focused on training young Egyptians to compete in the global economy.[58] There were constant rumours that Gamal was planning on founding his own liberal and pro-business political party, but instead he turned to the NDP as a vessel through which to realize his political ambitions. Encapsulated in the 2002 NDP slogan 'New Thinking', his programme was very much geared towards a neoliberal form of governance.

Gamal Mubarak was not popular among Egyptians, particularly given his clear stances on enhancing business opportunities for a particular class of Egyptians and accelerated neoliberal restructuring as a solution to economic crisis. He is often associated with the rise of businessmen who used the NDP to achieve economic reforms that benefitted few Egyptians, and given that for most Egyptians the idea of hereditary rule was distasteful to say the least, they did not see Gamal as someone fit to succeed his father. Nevertheless, he was able to amass much power within the NDP, particularly through the Policies Committee. It is interesting to think through why it is that this perceived connection between business and politics only became extremely pronounced in the mid 1990s, when arguably this had equally

[58] Shehata 2008, 418.

A New Ruling Class

characterized the infitah project, not to mention the connections between the state and capital under Nasser. I return to this further on, in order to tie it to the politics of consent.

Gamal Mubarak was able to position himself as a modern reformer, despite this lukewarm reception vis-à-vis the Egyptian public; this in turn can tell us a lot about the broader project of accelerated neoliberalization and deepening financialization that I discuss next. In the words of the former editor of Al-Ahram Weekly, Hani Shukrallah, 'They are modernists, more fluent in English and other languages, educated abroad, belonging to the younger generation. They are more open to Western management techniques, more exposed to Western culture and definitely economic liberals'.[59] Gamal consistently presented himself as a potential reformer of an Egyptian economy that was seen as inefficient, corrupt, and on the whole, failing. This echoes earlier representations of the economy that we saw during the return to infitah, which were necessary to justify the turn away from the public sector towards private investment. In an interview, Gamal Mubarak stated that Egypt's major problem – poverty – should be approached through inserting the country into the global economy, reducing the state's role in the economy, and giving the private sector greater freedom.[60]

Financialization cannot be underestimated as part and parcel of this process because of its very concrete effect of centralizing power in the hands of private interests, in effect 'restructuring Egypt's business elite'.[61] Take Banque du Caire, where between 2000 and 2005, 7 per cent of its loan portfolio belonged to forty-six businessmen.[62] Without access to capital offered by private banks in particular, the financial class would not have had the liquidity needed to make large investments. Large family holdings became characteristic of the Egyptian economy, and many within the new class were able to exercise a level of independence from the state previously unknown in Egypt.[63] Indeed in Egypt a key consequence of financialization has been the loss of government control over the allocation of capital, including credit.

---

[59] Zahid 2010, 219.
[60] www.meforum.org/articles/2009/gamal-mubarak-we-need-audacious-leaders
[61] Roll 2010, 350. [62] Ibid., 356.
[63] Take the example of Samih Sawiris, member of Egypt's richest business family, and his move to register Orascom – one of Egypt's biggest companies – as a Swiss company in order to avoid interference from the Egyptian government (Roll 2010, 366).

By the early 2000s, even sectors traditionally dominated by public capital such as construction and transportation, were now dominated by private capital.[64] Alongside this was the dismantling of the industrial sector through the dismantling of manufacturing. A robust manufacturing sector was a legacy of Nasserism's ISI policy and thus represented a material reversal of the Nasserist project.[65] Rather than investing in manufacturing – particularly in the face of increasing competition from Asia – a Ministry of Investments was set up to privatize the sector. By the late 1990s, the state had earned over $1.5 billion from these privatizations and over 100 factories had been privatized and half of all public enterprises were now privately owned.[66]

What ultimately consolidated the decline of the infitah project and the dominance of this new financial social force was the 2004 – literal – cabinet of businessmen. With Prime Minister Ahmed Nazif at its helm, for the first time in history the Egyptian cabinet was made up of mostly businessmen, including six monopoly capitalists in charge of ministries directly connected to their business interests.[67] Nazif and his new cabinet greatly accelerated the pace of privatization, and were promptly commended by the IMF. Foreign investment tripled during the first three years of the Nazif government.[68] Workers were offered the chance to participate in the privatization of the companies at which they worked through Employee Shareholder Associations (ESAs) which allowed them to buy shares. Not only did this attempt to turn worker opposition to privatization into support, it also shifted the

[64] By 2001, taxes on industrial and commercial profits amounted to a mere 4.4 per cent. By 2009, salaried workers paid a total of LE13 billion in taxes, while corporations paid only LE29 billion (Abdelrahman 2014, 15).

[65] De Smet 2016, 174.   [66] Ibid.

[67] Kandil 2012, 356. Kandil notes the following examples: Ahmed al-Maghraby, owner of the tourism conglomerate Accor Hotels, was appointed Minister of Tourism, and a year later Minister of Housing and Construction; Rashid Ahmed Rashid, head of the Middle East and North Africa affiliate of the multi-national Unilever, became Minister of Industry and Trade; Mohamed Mansour, chairman of Al-Mansour Motor Group, was charged with the Ministry of Transportation (he had also served as Secretary-General of Gamal's Future Generation Foundation and as President of the American Chamber of Commerce in Egypt between 1999 and 2003); Youssef Boutros Ghali, longtime IMF executive, was entrusted with Treasury; and Mahmoud Muhi al-Din, a Cairo University professor who was later elected Executive Director of the World Bank, handled economics and investment (ibid., 356).

[68] Ibid., 358.

A New Ruling Class

227

country's debt burden onto workers because ESAs were linked to debt-for-equity swaps where the US swapped the debt a country owed it for equity in a newly privatized company, then selling this equity to workers.[69] Egypt was the first country in the postcolonial world to trial ESAs, and throughout the 1990s ESAs were part of almost every single privatization.[70]

In many ways, these changes were not a fundamental departure from the infitah project. And yet the pace at which they were implemented – with the help of the IMF-led programme – produced a new class that capitalized on and then deepened the increasing financialization of the Egyptian economy. It is following their emergence that we see the rapid privatization of the public sector, the increase in foreign investment, the rise in coercion as a means of stabilizing society, and an imbalance within the ruling class itself. In particular, Gulf capital played a major role in the neoliberal restructuring of Egypt's economy from the 1980s onwards. By 2007, capital from the Gulf Cooperation Council (GCC) in Egypt represented over 25 per cent of investment.[71] Gulf capital has become heavily intertwined with capital across the Middle East (and beyond), and has created a clear material interest in maintaining conditions for capital accumulation, explaining resistance towards the 2011 revolution on the part of Gulf rulers.[72]

The expansion of Gulf capital was connected to the internationalization of capital flows more generally that took place during these decades. Indeed the formation of the GCC itself was part of this process, and manifested through expanded investment in construction, media and tele-communications, petrochemical projects, and private equity.[73] As Adam Hanieh notes, 'The increasing levels to which accumulation is conceived and articulated at a regional scale reflects the emergence of a pan-Gulf capitalist class, Khaleeji Capital, structured around a Saudi-UAE axis and consisting of those large Gulf conglomerates that tend to operate within these internationalising circuits'.[74] This internationalization has focused primarily on the Middle East, with 60 per cent of Gulf investment between 2003 and 2009 going to Jordan, Egypt, Lebanon, Palestine, and Syria.[75]

In Egypt, Gulf capital was involved in 22 per cent of privatization projects between 2000 and 2008, in sectors ranging from finance to real

---

[69] Hanieh 2013, 67. [70] Alongside public–private partnerships.
[71] Alexander and Bassiouny 2014, 81. [72] See Hanieh 2018.
[73] Hanieh 2013, 200. [74] Ibid. [75] Ibid., 201.

estate and telecommunications. It is through this process of privatization that we begin to see the coming together of Egyptian capital and Gulf capital. Hanieh has shown how particular sectors such as agribusiness have become almost completely reliant on Gulf capital to the extent that Egyptian agriculture as a whole is dominated by Saudi and Kuwaiti companies.[76] Hanieh also pinpoints how particular companies have been instrumental in these processes of privatization, with examples such as Abraaj, a company instrumental in internationalizing Gulf capital: 'In 2007, Abraaj made the biggest PE [private equity] investment in the MENA region's history at the time with its $1.4 billion purchase of Egyptian Fertilizers Company (EFC). Abraaj's purchase of EFC was followed soon after by investments in the country's leading construction firm, as well as real estate, a medical laboratory chain, information technology, food production, and the rollout of the Spinney's Supermarket chain across Egypt. These purchases made Abraaj one of the largest foreign companies operating in Egypt throughout most of the 2000s'.[77]

Another company, Amwal al Khaleej, similarly became a major investor in Egypt's industrial sector by purchasing textile companies that were being privatized by the government; it also purchased key flour mills, which gave it control over Egyptian good production. Alongside these direct purchases of companies privatized under Mubarak, Gulf capital has also entered into partnerships with Egyptian private equity firms such as EFG-Hermes, the largest financial company in Egypt throughout the 2000s and a key adviser to the Egyptian government on privatization. In 2006, Abraaj took the largest stake in EFG-Hermes with a $500 million investment; members of the board now included both Egyptians and Gulf representatives, and the company soon began to control major sectors of the Egyptian economy such as construction, agribusiness, steel production, infrastructure, and oil.[78] This pattern was repeated with other Egyptian private equity firms such as Citadel and Beltone, who soon represented both Egyptian and Gulf investors and who also had significant investments in strategic Egyptian sectors.

The real estate sector in particular highlights the increasing significance of finance capital and foreign direct investment under this new social force. A flurry of construction, focused primarily on luxury real

[76] Ibid., 203.   [77] Ibid., 205.   [78] Ibid., 207.

A New Ruling Class 229

estate, followed the emergence of this new class. Holiday resorts, gated compounds, and shopping malls popped up all over the country. More than 67 200 square kilometres were allocated by the state to investors, worth LE 80 billion.[79] Members of the new class acquired much of this land. Ahmed 'Ezz bought 21 million square metres at the price of LE 4 per metre, only to resell it to foreign companies at LE 1000 per metre a few years later; Minister of Tourism Zohair Garanah allocated plots in some of the best tourist sites at below market price; Minister of Housing and Construction Ahmed al-Maghraby allocated between January 2006 and December 2008 more than 27.2 million square metres to thirteen companies in which his family-owned Palm Hills Company controls between 49 and 100 per cent of each – in Palm Hills itself, the president's younger son's stock increased by LE 16 million in 2009 alone as a result of the appreciation of the value of land acquired by the company; and Prime Minister Ahmed Nazif cost the country a total loss of LE 51.2 billion by passing Ministerial Decree 2843 of 2009, which legalized the disputed acquisitions of 1.5 million *feddans* for 2.5 per cent of their market price.[80]

Land and real estate were also a central mechanism through which the inflow of Gulf capital was managed. Both direct purchases of land as well as investments in Egyptian real estate companies allowed Gulf capital to expand into real estate. Land auctions that were held throughout the 2000s saw Gulf investors as major participants and beneficiaries; at one of the largest auctions, in May 2007, 90 per cent of the 18.5 million square metres of Cairo land up for sale went to Saudi, Qatari, and UAE companies.[81] This has continued well after 2011: in 2012, fully owned Gulf real estate projects made up 80 per cent of the value of all real estate projects under development in Egypt.[82] Egyptian companies such as Sixth of October Development and Investment Company (SODIC) and the Tala'at Mustafa Group also have large investments from Gulf capital, thus adding to the total percentage of real estate development held by Gulf investors: 'Although they were registered in Egypt and established by prominent Egyptians with close links to Mubarak and the state apparatus, their subsequent development was essentially driven by Gulf capital flows'.[83]

The internationalization of Gulf capital was central to the acceleration of neoliberalism in the 2000s, primarily through privatization, as well as

[79] Kandil 2012, 362.   [80] Ibid.   [81] Ibid.   [82] Ibid.   [83] Hanieh 2014.

230   *Finance Capital and Empty Time*

to the increasing integration of Egypt into foreign capital flows. By the late 2000s, most strategic sectors in Egypt were heavily dominated by Gulf and other foreign capital, either through direct investment or through partnerships with local Egyptian capital. This would not have been possible without the privatization of the public sector, or the mass selling of Egyptian land. This shows, as Hanieh has argued, the centrality of privatization and Gulf capital to the process of neoliberal restructuring across the Middle East.[84] He argues that the process of liberalization in Egypt was dependent on the internationalization of Gulf capital, making Gulf states a primary beneficiary of the restructuring of class in Egypt. 'In this sense, neoliberalism needs to be understood as a project of class power that strengthened the position of national elites while simultaneously consolidating the Gulf's influence over the region as a whole'.[85]

By the late 2000s, the Egyptian economy was controlled by twenty to twenty-five family-owned monopolies, many of which included direct investment from foreign capital:

> The founders of these dynasties had a lot in common: most were into construction; their businesses were kicked off through state contracts; they drew funds freely from public banks; they partnered with foreign (especially American) investors; they employed a relatively small working force (3000 on average); and their products catered to the needs of the affluent. This fraction certainly did not represent the Egyptian bourgeoisie in its entirety but it was the fraction off of which the rest of the class members made their living, and the one none of them had any hope to compete with or dislodge.[86]

It is difficult to overstate the effects of this real estate explosion, and how it was connected to foreign capital. As Koen Bogaert has noted, the emphasis on 'mega-projects' means that the city is imagined in relation to outsiders – primarily tourists and foreign investors – rather than in relation to those who actually live inside of it.[87] The exchange value of the city is privileged over its use value. In cities like Cairo and Alexandria, this has resulted in severe social segregation based on class. New gated compounds, shopping malls, tourist resorts, and amusement parks have changed the city landscape, making the increasing economic equality extremely visible. It has also had the dramatic effect of tying Egyptian industry, manufacturing, and other strategic sectors to foreign capital in ways that had been undone in the 1950s

---

[84] Ibid., 207; Hanieh 2018.   [85] Ibid.   [86] Kandil 2012, 353.   [87] 2013, 227.

Dis-embedding Consent from Coercion

and 1960s. In fact, the only parallel that becomes relevant, then, is to the role foreign capital played in Egypt before independence in 1952.

Dis-embedding Consent from Coercion

A central feature of the emergence of a new financial class in the 1990s and 2000s was the increasing dis-embedding of consent from coercion. Recall that for Gramsci, hegemony does not imply the presence of consent alone, or the absence of coercion; rather, for Gramsci, hegemony means the embedding of coercion within consent so that it appears legitimate, necessary, or unintended. Coercion under the Nasserist project, for instance, was complicated by the presence of consent, particularly in relation to the broader nationalist project. From 1967 onwards, we see the slow dis-embedding of coercion from consent, largely because consent became weaker. Here I trace the dis-embedding of coercion from consent, highlighting just how central consent had been under Nasserism to justifying coercion.

Electoral Politics and Consent

A key space within which we can trace the waning presence of consent is within electoral politics. The weakening ability (or interest) of the ruling class to contest elections – despite the fact that they were rigged – was an early sign of the crisis of consent that would culminate in the broader absence of hegemony. Central to this was the increasing relevance of the National Democratic Party (NDP), Egypt's ruling party. The NDP was formed under Sadat as a replacement for the dismantled ASU, alongside the Misr Party. Other opposition parties were also formed during this time, such as the Tagamu' Party[88] (National Progressive Unionist Party), the New Wafd,[89] and the Al-Ahrar (the Liberal Party). All of these were

---

[88] This represented the ASU's 'left' made up of Marxists and leftist Nasserist intellectuals and trade unionists. Although branded by Sadat as communist and atheist, is represented socially mobile people of modest background working in the public sector industry or government administration (Arafat 2011, 15).

[89] A revival of the Wafd, and distinctly more secular in nature; it catered to middle-class and urban professionals.

232   *Finance Capital and Empty Time*

essentially factions that existed within the ASU, which in the late 1960s had splintered. The NDP's failings in regard to consent become especially apparent when we compare it to its predecessor, the ASU. The strong ideological role of the ASU meant that it very much functioned as an instrument of consent creation, and was seen as central to the broader project of Nasserism. The NDP, on the other hand, was not explicitly fashioned as an ideological instrument that was meant to generate consent *within the broader population,* but rather as an instrument through which Sadat – and later, Hosni and Gamal Mubarak – could create an elite base from which to amass political power. These are two very different functions, and while one recognizes the importance of creating consent *nationally,* the other seems to relegate consent to something that needs to be created within an elite class.

Here the supposed coming together of business and politics can shed light on the NDP's position on consent, as well as the NDP's inability to create consent and its increasing reliance on coercion. In particular, a new generation of businessmen, created through infitah, as well as a second generation, created through financialization, came to represent the powerful centre of Egyptian politics. They are often referred to as *ragal al-'amal,* which has been translated to businessmen, although the Arabic term has a broader meaning that could be better understood as 'owners of capital'.[90] The NDP essentially functioned as a space within which businessmen could come together and formulate a project around accelerated neoliberalization. In contrast to the ASU, which was a space through which a political project could expand outwards into society, the NDP's focus was inward-looking rather than outward-looking; any resistance from society was thereby dealt with through coercion, as we shall see.

By the start of Mubarak's presidency, the NDP was largely made up of wealthy landowners and the generation of infitah businessmen who had emerged during the 1980s and 1990s. Throughout the 1980s and especially the 1990s, the NDP began to shift away from landowners towards businessmen, particularly those who were active around the mid 1990s such as Ahmed 'Ezz, Mohamed Abu al-'Enein, and Hossam al-Badrawi. Unlike the ASU, the NDP did not have a clear ideological orientation, nor was its role to create consent in the way the ASU's role had been. The NDP's programmes and/or statements often contradicted actual policies

---

[90] Ibid., 122.

Dis-embedding Consent from Coercion 233

carried out by the ruling class, giving it the appearance of conflict or lack of transparency. Without a concrete ideology, programme, or symbols that might connect it to the public or a broader project, the NDP was a dramatically different organization to the ASU, its predecessor.

Another way of understanding this difference is by tracking the increasingly influential role geopolitics came to play in Egypt's electoral system in the 1990s and 2000s. Here, I return to the concept of the colonial international by tracing the ways in which electoral politics became a central mechanism through which global liberal hegemony was filtered into postcolonial contexts, leading to important ramifications in how the new financial class represented itself. Partly, this was a result of a neo-Orientalist assumption embedded within much scholarship on the Middle East that sees a liberal democratic system as the ultimate end-point. It was also a result of the increasing channelling of international pressure – through a reconfigured colonial international – into cultivating a particular form of subjectivity in Egypt that would lead to (it was assumed) liberal electoral politics and participation in the market.

The US in particular has been central to this project of political and economic liberalization: aside from the military aid Egypt receives each year, US aid helps in 'setting the parameters for Washington's influence in Egypt's domestic affairs and established a possible collusion between Washington and Egypt's programme for political liberalization'.[91] US influence has particularly worked through the question of democratic politics and rule of law. The US-Middle East Partnership Initiative (MEPI), for example, founded in 2002 by Colin Powell, works to promote grassroots education, economic and private sector growth, and to strengthen civil society and the rule of law. The aim is to provide funding to organizations that would then bring about structural and institutional reforms. As Arafat notes: 'In the political sphere, MEPI programmes seek to develop institutions essential to active citizenries and accountable, representative governments; to strengthen democratic practices, electoral systems, and political parties; to promote the rule of law and an autonomous judiciary; and to enhance the role of an independent, professional news media. In economics, MEPI pursues a reform agenda to create a thriving private sector and employment, trade liberalization, improved banking and

---

[91] Bush 2009, 85.

234 *Finance Capital and Empty Time*

commercial regulations, and entrepreneurial training for ordinary people'.[92]

This was followed by the Greater Middle East Initiative (GMEI), which was emblematic of George W. Bush's Middle East policy more general. Bringing together the US, Europe, the Arab world, and Iran, Israel, Pakistan, Turkey, and Afghanistan, the project was part of the War on Terror. Promoting democracy and good governance was the main focus of the project, echoing early attempts to discipline the Middle East through the use of democratization. The project quickly attracted criticism from Arab leaders who saw it as an attempt to impose a US agenda on the region.[93] More recently, European nations and the European Union have also become involved in using aid and political pressure to push forward a programme of political liberalization. The role of US and EU funding in promoting neoliberalism in Egypt is key, for it is around neoliberalization that we can trace the continuity with colonial capitalism. As Kwame Nkrumah noted quite some time ago, aid in all of its forms should primarily be understood as a form of 'revolving credit', where Western governments eventually recover their 'investment' in a variety of ways.[94] For Nkrumah, aid enhances donor control over local politics, enhancing the colonial international.[95]

Importantly, this provides a critique of the influential neo-patrimonial literature on Africa and the Middle East that sees poverty as a result of poor governance, cultural barriers, and corruption.[96] Views that see the failure of economic development in the Global South as the fault of culture and corruption miss this point: the proliferation of corruption and the spread of neoliberalization should not be seen as two separate processes. Dependent elites in places such as Egypt have been able to capitalize on the constant interventions from European, American, and other foreign actors. This is an expression of agency, albeit a problematic one. It is in this interaction between Egyptian elites and European actors that we see the erosion of Egyptian sovereignty.

This is where the focus on electoral politics partly stems from; the role of much of this aid has been to centre elections as the ultimate litmus test of a nation on its path to democratization. Across much of the 1990s and 2000s, we see an increasing focus on parliamentary and

[92] 2011, 90.
[93] Mubarak commented that the project was imperialist and that Arab states appeared to have no sovereignty (ibid.).
[94] Langan 2017, 63.　　[95] Ibid.　　[96] For more, see ibid., 18.

Dis-embedding Consent from Coercion 235

presidential elections in Egypt. Multiple changes to electoral laws have thus been read as cause for optimism in that they suggest Egypt was liberalizing. According to this reading, the introduction of multiple political parties under Sadat, and then potentially multiple candidates under Mubarak, both appear to have implied a move towards democracy. As Arafat notes, however, Egypt's liberalization process did not produce parties with grassroots support because it simply could not: 'Political parties derive from personal and familial networks that have long sustained traditional elite structures and that assure broad support for state-managed liberalization'.[97]

However, the story I propose here is slightly different. Rather than reading increasing changes to Egypt's electoral role as a supposed liberalizing of electoral politics and thus of Egypt's political system, I instead read Egypt's electoral politics throughout the 1990s and 2000s as a clear sign of declining consent, increasing coercion, and the continuing absence of hegemony. Egypt's electoral politics throughout this period show how quickly consent was withering away (what little was left of it by the 1990s), and represent a clear case of the centrality of coercion to keeping the ruling class in power. I agree with much of the literature that electoral politics are important to understand Egypt in the 1990s and 2000s, but not because they pointed to some kind of liberalization; rather, because they are a clear case of the shifting balance between consent and coercion. This becomes clear when we focus on two key moments: two elections in 2005, and one in 2010.

In 2005, Egypt held a national referendum on the possibility of presidential elections with more than one candidate for the first time. The major opposition parties, as well as the Muslim Brotherhood and *Kefaya* boycotted the vote, and the Judges' Club held an extraordinary session to discuss the complete lack of authority the judiciary had in the process, leading them to boycott the referendum as well. Alongside these boycotts, serious violence accompanied the voting process, aimed at *Kefaya* protesters. Women in particular were singled out, in a pattern that was to be repeated post-2011. Some argued that Gamal Mubarak was directly responsible for the escalation in violence against protesters, especially women, as it had dramatically increased following his rise within the NDP.[98] Whether or not this is the case, this referendum and the events surrounding it are worth unpacking. The 2005

[97] Arafat 2011, 16.   [98] Ibid.

parliamentary election was even more contentious, and signalled even further the breakdown of consent. A public debate on alternatives to Mubarak and his son was taking place, and movements such as *Kefaya* were reorienting demands for political reform.

These changes also signified the important role accorded to electoral politics by organizations such as the Brotherhood. The Muslim Brotherhood winning more seats than expected (88) – even by them – was the main news story of these elections. The Brotherhood had developed a comprehensive campaign strategy, which involved the careful selection of candidates and platforms. This transformation of the Brotherhood from a religious movement to 'something resembling a political party' took place in the 1980s.[99] The Brotherhood's popularity within professional syndicates, for example, can similarly be put down to superior organizational efforts as well as their emphasis on campaigning and the provision of social services. Moreover, a younger generation of Brothers emerged in the 1990s who posed a challenge to the groups' more old-school leadership. It is around this time that we see new statements on the importance of women's rights and political pluralism, even as these official statements were contradicted by Supreme Guide statements that often said the opposite.[100] Nevertheless, it was clear that electoral mobilization was central to the ability of the Brotherhood to contest the ruling class.

A second moment that signified the complete lack of consent is the 2010 parliamentary elections. Ninety-seven per cent voted for the NDP, in a shocking result even for elections everyone knew to be rigged. As Mona el-Ghobashy notes, 'No one thinks parliamentary elections in Egypt are democratic or even semi-democratic. The elections do not determine who governs'.[101] And yet, as she points out, political parties, politicians, and the opposition take elections very seriously. Campaigns, even if working under the assumption that elections are not contested, do a whole host of other forms of political work, such as renewing political alliances, distributing economic resources, and calibrating forms of opposition.[102] The 2010 elections were impacted by decisions to eliminate judicial supervision – reversing the greatest gain by opposition forces since 1976 – and stipulating that voting take place on a single day.

---

[99] El-Ghobashy 2005.   [100] Ibid.   [101] El-Ghobashy 2010.   [102] Ibid.

Dis-embedding Consent from Coercion 237

All of these changes, as well as high levels of violence on the voting day itself, marred this election and its outcome. On top of that, the unbelievable margin with which the election was won was a clear indication that the façade of a democratic process was no longer in place; was no longer worth keeping in place. It is precisely for this reason that these electoral moments in the 2000s are interesting: it is not only that they show the increasing reliance on coercion and specifically police brutality by the NDP, it is also that they show the disinterest in keeping up the charade of the people having any kind of say in Egyptian politics. Precisely what Nasser had invested so much in – through institutions like the ASU, through the media, through education and other public services – namely the idea that the nation had a say in deciding its own future – was completely absent in the 1990s and 2000s. The question is not whether Egyptians actually had significant power over their own destinies in the 1950s and 1960s; rather, it is that they thought they did. The complete lack of political will to create this façade during the decades leading up to 2011 is one way in which we can read the growing absence of consent as a tool of political rule.

The Ministry of the Interior and the Rise in Coercion

The Egyptian police bureaucracy employs 1.5 million to 1.7 million people, ranging from officers to civilian administrators, coming under the umbrella of the Ministry of Interior.[103] The turn to coercion under the new financial class was very much dependent on this already-existing infrastructure to support increasing levels of repression.[104] This infrastructure was both material, in terms of a larger budget and more policemen and women, and ideological, with the increasing association between police and violence. This infrastructure was nothing new; Nasser had expanded the police forces extensively in order to produce a counterpoint to the military. This expansion was not only numerical but also in terms of scope: while Nasser and the Free Officers had arguably made use of police brutality primarily in relation to political opponents – or opponents politicized as against the ruling class – the 1990s and 2000s saw the expansion of this brutality to all

---

[103] Ashour 2012, 6.

[104] The war against Islamists in particular was to be the main focus of the police in the early 1990s.

parts of the country, and to all types of people.[105] In other words, police brutality became part of the everyday. Where the previous section looked at the absence of consent, this section looks at the simultaneous increasing presence of coercion.

The use of violence against political opponents – particularly through beatings and/or detainment has a long history; however, as Mona el-Ghobashy notes, this is not what made Mubarak's Egypt a police state. Rather it was that police now dealt with everything: 'Police not only deal with crime and issue passports, drivers' licences, and birth and death certificates. They also resolve local conflicts over land and sectarian relations; fix all national and sub-national elections; vet graduate school candidates and academic appointments at every level; monitor shop floors and mediate worker-management conflicts; observe soccer games and Friday prayers; and maintain a network of local informants in poor neighbourhoods, to ensure that dispossession is not converted into political organization'.[106] The everyday-ness of policing was what was new; the infiltration of the police into the daily interactions of people.

Perhaps nothing brought this realization home more than the 2010 murder of Khalid Said at the hands of the police. Murdered by police officers after objecting to being searched without a warrant, he was attacked, murdered, and his corpse was later dumped on the street. Photographic evidence of Said's smashed up face spread rapidly through social media, throwing doubt on the official story that Said had died after swallowing drugs. Demonstrations in Cairo and Alexandria followed, but paramilitary and riot police forces crushed them violently. A Facebook page entitled *Kolena Khaled Said* (We are all Khaled Said) was set up and became one of the prominent sources of information before and during the revolution. For many Egyptians, Khaled Said represented a normal, middle-class youth who was not politically active. It was this detachment from political activity that underlined this shift in police repression and cemented it as something that could happen to anyone, anywhere, at any time. Said became a national symbol of intensifying police brutality.[107]

Farha Ghannam draws attention here to the symbolic nature of Khaled Said's death and his battered body. The meaning that was given to Said's death must be read in light of increasing police brutality, and the everyday nature this was taking on. She positions Khaled Said in relation to

---

[105] Abdelrahman 2017, 190. [106] El-Ghobashy 2011, 3.
[107] Ghannam 2013, 134.

Dis-embedding Consent from Coercion

a Cairene community in al-Zawiya al Hamra, noting that the reason many people gave for supporting the revolution was tied to such events:

> Most of my interlocutors came to embrace the January 25 revolution and its goals. Their reactions were framed by their socioeconomic positionality as well as their dreams and hopes for a better future. Almost everyone in al-Zawiya was aware of the brutality of the police, felt the growing pressure on men (and women) to provide for their families, encountered the state's corrupt and inefficient bureaucracy and suffered marginalisation and dis-empowerment under Mubarak's regime.[108]

Everyday encounters with the police became part of the fabric of everyday life in Egypt, especially for young men. As Ghannam skilfully shows in her ethnographic work, socioeconomic pressures faced by residents of al-Zawiya within the liberal economic policies of the infitah project were central to shaping interactions between the police and Egyptians.[109] I want to extend this point, and connect the intensification of police violence – in scope and form – to argue that the expansion of everyday police violence was very much connected to the rise of new class forces, namely the financial class, and their failure to create hegemony. Similarly, the worsening of socioeconomic conditions was connected to this financial class and their acceleration of neoliberal restructuring. These trajectories matter if we want to understand the 2011 revolution and the particular lineages that led to it.

The literal expansion of the security forces meant that by 2009, 1.7 million men were part of the security apparatus.[110] This expansion began in 1997, when Habib al Adly was appointed Minister of the Interior, a post he was to occupy for fourteen years. Adly was a graduate of the Police Academy, known for having normalized the use of *baltagiyya* (thugs) during elections to intimidate voters. Adly was very much part of the new financial class, and was close to members of the Policies Committee, the new inner circle of the NDP. Expenditure on the Interior Ministry had already been increasing since the late 1980s, and by 2002 it was 6 per cent of GDP.[111] Alongside this, there has been the increased use of private security companies to carry out state repression.[112] This began in 1979, with the US embassy hiring a private security company – Care Services – to protect its property.[113] Since then, even government institutions such

---

[108] Ibid., 162.   [109] Ibid., 17.   [110] Abdelrahman 2017, 196.
[111] Ibid., 336.   [112] Ibid., 196.   [113] Ibid., 195.

as the Ministry of Education have hired private security companies to provide security across national university campuses, which essentially allowed for more surveillance and repression of student activism.[114]

The consolidation of a 'security state' has taken place alongside the shift to neoliberal rationality and forms of governmentality.[115] This shift happened when violence and surveillance were deployed to extend the control of the state over space, particularly spaces that were low income.[116] This has happened together with the creation of the category of dangerous young men who are represented as working class, dangerous, and threatening.[117] The control, regulation, and exclusion of these young men is done through policing, in order to supposedly protect public spaces that are implicitly meant for rich Egyptians and foreigners, as well as capital investment.[118] Ghannam suggests that, rather than being a minor development, this exclusion and control was a major reason why young people supported the 2011 revolution: 'In addition to carrying their ID cards, young men were keenly aware of the importance of their bodily hexis in their interaction with the police

---

[114] Ibid., 196.   [115] Ibid.   [116] Ibid.

[117] In a fascinating account, Paul Amar (2011) has looked at the ways in which this violence and surveillance intersects with gender and masculinity in Cairo, coming to a similar conclusion about the restriction on the mobility of young men. The 'social cleansing' of public spaces frequented by wealthy Egyptians – especially women – was justified by drawing on classist depictions of young men (ibid., 315). Some feminist campaigns reproduced the problematic pathologization of working class masculinity as responsible for increasing levels of sexual harassment.

[118] Ibid., 67. Everyday police violence has had dramatic effects on masculinity and the ways in which men interact with the state. In particular, the notion of police violence as humiliating, especially when it is done to an older man, can partly explain why the notion of dignity was so central to the 2011 revolution. The everyday nature of police violence encroached on the ways in which men were able to navigate public spaces, and the class dimension of urban space is especially key. The targeting of working class men and the attempt to 'cleanse' certain areas of them carried with it particular humiliations. Indeed the rise of the new financial class brought with it dramatic changes in urban space, most notably the rapid expansion of gated compounds, shopping malls, and luxury resorts outside of Cairo (Ghannam 2002; Winegar 2012; Bayat and Denis 2000; Abaza 2006). The ways in which these spaces had to be policed required an expansion of policing capability – which soon expanded into private security companies – as well as specifically classed and gendered means of surveillance.

Dis-embedding Consent from Coercion

and thus often tried to dress and present their bodies in ways that would allow them to pass as good and respectable citizens'.[119]

It is here that we see the everyday nature of police violence, which shifted away from politically active Egyptians to all Egyptians. This led to laws such as Law 6 in 1998 that targeted 'thuggery' in an attempt to regulate 'antisocial and threatening' behaviour.[120] 'Social baltaga' emerged as a label for the violence between police and young men in working-class neighbourhoods – even as *baltagiyya* were increasingly used by the police to intimidate the general population.[121] Indeed Ghannam's interlocutors noted that they began to support the revolution after the attacks by *baltagiyya* on protesters on 2 February:

> The attacks brought to the foreground a set of associations between the past and the present, the local and the national, and the proper and improper uses of violence that shaped in vital ways the views many Egyptians held of the protesters and the pro-Mubarak supporters. Whereas the rebels (*el-suwwaar*) had proven themselves to be gid'aan, brave and decent men and women willing to sacrifice their lives for the dignity and good of the whole nation, Mubarak's government and its supporters were seen as *baltagiyya*, thus who protected their own interests.[122]

We thus see notions of nationhood crop up again, showing how national interest can be juxtaposed to individual interest. Whereas revolutionaries were seen as those willing to sacrifice their lives for the good of the whole nation, thugs were instead positioned as those who enacted violence for their own benefit. It is through such understandings that nationhood and nationalism framed the 2011 revolution. Police violence was often interpreted in the same way: as in the interests of certain individuals (often the ruling class) rather than in the interest of the nation. It is not a question of whether the police deploy violence or not, but rather *why, how much*, and *against whom*. Under the Nasserist project, violence by the state was represented as necessary for the good of the nation; by the 1990s and 2000s, this understanding had changed and state violence was seen as in the interest of the ruling class alone and at the expense of the nation. This has as much to do with the strength of the representations the ruling class produced about its own violence as it does with shifting political realities.

The 2011 revolution brought with it changes in the public perception of the police, as well as the self-perception of policemen themselves.

---

[119] Ibid., 68.   [120] Ibid., 122.   [121] Ibid.   [122] Ibid., 125.

242   *Finance Capital and Empty Time*

One of Ghannam's interlocutors in al-Zawiya, reflects that whereas before police officers acted like they were 'the masters', the revolution fundamentally undermined police power and limited their use of violence.[123] While this has clearly changed since, this anecdote captures an important post-revolutionary moment that highlights how important coercion was to the revolution. It was the everyday nature of police violence, and its extension into the 'ordinary', that marks the distinction between police violence before and after the 1990s and 2000s.

The extension of police violence into the everyday and the investment in policing infrastructure indicated the choice of the ruling class to rely on coercion to deal with the lack of consent and its political and social consequences. Perhaps there was no clearer lesson the new ruling class could have learned from the one that preceded it than the one learned by Sadat following the 1977 bread riots. While the ultimate goal of any ruling class is capital accumulation, there is always a political question that needs to be addressed – the question of legitimacy. Once this legitimacy is destroyed, stability comes under threat. The accelerated neoliberalization put in place by the new fraction ultimately required a dramatic deregulation of labour and increase in coercion. Fear seemed to be the only way to hold everything together and to make sure resistance was limited and ineffective, and for this the Ministry of the Interior was more than equipped. As we have seen, however, stability through coercion can never replace stability through hegemony; it was only a matter of time before an organic crisis brought the entire house of cards down.

A Failure of Hegemony

The extent to which coercion is embedded within consent is one way Gramsci identified whether a ruling class is hegemonic. While no ruling class ever rules purely through consent or coercion, the shifting relationship between consent and coercion can tell us a lot about the state of politics. The absence of hegemony means a ruling class opens itself up to an organic crisis. As Christine Buci-Glucksmann notes, 'from the moment hegemony becomes simply the backing for violence, or even

---

[123] Ibid., 36.

A Failure of Hegemony

243

worse, is only obtained by violence, this hegemony is in fact no longer assured'.[124]

The central argument of this chapter is that the accelerated nature of neoliberal restructuring under the new financial class, alongside their weak attempts to universalize these narrow interests, means that they were unable to create either a historical bloc or hegemony. The failure to create hegemony had its price, however. To stay in power without hegemony, the financial class had to increasingly turn to coercion. I have shown how this coercion played out both electorally and in the expansion of everyday police brutality. In this section, I focus on a third arena in which we can see rising resistance to the new financial class, as well as an increase in coercive attempts to eliminate this resistance.

Egyptian workers have long been central to Egyptian political projects. As I argued in previous chapters, the position of workers vis-à-vis the ruling class has often determined its ultimate fate, given the centrality of workers to production and capital accumulation. The 1990s and 2000s were no different, with workers constituting the largest and most significant form of resistance to the project of accelerated neoliberalization. It is not a stretch to say that workers set the stage for the 2011 revolution with their focus on social justice. To trace the broader failure of hegemony, this section focuses specifically on Egyptian labour and its connections financialization and privatization, as well as their resistance to these twin projects. I argue that in their critique of economic transformations during the 2000s, they were simultaneously making a deep-seated political critique of the new financial class, and that this critique contributed to the absence of both a historical bloc and hegemony.

The Economic Is Political: Egyptian Labour under Finance Capital

When Egyptian workers rose up against the acceleration of neoliberal restructuring, it was always in and of itself both an economic and political challenge. Demands for pensions, job security, wage increases, and so on, which increasingly defined strike demands throughout the 1990s and 2000s, were a challenge to the very heart of the political

---

[124] 1980, 56.

system. This was because they struck at the accumulation strategy of the ruling class, in this instance privatization. Despite this, workers' demands have often been represented as apolitical and connected solely to the 'economic sphere'. This delinking of the political from the economic has been one of the central ways in which the workers' struggle in Egypt has been depoliticized. Categorizing workers as non-threatening because their demands are economic – and not political – not only reproduces the unfounded binary between the two, but also serves to hide the fact that economic demands are by nature political. In other words, any attempt to change the structure of production affects accumulation, which in turn touches the very heart of politics: the ruling class.

The project of neoliberal restructuring brought new relations between capital and labour. Recall the ways in which labour was co-opted under the Nasserist project; this co-optation was partly possible because labour found symmetries between their own ideas around anticolonial nationalism and those of the Nasserist project. It was the transformation of this support into contestation that marked the shift from one project to another, and the intensification of this contestation that marked the rise of the financial class. The reduction of trade barriers, an increase in foreign direct investment, the deregulation of markets, and rapid privatization constituted an assault on the working class that signalled the end of the social welfare pact made under the Nasserist project.[125]

To place this in context, it is useful to remember that until 2011, no independent unions existed; only the state-controlled ETUF was in place. In the mid 1990s, we see the NDP begin to tighten its control over the ETUF, specifically by raising the term of elected union officials from four to five years and allowing retired members to stay in office.[126] These changes were in response to workers' clear and unequivocal challenge to the acceleration of the privatization programme under the new financial class:

During the strike waves of 1984–89 and the early1990s, Egypt experienced 25 to 80 actions a year. From 1998 to 2003, this increased to an average of 118 workers' collective actions a year. In 2004 there were 265 collective actions – more than double the 1998–2003 average. Over 70 per cent (190) of the collective actions in 2004 occurred after Nazif was appointed prime

[125] De Smet 2012, 146. [126] Bassiouny in Alexander 2010, 246.

A Failure of Hegemony

minister in July. The incidence of collective action has remained at roughly this level or higher since 2004, reaching an astounding 614 actions in 2007 and 609 in 2008.[127]

Beinin and others have located this wave of strikes both within the longer trajectory of infitah – as a reaction to the economic upheavals that resulted from opening up Egypt's economy to foreign capital – as well as the shorter trajectory of accelerated neoliberal restructuring that took the form of privatization.

By 2000, a proposed labour law that would have taken away significant rights from workers was in its seventeenth version, unable to get through parliament. Committees were formed to resist privatization,[128] and, more importantly, a massive wave of strikes engulfed Egypt. As Kamel Abbas has noted: 'The only way to understand the wave of strikes that have taken place is that they only have one thing in common: they are targeting – at least in part – the measures taken within the framework of privatisation'.[129] As argued by Dina Makram-Ebeid in her incisive research on steel workers in Egypt, privatization brought with it new forms of precarity as well as a deepening division between temporary and permanent workers in its attempt to fragment the working class.[130] Perhaps it is here that we

---

[127] Beinin 2009, 450.

[128] The National Committee in Defence of Workers Rights and the National Committee to Combat Privatisation are notable examples.

[129] Quoted in Paczyńska 2010, 188.

[130] Makram-Ebeid 2012, 29. In her research Makram-Ebeid argues that the onset of neoliberal reforms in 1991, which along with other changes in the state allowed some workers to access state resources while dispossessing others, creating a situation of unevenness. Her fieldwork focuses on the Egyptian Iron and Steel Company (EISCO) founded under Nasser as part of his industrialization program. It was a company that held major symbolic capital as the symbol of Egypt's independent future. In a telling passage, Makram-Ebeid narrates the ways in which the lives of company workers were changed by becoming part of this company: 'In time, permanent workers at EISCO acquired a status in their communities and had higher expectations about the sort of lives they should lead. 'Amm 'Umar, a production worker said that when buying clothes in Helwan, he never tells the salesperson he works at EISCO; otherwise they would triple the price. Responding to my surveys in the plant, many replied to the question, "What is the most important benefit you gained from working at EISCO?" with "kul hāga" ("everything") and workers often described the plant with generous terms such as al-sharika dih 'ummi 'atā'hā gheir mutanāhī ("this company is my mother, it gives endlessly"), or "I did not own land, but this job is my piece of land" or "I am retiring from the plant as a bey". Their reflections explain how the stability of their work

246   *Finance Capital and Empty Time*

see just how hegemonic the Nasserist project had been. Nasserism created a particular understanding of the relationship between workers and the state, one that resonated with workers ideologically and that provided them with tangible material benefits. In a sense, we can understand the years between the decline of the Nasserist bloc and the 2011 revolution as a slow erosion of this understanding, a chipping away at the welfare-based ideology and policies that had been put in place in the 1950s. This dismantling, however, was suddenly accelerated in the 2000s, giving workers little choice but to accelerate their already-growing resistance.

Notable about this wave of strikes were their geographical spread; the incorporation of both public and private workplaces; and their long duration.[131] Although the textile sector was the 'centre of gravity', strikes soon spread outwards.[132] This is a marked difference from the 1980s during which strikes tended to be concentrated in the public sector; the 1990s and 2000s saw these spread into the private sector as well. These strikes often began with grievances directly linked to workplace conditions, but that quickly expanded to broader demands around minimum wages and the wider political system. The ETUF – which by law must approve strikes before they happen – had only approved two strikes since its creation in 1957, and thus was largely seen as a defunct organization. Indeed its membership dropped from 4.5 million in 2003 to 3.8 million in 2006.[133] Instead, workers cultivated forms of activity that included mass meetings, demonstrations, sit-ins, and the building of 'tent cities', often acting as a 'meeting place to plan and discuss their goals and tactics with each other and "outsiders" (including journalists and officials from the ruling party), as a social space where strikers shared food and companionship and as

> allowed them to plan for the future and to make their aspirations for upward social mobility concrete, whether through offering their children the opportunity of higher education or through stable jobs in the plant, building family houses for their nuclear families, marrying their children into well-off families, or buying land. Hajj Medhat, a retired worker, summarized the life conditions of many workers in a somewhat intense way when he said: "we were nothing when we came to the plant, now we have become something, a big thing". Those who joined the plant later as temporary workers starting from 2007 lived a different reality conditioned by the devaluation of EISCO's market status since the 1980's' (ibid., 22). This emphasis on stability is what demonstrates the change following the neoliberal reforms.

[131] Alexander 2010, 247.   [132] Beinin and El-Hamalawy 2007.
[133] Alexander 2010, 252.

A Failure of Hegemony   247

a stage on which they could demonstrate their collective defiance with chanting, drums and hand-written placards'.[134] These forms of coming together as workers not only indicate a growing sense of solidarity but also predicted similar forms of coming together that we would see in 2011. Critical forms of democratic organizations were clear in these spaces, such as when strikers would challenge their self-elected leaders on points they disagreed with. The idea of strike spaces as 'liberated zones' also had gendered dimensions, in that women were very much central to the strike wave of the 2000s. The founding of the Real Estate Tax Authority Union indicated the clear move away from the ETUF and the support for popular and independent unions. The Real Estate Tax Authority Union was founded in 2008, and is an example of how far collective action moved during the 2000s. By 2009 around 36 000 out of 55 000 employees of the Property Tax Authority had joined the new organization.[135] A complex network of local activists made up this union, characterizing it as a bottom-up rather than top-down structure. This was to set the scene for the mushrooming of independent unions following 2011.

Several key moments define the wave of strikes throughout the 1990s and 2000s; here I focus on two of the most significant ones: the Mahalla strikes of 2006 and 2008. The Mahalla Fine Weaving and Spinning Factory is the largest textile factory in the Middle East and Africa, employing one-quarter of Egypt's entire public sector textile workforce.[136] Leading up to 2006 there had been growing unrest among public sector workers over privatization. Ahmed Nazif – prime minister and head of the cabinet of businessmen – attempted to quell this unrest by promising all public sector workers a raise in their annual bonus. This raise never materialized, leading to a spontaneous demonstration of 10 000 workers that was initially started by female workers. The number doubled the next day when security forces attempted to control the crowd. This quickly expanded into strike committees, mass meetings, sit-ins, and 'tent cities' where collective debate took precedence.[137] In other words, 'it turned thousands of workplaces into temporary laboratories for democratic self-

---

[134] Ibid., 250.   [135] Ibid., 251.   [136] Abdelrahman 2014, 56.
[137] De Smet 2012, 147. Indeed connections between this and 2011 have been noted by De Smet and others.

organisation'.[138] Minister of Labour Ai'sha Abdel-Hadi announced the demands of workers would be met and that the strike days would be considered a paid holiday.

This strike is notable not only for its size – reaching up to 24 000 workers – but because it transcended the division between public and private sector. Some have placed this strike within a wider evolving 'culture of protest' following demonstrations in support of the 2000 Al-Aqsa *intifada* in Palestine and the demonstrations against the 2003 invasion of Iraq.[139] This particular strike triggered the largest strike wave since the 1940s, and lasted for an extended period of time unlike the usual tendency of strikes to last twenty-four hours.[140] Moreover, the fact that it was a strike rather than a work-in is significant, as it halted production rather than slowed it down, which tended to be the case in previous workers' actions.

The 2008 strike, however, was to end very differently, marking a return to the tendency to use coercion to break up workers' actions. Starting on 6 April, the strike was a response to rising food prices and low wages. This led to activists and workers around the country calling for a 'day of anger' in support, urging Egyptians not to go to work. Before the strike at Mahalla could even begin, police officers in plain clothing entered the factory and began intimidating workers, in an attempt to prevent them from striking. Throughout the day these police officers forced the men to work, and escorted them home afterwards. Despite this attempt at containment, the day ended violently. Demonstrations broke out in the town itself, where one person was shot and hundreds were injured or arrested. What some have called a local uprising was brutally crushed.

The 2006 and 2008 Mahalla strikes are significant for two reasons: first, because they were the closest workers' actions had ever come to igniting a nation-wide popular movement; and second, because they made clear the complete separation of coercion from consent. Understanding these strikes as national in nature suggests a return to the concept of hegemony as it was originally understood: in its proletarian sense. Workers were able to transcend their own narrow interests and universalize them in a way that the ruling class was unable to do at this moment in time. These strikes – being labelled uprisings – were broadly understood to be political in nature and as against the

---

[138] Alexander and Bassiouny 2014, 98. [139] El Mahdi 2009. [140] Ibid., 102.

A Failure of Hegemony

ruling class and its economic and political policies. Although Gramsci's innovation was to apply the concept of hegemony to the ruling classes, hegemony could – and should – also be constructed by subaltern groups. Indeed hegemony's initial iteration was precisely a hegemony of the proletariat. It is only by constructing their own hegemony that subaltern forces can truly overthrow an oppressive order. Gramsci did not partake in liberal utopic ideas of different projects coexisting side by side in harmony; he recognized that societies are constituted through power relations, and the best outcome was for the most radical project to establish its own hegemony. We see in the strikes of 2006 and 2008 the beginnings of such an attempt, with Egyptian industrial workers bridging several gaps: between public and private sector workers, between manufacturing and services, and – most importantly – between workers and the broader population. The irony is that while the 2000s are marked by the failure of the ruling class to transcend its narrow interests, they are equally marked by the success of workers in doing this.

Simultaneously, events such as the brutal suppression of the 2008 Mahalla strike make clear the complete disintegration of consent. State coercion was seen for what it was, and in no way had the legitimacy Nasser enjoyed when he similarly used brutal coercion against workers in the 1950s and 1960s. Nasser's call to put anti-imperialism and nationalism first, before other intersecting struggles, was a form of consent that justified the coercion used against groups that opposed the new project, including workers, communists, Muslim Brotherhood members, and others. By the 2000s, these calls rang empty; the idea that the state was using violence for the good of the nation was one very few believed.

If what distinguished the Nasserist project was its recognition that workers were an important subaltern group to fold into the emerging political project, then the ruling classes that came after were increasingly unwilling to universalize their narrow interests through forming alliances with other social forces such as labour. While the Nasserist bloc did use force against striking workers, they concomitantly understood the importance of framing this within nationalist development and thereby providing an ideological legitimization of it. By the late 2000s, the failure of the financial class – now in power for more than fifteen years – to form a bloc and to create similar ideological justifications for the violence being meted out meant that it needed to turn to increasing levels of coercion simply to remain in power. This turn to

Finance Capital and Social Crisis

My naming of the new dominant social force the financial class indicates the importance finance capital carried in shaping Egyptian politics in the decades leading up to the revolution. In this concluding section, I turn to the broader shift from productive to unproductive capital in Egypt, with all of its demands and consequences. Returning to Fanon's condemnation of the dependent national bourgeoisie once again, I show that by 2011 the process of shifting from a nationalist, anti-imperialist bourgeoisie to one dependent on global capital was complete; in other words, 2011 marks the end of the hegemonic project that was created in 1952. The 1990s and 2000s see the continuing presence of the national middle-class Fanon so vehemently criticized, one whose primary mission was to act as an intermediary between local and global capital. The transition to unproductive capital marks the return of Egypt into the colonial international, once again on a dependent basis.

This chapter has traced the increased tempo of finance capital, and how this shift in tempo – marked by acceleration – ultimately destroyed the balance both Gramsci and Fanon spoke of as being integral to hegemony. From a Gramscian perspective, it was the inability of the ruling class post-1967 onwards to create a historical bloc or hegemony. However, it is only by using a Fanonian lens – i.e. 'stretching' Marxism – that we can understand *why* this didn't happen. In other words, the emergence in Egypt of the dependent bourgeoisie Fanon had predicted explains the *structural* inability to form hegemony; this class cannot accumulate capital on the scale necessary, and so it turns to transnational patronage to ensure its domination.

This is connected not only to the shift in tempo, but also the shift from productive to unproductive capital. Recall that financialization brought with it the increasing centralization of power in a small number of individuals, the financial class. In an interview, the former head of Bank Misr al Motahad, Hassan Hussein, said the following:

Finance Capital and Social Crisis

In the 1980s, there were respected businessmen who worked in trade and industry. They would open a letter of credit and when the goods arrived, they would pay the banks. But in the 1990s, businessmen were trading with the banks' money. For example, those who had political connections bought pieces of land for a nominal price. Then they would get loans from the banks based on the value of this piece of land after the bank had highly inflated its price. These people were involved in unproductive activities and made money using state-owned lands.[141]

His point about productive capital is what interests me, as it reveals one of the major distinctions between the Nasserist project and the financial class of the 1990s and 2000s – with the infitah class acting as a bridge between the two – namely: the shift from national productive capital to finance capital that was, on the whole, unproductive. The Nasserist bloc made the public sector the centre of the economy, based on industry. This project ultimately came up against constraints set by the colonial international, and the rise of the infitah ruling class saw the rise of financial speculation, rents, and import/export as the main means of accumulating capital. The financial class that emerged at the expense of the infitah project did not radically depart from this form of capital accumulation; what we see instead is an acceleration of neoliberal restructuring. When Hussein claims that the new type of businessman was unproductive, he means that land and money were now being used to generate more money, rather than being invested in industry, trade, or other long-term projects. Speculation – largely through the funds of national banks – was unable to contribute to the development of the nation as a whole – but it did develop a small class of Egyptians who continued to become wealthier. The public sector – once the jewel in the crown of national development, slowly degenerated until it was held up by nothing but corruption – ironically the charge held up against Nasser.

Despite increasing rhetoric around the free market and against the state, the state was a central actor from 1952 to 2011. Although common sense would suggest that the state was less interventionist following infitah than it had been under Nasserism, what we see is that the state remained as interventionist as ever – but this intervention was not directed elsewhere and to different ends. As Timothy Mitchell noted, 'The state turned resources away from agriculture and industry. It now subsidized financiers instead of factories, cement kilns instead of

---

[141] El Tarouty 2015, 71.

bakeries, speculators instead of schools'.[142] Reforms of the public and private sectors and the growing availability of capital lend credence to Mitchell's arguments that the expanding financial sector did not get rid of state support but redirected it where the support was to go.[143] This created tension with national banks, who had no means of pressuring businessmen to repay the massive loans they were now taking out.[144] National banks – whose role arguably was to finance national infrastructure and public projects through tax payer savings and pensions – were now providing credit to business projects instead, projects the majority of Egyptians would never set foot in, let alone own.[145] This spilled into elections and political life, as the new electoral system encouraged businessmen to stand for election; after all, all that was needed was money.[146]

As highlighted in this chapter, a central mechanism through which privatization took place was through investment by foreign capital, primarily from the Gulf. This investment targeted key national sectors, sectors that had previously been presented as central to national development. Perhaps nothing encapsulates the shift from productive to unproductive capital as much as the privatization of national industries such as cement and steel, long the centrepiece of Egyptian modernization. Steel in particular is symbolic for many reasons: it is the material that builds the nation; that represents industry and infrastructure.

---

[142] 2002, 276.

[143] Ibid., 277. As Roll notes: 'financial sector reforms allowed Gamal Mubarak to strengthen his personal ties to the strategically important financial sector. Many of the changes taking place in the boardrooms of public and private financial institutions as part of the financial reforms put in power friends or, at the very least, confidants of the President's son, whom he had known since his own financial sector career. Exemplary of this are Hassan Abdallah, Vice Chairman and Managing Director of the Arab African International Bank (AAIB) and Board Member of the Central Bank of Egypt as well as Yasser El-Mallawany, Chief Executive Officer of EFG-Hermes. Both of them are members of the NDP's Policy Secretariat and are seen as close friends of Gamal Mubarak' (ibid., 366).

[144] This was particularly the case after 2004, when Farouk al Okda – a close associate of Gamal Mubarak – was made head of Egypt's Central Bank. As Safinaz el Tarouty (2015, 72) notes, 'there was a general pressure on the banks to reconcile with the businessmen and not to arrest them. They don't pay back the whole amount but negotiate on paying part of it, and they will get out'.

[145] By 2011, Egypt was servicing a debt of LE962.2 billion – double the amount it had been in 2004, just seven years ago (Abdelrahman 2014, 15).

[146] Arafat 2011, 39.

Finance Capital and Social Crisis 253

Indeed advertisements for steel on Egyptian television are often particularly nationalist in tone.

For the Nasserist project, industry was key to Egypt's future, and steel was a central element of this vision. Companies such as the Egyptian Iron and Steel Company (EISCO) were seen as symbols of Egyptian nationalism and independence, underlining how steel production was central to Egyptian development. Indeed upon the founding of this particular company Nasser is claimed to have said 'Egypt's dream [has] come true'.[147] The aim of the company was to produce enough steel so that Egypt would not have to import any at all. The profits of this company went to the state, a state committed to national development. By the time we get to the 2000s, 65 per cent of Egypt's steel market was controlled by one of the major personalities inside the financial class: Ahmed 'Ezz.[148]

'Ezz has been described as a 'living embodiment of the intimate connection between the state and capital under neoliberalism'.[149] From a scandal where he was accused of buying Egypt's largest public steel company at an exorbitantly low price to accusations of manipulating steel prices to make profit, to preventing the passing of an anti-monopoly bill in parliament, 'Ezz has been at the centre of Egypt's transition to neoliberalism. Indeed 'Ezz was massively in debt to national banks by 2011, having taking out loans of such proportion as to bring about criticism even from within the NDP. It is no surprise that when the 2011 revolution happened, he was one of the main targets of public anger. EISCO's market share had slowly been taken away by 'Ezz's company, and it suffered further from increased prices after IMF-led structural adjustment and competition from imports.[150] Egypt went from producing steel in large public sector companies, with the aim of developing the nation as a form of anti-imperialism, to producing steel in private companies monopolized by individual businessmen who were part and parcel of the ruling class.

This begs the question of the connection between the state and national development. Is the problem of development a problem of the state? Does the presence of the state equivocally mean the absence of economic and political development? It would appear that the

---

[147] Makram-Ebeid 2012, 14.   [148] Chekir and Diwan 2013, 2.
[149] Alexander and Bassiouny 2014, 55.   [150] Ibid., 23.

254　　　　　　　　　　　　　　　　*Finance Capital and Empty Time*

nation, the state, and the nation-state have been thoroughly discredited in the decades since the end of colonial rule. As Adam Hanieh argues, 'the agency of freedom is located in the realm of the market, while tyranny lurks ever-present in the state. The history of the region [the Middle East] is thus characteristically recounted as a long-standing struggle between the "authoritarian state" and "economic and political liberalisation"'.[151] Yet what happens when we ask why it was only a strong state, with a strong nationalist project, that was able to create hegemony in Egypt since independence? In other words, nationalism as a project that directs the state appears to have created the levels of consent needed to lead, rather than just to rule, as Gramsci would say. It is not that the state disappeared following the opening of Egypt's markets; it continued to be central to accumulation, but directed its power, resources, and coercive muscle to a different project. What changed from the Nasserist bloc to the financial ruling class was not the role of the state but rather the project to which the state's energies were directed.

The postcolonial state had a project, and I define project in the largest sense possible. As Vivienne Jabri has written, the postcolonial state is an interventionist one that constructs a hegemonic structure in order to legitimize a political economy of development, planning, and management of natural resources.[152] Alongside this, Omnia El Shakry has argued that the postcolonial state in Egypt was built around the project of social welfare and national development.[153] This is where the postcolonial state poses a (limited) challenge to the colonial international. Thus while we can see the Nasserist project as having challenged the international, the infitah project and the ruling class that came after it did precisely the opposite. The afterlife of hegemony was marked by an unwillingness to take seriously the colonial nature of the international, and consequently to resist or subvert it. Instead, the dominant logic of neoliberal restructuring was adopted by an increasingly small number of elites, who eventually failed to produce a coherent project that would allow them to create hegemony. Part of this failure is due to the increasing materiality felt by many Egyptians around the failures of the economic policies themselves; wealth was being monopolized, poverty was rising, and repression was spreading beyond the confines of political activism. Another part of this failure was due to the strength of

[151] 2014, 5.　　[152] 2012, 102.　　[153] 2007.

the previous hegemonic project created under Nasser. This project created a particular set of relationships between the state, the nation, and the people that continue to exert power today, in complicated ways. Given this, perhaps a question that should be asked is: what was it about that set of relationships, in that moment, under that leader, that spoke to so many Egyptians?

This question goes beyond normative claims about right and wrong. There is little doubt that coercion has been part of the creation of postcolonial Egyptian nation from 1952 until today. This coercion has taken many forms: from the displacement of communities such as the Nubians in order to construct national infrastructure, to the disappearing of politically active leftists, workers, feminists, and communists. Coercion has been part and parcel of the nation and the state, and had underpinned every political project in Egypt's modern history. The question then becomes: where coercion has always been present, why is it that consent has not? And what does the *absence* of consent rather than the *presence* of coercion tell us about nation-making in Egypt? By focusing both on the (continuing) presence of coercion as well as the increasing absence of consent, I hope to have presented a different retelling of the making of the modern Egyptian nation, and its culmination in the 2011 revolution.

Conclusion: Haunted Histories and Decolonial Futures

To be haunted is to be tied to historical and social effects.

Avery Gordon[1]

In the postcolonial world, the national question is, of course, historically fused with a colonial question.

Partha Chatterjee[2]

The living present is scarcely as self-sufficient as it claims to be; that we would do well not to count on its density and solidity, which might under exceptional circumstances betray us.

Frederick Jameson[3]

An inheritance is never gathered together, it is never one with itself.

Jacques Derrida[4]

This generation was never able to imagine itself escaping the borders of the established political map that it eventually came to see as a pipe-dream: to the east the socialist camp, to the west the capitalist one and in the middle, at the very beating heart, the national independence movements of the third world.

Arwa Salih[5]

In no way must my colour be felt as a stain ... another solution is possible. It implies a restructuring of the world.

Frantz Fanon[6]

Millions of people filled the streets of Egypt in late January 2011. The events that followed were both entirely unexpected and

---

[1] Gordon 2008, 1.   [2] Chatterjee 1986, 18.   [3] Sprinker 1999, 39.
[4] Derrida 2012, 18.   [5] Salih 2018.   [6] Fanon 1963, 63.

Haunted Histories and Decolonial Futures

scarcely shocking at the same time. The country was, and had been, in a state of crisis for decades; and frustration, fear, anger, and hopelessness had become commonplace. And yet, it came as a surprise, for one simple reason: no one had predicted the revolution would happen when it did. Throughout this book, I have argued that the ruling class that was in power when the 2011 revolution broke out not only failed to create hegemony, but was the product of the fall of Nasserism as the hegemonic project of decolonization. This failure makes legible the timing of the revolution, suggested that the events of 2011 should be historicized within the legacies of colonial rule, capitalist expansion, and anticolonial nationalism that have shaped contemporary Egyptian politics. I have argued that by searching for hegemony, we find alternate explanations for the rise and fall of different political projects; in other words, I have thought of hegemony as a lens or a searchlight through which to excavate Egyptian political history. Even in its absence, hegemony tells us much about the negotiations, conflicts, and alliances among various social forces, the different ideological pronouncements and promises made by these forces, and the political projects these forces coalesced around.

This concluding chapter revisits hegemony and its afterlives in Egypt through the concept of haunting. I trace some of the ways these afterlives fed into the 2011 revolution, and ask why it was so important for each ruling class to portray itself as either a rupture or a continuity. Haunting allows me to lay out both how these different projects were formed, and how they seeped into one another; in other words, how some projects haunted others. This notion of haunting is useful in various ways. It pushes for an understanding of how the legacies of some projects persist, but not always in tangible ways. In particular, I use the concept of haunting to refer to how the spectre of the Nasserist project continued – and continues – to set the standard of what a successful hegemonic project looks like, thereby explicitly and implicitly setting expectations around what other projects should say, do, or be. In other words, I posit that Nasserism set the terms of the political and economic debate in contemporary Egypt; the projects that came after consistently found that they had to work within these terms – or face serious crises. Such expectations are not merely rhetorical, but also have material repercussions.

Figure 5.1 Egypt goes to the polls for parliamentary elections. Credit: Peter Macdiarmid / Getty Images.

Haunted Histories

The image above (Figure 5.1) is one of many you might see across Cairo and other Egyptian towns, villages and cities. Images of Nasser were also present during the 2011 revolution, a haunting presence across a cityscape that brings to life the promises of a past long gone. Haunting is a visceral experience, one that destabilises past, present and future. The image above captures this: we know it is in present-day Cairo; yet the image itself – its black-and-white nature, the depiction of a young Nasser – takes us back to a different time.

Spectres of ghosts, death, and haunting appear every now and then in the *Prison Notebooks*, perhaps most notably in reference to the interregnum when Gramsci writes, 'the crisis consists precisely in the fact that the old is dying and the new cannot be born: in this interregnum, morbid phenomena of the most varied kind come to pass'.[7] An organic political crisis – such as the one we saw in 2011 – is a moment in time where the old order is dying, but where there is nothing robust enough to replace it. This line, moving between death and crisis on the one hand, and 'morbid' phenomena on the other, brings to mind scenes of ghostly terror, during

[7] 1992, 32.

Haunted Histories

which something that should not have been unleashed has escaped. Gramsci attunes us to the uncontrollable forces lying beneath the surface of any political order, and the risks of entering this 'interregnum'. He highlights that it is not given that one order will replace another; nor that hegemony is followed by hegemony. As I have shown in the case of Egypt, the Nasserist project – Egypt's sole instance of hegemony – was followed by an interregnum that stretched out into forty years, at the end of which was the crisis Gramsci gestures towards. How do hegemony and its afterlives come together? How do we begin to understand the ties between these two historical periods, and the ways in which hegemony seeped into the everyday workings of what came after?

The concept of hauntology owes its roots to Derrida, who made ghosts the subject of analysis in his book *Spectres of Marx*.[8] Derrida asks us to listen and speak with the spectre, to resist the disinclination we have towards this because of how we have been academically trained, and to be open to secrets or other forms of knowledge this listening may reveal. Listening to the ghost means listening to the past and the future at the same time. In her magisterial *Ghostly Matters,* Avery Gordon seeks a new way of knowing, one that is more than listening or seeing but that instead searches for what is still among us in the form of 'intimations, hints, suggestions, and portents'[9] – all of which make up what she calls 'ghostly matters'. Haunting is frightening, in that it registers and brings to the surface the harm inflicted or loss sustained by social violence that happened in the past or present:

> It seemed to me that haunting was precisely the domain of turmoil and trouble, that moment (of however long duration) when things are not in their assigned places, when the cracks and rigging are exposed, when the people who are meant to be invisible show up without any sign of leaving, when disturbed feelings cannot be put away, when something else, something different from before, seems like it must be done.[10]

For Gordon, to study social life means confronting the ghostly aspects of it. This poses a critical challenge to knowledge production and the ways in which we legitimize certain forms of knowing over others. Ghosts can be understood as empirical evidence, or they can be show us that empirical evidence, understood in conventional terms, is not always necessary to show something is real. 'Of one thing I am sure: it's not that ghosts don't exist. The postmodern, late-capitalist, postcolonial world represses and

---

[8] Derrida 2012.   [9] Ibid.   [10] Ibid., xvi.

projects its ghosts or phantoms in similar intensities, if not entirely the same forms, as the older world did'.[11]

Gordon uses haunting to explore what is hidden, invisible, lingering, and unmeasurable. In doing so, she asks questions about what we consider to be real or valid knowledge, and how we can account for the afterlives of certain political projects. It is these afterlives this book has been interested in, particularly in relation to the Nasserist project in Egypt, one that was arguably much more powerful than those that came after. I suggest that the afterlives of Nasserism complicate the idea of haunting, in that they haunt through both promise and failure. I see Nasserism as an instance of what José Esteban Muñoz terms 'performative force of the past'.[12] The past is performative because the past *does things*. This does not mean seeing the past as having *led* to the present, but rather to break away from conceptions of linear time entirely. As Derrida argued in *Spectres of Marx,* haunting is one of way of breaking this teleology.

On the one hand, I see Nasserism as haunting in the sense that it normalized certain ideas around what politics in Egypt's postcolonial period should look like and what an economic model founded on ideas of independent development could deliver. On the other hand, Nasserism should be understood as a form of haunting in that it significantly affected the ability of leftist social forces to prevent the very neoliberal project Nasser consistently warned Egyptians about. Nasser's weakening of the left – perhaps the only force that could have mobilized successfully against the reforms Sadat was to put in place – is one of the major failures of the Nasserist project more broadly, and one that continues to have repercussions on contemporary Egyptian politics. Nasserism thus haunts us in two ways: as a historical moment and project that promised much but ultimately came apart – therefore as a kind of historical alternative that never quite materialized; and as a project filled with social violence that continues to haunt contemporary Egyptian politics today.

I take my cue from Gordon's suggestion to see the 'particular density, delicacy and propulsive force of the imagination in sociological analysis, which is too often limited by its restrictive commitment to an empiricist epistemology and its supporting ontology of the visible and the concrete'.[13] It blurs the strong lines we often draw between different political projects, suggesting that ideas and decisions from one project can seep into other

---

[11] Ibid., 12.   [12] Muñoz 2009, 21.   [13] Ibid.

Nasserism and the Promises of the Past 261

projects that are constructed as new or antithetical: 'Haunting raises spectres, and it alters the experience of being in time, the way we separate the past, the present, and the future'.[14] Finally, it gives us a way of thinking through why some projects have the power to haunt, while others do not; what is it about the constitution of particular projects that produces afterlives? More broadly, I am interested in how we come to understand how certain political projects create both 'particular kinds of subjects' as well as the 'possible and the impossible'.[15]

Nasserism and the Promises of the Past

The Nasserist project was created by and flourished within a particular historical moment, that of decolonization. Its mobilization of anticolonial nationalism and independent, state-led industrialization mirrored a broader trend across the postcolonial world that saw the dependency of former colonies on the metropole as a major challenge to meaningful independence. In many ways, the Nasserist project predated Nasser. The project formed in the 1950s, against a backdrop of the intense nationalist fervour that had engulfed the country for decades. Because of the centrality of nationalism to almost all social movements in the decades leading up to 1952, the groundwork for the Nasserist project was already in place when it was 'officially' established in 1952. Key changes such as the nationalization of the Suez Canal, the adoption of positive neutralism, land reforms, the expansion of the public sector, and the introduction of free social services such as education and health care, were part of this broader move to take control of the national economy. This control, however, had a very limited purview; it belonged to the ruling class, who liberally employed both consent and coercion to cultivate support and crush resistance.

This mixed record is what complicates an understanding of Nasserism as haunting. It is clear that Nasserism had afterlives, and that the figure of Nasser himself continued to linger in the Egyptian public imagination. Certain events, such as the nationalization of the Suez Canal and the 1967 defeat to Israel, as well as certain policies, such as the land reform programme, became landmarks in Egyptian history, moments that set the contours of what an independent Egypt could be. Haunting, however, expressed itself in different ways. On the one hand, as a reminder of

[14] Ibid., xv. [15] Ibid.

the social violence that had come before; on the other hand, as a reminder of a promise that was extremely powerful, and yet that ultimately failed. Haunting is thus also split between these realities: that of promise and of failure. At times, it is the promises of Nasserism that haunt Egypt; at other times, it is the failures of Nasserism that continue to haunt Egypt.

In her memoir, Egyptian communist Arwa Salih uses the term *stillborn* to describe how her generation of Egyptian leftists related to the Nasserist project, one they saw as an unfinished failure that haunts the present nonetheless:

I felt profoundly disconnected from the 'national struggle' that haunts every sentence of this book. This national struggle was a historical necessity for liberation-era communists. Both second and third wave communists were hopelessly trapped in the logic of anti-imperial nationalist populism, isolated from 'the only game in town' and forced to lead a 'double life' that destroyed both their integrity and 'their ability to believe'.[16]

I detailed the ways in which the relationship between Nasser and the communists was especially tenuous. The extended programme of disappearances and imprisoning under Nasser, whether of communists or Islamists, brings us back to the notion of haunting. Gordon writes that disappearance is a 'state-sponsored method for haunting a population. The power of disappearance is the power to control everyday reality, to make the unreal real; it is the power to be spoken for, to be vanished as the very condition of your existence'.[17] This power was exercised against the left in Nasser's Egypt, despite apparent similarities in how they understood Egypt's future. 'The power of disappearance is to create a deathly consent out of our own stolen heterodoxy and will to dissent. The fundamental mode by which disappearance does its dirty nervous work is haunting'.[18]

And yet what we see is a continuing loyalty towards the Nasserist project on the part of many radical forces. As Salih notes, an intellectual in the sixties could either 'sing from behind the bars of his cage' or 'wither away in a crushing tomb of solitude'.[19] The predicament here was the realization that at that particular historical moment, anti-imperialism and nationalism were the most important projects, and that Nasser and the Free Officers seemed to represent the most likely

---

[16] Salih 2018, 1.   [17] Ibid., 131.   [18] Ibid.   [19] Salih 2018, 23.

Liberalism within Limits   263

possibility of achieving them. Egyptians were caught up in a nationalist
movement that 'ultimately destroyed it',[20] and, as Salih notes, the
'Nasserist vision got all tangled up with Marxism, and it became
increasingly difficult to distinguish between the two until well after
the flood waters had receded'.[21] The glaring paradox of this time was
precisely the concomitant existence within the left of nostalgia and
bitterness towards Nasser.[22]

This is the generation Salih focuses on in her book, a 'melancholy
generation of the sixties' who were content to 'sing half a song in
Nasser's prisons and whose petty-bourgeois origins destined them to
failure and defeat'.[23] Remembering, as she writes, is painful; it is not
just painful in the way memories can be, but it is also painful in that it
forces the leftist to confront their own role in the failure of the Nasserist
project. Some, like Salih, did this by acknowledging their guilt; others
repressed it, and turned to nostalgia instead.

A crucial point made in Samah Selim's introduction to Salih's memoir is that it was this left that was inherited by Sadat in 1970.[24] One of
the major afterlives of the Nasserist project, then, was the decimation
of a left that could have launched an attack on infitah, neoliberalization, and the broader shift towards the right. Instead, Sadat's 'corrective revolution' and later purges against leftists were to reveal just how
weak the left was, and how discredited many of their ideas had become.
The ghosts of Nasserism are many, but surely his exclusion and
silencing of those who supposedly shared his vision for what Egypt
could be produced an especially intense form of haunting. In her
attempt to understand Nasserism through the contradiction of those
who he imprisoned nevertheless 'singing his praises' from behind bars,
Arwa Salih pinpoints not only a major enigma of the Nasser era, but
also one of the central reasons for its ultimate failure.

Liberalism within Limits

Looking back at the start of the global neoliberal revolution – or
counter-revolution, to be more accurate – it seems as though it all
happened very quickly, and very decisively. Margaret Thatcher's statement – 'there is no alternative' – was not an attempt at debate cr

---

[20] Beinin 2005b, 585.   [21] Salih 2018, 28.   [22] Ibid., 3.   [23] Salih 2018, xvi.
[24] Ibid., xvi.

conversation, but rather the final word on a matter that had already been decided. Much work today looks at the ways in which neoliberalism produced – and was produced by – forms of liberal subjectivity that facilitated the rise of free market orthodoxy, and all of the self-disciplining this required. Similarly, much work has looked at the ways in which certain notions of public sector inefficiency, state corruption and incompetence, and free market competition became commonplace, despite the lack of evidence. In the third chapter, I focused on some of the debates that took place in Egypt during the transition to infitah – or free market capitalism – in the late 1960s, and proposed that the transition was not as seamless as imagined. I argued that while neoliberal restructuring went ahead materially – albeit very slowly – the ideological legitimation never really fell in place. While Nasserism as a project was hegemonic, the one that came after – led by Sadat – was not. The reason for this, I posit, is precisely the failure of free market orthodoxy to successfully challenge the Nasserist version of state-led capitalist development, a project which essentially had already set the parameters within which economic debates could take place.

For Avery Gordon, the spectres or ghosts always appear when the trouble they represent is no longer being contained or repressed or blocked from view:

Haunting and the appearance of specters or ghosts is one way, I tried to suggest, we are notified that what's been concealed is very much alive and present, interfering precisely with those always incomplete forms of containment and repression ceaselessly directed towards us.[25]

But what happens when haunting has contradictory effects? In other words, what happens when a project that haunts us also has liberatory effects? In this section I argue that the Nasserist project has haunted Egypt in ways that have slowed the encroachment of the neoliberal project, thereby stalling the disastrous economic, social, and political effects it would eventually bring with it. Although Nasserism as a project failed in its own stated goals of social justice and Arab socialism, it did manage to normalize certain notions of how a national economy should work.

I have shown how, starting in the 1980s and accelerating through the 1990s and 2000s, Egyptian workers launched a major offensive against the expansion of the private sector and the privatization of national

---

[25] Ibid., xv.

Liberalism within Limits

enterprises. Committees were formed to resist privatization, major strikes were held, one after the other, and contestation around labour rights increased in parliament. Privatization brought new forms of precarity as well as a deepening division between temporary and permanent workers in its attempt to fragment the working class. Recall Derrida, who wrote that ghosts may seem to have been vanquished, but are always ready to come back: 'Capitalist societies always heave a sigh of relief and say to themselves: communism is finished since the collapse of the totalitarianisms of the twentieth century and not only is it finished, but it did not take place, it was only a ghost. They do no more than disavow the undeniable itself: a ghost never dies, it remains always to come and to come-back'.[26]

This ghost came back in the form of a particular promise Nasserism consistently made (though never quite delivered). Workers consistently mobilized an idea of what the Egyptian economy should look like in their attempts to challenge neoliberal reforms. This drew on both the rich history of worker contestation in Egypt, that predated Nasserism and that Nasserism was largely based on, as well as certain material changes that took place in the 1950s and 1960s. Combined, these created a certain understanding of the relationship between workers and the state. In a sense, we can understand the years between the decline of the Nasserist project and the 2011 revolution as a slow erosion of this understanding, a chipping away at the material and ideological support for state-led capitalist development.

By the 2000s, finance capital had come to dominate Egypt's economy, and privatization was rapidly accelerated, both centralizing power in the hands of private interests and effectively 'restructuring Egypt's business elite'.[27] Large family holdings became characteristic of the Egyptian economy, and many within the new class were able to exercise a level of independence from the state previously unknown in Egypt.[28] By the early 2000s, even sectors traditionally dominated by public capital such as construction and transportation, were now dominated by private capital.[29] This was coupled with the erosion of

---

[26] Derrida 2012, 123.   [27] Roll 2010, 350.
[28] Take the example of Samih Sawiris, member of Egypt's richest business family, and his move to register Orascom – one of Egypt's biggest companies – as a Swiss company in order to avoid interference from the Egyptian government (Roll 2010, 366).
[29] Abdelrahman 2015, 15.

the industrial sector through the dismantling of manufacturing. A robust manufacturing sector was a legacy of Nasserism's import substitution industrialization policy (ISI) and thus represented a material reversal of the Nasserist project.[30] By the late 1990s, the state had earned over $1.5 billion from these privatizations and over 100 factories had been privatized and half of all public enterprises were now privately owned.[31] By the late 2000s, the Egyptian economy was controlled by twenty to twenty-five family-owned monopolies,[32] leading to the intensification of strikes in the 2000s.

Major strikes such as those in 2006 and 2008 at Mahalla mobilized workers across sectors, and also went beyond factories and companies, permeating the Egyptian public sphere. These strikes – labelled uprisings – were broadly understood to be political in nature and as against the ruling class and its economic and political policies. Importantly, they were increasingly met with intense levels of coercion (especially the 2008 Mahalla strike), signalling the increasing tenuousness of the neoliberal project that had begun thirty years earlier, and that still hadn't quite justified itself. Workers demanded a return to something, to an era during which privatization was not the dominant logic of the nation. For some, this may be read as a situation in which workers did not going far enough in expressing radical demands. Yet I propose that it can also be read as the lingering presence of a hegemonic project that was seen as thoroughly Egyptian, a project in which workers saw themselves even as they sought to go beyond it.

Ghosts produce material effects. I have suggested in this section that the ghost of Nasserism continued to haunt the new project that formed around Sadat, albeit in a contradictory manner. The strong ideological legitimacy Nasserism deployed around state-led capitalist development, free social services, land reform, and industrialization came back to haunt Sadat throughout his attempt to transition towards a free market, and liberalism more broadly. This produced a form of liberalism that was contained within limits, limits set by the project that had come before. These limits were also constantly reproduced by worker's strikes, the student movement, leftist activism, and other forms of resistance against Egypt's new direction. In this sense, the revolution of 1952 may have died in 1967, but its ghosts emerged and persisted shortly thereafter.

[30] De Smet 2016, 174. [31] Ibid. [32] Kandil 2012, 353.

Mastery, Revolution, and Anticolonial Praxis

While the last two sections have worked with the concept of haunting to blur as well as strengthen the lines between different political projects, this section explores a deeper critique of the assumptions embedded within these projects, and how they led to the moment of 2011. I focus specifically on nationalism, tracing its evolution from anticolonial to neoliberal nationalism. Ideas of the nation have held both liberatory and regressive potential, often at the same time. The political work performed by nationalism has also been central to the various political projects that have emerged in modern Egyptian history. I am interested in thinking through the contradictions embedded within anticolonial nationalism, and how these produced afterlives that have significantly affected the ways in which the Egyptian nation has been imagined since. In a sense, then, this section is still about a form of haunting: the ways in which the promise and failure of anticolonial nationalism has haunted Egypt ever since.

Edward Said's reading of Fanon on the question of nationalism is particularly astute. For Fanon, nationalism is a necessary but far from sufficient condition for liberation – 'perhaps even a sort of temporary illness that must be gone through'.[33] Because of the unforgiving dialectic of colonialism, independence does not necessarily bring with it liberation:

The new nation will produce a new set of policemen, bureaucrats, and merchants to replace the departed Europeans. Nationalism is too heavily imprinted with the *unresolved* (or unresolvable) dialectic of colonialism for it to lead very far beyond it. The complexity of independence, which is so naturally desirable a goal for all colonised people, is that simultaneously it dramatized the discrepancy between colonizer and colonized so basic to colonialism, and also a discrepancy between the people and their leaders, leaders who perforce are shaped by colonialism.[34]

Yet what this book has argued is that at the moment of independence, Egypt did not produce this class that was simply a caricature of European colonial rulers. Anticolonial nationalism in the form of the Nasserist project was able to temporarily resolve this dialectic of colonialism that Said speaks of. The discrepancy between the people and their leaders was at its most minimal during this period. If anything, the

[33] 2000. [34] Ibid.

Nasserist project more closely resembled Fanon's notion of progressive nationalism. The dependent bourgeoisie Fanon predicted, or the new set of policemen, bureaucrats, and merchants Said mentions here, did materialize in Egypt – but at least two decades after independence. Nevertheless, it is important to also read Fanon against Fanon,[35] and to critically assess his notions of anticolonial nationalism.

For Fanon, national consciousness was something that came from the people in their quest for liberation from colonial rule. Once it is captured by the colonial bourgeois elite – the nationalist leaders – it will simply be used to continue colonialism under the guise of independence. Yet the question here is: are all nationalist leaders the same? Recalling Siba Grovogui's more optimistic assessment of African independence leaders, it is perhaps useful to question whether all nationalist leaders continued colonialism under the guise of independence. Surely this cannot be said for Kwame Nkrumah or Kenneth Kaunda; nor for Patrice Lumumba who was ultimately assassinated for his anticolonial views. What we see in many of these nations, as in Egypt, is the delayed emergence of the dependent bourgeois Fanon speaks of. Colonialism did create this bourgeoisie, and they did eventually come to power – but not at the moment of independence. The nationalist leaders that emerged at independence were instead very much anticolonial, in both ideology and action.

This does not, however, exonerate the Nasserist project and historical bloc for its failures. Indeed, as Fanon noted, the national government should always *cede its power back to the people*. It should, in effect, *dissolve itself*. Because nationalist consciousness during the anticolonial moment comes from the people, this is where it should reside. However, as we have seen, the Nasserist bloc – while it did universalize its interests – also co-opted and repressed various subaltern groups. From the communist movement to labour, and from feminists to the Muslim Brotherhood, the bloc was very much unable to ultimately represent the national interest in its fullest form. It is here that critical approaches to nationalism are important; the nation cannot be a whole, and thus there can never be a 'national interest'.

To understand the failures of the Nasserist project, it is useful to return to the question of passive revolution. Partha Chatterjee's influential argument that all instances of decolonization during the 1950s

---

[35] A special thanks to Vanessa Eileen Thompson for her phrasing.

Mastery, Revolution, and Anticolonial Praxis 269

and 1960s took the form of passive revolution is key here, for Egypt was certainly no exception to this global tendency. Understanding Nasserism as hegemonic does not preclude understanding it as an instance of passive revolution; Nasserism was both at the same time. This book has focused on the hegemony of Nasserism, but in understanding its failures passive revolution is central. Because Nasserism represented an instance of passive revolution, it cannot be understood as revolutionary in the sense Gramsci valorized. It was hegemonic, which meant subaltern forces were part of the Nasserist historic bloc; but this did not mean that their political project was the central aim of the bloc. Nasser's repression of workers, communists, and other subaltern groups demonstrates that Nasser's project was a different one. State-led capitalist development was still capitalist development.

However, staying with Chatterjee, there is a crucial moment in which Egypt diverges from the progression of passive revolution he traces in India. Writing on India several decades after the moment of decolonization, Chatterjee argues:

> The capitalist class has come to acquire a position of moral-political hegemony over civil society, consisting principally of the urban middle classes. The dominance of the capitalist class within the state structure as a whole can be inferred from the virtual consensus among all major political parties about the priorities of rapid economic growth led by private investment, both domestic and foreign. This is the evidence of the current success of the passive revolution.[36]

This is precisely what did not happen in Egypt. The capitalist class that emerged around the infitah project, as well as the class that emerged around financialization were both unable to acquire this position of moral-political hegemony over civil society. In fact the urban middle classes were very much increasingly excluded from capital accumulation as we move closer to 2011. Moreover, the consensus Chatterjee points to around private investment and rapid economic growth did not exist in Egypt by 2011, as other social forces such as the military had alternative notions of capital accumulation. The success of passive revolution in the Indian context in the 1970s onwards was thus not replicated in the Egyptian context.

While Egypt and India shared the same experience with passive revolution at the moment of decolonization in the 1950s, affirming

---

[36] In Srivastava and Bhattacharya 2012, 128.

Chatterjee's argument that this was a *global* tendency, we see a clear divergence in the 1970s. Where India would go on to experience a *second* passive revolution that was hegemonic, this was not the case in Egypt. Instead, while Egypt did experience a second passive revolution, Egypt also experienced a steady decline in hegemony up until the 2000s, where there was no bloc or hegemony to speak of. It remains the case that the Nasserist passive revolution and the Nasserist bloc is the only instance of hegemony in modern Egyptian history.

But it is important to pause here, and to revisit the assumptions embedded within the Nasserist vision of the future. I draw in particular from Julietta Singh's book *Unthinking Mastery*, to probe deeper into the notions of sovereignty and mastery that seeped through the Nasserist project and without which hegemony would have been unthinkable. In *Unthinking Mastery,* Singh explores the ways in which postcolonial thinkers – even as they criticized the colonial project – reproduced elements of it in their envisioning of a future beyond empire.[37] She looks specifically at the idea of mastery – mastery of the self, mastery of others, mastery of nature – and reads it as an idea rooted in colonial epistemologies of being.

Across anticolonial discourse the mastery of the coloniser over the colonies was a practice that was explicitly disavowed, and yet, in their efforts to decolonise, anticolonial thinkers in turn advocated practices of mastery – corporeal, linguistic, and intellectual – toward their own liberation.[38]

Singh speaks here of corporeal, linguistic, and intellectual forms of mastery. Yet as we have seen, Nasserism – a project that saw itself as anticolonial – also advocated mastery of nature and society. Singh recognizes that for anticolonial thinkers, countering colonial mastery by producing masterful subjects was seen as necessary to producing decolonized subjects. But, she argues, this masterful discourse of anticolonialism did not interrogate its own masterfulness thoroughly; did not 'dwell enough on how its complex entanglements with mastery would come to resonate in the postcolonial future it so passionately anticipated'.[39]

Mastery over society and over nature became emblematic of Nasserism's attempt at regaining sovereignty and control over Egyptian land, resources, and – most importantly – Egyptian futures. Perhaps nothing indicates this more clearly than the mega-projects Nasser is

---

[37] Singh 2017.   [38] Ibid., 2.   [39] Ibid.

famous for, including the building of the High Dam. These projects were geared precisely towards mastery over a terrain that needed to yield to the forces of modernity and futuristic thinking. Videos and images of workers steadily chipping away at masses of solid rock reveal the workings of attempted mastery. The Dam was necessary for the nation, at any cost. The devastation caused in loss of life and loss of nature was incidental; a price that needed to be paid.

Singh writes: 'As a pursuit, mastery invariably and relentlessly reaches towards the indiscriminate control over something – whether human or inhuman, animate or inanimate. It aims for the full submission of an object – or something *objectified* – whether it be external or internal to oneself. In so doing, mastery requires a rupturing of the object being mastered, because to be mastered means to be weakened to a point of fracture'.[40] This process of objectification can be seen at various points in Nasser's project. The objectification of land in the project of land reform; the objectification of labour and workers in the project of industrialization; the objectification of nature in the project of modernization; and the objectification of language, religion, and culture in the project of de-Westernization. We know now that there were other forms of violence enacted by postcolonial forms of mastery. Singh points to the relations between anticolonial masteries and colonial violence in the making of particularly masculine decolonized subjects.[41] The forms of violence enacted against Nubians point to another aspect of anticolonial masteries, as does the solidifying of the very state form that would continue to produce Egyptian Copts as unequal members of the nation.

If we follow Gramsci, we must accept that hegemony requires mastery; indeed, one could even suggest that hegemony *is* mastery. But to what ends? And for how long? This brings us back to the question of historical and political necessity: to what extent could anti-imperialism have succeeded without counter-mastery? Perhaps here Joseph Massad's warning about nationalism is pertinent; that anticolonial nationalism was necessary, at that moment in time, but that it should have been seen as a *strategic* goal. Futures beyond the nation – and beyond nationalism-as-mastery – should have been the long-term objective. To adopt mastery as the means of thinking a new future beyond empire was to adopt imperial ways of relating to the world; and

[40] Ibid., 10.   [41] Ibid., 41.

Decolonial Futures

Today, in Egypt, we see the creation of new ghosts, ghosts that will likely continue to accrue a performative force. In June 2013, following a military coup that dethroned the Muslim Brotherhood's Muhammad Morsi, Abdelfattah al Sisi became president of Egypt. Although the focus of this book is Egypt between the revolutions of 1952 and 2011, a note on post-2011 affirms the importance of hegemony as a frame through which to analyse political change. Sisi undoubtedly had support from many segments of society, who had quickly becomes disillusioned by Morsi's government. The previous two years had seen the Muslim Brotherhood lead the country after the military made a tactical decision to allow them to be a significant part of the emerging historical bloc, albeit on a subservient basis. The military was able to draw ideologically on nationalism and state-led development, explaining some of their support. Although their image had suffered following their intervention in the 2011 revolution and the multiple crackdowns they were involved in, including the infamous Maspero Massacre, they retained their reputation as the only institution capable of handling the major problems facing Egypt. Largely based on this, Sisi and the military seemed on the path to establishing a new historical bloc in 2013. The military were once again at the centre of Egypt's ruling class, and in 2013 it appeared as though they had created hegemony strong enough to withstand continuing resistance from some revolutionary forces. And yet only a few years later, this appeared to have completely evaporated, with the military turning towards extreme coercion to maintain stability.

At time of writing it is clear that the new ruling class has lost much of the support it had in 2013. Each crisis brings resistance from different parts of society, and the economic crisis facing them is increasingly astute. Regional flows of capital that have propped Egypt up for decades have all but withered away, and talks with the IMF suggest a return of the 1990s ERSAP episode that dramatically destabilized labour and led to the massive mobilization of workers across the country. It seems as though this ruling class will be unable to create a historical bloc or hegemony, and yet imagining alternatives proves

Decolonial Futures 273

difficult. The military may choose to sacrifice Sisi, but as a social force they have lost both some legitimacy in the eyes of the population as well as control over large parts of the Egyptian economy now in the hands of the social force that coalesced around Gamal Mubarak. The neoliberalization of Egypt that was started by Sadat and accelerated by Gamal Mubarak has all but destroyed the productive base of Egypt's economy, and there seems to be no way out that does not entail a period of extreme economic hardship for most Egyptians.

Perhaps the greatest indication that this is not a historical bloc has been the intense level of coercion that the ruling class has had to increasingly turn towards over the last few years, and the return to coercion being separate from consent. Part of this weakness stems from the continuing presence of contradictory accumulation strategies within the ruling class, with neoliberalization continuing despite its contribution to the revolution itself. Because the military has stepped in at key moments, for example following sugar shortages, moments have crisis have bene indefinitely postponed. Warehouses were raided and stocks that were being hoarded were confiscated. While this, along with the move by the military to invest in infrastructure, seem to indicate a focus on state-led capitalist development à la Nasser, this ruling class does not resemble the Nasserist project or bloc in any important way. It is perhaps the failure of a military-led ruling class to establish a bloc or hegemony that once again underlines how singular the Nasserist project was.

Terror and disappearance, torture and elimination, all work to create more ghosts of an unfinished past. Disappearance in particular, perhaps the most notable of the military's tactics in today's Egypt, 'is a state-sponsored procedure for producing ghosts to harrowingly haunt a population into submission'.[42] As Gordon notes, disappearance is not only about death; it is a form of organized terror unleashed by the state and military to destroy not only any form of organized resistance, but to destroy 'the disposition to opposition, the propensity to resist injury and injustice, and the desire to speak out, or simply to sympathise'.[43] Its aim is to destroy hope, the will to resist, the will to want, or dream of, more. In that sense, one becomes a target not only if one openly resists; one becomes a target simply by being in the present.

---

[42] Ibid., 115.   [43] Ibid., 124.

The aim, then, is not to fully disappear people; but rather to partially disappear them in order to impart an augury upon the remaining population. 'Disappearance is a public secret'. In this endless production of ghosts, between one project and another, social violence is continuously reproduced. Concomitantly, hope is also generated: as long as there is haunting, there is hope. Minute, barely visible, barely tangible – it is there. While haunting never ends, there is always the hope that certain ghosts and certain forms of haunting can be addressed, acknowledged, resolved, and that they might one day fade away. 2011 was perhaps just such an attempt, to deal with the ghost of Nasser and the haunting of the Nasserist project more broadly. Perhaps it was a moment in which people rose up, confronted a particular form of haunting they had endured for decades, and attempted – briefly – to address the ghost of anticolonialism. And yet without an alternative project, and without the fulfilment of the promises the Nasserist project itself promised, in the end there was no way out. The ghosts of Nasserism persist, and in their midst are more who have only just been born, not least through the martyrs of the 2011 revolution as well as the massacred during events such as Raba'a. As long as there are ghosts, however, there is a chance that people will pause, wonder what really happened in the past, why there should be ghosts in the present. There is a chance – a much smaller one – that people will even rise up, confront the haunting they endure, and fight for a world in which haunting is a thing of the past. There is hope, then, that these ghosts will signal the persistence of unfinished business and allow those haunted by them to explore – and perhaps protest – their conditions of emergence.

To write stories of exclusions and invisibilities is to write ghost stories.[44] In her book Gordon asks how we can develop a critical language to describe the historical structures of haunting, and how we can, in turn, articulate a 'sense of the ghostly and its social and political effects'.[45] If for Gordon the ghost is mainly a symptom of what is missing, I have argued here that the ghost in this story is a symptom for what has failed, for promises that were made but never delivered. Ghosts represent loss, paths not taken, alternative roads never travelled down. In a sense, this means that they can also – at the same time – represent hope, and future possibilities.[46] In this story, however, they instead represent the death of this very hope; the destruction of these future possibilities.

[44] Ibid., 12.   [45] Ibid., 18.   [46] Ibid., 64.

Decolonial Futures

For Arwa Salih and Egyptian leftists, Nasserism was a failure, but a complicated one. For the workers who resisted Sadat's neoliberal reforms, Nasserism was seen rather as a promise whose articulation could disrupt the present, though one that had never quite materialized. And yet we also see moments when haunting inspires, pushes, nurtures, and cultivates hope. The 2011 revolution can be read as a response to a haunting, an attempt to rewrite history:

Legacies are ambivalent things. The hundreds of thousands of young men and women who took the streets in 2011 were also haunted by the ghosts of the past; their language, their songs and symbols, their remembering of bygone battles all drew on a history rich with the struggle for freedom.[47]

Ghosts are there because they represent unresolved tensions. They point to holes in the social fabric, suggest moments in our neat nationalist histories that are not as pristine as we like to think. 2011 may have been an attempt to confront the ghosts of past revolutions, but it has, in turn, created its own ghosts:

Yet that moment of unbearable lightness was also followed by utter ruin on a new and perhaps unprecedented scale. And so the same questions will surely return to haunt this generation as it did the ones before: Who were we? What was our experience? How do we assess the truth of who we used to be?[48]

Many of the contradictions of decolonization are manifesting themselves today. This book has shown how capitalist development, from its initial expansion in the 1800s to its neoliberal articulation today, is central to understanding Egyptian politics and the 2011 revolution. Throughout this book I have read events through both Gramsci and Fanon. While Gramsci proved an invaluable companion, providing his concepts of hegemony, passive revolution, and the historical bloc, Fanon was very much present in my understanding of Egypt's process of decolonization and the lineages it has given birth to. Fanon's incisive understanding of the psychic, material, and ideological effects of European imperialism provided a dynamic lens through which to revisit Egyptian political events. Re-reading events through this lens made once-familiar events unfamiliar, and pushed me to ask questions about the connections between decolonization then and revolution now.

---

[47] Salih 2018, xxvii.   [48] Ibid.

I have argued that the postcolonial world tried to build something new at the moment of decolonization: a new international that was postcolonial rather than colonial. Fanon also called for something new as a way out of the world European imperialism had created. Fanon's project of radical humanism entailed the creation of a *new* humanism, a process that was by no means painless or nonviolent. For Fanon, the postcolonial was always connected to the colonial; rather than a sequential reading, Sekyi-Otu has called for a dialectical reading of his work, which would make clear the ways in which neocolonialism could be detected in the political and moral economy of the colonial experience.[49] This would ultimately allow for a critical reading of the promises of anticolonial nationalism, which always deferred to a later time questions of social oppression embedded within the project itself. Indeed Fanon posited that the national bourgeoisie did not have only one path open to them; they had several, all which led to different futures.[50] As discussed throughout this chapter, these alternatives were rejected, in particular by de-centring questions of social justice, anti-capitalism, and democracy. The only vision of postcolonial autonomy is one that returns to the question of humanity.

For Fanon, Europe's answer to this question of humanity was deeply flawed. He writes, 'Leave this Europe where they are never done talking of humanity, yet murder human beings everywhere they find them, at the corner of every one of their streets, in all the corners of the globe. When I search for humanity in the technique and style of Europe, I see only a succession of negations of humanity, and an avalanche of murders'.[51] Rather than trying to 'catch up with the West' – which Fanon sees as a failed project from its inception, a project whose very premises are flawed – the real radical project is to answer the question of humanity *differently*. Any attempt to catch up with the West would be tried 'before the court of Western achievement'.[52] As Sekyi-Otu argues, a truly new day begins when the West is no longer mimicked: 'The awesome task Fanon enjoins upon postcolonial humanity in their particular national communities is nothing less than wresting from the West monopolistic stewardship of the "human condition" in its concrete instance as the modern project'.[53]

Fanon wrote his last book, *The Wretched of the Earth*, in 1963. The world was still very much in the throes of decolonization, during which

[49] 1996, 24.   [50] Ibid., 174.   [51] 1963, 311.   [52] Ibid.   [53] 1996, 183.

Decolonial Futures 277

things were clearer than they are today. Similarly, Gramsci wrote at a time when class struggle was brewing everywhere, and where questions of capitalism were debated virulently. One could question whether, given the complexities of global politics today, Fanon and Gramsci remain relevant. I have sought to show that their work remains not only relevant, but speaks very directly and urgently to our contemporary moment. Indeed Fanon's political writings more adequately describe Egypt's contemporary ruling classes than they do the ruling class that was in power while Fanon was still alive. It is from the 1970s onwards that we see the dependent nationalist class Fanon so despised emerge in Egypt, a class that has only become more dependent with time. It was this class that did precisely what Fanon demanded postcolonial nations *not* do: play the game of imitating Europe, thinking it could win.

Let us decide not to imitate Europe; let us combine our muscles and our brains in a new direction. Let us try to create the whole man, whom Europe has been incapable of bringing to triumphant birth. Two centuries ago, a former European colony decided to catch up with Europe. It succeeded so well that the United States of America became a monster, in which the taints, the sickness and the inhumanity of Europe have grown to appalling dimensions. Comrades, have we not other work to do than to create a third Europe?[54]

I use the term *decolonial futures* not to employ a linear narrative or teleology of progress. As I have shown throughout this book, we see that with the progression of time, Egypt has become increasingly entangled within global capitalism in ways that have diminished its people and its potential. Progression through time has implied movement further away from independence. This unites linear narratives of progress and European imperialism; imperialism progresses as time moves forward – its colonies regress. Decolonial futures therefore do not deploy this articulation, but instead ask how we can bring about a global future that is just.

I want to return to an argument I made in the chapter on Nasserism and the moment of anticolonial nationalism; both of which continue to haunt us today. It was the imagining of something new that separated postcolonial projects from the ones that have come since. In our current moment, there can be little doubt

[54] 1963, 252.

of the damages wrought by capitalism and the colonial international. The 2010/2011 uprisings across the Middle East and North Africa were a rupture in this contemporary political moment; an attempt again to imagine something *new*. Although these events have been analysed through old frames, there remains an essence that cannot be captured. I want to end this book by turning one last time to Fanon, who eloquently warned us of the problems of decolonization. Fanon knew that the real struggle of decolonization lay not in winning the war of independence, but in establishing a new state and in creating a new people, a new humanity. His last words, published in *The Wretched of the Earth*, are both a warning and a promise – a promise that things can be different:

Humanity is waiting for something other from us than such an imitation, which would be almost an obscene caricature. If we want to turn Africa into a new Europe, then let us leave the destiny of our countries to Europeans. They will know how to do it better than the most gifted among us. But if we want humanity to advance a step further, if we want to bring it up to a different level than that which Europe has shown it, then we must invent and we must make discoveries.

No, we do not want to catch up with anyone. What we want to do is go forward all the time, night and day, in the company of Man, in the company of all men.[55]

For Fanon, then, humanity would only advance a step further when postcolonial nations produced something different; a future yet to come. It is important to emphasize what anticolonial projects such as Nasserism were up against, and to underline the fact that they did not have many options available to them. In that sense, failure cannot be easily located; it cannot and should not be placed solely on the shoulders of anticolonial projects.

And yet part of me wonders what it would mean to dream beyond this; to think about what we know now about the problems embedded in 'moving forward', in 'sovereignty' and in 'invention and discovery'. What would it mean to think beyond mastery, beyond creation? What would it mean to think about care, repair, reparations, abolition – to think about lineages of dreaming and imagining futures that de-centre masculine worldmaking. This is a story for another day; suffice it to say that I could not help but think about this as I spent time with Fanon and

---

[55] Ibid., 254.

Decolonial Futures 279

Gramsci; with Nasser and Nkrumah; with anticolonial nationalism and independent industrialization. What I know is that the historical moment during which decolonization took place was complex and contradictory; that anticolonialism did not have open to it endless options.

Perhaps haunted histories do not disappear because they are either incapable of doing so or stubbornly persist until we succeed in creating the world they deem unfinished – a world in which decolonization is fully realized. This is a world in which we break away from haunted histories of colonialism and anticolonialism; in which we transcend the nation (and all of its own haunted histories); and in which we break free from capitalist modernity. It is a moment in which we rectify the mistakes of anticolonial nationalism and centre *all* forms of social struggle from the start, from racism to sexism, from homophobia to classism, rather than perpetually relegate them to the future. This is a moment when we transition from an international crushed under the weight of empire and imperialism, to a true international open to all. I imagine that in this world we would find, finally, the new humanity Fanon spoke of, the world beyond mastery Singh writes about, and the recokoning with past ghosts Gordon calls for. I imagine we would finc an international that is no longer colonial. A truly decolonized international; a truly decolonized world.

References

Abaza, M. (2006) *Changing Consumer Cultures of Modern Egypt: Cairo's Urban Reshaping*. Leiden: Brill.

Abdalla, A. (2008) *The Student Movement and National Politics in Egypt, 1923–1973*. Cairo: American University in Cairo Press.

Abdel-Malek, A. (1968) *Egypt: Military Society*. New York: Random House.

Abdelrahman, M. (2014) *Egypt's Long Revolution: Protest Movements and Uprisings*. London: Routledge.

(2017) Policing neoliberalism in Egypt: the continuing rise of the 'securocratic' state. *Third World Quarterly*, 38(1), 185–202.

Abou-El-Fadl, R. (2019) Solidarity and Transnationalism in Egypt's Afro-Asian Hub: The 1957 Afro-Asian Peoples' Solidarity Conference in Context. *Journal of World History*. 30(1–2), 157–192.

(2015) Neutralism Made Positive: Egyptian Anti-Colonialism on the Road to Bandung. *British Journal of Middle Eastern Studies*, 42(2), 219–240.

Abul-Magd, Z. (2017) *Militarizing the Nation: The Army, Business, and Revolution in Egypt*. New York: Columbia University Press.

Adamson, W. (1983) *Hegemony and Revolution: A Study of Antonio Gramsci's Political and Cultural Theory*. Berkeley: University of California Press.

Ahmed, L. (1992) *Women and Gender in Islam: Historical Roots of a Modern Debate*. New Haven, CT: Yale University Press.

Alahmed, A. (2011) Voice of the Arabs Radio: its effects and political power during the Nasser Era (1953–1967). https://ssrn.com/abstract=2047212

Al-Ali, N. (2000) *Secularism, Gender and the State in the Middle East: The Egyptian Women's Movement*. Cambridge: Cambridge University Press.

Albrecht, H. (2005) How can opposition support authoritarianism? Lessons from Egypt. *Democratization*, 12(3), 378–97.

Alexander, A. (2010) Leadership and collective action in the Egyptian trade unions. *Work, Employment, and Society*, 24(2), 241–59.

Alexander, A., & Bassiouny, M. (2014) *Bread, Freedom, Social Justice: Workers and the Egyptian Revolution*. London: Zed Books.

References 281

Amar, P. (2011) Middle East masculinity studies discourses of 'men in crisis': industries of gender in revolution. *Journal of Middle East Women's Studies*, 7(3), 36–70.

Amin, S. (2012) *The People's Spring: The Future of the Arab Revolution.* New York: Pambazuka Press.

Anderson, K. B. (2016) *Marx at the Margins: On Nationalism, Ethnicity, and Non-Western Societies.* Chicago: University of Chicago Press.

Anderson, L. (2006) Searching where the light shines: studying democratization in the Middle East. *Annual Review of Political Science*, 9, 189–214.

(2011) Demystifying the Arab Spring: parsing the differences between Tunisia, Egypt, and Libya. *Foreign Affairs*, May/June, 2–7.

Anderson, P. (1977) *The Antinomies of Antonio Gramsci.* London: Verso Books.

Anghie, A. (2007) *Imperialism, Sovereignty and the Making of International Law.* Cambridge: Cambridge University Press.

Aoude, I. G. (1994) From national bourgeois development to 'Infitah': Egypt 1952–1992. *Arab Studies Quarterly*, 16(1), 1–23.

Arafat, A. (2011) *Hosni Mubarak and the Future of Democracy in Egypt.* London: Springer.

Ashour, O. (2012) From bad cop to good cop: the challenge of security sector reform in Egypt. Brookings Institution. www.brookings.edu/research/fro m-bad-cop-to-good-cop-the-challenge-of-security-sector-reform-in-egypt/

Aydin, C. (2017) *The Idea of the Muslim World: A Global Intellectual History.* Cambridge, MA: Harvard University Press.

Ayubi, N. (1980) The political revival of Islam: the case of Egypt. *International Journal of Middle East Studies*, 12(4), 481–99.

(1996) *Over-stating the Arab State: Politics and Society in the Middle East.* London: I. B. Tauris.

Badran, M. (1988) Dual liberation: feminism and nationalism in Egypt, 1870s–1925. *Gender Issues*, 8(1), 15–34.

Baker, R. W. (1990) *Sadat and After: Struggles for Egypt's Political Soul.* Cambridge, MA: Harvard University Press.

Baldwin, J. (1984) *Notes of a Native Son.* New York: Beacon Press.

Barak, O. (2013) *On Time: Technology and Temporality in Modern Egypt.* Berkeley: University of California Press.

Baron, B. (2005) *Egypt as a Woman: Nationalism, Gender, and Politics.* Berkeley: University of California Press.

Bartolovich, C., & Lazarus, N. (Eds.). (2002) *Marxism, Modernity and Postcolonial Studies.* Cambridge: Cambridge University Press.

Bates, T. R. (1975) Gramsci and the theory of hegemony. *Journal of the History of Ideas*, 36(2), 351–66.

Bauman, Z. (2012) Times of interregnum. *Ethics and Global Politics*, 5(1), 49–56.

Bayat, A., & Denis, E. (2000) Who is afraid of ashwaiyyat? Urban change and politics in Egypt. *Environment and Urbanization*, 12(2), 185–99.

Beattie, K. J. (1994) *Egypt during the Nasser Years: Ideology, Politics and Civil Society*. New York: Westview Press.

Beckert, S. (2014) *Empire of Cotton: A New History of Global Capitalism*. London: Penguin.

Beinin, J. (1987) The communist movement and nationalist political discourse in Nasirist Egypt. *Middle East Journal*, 41(4), 568–84.

(1989) Labor, capital, and the state in Nasserist Egypt, 1952–1961. *International Journal of Middle East Studies*, 21(1), 71–90.

(2005a). Political Islam and the new global economy: the political economy of an Egyptian social movement. *The New Centennial Review*, 5(1), 111–39.

(2005b) *The Dispersion of Egyptian Jewry: Culture, Politics, and the Formation of a Modern Diaspora*. Cairo: American University in Cairo Press.

(2009) Workers' protest in Egypt: neo-liberalism and class struggle in the 21st century. *Social Movement Studies*, 8(4), 449–54.

Beinin, J., & El-Hamalawy, H. (2007) Strikes in Egypt spread from center of gravity. *Middle East Report Online*. https://merip.org/2007/05/strikes-in-egypt-spread-from-center-of-gravity/

Beinin, J., & Lockman, Z. (1998) *Workers on the Nile: Nationalism, Communism, Islam, and the Egyptian Working Class, 1882–1954*. Cairo: American University in Cairo Press.

Bellin, E. (2012) Reconsidering the robustness of authoritarianism in the Middle East: lessons from the Arab Spring. *Comparative Politics*, 44(2), 127–49.

Bieler, A., & Morton, A. D. (2003) Globalisation, the state and class struggle: a 'Critical Economy' engagement with Open Marxism. *The British Journal of Politics and International Relations*, 5(4), 467–99.

(2004) A critical theory route to hegemony, world order and historical change: neo-Gramscian perspectives in International Relations. *Capital and Class*, 28(1), 85–113.

Bier, L. (2011) *Revolutionary Womanhood: Feminisms, Modernity, and the State in Nasser's Egypt*. Stanford, CA: Stanford University Press.

Blaydes, L. (2010) *Elections and Distributive Politics in Mubarak's Egypt*. Cambridge: Cambridge University Press.

Blumi, I. (2018) *Destroying Yemen: What Chaos in Arabia Tells Us about the World*. Berkeley: University of California Press.

References

Bogaert, K. (2013) Contextualizing the Arab revolts: the politics behind three decades of neoliberalism in the Arab world. *Middle East Critique*, 22(3), 213–34.

Boothman, D. (2008) The sources for Gramsci's concept of hegemony. *Rethinking Marxism*, 20(2), 201–15.

Botman, S. (1986) Egyptian communists and the free officers: 1950–54. *Middle Eastern Studies*, 22(3), 350–66.

Boyd, D. A., & Kushner, J. (1979) Media habits of Egyptian gatekeepers. *Gazette*, 25(2), 106–13.

Braudel, F. (1982) *On History*. Chicago: University of Chicago Press.

Brennan, T. (2001) Antonio Gramsci and postcolonial theory: 'Southernism'. *Diaspora: A Journal of Transnational Studies*, 10(2), 143–87.

(2006) *Wars of Position*. New York: Columbia University Press.

Bromley, S., & Bush, R. (1994) Adjustment in Egypt? The political economy of reform. *Review of African Political Economy*, 21(60), 201–13.

Brownlee, J. (2002) The decline of pluralism in Mubarak's Egypt. *Journal of Democracy*, 13(4), 6–14.

Buci-Glucksmann, C. (1980) *Gramsci and the State*. London: Lawrence and Wishart.

Burnham, P. (1991) Neo-Gramscian hegemony and the international order. *Capital and Class*, 15(3), 73–92.

Bush, R. (2009) When 'enough' is not enough. *Iḥtijāj Al-siyāsī Wa-al-ijtimāʿī Fī Miṣr*, 29(2–3): 85.

Bush, R., & Ayeb, H. (2012) *Marginality and Exclusion in Egypt*. London: Zed Books.

Buttigieg, J. A. (2009) Reading Gramsci now. In Francese, J. (Ed.), *Perspectives on Gramsci: Politics, Culture and Social Theory* (pp. 20–32). London: Routledge.

Carothers, T. (2002) The end of the transition paradigm. *Journal of Democracy*, 13(1), 5–21.

Cavatorta, F. (2010) The convergence of governance: upgrading authoritarianism in the Arab world and downgrading democracy elsewhere? *Middle East Critique*, 19(3), 217–32.

Chaichian, M. A. (1988) The effects of world capitalist economy on urbanization in Egypt, 1800–1970. *International Journal of Middle East Studies*, 20(1), 23–43.

Chakrabarty, D. (2000a) *Provincializing Europe*. Princeton, NJ: Princeton University Press.

(2000b). Subaltern studies and postcolonial historiography. *Nepantla: Views from the South*, 1(1), 9–32.

Chalcraft, J. (2007) Counterhegemonic effects: weighing, measuring, petitions and bureaucracy in nineteenth-century Egypt. In *Counterhegemony in the Colony and Postcolony* (pp. 179–203). London: Palgrave Macmillan.

(2011) Labour protest and hegemony in Egypt and the Arabian Peninsula. In *Social Movements in the Global South* (pp. 35–58). London: Palgrave Macmillan.

(2016) *Popular Politics in the Making of the Modern Middle East.* Cambridge: Cambridge University Press.

Chatterjee, P. (1986) *Nationalist Thought and the Colonial World: A Derivative Discourse.* London: Zed Books.

(1998) Beyond the nation? Or within? *Social Text, 56,* 57–69.

(2008a) Democracy and economic transformation in India. *Economic and Political Weekly,* 53–62.

(2008b) Gramsci in the twenty-first century. *Studi culturali, 2,* 201–22.

(2011) *Lineages of Political Society: Studies in Postcolonial Democracy.* New York: Columbia University Press.

(2017) The legacy of Bandung. In Eslava, L., Fakhri, M., & Nesiah, V. (Eds.), *Bandung, Global History, and International Law: Critical Pasts and Pending Futures* (pp. 657–74). Cambridge: Cambridge University Press.

Chekir, H., & Diwan, I. (2013) Distressed whales on the Nile – Egypt capitalists in the wake of the 2010 Revolution. Economic Research Forum.

Cherki, A. (2006) *Frantz Fanon: A Portrait.* Ithaca, NY: Cornell University Press.

Chibber, V. (2014) *Postcolonial Theory and the Specter of Capital.* London: Verso Books.

Cook, S. (2011) *The Struggle for Egypt: From Nasser to Tahrir Square.* Oxford: Oxford University Press.

Cooper, M. (1979) Egyptian state capitalism in crisis: economic policies and political interests, 1967–1971. *International Journal of Middle East Studies, 10*(4), 481–516.

Cox, R. W. (1981) Social forces, states and world orders: beyond international relations theory. *Millennium – Journal of International Studies, 10*(2), 126–55.

(1983) Gramsci, hegemony and international relations: an essay in method. *Millennium – Journal of International Studies, 12*(2), 162–75.

(1987) *Production, Power, and World Order: Social Forces in the Making of History.* New York: Columbia University Press.

Crabbs, J. (1975) Politics, history, and culture in Nasser's Egypt. *International Journal of Middle East Studies, 6*(4), 386–420.

Davis, E. (1983) *Challenging Colonialism: Bank Misr and Egyptian Industrialization, 1920–1941.* Princeton, NJ: Princeton University Press.

Deeb, M. (1979) Labour and politics in Egypt, 1919–1939. *International Journal of Middle East Studies, 10*(2), 187–203.

References

Dekmejian, R. D. (1982) Egypt and Turkey: the military in the background. In Kolkowicz, R., & Korbonski, A. (Eds.), *Soldiers, Peasants, and Bureaucrats: Civil–Military Relations in Communist and Modernizing Societies* (pp. 29–31). London: George Allen and Unwin.

Derrida, J. (2012) *Specters of Marx: The State of the Debt, the Work of Mourning and the New International.* London: Routledge.

De Smet, B. (2012) Egyptian workers and 'their' intellectuals: the dialectical pedagogy of the Mahalla strike movement. *Mind, Culture, and Activity, 19*(2), 139–55.

  (2016) *Gramsci on Tahrir: Revolution and Counter-Revolution in Egypt.* London: Pluto Press.

Dessouki, A. E. (1981) Policy making in Egypt: a case study of the open door economic policy. *Social Problems, 28*(4), 410–16.

DiMeo, D. (2016) *Committed to Disillusion: Activist Writers in Egypt in the 1960s–1980s.* Oxford: Oxford University Press.

Dirlik, A. (1994) The postcolonial aura: Third World criticism in the age of global capitalism. *Critical Inquiry, 20*(2), 328–56.

Drainville, A. C. (1995) Politics of resistance in the New World Order. In Alden Smith, D., & Borocz, J. (Eds.), *A New World Order? Global Transformations in the Late Twentieth Century* (pp. 164–217). Westport, CT: Greenwood.

Du Bois, W. E. B. (1933) *Marxism and the Negro Problem.* New York: Crisis.

Elyachar, J., (2005) *Markets of dispossession: NGOs, economic development, and the state in Cairo.* Duke University Press.

El-Ghobashy, M. (2005) The metamorphosis of the Egyptian Muslim brothers. *International Journal of Middle East Studies, 37*(3), 373–95.

  (2010) The dynamics of Egypt's elections. *Middle East Report Online, 29* (9). https://merip.org/2010/09/the-dynamics-of-egypts-elections/

  (2011) The praxis of the Egyptian revolution. *Middle East Report, 41* (258), 2–13.

El Mahdi, R. (2009) The democracy movement: cycles of protest. In El Mahdi, R., & Marfleet, P. (Eds.), *Egypt: The Moment of Change* (pp. 87–102). London: Zed Books.

  (2011) Labour protests in Egypt: causes and meanings. *Review of African Political Economy, 38*(129), 387–402.

El Shakry, O. (2007) *The Great Social Laboratory: Subjects of Knowledge in Colonial and Postcolonial Egypt.* Stanford, CA: Stanford University Press.

  (2015) 'History without documents': the vexed archives of decolonization in the Middle East. *The American Historical Review, 120*(3), 920–34.

El Tarouty, S. (2015) *Businessmen, Clientelism, and Authoritarianism in Egypt.* London: Springer.

Fahmy, K. (1997) *All the Pasha's Men: Mehmed Ali, His Army and the Making of Modern Egypt*. Cambridge: Cambridge University Press.

Fahmy, Z. (2011) *Ordinary Egyptians: Creating the Modern Nation through Popular Culture*. Stanford, CA: Stanford University Press.

Faksh, M. A. (1976a) An historical survey of the educational system in Egypt. *International Review of Education*, 22(2), 234–44.

(1976b) Education and elite recruitment: an analysis of Egypt's post-1952 political elite. *Comparative Education Review*, 20(2), 140–50.

(2006) Voices of the new Arab public: Iraq, Al-Jazeera, and Middle East politics today. *Perspectives on Politics*, 4(4), 793–4.

Fanon, F. (1963) *The Wretched of the Earth*. New York: Grove Press.

(1968) *Black Skin, White Masks*. New York: Grove Press.

Farahzad, F. (2017) Voice and visibility: Fanon in the Persian context. In Batchelor, K., & Hardin, S. (Eds.), *Translating: Frantz Fanon across Continents and Languages* (pp. 129–50). London: Routledge.

Femia, J. (2005) Gramsci, Machiavelli and international relations. *The Political Quarterly*, 76(3), 341–9.

Fontana, B. (1993) *Hegemony and Power: On the Relation between Gramsci and Machiavelli*. Minneapolis: University of Minnesota Press.

(2009) Power and democracy: Gramsci and hegemony. In Francese, J. (Ed.), *Perspectives on Gramsci: Politics, Culture and Social Theory* (pp. 80–97). London: Routledge.

Gerges, F. A. (2000) The end of the Islamist insurgency in Egypt? Costs and prospects. *The Middle East Journal*, XX, 592–612.

Germain, R. D., & Kenny, M. (1998) Engaging Gramsci: international relations theory and the new Gramscians. *Review of International Studies*, 24(1), 3–21.

Getachew, A. (2019) *Worldmaking after Empire: The Rise and Fall of Self-Determination*. Princeton, NJ: Princeton University Press.

Ghannam, F. (2013) *Live and Die Like a Man: Gender Dynamics in Urban Egypt*. Stanford, CA: Stanford University Press.

Gill, S. (1993) *Gramsci, Historical Materialism and International Relations*. Cambridge: Cambridge University Press.

(2002) Globalization, market civilization and disciplinary neoliberalism. In Hovden, E., & Keene, E. (Eds.), *The Globalization of Liberalism* (pp. 123–51). London: Palgrave Macmillan.

Gill, S., & Law, D. (1989) Global hegemony and the structural power of capital. *International Studies Quarterly*, 33(4), 475–99.

Gordon, A. F. (2008) *Ghostly Matters: Haunting and the Sociological Imagination*. Minneapolis: University of Minnesota Press.

Gordon, J. S. (1992) *Nasser's Blessed Movement: Egypt's Free Officers and the July Revolution*. Oxford: Oxford University Press.

References

Gramsci, A. (2000) *The Gramsci Reader: Selected Writings, 1916–1935.* New York: New York University Press.

Gramsci, A., & Buttigieg, J. A. (1971) *Selections from the Prison Notebooks.* London: Lawrence and Wishart.

(1992) *Prison Notebooks.* New York: Columbia University Press.

Grovogui, S. (2011) A revolution nonetheless: the Global South in international relations. *The Global South, 5*(1), 175–90.

Guha, R. (1997) *Dominance without Hegemony: History and Power in Colonial India.* Cambridge, MA: Harvard University Press.

Hall, S. (1986) Gramsci's relevance for the study of race and ethnicity. *Journal of Communication Inquiry, 10*(2), 5–27.

(2002) Gramsci and us. In Martin, J. (Ed.), *Antonio Gramsci: Critical Assessments of Leading Political Philosophers* (pp. 227–38). London: Routledge.

(2016) *Selected Political Writings: The Great Moving Right Show and Other Essays.* Durham, NC: Duke University Press.

Hammad, H. (2016) Arwa Salih's the Premature: Gendering the History of the Egyptian Left. *Arab Studies Journal, 24*(1), 120–145.

(2011) The Other Extremists: Marxist Feminism in Egypt, 1980–2000. *Journal of International Women's Studies, 12*(3), 217–233.

Hamed, O. (1981) Egypt's open door economic policy: an attempt at economic integration in the Middle East. *International Journal of Middle East Studies, 13*(1), 1–9.

Handoussa, H. (1990) Fifteen years of US aid to Egypt: a critical review. In Oweiss, I. (Ed.), *The Political Economy of Contemporary Egypt* (pp. 109–24). Washington, DC: Center for Contemporary Arab Studies.

Hanieh, A. (2018) *Money, Markets, and Monarchies: The Gulf Cooperation Council and the Political Economy of the Contemporary Middle East.* Cambridge: Cambridge University Press.

(2016) *Capitalism and Class in the Gulf Arab States.* London: Springer.

(2013) *Lineages of Revolt: Issues of Contemporary Capitalism in the Middle East.* London: Haymarket Books.

Hanna, N. (2011) *Artisan Entrepreneurs: In Cairo and Early-Modern Capitalism (1600–1800).* New York: Syracuse University Press.

Harding, S. A. (2017) Fanon in Arabic. In Batchelor, K., & Hardin, S. (Eds.), *Translating: Frantz Fanon across Continents and Languages* (pp. 98–128). London: Routledge.

Harik, I. F. (1974) *The Political Mobilization of Peasants: A Study of an Egyptian Community.* Bloomington: Indiana University Press.

Harvey, D. (2009) The art of rent: globalisation, monopoly and the commodification of culture. *Socialist Register, 38*, 93–110.

Hatem, M. F. (1992) Economic and political liberation in Egypt and the demise of state feminism. *International Journal of Middle East Studies*, 24(2), 231–51.

Heikal, M. H. (1986) *Cutting the Lion's Tail: Suez through Egyptian Eyes*. London: Deutsch.

(1972) *Nasser: The Cairo Documents*. London: New English Library.

Hinnebusch, R. A. (2017) Political parties in MENA: their functions and development. *British Journal of Middle Eastern Studies*, 44(2), 159–75.

Hobson, J. M. (2012) *The Eurocentric Conception of World Politics: Western International Theory, 1760–2010*. Cambridge: Cambridge University Press.

Hosseinzadeh, E. (1988) How Egyptian state capitalism reverted to market capitalism. *Arab Studies Quarterly*, 10(3), 299–318.

Hussein, M., & Chirman, M. (1973) *Class Conflict in Egypt, 1945–1970*. New York: Monthly Review Press.

Ibrahim, S., & Calderbank, A. (2005) *Zaat*. Cairo: American University in Cairo Press.

International Monetary Fund. (1976) Staff report for the 1976 Article XIV consultation.

Arab Republic of Egypt.

Issawi, C. P. (1954) *Egypt at Mid-Century: An Economic Survey*. Oxford: Oxford University Press.

Jabri, V. (2012) *The Postcolonial Subject: Claiming Politics/Governing Others in Late Modernity*. London: Routledge.

Jadaliyya. (2012) Hassan Hamdan 'Mahdi Amel': a profile from the archives. www.jadaliyya.com/Details/27151

James, C. L. R. (2001) *The Black Jacobins: Toussaint L'Ouverture and the San Domingo Revolution*. London: Penguin.

Joya, A. (2011) The Egyptian revolution: crisis of neoliberalism and the potential for democratic politics. *Review of African Political Economy*, 38(129), 367–86.

Kandil, H. (2014) *Inside the Brotherhood*. London: John Wiley.

(2012) *Soldiers, Spies, and Statesmen: Egypt's Road to Revolt*. London: Verso Books.

Khater, A., & Nelson, C. (1988) Al-Harakah Al-Nissa'Iyah: the women's movement and political participation in modern Egypt. *Women's Studies International Forum*, 11(5), 465–83.

Korany, B., & El Mahdi, R. (2012) *Arab Spring in Egypt: Revolution and Beyond*. Cairo: American University in Cairo Press.

Korayem, K. (1997) *Egypt's Economic Reform and Structural Adjustment (ERSAP)*. Cairo: Egyptian Center for Economic Studies.

References

Laclau, E., & Mouffe, C. (2014) *Hegemony and Socialist Strategy: Towards a Radical Democratic Politics*. London: Verso Books.

Langan, M. (2017) *Neo-Colonialism and the Poverty of 'Development' in Africa*. New York: Springer.

Laroui, A., & Cammell, D. (1977) *The Crisis of the Arab Intellectual: Traditionalism or Historicism?* Berkeley: University of California Press.

Lazarus, N. (1999) *Nationalism and Cultural Practice in the Postcolonial World*. Cambridge: Cambridge University Press.

(2011) *The Postcolonial Unconscious*. Cambridge: Cambridge University Press.

Lazarus, N., & Varma, R. (2007) Marxism and postcolonial studies. In Bidet, J. (Ed.), *Critical Companion to Contemporary Marxism* (pp. 309–32). Leiden: Brill.

Lears, T. J. (1985) The concept of cultural hegemony: problems and possibilities. *The American Historical Review*, 90(3), 567–93.

Lockman, Z. (Ed.). (1994) *Workers and Working Classes in the Middle East: Struggles, Histories, Historiographies*. New York: SUNY Press.

Lucas, S. (Ed.). (1996) *Britain and Suez: The Lion's Last Roar*. Manchester, UK: Manchester University Press.

Mabro, R., & Radwan, S. (1976) *The Industrialization of Egypt 1939–1973: Policy and Performance*. Oxford: Oxford University Press.

Macey, D. (2000) *Frantz Fanon: A Life*. New York: Granta Books.

Makram Ebeid, D. (2012) Manufacturing stability: everyday politics of work in an industrial steel town in Helwan, Egypt. Doctoral dissertation, London School of Economics and Political Science.

Masoud, T. (2015) Has the door closed on Arab democracy? *Journal of Democracy*, 26(1), 74–87.

Massad, J. (2001) Colonial effects: *The Making of National Identity in Jordan*. New York: Columbia University Press.

Mehrez, S. (2011) *The Literary Life of Cairo: One Hundred Years in the Heart of the City*. Oxford: Oxford University Press.

Mitchell, T. (1991a) *Colonising Egypt*. Berkeley: University of California Press.

(1991b) The limits of the state: beyond statist approaches and their critics. *The American Political Science Review*, 85(1), 77–96.

(1999) Dreamland: the neoliberalism of your desires. *Middle East Report*, 29(1): 28–33.

(2002) *Rule of Experts: Egypt, Techno-Politics, Modernity*. Berkeley: University of California Press.

Molyneux, M., & Halliday, F. (1984) Marxism, the Third World and the Middle East. *MERIP Reports*, 120, 18–21.

Morton, A. (2012) Traveling with Gramsci: the spatiality of passive revolution. In Ekers, M., et al. (Eds.), *Gramsci: Space, Nature, Politics* (pp. 45–64). London: John Wiley.

Mossallam, A. (2012) Hikāyāt shaʿ b-stories of peoplehood: Nasserism, popular politics and songs in Egypt, 1956–1973. Doctoral dissertation, London School of Economics and Political Science.

Mostafa, T. (2007) *The Struggle for Constitutional Power: Law, Politics, and Economic Development in Egypt.* Cambridge: Cambridge University Press.

Munif, Y. (2012) Frantz Fanon and the Arab Uprisings: an interview with Nigel Gibson. *Jadaliyya.* www.jadaliyya.com/pages/index/6927/frantz-fanon-and-the-arab-uprisings_an-interview-w

Muñoz, J. E. (2009) *Cruising Utopia: The Then and There of Queer Futurity.* New York: New York University Press.

Nasser, G. A. (1959) *The Philosophy of the Revolution, Book I.* London: Smith, Keynes and Marshall.

Nassif, H. B. (2013) Wedded to Mubarak: the second careers and financial rewards of Egypt's military elite, 1981–2011. *The Middle East Journal,* 67(4), 509–30.

Nkrumah, G. (2002) Safeguarding Nasser's legacy. *Al Ahram Weekly Online.* www.mafhoum.com/press3/nas105-4.htm

  (2007) Chasing the paper trail. *Al Ahram Weekly Online.* http://weekly.ahram.org.eg/Archive/2007/855/eg2.htm

Nkrumha, K. (1965) *Neo-Colonialism: The Last Stage of Imperialism.* London: Thomas Nelson.

Nye, D. E. (1996) *American Technological Sublime.* Boston: MIT Press.

Osman, T. (2010) *Egypt on the Brink: From Nasser to Mubarak.* New Haven, CT: Yale University Press.

Overbeek, H. (2013) Transnational historical materialism: neo-Gramscian theories of class formation and world order. In Palan, R. (Ed.), *Global Political Economy: Contemporary Theories* (pp. 162–76). New York: Routledge.

Paczyńska, A. (2013) *State, Labor, and the Transition to a Market Economy: Egypt, Poland, Mexico, and the Czech Republic.* University Park: Penn State University Press.

Pandolfo, S. (2018) *Knot of the Soul: Madness, Psychoanalysis, Islam.* Chicago: University of Chicago Press.

Panitch, L. (1994) Globalisation and the state. *Socialist Register,* 30(30), 60–93.

Parry, B. (2004) *Postcolonial Studies: A Materialist Critique.* London: Routledge.

  (2012) What is left in postcolonial studies? *New Literary History,* 43(2), 341–58.

References

291

Pasha, M. K. (2005) Islam, 'soft' orientalism and hegemony: a Gramscian rereading. *Critical Review of International Social and Political Philosophy*, 8(4), 543–58.

Piketty, T. (2014) *Capital in the 21st Century*. Cambridge, MA: Harvard University Press.

Posusney, M. (1997) *Labor and the State in Egypt: Workers, Unions, and Economic Restructuring*. New York: Columbia University Press.

Prakash, G. (1994) Subaltern studies as postcolonial criticism. *The American Historical Review*, 99(5), 1475–90.

Pratt, N. C. (2007) *Democracy and Authoritarianism in the Arab World*. Boulder, CO: Lynne Rienner.

Rahnema, A. (2015) *Shi'i Reformation in Iran: The Life and Theology of Shari'at Sangelaji*. London: Ashgate.

Rao, R. (2017) Recovering reparative readings of postcolonialism and Marxism. *Critical Sociology*, 43(4–5), 587–98.

Reid, D. M. (2002) *Cairo University and the Making of Modern Egypt*. Cambridge: Cambridge University Press.

Robinson, C. J. (1938/1983) *Black Marxism: The Making of the Black Radical Tradition*. Chapel Hill: University of North Carolina Press.

Roccu, R. (2013) *The Political Economy of the Egyptian Revolution: Mubarak, Economic Reforms and Failed Hegemony*. London: Springer.

Rodney, W. (1972) *How Europe Underdeveloped Africa*. London: Bogle-L'Ouverture.

Rodrigo, N. (2015) Fanon in Palestine: a four-part essay series. *Jadaliyya*. www.jadaliyya.com/Details/32680/Fanon-in-Palestine-A-Four-Part-Essay-Series

Roll, S. (2010) 'Finance matters!' The influence of financial sector reforms on the development of the entrepreneurial elite in Egypt. *Mediterranean Politics*, 15(3), 349–70.

Rupert, M. (1995) *Producing Hegemony*. Cambridge: Cambridge University Press.

Said, E. (1979) *Orientalism*. New York: Vintage.

(1983) *The World, the Text, and the Critic*. Cambridge, MA: Harvard University Press.

(1995) *East Isn't East: The Impending End of the Age of Orientalism*. London: Times Literary Supplement.

(2000) Traveling theory reconsidered. In *Reflections on Exile and Other Essays* (pp. 436–52). Cambridge, MA: Harvard University Press.

Salem, S. (2017) Four women of Egypt: memory, geopolitics, and the Egyptian women's movement during the Nasser and Sadat eras. *Hypatia*, 32(3), 593–608.

Salih, A. (2018) *The Stillborn*. New York: Seagull Books.

Sassoon, A. S. (2001) Globalisation, hegemony and passive revolution. *New Political Economy*, 6(1), 5–17.

Sayigh, Y. (2012) *Above the State: The Officers' Republic in Egypt*. Washington, DC: Carnegie Endowment for International Peace.

Sayyid-Marsot, A. L. (1984) *Egypt in the Reign of Muhammad Ali*. Cambridge: Cambridge University Press.

Schlumberger, O. (2007) *Debating Arab Authoritarianism: Dynamics and Durability in Nondemocratic Regimes*. Stanford, CA: Stanford University Press.

(2008) Structural reform, economic order, and development: patrimonial capitalism. *Review of International Political Economy*, 15(4), 622–49.

Scott, D. (1996) The aftermaths of sovereignty: postcolonial criticism and the claims of political modernity. *Social Text*, 48, 1–26.

Sekyi-Otu, A. (1996) *Fanon's Dialectic of Experience*. Cambridge, MA: Harvard University Press.

Sfakianakis, J. (2004) The whales of the Nile: networks, businessmen, and bureaucrats during the era of privatization. In Heydemann, S. (Ed.), *Networks of Privilege in the Middle East: The Politics of Economic Reform Revisited* (pp. 77–100). London: Springer.

Shehata, S. (2008) After Mubarak, Mubarak? *Current History*, 107(713), 418–24.

Shilliam, R. (2004) Hegemony and the unfashionable problematic of primitive accumulation. *Millennium*, 33(1), 59–88.

(2016) Colonial architecture or relatable hinterlands? Locke, Nandy, Fanon, and the Bandung spirit. *Constellations*, 23(3), 425–35.

Singh, J. (2017) *Unthinking Mastery: Dehumanism and Decolonial Entanglements*. Durham, NC: Duke University Press.

Sinha, S., & Varma, R. (2017) Marxism and postcolonial theory: what's left of the debate? *Critical Sociology*, 43(4–5), 545–58.

Soliman, S. (1998) *State and Industrial Capitalism in Egypt*. Cairo Papers in Social Science 21. Cairo: American University in Cairo Press.

(2005) *The Strong Regime and the Weak State: Managing the Fiscal Crisis and Political Change under Mubarak*. Cairo: Merit.

(2011) *The Autumn of Dictatorship: Fiscal Crisis and Political Change in Egypt under Mubarak*. Stanford, CA: Stanford University Press.

Springborg, R. (1979) Patrimonialism and policy making in Egypt: Nasser and Sadat and the tenure policy for reclaimed lands. *Middle Eastern Studies*, 15(1), 49–69.

(1990) Agrarian bourgeoisie, semiproletarians, and the Egyptian state: lessons for liberalization. *International Journal of Middle East Studies*, 22(4), 447–72.

References

(2011) Whither the Arab Spring? 1989 or 1848? *The International Spectator*, 46(3), 5–12.

Sprinker, M. (Ed.). (1999) *Ghostly Demarcations: A Symposium on Jacques Derrida's Spectres of Marx*. London: Verso.

Srivastava, N., & Bhattacharya, B. (Eds.). (2012) *The Postcolonial Gramsci*. London: Routledge.

Stacher, J. (2012) *Adaptable Autocrats: Regime Power in Egypt and Syria*. Stanford, CA: Stanford University Press.

Stoler, A. L. (2006) Intimidations of empire: predicaments of the tactile and unseen. In *Haunted by Empire: Geographies of Intimacy in North American History* (pp. 1–22). Durham, NC: Duke University Press.

(2008) Imperial debris: reflections on ruins and ruination. *Cultural Anthropology*, 23(2), 191–219.

(2016) *Duress: Imperial Durabilities in Our Times*. Durham, NC: Duke University Press.

Taha, M. (2017) Reimagining Bandung for women at work in Egypt. In Eslava, L., Fakhri, M., & Nesiah, V. (Eds.), *Bandung, Global History, and International Law: Critical Pasts and Pending Futures* (pp. 337–54). Cambridge: Cambridge University Press.

Thomas, P. D. (2009) *The Gramscian Moment: Philosophy, Hegemony and Marxism*. Leiden: Brill.

Tignor, R. L. (1977) Bank Miṣr and foreign capitalism. *International Journal of Middle East Studies*, 8(2), 161–81.

(1980) Dependency theory and Egyptian capitalism, 1920 to 1950. *African Economic History*, 9, 101–18.

(1987) Decolonization and business: the case of Egypt. *The Journal of Modern History*, 59(3), 479–505.

(2015) *Capitalism and Nationalism at the End of Empire: State and Business in Decolonizing Egypt, Nigeria, and Kenya, 1945–1963*. Princeton, NJ: Princeton University Press.

Tschirgi, D. (1996) *Development in the Age of Liberalization: Egypt and Mexico*. Cairo: American University in Cairo Press.

Van der Pijl, K. (1998) *Transnational Classes and International Relations*. Oxford: Psychology Press.

Vatikiotis, P. J. (1975) *The Egyptian Army in Politics: Pattern for New Nations?* Westport, CT: Greenwood Press.

Vitalis, R. (1995) *When Capitalists Collide: Business Conflict and the End of Empire in Egypt*. Berkeley: University of California Press.

Waterbury, J. (2014) *The Egypt of Nasser and Sadat: The Political Economy of Two Regimes*. Princeton, NJ: Princeton University Press.

Williams, G. A. (1960) The concept of 'egemonia' in the thought of Antonio Gramsci: some notes on interpretation. *Journal of the History of Ideas*, 21(4), 586–99.

Winegar, J. (2012) The privilege of revolution: gender, class, space, and affect in Egypt. *American Ethnologist*, 39(1), 67–70.

Younes, S. (2012) *Nidaa Al-Sha'ab* [The call of the people: a critical history of the Nasserite ideology]. Cairo: Dar el-Shorouk.

Young, R. (2016) *Postcolonialism: An Historical Introduction*. London: John Wiley.

Zaalouk, M. (1989) *Power, Class, and Foreign Capital in Egypt: The Rise of the New Bourgeoisie*. London: Zed Books.

Zahid, M. (2010) The Egyptian nexus: the rise of Gamal Mubarak, the politics of succession and the challenges of the Muslim Brotherhood. *The Journal of North African Studies*, 15(2), 217–30.

Zureik, E. (1981) Theoretical considerations for a sociological study of the Arab state. *Arab Studies Quarterly*, 3(3), 229–57.

Index

Abboud, Ahmed, 143
Ali, Mehmed, 64, 67–69
Amel, Mahdi, 55
Urabi revolt, 90, 120
1973 War, 164
Abdel Nasser, Gamal, 25, 57, 79, 81, 98
    Nasserist, 2–3, 18–19, 21–24, 27, 54, 64, 71, 76, 81–83, 87–93, 96–97, 100–102, 107, 109–111, 113–116, 118–119, 122, 124, 132, 134–136, 144, 146, 148, 150–152, 154–155, 160, 164, 166–168, 170–177, 180, 182, 184–186, 192–194, 196–197, 200, 202–203, 208–209, 219, 221–222, 226, 231, 241, 244, 246, 249, 251, 253–254, 257, 259–270, 273–274
Abdel-Malek, Anouar, 6, 74
Abraaj, 228
Abu Ghazala, Mohamed, 220
Accumulation, 48, 66, 74, 78, 102–103, 107, 143, 153–154, 169–170, 176, 178, 180–181, 184, 190, 213, 219–220, 222–223, 227, 242–244, 251, 254, 269, 273
Agrarian, 46, 66, 102, 107, 109, 153–154, 181, 197, 199, 201
Agriculture, 113, 125, 142–143, 152, 172, 200, 218, 228, 251
Ahmed Osman, Osman, 197
al Sisi, Abdelfattah, 272
al-Zawiya al Hamra, 239
Al-Ahrar, 231
al-Banna, Hassan, 111–112
Algeria, 54, 56, 123
al-Jama'a al-Islamiyya, 187
al-Maghraby, Ahmed, 229
al-Shatir, Kharait, 185

Amer, Abdel Hakim, 20, 103, 108, 163
American University in Cairo, 224
Amin, Samir, 6–8, 68, 88
Amwal al Khaleej, 228
Anglo-Egyptian Treaty, 91, 137
Anglo-Ottoman Tariff Treaty, 65
Anticolonial, xi, 1, 4, 7, 19–20, 25–27, 58, 75, 77, 79, 81, 83, 87–88, 91–92, 100, 102–103, 132, 136, 139–140, 148–149, 154–155, 161–162, 166–167, 169, 184, 187–188, 191, 203, 244, 257, 261, 267–268, 270–271, 276–279
April 6, 190, 248
Arab Industrial Organisation, 220
Arab Marxism, 10, 14, 55
Arab-Israeli War, 162
Aswan, 116, 132, 135–137, 140–141
Authoritarianism, 12–13, 37, 107, 110
Ayubi, Nazih, 10, 14, 35, 91, 150, 174, 188

Baghdad Pact, 123
Bandung, 84, 86, 88
    Afro-Asian conference, 84
Bank Misr, 67–76
Banque du Caire, 225
Beltone, 228
Black Radical Tradition, 6
Black Skin, White Masks, 57
Bourgeoisie
    national bourgeoisie
        dependent bourgeoisie, 17, 22–23, 32, 36, 38, 44, 54–58, 61–62, 64, 66, 70, 74–75, 78, 83, 92, 151, 153–154, 162, 166, 168, 196–197, 200–201, 204, 207, 250, 268, 276

295

Bread riots, 182–183, 196, 202, 209, 211, 215, 242
Britain, 65–66, 72, 91, 120, 123, 137–140
British, 67, 136, 140
Budget deficit, 215, 217
Bureaucrats, 105, 141, 268
  bureaucracy, 181

Cabinet of businessmen, 24, 208, 222–224, 226, 247
Cairo tramway, 100
Cairo University, 127
Camp David Accords, 165
Capitalism
  capitalist development
    capitalist world system, 4, 7–8, 11, 14–15, 19, 33, 47–48, 62, 70–71, 73, 75–76, 81, 88, 95, 98, 100, 104, 106–107, 109, 137, 140, 144–145, 151–153, 164, 167–169, 173, 191, 197, 203–204, 207, 234, 264, 276–278
Chatterjee, Partha, 52, 268
Citadel, 228
Coercion, 3, 13, 17–18, 21–25, 27, 34, 36–40, 49–51, 53, 59–60, 65, 67, 83, 89, 98, 103, 110–111, 113–114, 118–120, 131, 133, 136, 160, 183–185, 192–193, 205, 208, 211, 227, 231–232, 235, 237–238, 242–243, 248–250, 255, 261, 266, 272–273
Colonial international, 11, 22–23, 75–78, 84–86, 147, 154–155, 160, 204, 212, 215, 233–234, 250–251, 254, 278
Communism, 96, 116–117, 191, 221, 249, 255, 262, 265, 269
  communist, 5, 21, 95, 117, 182, 262, 268
Comparative advantage, 214
Congo, 107
Consent, 3, 17–18, 21–23, 25, 27, 34, 36–40, 49–54, 59–60, 67, 83, 87, 89, 93, 102–103, 105–106, 109–110, 113–114, 118–120, 128–129, 132, 136, 160, 162,

166, 170, 183–185, 190, 192, 201–202, 208–209, 211, 225, 231–232, 235–238, 242, 248–249, 254–255, 261–262, 273
Construction, 119, 124, 135, 144–145, 178, 180, 186, 193, 220, 224, 226–228, 265
Cooperatives, 115, 133
Corrective revolution, 172
Cotton, 64–66, 68–70, 72, 98–99, 121
Coup d'état, 2
Czech arms deal, 137

Darwish, Sayyid, 121
De Smet, Brecht, 10, 17
Debt, 4, 64, 68, 99, 167, 181, 212–214, 227, 253
  indebtedness, 214
Decolonization, 1–2, 4–5, 14, 19–20, 25–26, 28, 58, 77–78, 81–84, 88, 103, 107, 137, 140–141, 153–155, 201, 203, 207, 212–213, 257, 261, 268–269, 272, 275–276, 278–279
Dinshaway, 121

Economic Reform and Structural Adjustment Program (ERSAP), 215, 217, 272
Education, 22, 94, 96–98, 115–116, 124–128, 144–145, 154, 192–193, 195, 204, 212–213, 215–216, 224, 233, 237, 261
EFG-Hermes, 228
Egyptian Iron and Steel Company (EISCO), 253
Egyptianization, 70, 74
El Nahhas, Mustafa, 91
El Sadat, Anwar, 18, 20–21, 23, 25, 57, 103–104, 171
Electoral politics, 231–7
Elite, 2, 4, 9–13, 20, 22, 25, 103, 105, 108–110, 114–115, 127, 131, 141, 146, 150, 172, 174, 180, 196, 201, 204, 212, 225, 232, 235, 265, 268
Employee Shareholder Associations (ESA), 226

Index

Employment, 22, 96–98, 115–116, 134, 154, 174, 193, 196, 204, 212–213, 216, 233
Empty time, 24, 161, 207–208, 210
Eurocentrism, 6, 8
Extraction, 91, 152, 168
Ezz, Ahmed, 223

Factory, 65, 200, 217, 221, 226, 247–248, 251, 266
Fanon, 4, 7–8, 10, 18–19, 22–23, 26–28, 32, 45, 54–58, 61–62, 64, 75–79, 83, 86, 92, 140, 153–154, 162, 167–168, 170, 196, 199–202, 204, 207, 250, 267–268, 275–276, 278–279
  Fanonian, 9, 58, 200, 250
Farouk, King of Egypt, 70, 90–91, 104
Feminism, 93–98, 100
  feminists, 20, 90, 93–97, 100, 192, 255, 268
Feudalism, 20, 104, 197
Finance capital, 181, 200, 207, 224, 228, 250–251, 265
  financial class, 211, 222–225, 231, 233, 237, 239, 243–244, 249–251, 253
FLN, 57
Foreign capital, 63, 66, 68–72, 74–75, 137, 139, 141–142, 145, 150, 166, 175, 178–179, 197–199, 204, 212, 230–231, 245, 252
Free Officers, 19–20, 25, 63, 82, 87, 89–91, 97, 102–106, 108, 112, 145, 147, 167, 169, 197, 221, 237, 262
Free trade, 65, 69, 175, 195

Garanah, Zohair, 229
Ghannam, Farha, 206, 238
Ghosts, 101, 258–260, 263–266, 272–275
Gordon, Avery, 259, 264
Gramsci, 1, 3–4, 8–10, 12–18, 23, 23, 26–27, 31–52, 54–55, 59–60, 77–78, 81, 116, 118–119, 155, 160–162, 164, 196, 201, 205–206, 208–209, 231, 242, 249–250, 254, 258, 269, 271, 275, 277–279

Gramscian, 9, 13–14, 21, 47–49, 119, 131, 187–188, 201, 250
Greater Middle East Initiative (GMEI), 234
Grovogui, Siba, 60, 268
Guha, Ranajit
  subaltern studies, 32, 52, 54, 59
Gulf Cooperation Council (GCC), 227
Gulf states, 112, 196, 214, 230
  Gulf capital, 190, 227–230

Habib al Adly, 239
Hafiz, Abdel-Halim, 121
Hall, Stuart, 13, 34–35, 41, 45–46, 51, 80, 109
Hanieh, Adam, 10, 152, 191, 213–214, 227, 254
Harb, Tala'at, 64, 137
Hassanein Haikal, Muhammad, 129
Haunting, 101, 117, 147, 257–258, 260–264, 267, 274–275
  haunted, 5, 257, 264, 267, 274, 279
Health care, 22, 115–116, 134, 144–145, 154, 212–213, 261
Hegemonic project, 1, 3, 21, 25–27, 36, 38, 40–41, 43–44, 60, 79, 83, 86, 88–89, 92, 101, 110–111, 116, 122, 124, 134, 150, 160–161, 164, 172, 185, 187, 190–191, 208, 221, 246, 250, 255, 257, 266
Hegemony, 1, 3–4, 9–10, 12, 16–28, 31–41, 43–44, 46–54, 59–61, 63, 67, 77–79, 83, 87, 89, 100, 102, 105, 113–114, 116, 119, 124, 128, 133, 135–136, 138–139, 147, 152, 154, 160–162, 166, 170, 177, 181, 183–185, 187–189, 191, 193–196, 201–202, 204–205, 207–209, 211, 222, 231, 233, 235, 239, 242, 248–250, 254, 257, 259, 269–273, 275
High Dam, 136–137, 140–141, 197, 271
Historical bloc, 41–3

Ibn Khaldun, 35
Ideology, 6, 21, 23, 25, 27, 34–36, 40–43, 48, 51, 87–89, 92, 100, 106, 118, 123–126, 128–130, 132, 135–136, 152, 166, 170,

172, 175, 177, 179, 184–185, 187, 189–191, 200–202, 208–209, 218, 221–222, 231–233, 237, 246, 249, 257, 264–266, 268, 275

IMF, 174, 177, 180–183, 211, 213–215, 217–218, 223, 226–227, 253, 272

Import Substitution Industrialization (ISI), 266

India, 53, 59, 63, 65, 269

Industrialization, 2, 19, 63–68, 70–72, 74, 76, 85–86, 101, 106, 136–137, 141–142, 144–147, 150–152, 166, 175, 179, 182, 212, 222, 261, 266, 271, 279

Infitah, 23, 44, 161, 169–186, 190–192, 195–198, 200–205, 207–208, 210, 212, 215–216, 219–220, 222–223, 225–227, 232, 239, 245, 251, 254, 263–264, 269

Infrastructure, 63, 67–69, 85, 139–140, 142, 163, 168, 200, 222, 228, 237, 242, 252, 255, 273

Intellectuals, 6, 34, 36, 38, 56, 61, 95, 117, 127, 187

International financial institutions, 181

Internationalism, 86–87, 100, 136

Interregnum, 24, 160–162, 196, 201–202, 204–205, 207, 222, 254, 258–259

Iran, 57–58, 234

Iraq, 123, 138, 213, 248

Islamic finance, 186

Islamism, 55, 111, 189–191

Italy, 8, 15, 33–34, 45, 47, 54, 104, 208

Jordan, 123, 138, 162, 185, 227

Judges' Club, 235

Kafr al-Dawwar, 114

Kaunda, Kenneth, 268

Kefaya, 235

Kenyatta, Jomo, 167

Kuwait, 228

Labour, 5, 12, 35, 48, 61, 64–66, 68, 77, 83, 90, 96, 99–100, 110,

115, 131, 152, 164, 176, 182, 214, 216, 220, 242–245, 249, 265, 268, 271–272

Land, 22, 66, 68–69, 71, 76, 97, 99, 103, 105–106, 115, 124, 129, 131, 133–134, 139–140, 143–146, 150, 154, 163, 169, 180–181, 186, 192, 195, 197, 200, 216, 218, 220–221, 229–230, 238, 251, 261, 266, 270–271

Land reform, 22, 106, 115, 124, 129, 133–134, 144–146, 154, 186, 218, 261, 266, 271

Land reform programme, 22, 133, 218, 261

Lebanon, 227

Legitimacy, 23, 78, 101, 117, 124, 143, 184, 195, 201–202, 242, 249, 266, 273

Liberalization, 13, 176–177, 180, 182, 202, 213, 223, 230, 233–235

Liberation Rally, 128–129, 193

Lumumba, Patrice, 107, 268

Mahalla, 247–249, 266

Maher, Ali, 104, 106

Malik, Hassan, 186

Manufacturing, 121, 144, 220–221, 226, 230, 249, 266

Marei, Sayyid, 181

Marxism

    Stretch Marxism, 4–8, 14, 18, 32, 34, 45, 52, 54, 59, 61–62, 64, 78, 95, 117, 130, 207, 250, 263

Maspero Massacre, 272

Mastery, 19, 141, 154–155, 270–271, 278

Middle East, 4–5, 8–12, 14, 37, 54, 107, 111, 122–123, 132, 137, 161, 213–214, 223, 227, 230, 233–234, 247, 254, 278

Military, 37–38, 55, 81, 89–92, 102–105, 108–110, 112, 123, 144, 150, 153, 155, 162–163, 166, 172–174, 177–178, 182, 185, 193–194, 211–212, 219–222, 233, 237, 269, 272–273

Ministry of Education, 55, 125, 240

Index

Ministry of Investments, 226
Ministry of the Interior, 242
Misr Party, 173, 231
Misr Spinning and Weaving Company, 71–72
Mode of production, 34, 40, 66, 73, 99, 150, 152
Modernization, 22, 52, 68, 73, 87, 94, 96, 115, 147, 149, 151, 188, 191, 204, 252, 271
Mohieddin, Khalid, 20, 103
Mohieddin, Zakaria, 164
Monarchy, 20, 91, 102, 127
Monopoly, 69, 77, 104, 154, 178, 187, 226, 230, 253, 266
Morsi, Muhammad, 272
Movement, 2, 5, 8–9, 12, 14, 19–22, 27, 33–35, 38, 41, 45, 56, 77, 83–84, 86, 88–95, 98, 100–103, 111–114, 116–117, 120, 123, 131–132, 161, 172, 182, 184, 186–187, 191–193, 195–196, 205, 207, 236, 248, 261, 263, 268, 277
Mubarak, Gamal, 190, 215, 222–225, 232, 235, 273
Mubarak, Hosni, 18, 21, 24–25, 43, 173, 187, 208–212, 222–223
Muslim Brotherhood, 20–21, 102, 104, 110–113, 180, 184–185, 187–188, 191–192, 235–236, 249, 268, 272

Naguib, Muhammad, 104, 106
Nakba, 162
Naksa, 162
Nation-state, 85–86
National capital, 130, 166, 171, 198, 222
National Charter, 125, 127, 130, 144–145
National Democratic Party (NDP), 173, 222–224, 231–233, 235–237, 239, 244, 253
National Service Projects Organisation, 220
Nationalization, 85, 87, 101, 106, 117, 121, 128–129, 136–140, 142–145, 147–148, 153, 176, 186, 261

Nationalism
anticolonial nationalism, 2, 4–6, 11, 20, 25, 45, 55, 59, 69–71, 75, 77, 79, 81, 83, 85, 87, 90, 92–95, 98, 100, 102, 104–105, 114, 121, 123, 126–128, 132, 135–140, 148–149, 155, 161–162, 166–168, 184, 187–188, 191–192, 203, 241, 244, 249, 253–254, 257, 261–262, 267–268, 271–272, 276–279
Nazif, Ahmed, 226, 229, 247
Neocolonialism, 62, 83, 168, 213, 276
Neo-Gramscian, 47–50
Neoliberal
Neoliberalization, 101, 170, 182–183, 213, 223, 225, 232, 234, 242–243, 263, 273
Neoliberalism, 23–24, 27, 63, 170, 175, 203, 208, 213, 217–218, 229–230, 234, 253, 264
Neoliberal restructuring, 2, 11, 23, 27, 161, 190–191, 203, 207–208, 211–212, 221–224, 227, 230, 239, 243–245, 251, 254, 264
Nkrumah, Kwame, 8, 62, 119, 167, 234, 268
Non-Aligned Movement, 84, 88, 138
Nostalgia, 5, 263
Nubians, 135, 140–141, 255, 271
Nyerere, Julius, 167

October Paper, 173, 178
October War, 165
Organic crisis, 39–40, 119, 164, 182, 242
Ottoman, 65, 67, 69

Palestine, 20, 56, 90, 104, 112, 126, 163, 194, 227, 248
Pan-Africanism, 86–87, 123
Pan-Arabism, 86–87, 123, 126, 166
Pasha, Ismail, 68
Passive revolution, 43–5
Philosophy of the Revolution, 77, 119

Police, 24, 27, 37–38, 100, 182–183, 194, 237–243, 248
  Police brutality, 24, 27, 237–238, 243
Policies Committee, 223–224, 239
Postcolonial theory, 6–7, 10–11
  postcolonial studies, 6–7, 33
Primitive accumulation, 49, 66
Prison Notebooks, 3, 35–36, 43, 258
Private capital, 63, 138, 142, 226, 265
Private sector, 112, 139, 144–145, 150, 154, 174–178, 181, 187, 197–199, 204, 216, 218–219, 223, 225, 233, 246, 248–249, 264
Production, 17, 35, 39, 66, 68, 77, 98–99, 105, 107, 118, 121, 128, 143–145, 151, 154, 168–169, 181, 194, 204, 211, 219–221, 228, 243–244, 248, 253, 259, 274
Public sector, 96, 105, 110, 116, 141, 144–146, 166, 169, 172, 174–178, 180, 196, 199–200, 212–213, 215–217, 221, 225, 227, 230, 246–247, 251, 253, 261, 264

Qatar, 186
Qutb, Sayyid, 111

Raba'a al'Adawiyya, 189
Racism, 7, 47, 86, 279
Ramadan War, 165
Ranajit Guha
  Subaltern Studies, 32, 34, 50, 52, 59, 78–79
Rao, Rahul, 8, 18
Real estate, 112, 143, 177–178, 202, 217–218, 221, 228–230
Real Estate Tax Authority Union, 247
Revolution 1919, 66, 75, 90–91, 93–94
Revolution 1952, 2, 10, 20, 25, 32–33, 66–67, 70, 75, 81, 88–93, 98, 102, 104–105, 108, 112, 114–115, 125–126, 132–133, 143–144, 148, 150, 154, 170, 174, 176, 192, 197, 204, 231, 250–251, 255, 261, 266, 272

Revolution 2011, 2, 4, 9–13, 24–25, 40, 42–43, 109, 131, 155, 160–161, 182–183, 203, 207, 209, 212, 217, 219, 221–222, 227, 229, 235, 237, 239–241, 243–244, 246–247, 250–251, 253, 255–258, 274–275, 278
Rupture, 28, 90, 92, 160, 172–174, 177, 207, 257, 278
Russia, 35–36, 49
  Soviet Russia, 178

Sabri, Ali, 129, 172
Said, Edward, 6, 8, 16, 32–33, 267
Said, Khaled, 238
Salafis, 189
Salih, Arwa, 117, 192, 262–263, 275
Sardinia, 15, 45
Saudi Arabia, 185
Scott, David, 5, 88
Shareholders, 71, 94, 137, 226
Shariati, Ali, 57
Shock therapy, 215
Shukrallah, Hani, 225
Six-Day War, 162
Sixth of October Development and Investment Company (SODIC), 229
Social services, 175, 183, 186, 193, 200, 212, 216–217, 236, 261, 266
Socialism, 86–87, 92, 95, 98, 106, 123, 126–128, 130, 136, 150–151, 153, 172, 176, 264
Some Aspects of the Southern Question, 46
Sovereignty, 5, 84, 139–140, 154–155, 192, 234, 270, 278
Speculation, 112, 177, 180–181, 200, 212, 251
Stretch Marxism, 44, 78, 195, 259
Strike, 11, 91, 94, 97, 100, 183, 243, 245–249, 265–266
Structural adjustment, 177, 182–183, 211–218, 253
Student movement, 184–185, 188, 192–196, 266
Subaltern, 9, 12, 16, 25, 34, 36, 41, 44, 48, 53, 56, 59, 92, 107, 110, 116, 172, 191, 249, 268–269

Index

Subsidies, 74, 164, 177, 180, 182–183, 200, 211, 214–217
Suez Canal, 20, 71, 104, 128, 136–140, 145, 147–148, 165, 178, 204, 261
    Suez Canal Company, 71, 137–138
Syria, 65, 162, 165, 227

Tagamu' Party, 231
Tala'at Mustafa Group, 229
Tanzimat, 68
Taxes, 142, 164, 178–179, 215–217
Technocrats, 105, 141, 151, 172
Third International, 36
Third Worldism, 84
Thomas, Peter, 44, 47, 50
Trade union, 100, 115, 130
Transformismo, 24, 209–210
Travelling theory, 33

Umm Kulthum, 121
Uneven development, 46–47, 49

United Arab Emirates (UAE), 227, 229
USAID, 181

Vanguard, Socialist, 172
Voice of the Arabs, 21

Wafd, 20, 90–92, 100, 231
War of position, 131, 188
Women's movement, 92, 98, 110
World Bank, 138, 211, 213–215, 217–218
Wretched of the Earth, 23, 55–58, 78, 168, 276, 278

Yemen, 87, 123, 153, 163, 185–186
Young Egypt, 192
Youth Organization, 130, 193
Yugoslavia, 129

Zaghloul, Sa'ad, 90–91, 94